D0039381

Sherman Alexie

CONCORDIA UNIVERSITY LIBRARY
PORTLAND, OR 97211

Sherman Alexie

A Collection of Critical Essays

■ *Edited by Jeff Berglund and Jan Roush*

THE UNIVERSITY OF UTAH PRESS

Salt Lake City

Copyright © 2010 by the University of Utah Press.
All rights reserved.

 The Defiance House Man colophon is a registered
trademark of the University of Utah Press. It is
based upon a four-foot-tall, ancient Puebloan
pictograph (late PIII) near Glen Canyon, Utah.

14 13 12 11 10   1 2 3 4 5

LIBRARY OF CONGRESS CATALOGING-IN-PUBLICATION DATA
Sherman Alexie : a collection of critical essays / edited
by Jeff Berglund and Jan Roush.
          p. cm.
Includes bibliographical references and index.
ISBN 978-1-60781-008-7 (pbk. : alk. paper)
1. Alexie, Sherman, 1966—Criticism and interpretation.
2. Indians in literature. I. Berglund, Jeff. II. Roush, Jan
PS3551.L35774Z87 2010   818'.5409—dc22
2010023990

Cover photo by Rob Casey, www.robcasey.net.

Printed and bound by Sheridan Books, Inc.,
Ann Arbor, Michigan.

For Monica, Isabella, and Juliana

—JB

For Michael

—JR

Contents

Acknowledgments

■ *Jeff Berglund*

I would like to thank, first and foremost, Sherman Alexie for invigorating our contemporary world with his energy and vision. I and my students have been pushed to reevaluate the ways we view the world. He may not have seen this firsthand when he visited my campus, Northern Arizona University, two times in the past eight years, but we have found a new reason to read.

Throughout the process of editing this book, Sherman Alexie's assistant, Christy Cox, has been tremendously helpful. I especially appreciate her efficiency and sincere warmth. Rob Casey, Sherman Alexie's official photographer, has graciously contributed the cover image, and for this I am incredibly grateful.

I'm deeply indebted to reviewers for the press, Simon Ortiz and Birgit Hans, for seeing the value of this enterprise and for astute suggestions for improvement of this manuscript. Thank you to everyone at the University of Utah Press for supporting this project.

I would like to thank my co-editor, Jan Roush, for first facilitating this collaboration a number of years ago, not long after we met at the

Western Literature Association conference in Tucson, Arizona. I appreciate Jan's interest in Alexie's intertextuality and generic explorations, not to mention her sharp editing eyes.

Over the years I have treasured the professional friendships that have been formed through discussions of Sherman Alexie's work at wonderful conferences. So, I thank the organizers of the Native American Literature Symposium, the American Studies Association national conference, the Modern Language Association conference, the Western Literature Association conference, the Southwest/Texas Popular Culture Association, and the Native American and Indigenous Studies Association conference.

I would like to thank my students, too, who have shared this journey through the constantly expanding oeuvre of Alexie's writings, even the students who made it seem as if *Indian Killer* was coming to life before our very eyes when the campus police were called about hate speech and threats of violence. Alexie's work explores issues that touch nerves and that resonate in visceral, emotional, and cerebral ways.

In particular, I want to thank all of the contributors to this collection: Jan Johnson, Lisa Tatonetti, James H. Cox, P. Jane Hafen, Elizabeth Archuleta, Angelica Lawson, Nancy J. Peterson, Patrice Hollrah, Susan Berry Brill de Ramírez, Meredith James, Stephen F. Evans, Margaret O'Shaugnnessey, and Philip Heldrich. Thank you for your inspiring scholarship—herein and elsewhere—as well as your patience and incredible dedication to this project.

Thank you to my friends and colleagues: Monica Brown, Jennifer Denetdale, Eric Meeks, Leilah Danielson, Annette McGivney, Jerry Thull, Gioia Woods, Aaron Cohen, Irene Matthews, Nancy Paxton, Nancy Barron, Sara Aleman, Steven Rosendale, Paul Ferlazzo, Octaviana Trujillo, Michelle Harris, Harvey Charles, Linda Shadiow, Esther Belin, Connie Jacobs, and Jan Johnson. I value your friendships and the ways you help me reflect on the direction and value of the work we all undertake.

Thank you to my Provost Liz Grobsmith and President John Haeger for your support and recognition of my research, teaching, and service on numerous levels throughout my years at Northern Arizona University.

Thank you to my parents, Patricia and Duane Berglund, for having confidence in me in all ways.

I reserve my deepest thanks for Monica, Isabella, and Juliana for your unwavering support and for the strength of your convictions about making this a just world. Your creative, intelligent, and energizing spirits sustain me and make anything seem possible. And, you're a lot of fun! Monica sees possibilities in me that I could easily miss out on; thank you for your advice and encouragement in all aspects of my professional and personal life. You made this happen.

■ *Jan Roush*

In any collaborative undertaking, there are always many people along the way who should be recognized for their contributions to the final product, and this anthology is no exception, beginning, as my co-editor has so eloquently expressed above, with the inspiration emanating from the subject of this work, Sherman Alexie himself. Without the depth of his artistry and versatility across genres there quite simply would be no need for this collection. To all of those who helped this publication come to life, from the contributors to the publishing staff and particularly to my co-editor, Jeff Berglund, whose singlehanded nurturing efforts moved the manuscript forward, I would like to express my sincere gratitude for their creativity, scholarly analysis, attention to detail, and their patience in making certain that the resulting publication do justice to its subject. Most of all, I would like to thank my family, and especially my husband Michael, for their unfailing support throughout. Without all of these collaborative efforts, this anthology would not have happened.

A portion of the royalties from the sale of this book are directly donated to the American Indian College Fund, something Alexie has recommended, at minimum, for non-Indian writers and scholars working on Native issues.

■ *Jeff Berglund*

INTRODUCTION

"Imagination Turns Every Word into a Bottle Rocket"

An Introduction to Sherman Alexie

Imagination is the politics of dreams;
imagination turns every word into a bottle rocket.

—SHERMAN ALEXIE, "IMAGINING THE RESERVATION," *THE LONE*
RANGER AND TONTO FISTFIGHT IN HEAVEN

On October 7, 1966, Sherman Alexie was born in Wellpinit on the Spokane Indian Reservation in the eastern part of Washington. His father, Sherman Sr., was Coeur d'Alene, and his mother, Lillian, is Spokane. When Alexie was still a child, his father's interest in reading sparked his passion for the power of language. In fact, Alexie learned to read at three because his father was a "major genre reader."[1] After graduating from Reardan High School, off the reservation, Alexie initially attended Gonzaga University before graduating in 1991 from Washington State University in Pullman with a degree in American studies. Today Alexie lives in Seattle with his wife, Diane, and his two sons.

Alexie's formative experiences—as a child reared in the midst of alcoholism in the harsh economic realities of rural reservation life—are focal points in his early fiction and poetry. In his National Book Award-winning novel for young adults, *The Absolutely True Diary of a Part-Time Indian* (2007), Alexie fictionally revisits aspects of his childhood; he decided to novelize them, rather than include them in a memoir he's writing because "nobody would actually [believe] it as a memoir."[2] In addition to an exploration of reservation life, in books such as *The Toughest Indian in the World* (2000), *Ten Little Indians* (2003), *Flight* (2007), and *War Dances* (2009), he has turned his attention to the experiences of urban Indian people living in a multiethnic environment in situations where identity and cultural loyalties are questioned because of class standing or romantic and sexual relationships. Notably—given Alexie's focus to date on American Indian characters—*War Dances,* his most recent publication, contains several stories that lack identifiable Indian characters.

During his college years, he confronted his own alcoholism, gave up drinking, and has remained sober since he was twenty-three. Switching from his initial plans to go into medicine, Alexie found his calling through poetry-writing workshops and was inspired by his professor and mentor, Alex Kuo, who exposed him to poetry by contemporary Native writers such as Simon Ortiz, Leslie Silko, Joy Harjo, James Welch, and Adrian Louis, whom he now includes alongside Walt Whitman and Emily Dickinson as his literary influences. Kuo encouraged him to seriously consider becoming a writer. A mature Alexie agrees that this decision was the right one and credits Kuo for starting him on a path that has led to one of the most prolific writing careers of any contemporary American author.

Alexie found in books a lifeline out of the reservation, if not literally, then out of what Adrian Louis calls "the reservation of my mind": an internalization of colonial oppression and alienation.[3] In "Superman and Me," an early essay published in the *Los Angeles Times,* Alexie noted that he was reading *The Grapes of Wrath* when his kindergarten classmates were struggling with "Dick and Jane": "I refused to fail. I was smart. I was arrogant. I was lucky. I read books late into the night...I read anything that had words and paragraphs. I read with equal parts joy and desperation. I loved those books, but I also knew that love had only one purpose. I was trying to save my life."[4] In "Up All Night," which aired in October 2002 on *Now with Bill Moyers* on PBS, Alexie explained,

On Friday nights when I can't sleep, there's a place I can go unlike any others in Seattle. Twice Sold Tales is open 24 hours on Fridays. And in that, I find such great comfort and joy. I mean there's something amazing about a place where I can find Chester Himes at four in the morning, or . . . Graham Greene at 4:30. That instead of some . . . carbohydrate grand slam feast that kills your heart, I can find something that feeds your heart. Toni Morrison. Imagine that, Toni Morrison at sunrise. Can you imagine anything better than that? I mean I could be patriotic in a place like this. I can love this country more in a place like this than in any other place. We have too much. But not here. There is no such thing as too many books.[5]

Alexie has also passed on to several of his young protagonists a similar predilection for reading. In *Flight*, Zits, a teenage orphan in and out of foster homes, finds himself transported into the bodies and experiences of others in different time periods. Though his life is filled with instability, among the other essentials (clothes and photos of his parents) in his backpack are three novels: *The Grapes of Wrath, Winter in the Blood* and *The Dead Zone.* He knows "there has never been a human being or a television show, no matter how great, that could measure up to a great book."[6] When Zits finds himself in a foster home that has no books, he wonders, "What kind of life can you have in a house without books?" (*Flight,* 13). His transportation through time transforms him and ultimately leads to a stable situation: his recognition is complex, but he finds a "new act" after he realizes that he is his father (in one instance, he is embodied in his father who is living on the street): "I am my father. . . . Who can survive such a revelation? It was father love and father shame and father rage that killed Hamlet. Imagine a new act" (*Flight,* 150–51).

In *The Absolutely True Diary of a Part-Time Indian,* Alexie further fleshes out the relationship that links reading, creativity, and self-empowerment. For Junior—Alexie's narrator and diary writer—reading and writing (and drawing) are important vehicles for expressing and/or understanding his own life. Junior's mother (like Alexie's father) "still reads books like crazy. She buys them by the pound. And she remembers everything she reads. She can recite whole pages by memory. She's a human tape recorder."[7] Junior admits that he's also a "book kisser" (*ATD,* 30). The entire novel is a record of his thoughts in journal form, intermixed with sketches and jottings: "I draw because words are too unpredictable. I draw because words are too limited.... So I draw because I want to talk to the world. And I want the world to pay attention to me. I feel important with a pen in my hand. I feel like I might grow up to be somebody important. An artist. Maybe a famous artist. Maybe a rich artist.... So I draw because I feel like it might be my only real chance to escape the reservation" (*ATD,* 5–6).

Junior befriends a white boy named Gordy at his new school in Reardan, off the reservation, who teaches him—he claims—how to read: "You have to read a book three times before you know it." Moreover, Gordy recognizes that drawing helps Junior "navigate the river of the world" (*ATD,* 95). Gordy tells him he should "read and draw because really good books and cartoons give you a boner" (*ATD,* 96). Pointing at the school's library, he tells Junior that "the world, even the smallest parts of it, is filled with things you don't know" to which Junior responds,

> So it's like each of these books is a mystery. Every book is a mystery. And if you read all the books ever written, it's like you've read one giant mystery. And no matter how much you learn, you just keep on learning there is so much more you need to learn.... Now doesn't that give you a boner? ...I don't mean a boner in the sexual sense. I don't think you should run through life with a real erect penis. But you should approach each book—you should approach life—with the real possibility that you might get a metaphorical boner at any point (ATD, 97).

After Junior endures the successive deaths of his sister and his grandmother, and his father has left on a "legendary drinking binge" to cope with the death of his friend, Junior misses more than twenty days of school. Unlike his mother, who looks for solace in church, Junior writes, "I felt helpless and stupid. I needed books. I wanted books. And I drew and drew and drew cartoons. I was mad at God; I was mad at Jesus"

(*ATD,* 171). He reads Euripides' *Medea* and learns something about the nature of grief but comes to believe that he has cursed his family: "I had left the tribe, and had broken something inside all of us, and I was now being punished for that" (*ATD,* 173). During the process of healing, when he learns that he is not personally accountable for the death of his loved ones, Junior tries to inventory the little pieces of joy in his life by making lists: favorite foods, favorite musicians, favorite basketball players, and favorite books:

1. *The Grapes of Wrath*
2. *Catcher in the Rye*
3. *Fat Kid Rules the World*
4. *Tangerine*
5. *Feed*
6. *Catalyst*
7. *Invisible Man*
8. *Fools Crow*
9. *Jar of Fools* (*ATD,* 177)

Books by John Steinbeck, J. D. Salinger, K. L. Going, Edward Bloor, M. T. Anderson, Laurie Halse Anderson, Ralph Ellison, James Welch, and Jason Lutes explore the experience of being disenfranchised or alienated and the desire to find a home, a place to belong. Junior works his way through grief by "making list after list of the things that made me feel joy. And I kept drawing cartoons of the things that made me angry. I keep writing and rewriting, drawing and redrawing, and rethinking and revising and reediting. It became my grieving ceremony" (*ATD,* 178).

> *So why do Indians sing '49s'? We sing them for the same reason*
> *all musicians make music: to tell stories, to pray to God,*
> *to curse God, to cry in our beers or our Kool-Aid, to have fun*
> *with the guys or girls, to get laid, to get attention, to protest,*
> *to make money, to connect with other human beings.*
>
> —Sherman Alexie, screenplay for *49?*

*There is a whole other population out there I want to reach. And so
for me, what kind of art can I create that gets to them? I don't want
to have an elitist career. I've won awards, I've gotten a lot of attention, I've been in* The New Yorker, *and I'm very happy with all of
that. I'm very proud. But I would consider myself a failure if more
people didn't read me. I'd rather be accessible than win a MacArthur.*

—SHERMAN ALEXIE, "WHAT IT MEANS TO BE SHERMAN ALEXIE"[8]

Contributors to this book and their students are only a small portion
of the readers—nationally and globally—who have had the pleasure of
following the brilliant comet trail of Alexie's career. He is now among
the most widely read and consistently popular American Indian writers.
Early in his career, Alexie claimed that he was writing books to interest
the sort of young Native reader he once was: "If Indian literature can't
be read by the average 12-year-old kid living on the reservation, what the
hell good is it? You couldn't take any of [Vizenor's] books to the rez and
teach them, without extreme protestation. What is an Indian kid going
to do with the first paragraph of any of those books?"[9] But following the
release of his film *The Business of Fancydancing* (2002)—reacting in part
to the homophobic dismissal by Native audiences—Alexie said that his
dependable audience nowadays is quite different from the one he envi-
sioned earlier: "You know who I depend on? There are about 75,000 college-educated white women in the country who buy all of my books and
go to all of my movies. I mean, if I had to depend on Indians for a career?
No way! No chance."[10] Despite such defensive comments, it seems clear
that in writing his novels for young adults—another one is slated for
release in 2010—Alexie hasn't given up on reaching the young "Indian
kid" he once was.

Alexie's first books of poetry—*The Business of Fancydancing* and *I
Would Steal Horses*—were published in 1992 and laid the foundation
for future success. In 1993 his first collection of short stories—*The Lone
Ranger and Tonto Fistfight in Heaven*—earned a PEN/Hemingway Award
for best first book of fiction. He went on to be named one of Granta's
best young American novelists and received the Before Columbus Foundation's American Book Award for his first novel, *Reservation Blues,*

published in 1995. His short fiction has often appeared in *The New Yorker* and has been selected for inclusion in both the annual O'Henry Award and Best American Short Story collections.

Readers of Alexie's twenty-one published books (including screenplays and poetry chapbooks) will likely concur that his literary talents express themselves in multiple genres. His early collections more often included several genres than his work since 1998, though *War Dances* (winner of the PEN/Faulkner Award for fiction in 2010) is liberally interspersed with poetry, most of which employs formal poetic conventions. A number of the prose pieces within *War Dances* defy easy categorization, raising questions about whether they are nonfictional essays, prose poems, or experimental short fiction; the possibly autobiographical "I" of the implied speaker of most of the conventional poetry also rubs up against the narrating "I" of the more experimental prose pieces. The editors of this collection—Jan Roush and I—believe that readers will be most rewarded with intertextual readings—readings across the genres of Alexie's works—to find intricate reworkings and meditations on common themes, emblems, and motifs, as well as characters. Alexie's multigenre interests remind readers of other contemporary Native writers who have published poetry and fiction: N. Scott Momaday, Leslie Marmon Silko, Louise Erdrich, James Welch, and Simon Ortiz.

Alexie's inventive style conveys to readers his characters' suffering and anguish but also the enduring power of humor and imagination. His most well-known character—Thomas Builds-the-Fire from *The Lone Ranger, Reservation Blues,* and the film *Smoke Signals*—illustrates the power of storytelling to connect the past, present, and future; to reinvent traditional forms; and to infuse tragedy with a dose of laughter and a refusal to submit to traumatizing forces. Alexie again explores this subject in *Face* (2009) in his poem with the double-edged meaning: "Comedy Is a Funny Way of Being Serious." Scholar P. Jane Hafen (Taos Pueblo) notes in her essay in this collection that she enjoys Alexie's writings because "they make me laugh. In the face of dismal reservation life and urban crises of self, community, and identity, he can make me laugh, often by inverting imagery and turning inside jokes. He helps make the pain bearable."[11]

Alexie's work-in-progress—a memoir about his family's history with war—is currently planned as a multigenre work: "I am currently working on my first non-fiction, a big book about four generations of Indian men in my family, and our relationship with war, and I've broken it down into [a] fiction, non-fiction project, and poetry, so I'm really looking for a hybrid work here," he notes in an interview with Diane Thiel. He continues, "In some sense, I feel this new book is a summation of all my themes until now. After this book, I think I'll be looking in some radical new directions."[12]

Some of his most recent publications seem to have been inspired by this projected project. From the limited-edition *Dangerous Astronomy* (2005) to *Face* to *War Dances*, Alexie continues to explore his familial connection to war, but even more, his own or his character's relationship with fathers. In the collection's title story, "War Dances," in a subsection labeled "Battle Fatigue," Alexie's narrator notes the intergenerational consequences of his father's father's death in World War II: "Six years old, my father was cratered [with the death of his father in war and his mother's to tuberculosis]. In most ways, he never stopped being six. There was no religion, no magic tricks, and no song or dance that helped my father." At the end of the story, he wants to call his father up, "but I couldn't tell him anything. He was dead.... I miss him, the drunk bastard. I would always feel closest to the man who had most disappointed me."[13]

In a number of very different stories in this collection, Alexie explores related issues. For example, in "The Ballad of Paul Nonetheless," he creates a character who is a failure as a husband and a father and asks himself, "But who has sympathy for the failed father? Who sings honor songs for the monster?" (*WD*, 140). This theme is similarly explored in another father/son story involving a white Republican senator and his son, both of whom are homophobic. In this story, Alexie flips his familiar trope about children forgiving their parents for their legacy of trouble and sin: "If it is true that children pay for the sins of their fathers, is it also true that fathers pay for the sins of their children?" (*WD*, 96).

This thematic turnabout is likely fueled by Alexie's increasing focus on fatherhood now that he is a father and aging, and his father has passed away. Several of these themes find expression in the poem "On the Second Anniversary of My Father's Death" in his collection *Face*. The speaker, who keeps finding dead birds that have flown into his glass door because it mirrors the sky, recognizes that they make him think of his father: "Do I see my father in that bird because I see myself in that bird? In my grief and rage, have I grown wings and the need to destroy my own reflection? Do I want to destroy my face because it looks so much like my father's face? I don't want to be that cruel; I don't want to be that hateful. I want to be the child so in love with his father that he falls in love with the parts of his face that most resemble his father's."[14] Within this one poem, Alexie moves his readers through grief, rage, self-hatred, and the need for redemption, rescue, and love.

Alexie initially reached his largest audience via the 1998 film *Smoke Signals*, directed by Chris Eyre (Cheyenne/Arapaho) and adapted by Alexie from several short stories, including "What It Means to Say Phoenix, Arizona," from *The Lone Ranger and Tonto Fistfight in Heaven*. *Smoke Signals* follows the journey of Victor and Thomas Builds-the-Fire on their trip to recover the ashes of Victor's deceased father from whom he was estranged. Their journey is also metaphorical because their shared experiences lead to discoveries about their abilities to forgive, understand, and transcend the legacies left them by their parents, more specifically their fathers. When the two return home—to the reservation and tribal homeland their father had left behind—Victor returns his father's ashes to the river where salmon return to mate and die. In the final scene of the movie, the ashes mix with the rising mists of the rapids, and his father's spirit leaps like the salmon; viewers hear Thomas speaking in a voice-over: "Do we forgive our fathers for leaving us too often or forever when we were little? . . . If we forgive our fathers, what else is left?" The movie begs viewers to consider if they can afford to live in the shadow of terrible legacies, or if they should take the risks required to forge new futures and identities from the raw materials of empathy and forgiveness.

Some people have therapists, I have audiences.

—SHERMAN ALEXIE, "SPOKANE WORDS"[15]

I have enormous cultural power now and it's all out of proportion to the number of books I actually sell.... Because of my ethnicity, my age, the times we live in, I have power.

—SHERMAN ALEXIE, "VOICE OF THE NEW TRIBES"[16]

Beyond the typical literary readership, Alexie has attracted a public fan base with public-speaking engagements that infuse a typical poetry-reading format with high-octane energy, likely a carryover from the World Heavyweight Championship Poetry Bout in Taos, where Alexie has repeatedly laid claim to the title since 1999. Most of his stand-up-style appearances at book festivals and universities and schools are also energized by doses of politically charged commentary. Such platforms, then, have cast him as a public spokesperson for Native America, which was clearly the case in 1998, when he participated in President Clinton's summit on race. When asked by CBS television in 2001 about his rapid ascent in the literary world, he admitted that he always knew it was possible: "I thought I had that combination of skills which was very conducive to being successful in the United States in the earliest 21st century. I write well enough. I'm funny. I'm good in front of the camera."[17] Alexie's self-description identifies some of the unique aspects of his writing and public performances as a writer/speaker that have set him apart from other Native American writers. Without a doubt, these extraliterary forums have helped construct his identity and played a role in shaping the way his work is received.

During the past eight years, his speaking schedule has been packed; it's quite likely—if you're reading this book in the United States—that he's been on a university campus or at a book festival near you. In the fall of 2002, he was in Swainsboro, Georgia; then Manchester, New Hampshire; and a few days later, Seattle. His bookings after that included Auburn, Georgia; Washington, D.C.; Kent, Ohio; New York City; Davis, California; Keene, New Hampshire; Culowhee, North Carolina; Park City, Utah; Easton, Pennsylvania; Lawrence, Kansas: Salt Lake City; and Indianapolis. In the spring of 2004, Alexie visited Notre Dame; the University of San Diego; Colby College; the University of Maine; St. Paul's School in

New Hampshire; the 92nd Street Y in New York City; and the Hydrocephalus National Convention.

Both of this volume's editors have had the opportunity to enjoy Alexie's appearances: Jan Roush saw him perform in Park City in 2003, where he cracked to the audience, "That's why I like Utah. It's the only place in the world white guys carry *my* bags." I saw him at Northern Arizona University in Flagstaff, Arizona, where I teach, in 2001, when 9/11 was still very much on everyone's minds. One October night—after lunch with faculty and students and meeting with a school group from Tuba City in the late afternoon—Alexie packed an auditorium at Northern Arizona University to overflow: flaunting the fire code, the crowd filled the aisles and the stage behind and around him. Students bussed in from Tuba City, Winslow, and Fort Defiance mixed with university and Flagstaff community members to hear Alexie's contribution to the annual, endowed talk on the humanities. On that night—as he has done on similar occasions elsewhere—Alexie discoursed on multiple topics: historical omissions and amnesia, U.S. foreign policy, President Bush, Indian mascots, stereotypes, assumptions about Native writing, and homophobia. He distinctively tapped into the energy of the audience. But ultimately, who knows what image of Alexie drew each person there: Alexie as Indian spokesperson; Alexie as political post-9/11 commentator; Alexie as filmmaker, fiction writer, poet; or Alexie as flat-out funny comic?

In February 2009, he returned to Northern Arizona University to bigger crowds, in a bigger auditorium, and again wowed his audience with his mix of humor, pathos, and satire. His rapt audience hung onto each word of this consummate storyteller and poet, including his poignant observation about flying into the urban sprawl of the greater Phoenix area: beneath each light were vibrant lives, and while there were many he'd likely dislike, there were those who could be his friends, and people he'd find attractive, and even some he could fall in love with. This focus on the human dimension of overpopulation in the desert further endeared him to me, partly because I saw him in a new light, simultaneously making the familiar strange and new.

Alexie's performances are quite different from what audiences expect from more traditional poetry readings. His style borrows heavily from

Margaret Cho, John Leguiziamo, or George Carlin and Richard Pryor from an earlier generation. In his poem "Oral Tradition" from *Face,* Alexie shares his admiration for Pryor; this poem forges a theory about poetry and good comedy making common use of the caesura: the measured pause on which comic and poetic timing depend. During his performances, his fiction and poetry usually come last, if at all, and are recited from memory or edited extemporaneously. When he was asked about the unique style of his performances—more akin to routines by stand-up comics—Alexie told an interviewer,

> Most of the readings I've been to are so damn boring! We've got a lot of competition out there in the world. I have to be at least as good as Eminem or I'm dead! In my personal life, I'm an introvert. I spend most of my time alone, with my thoughts for company, and much prefer a book and a bathtub to any gathering of messy human beings. As a public performer, I "act." It's a strange thing. I become a slightly larger and more exaggerated version of myself.[18]

One appearance on television particularly captured the flavor of his live performances. During the winter of 2001, in anticipation of the paperback release of *The Toughest Indian in the World,* CBS's *Sixty Minutes II* aired a brief, twelve-minute piece on Alexie's career and experiences as a child growing up on a reservation amidst the alcoholism of his parents. In this interview, Alexie comes across as poetic, serious, humorous, arrogant, troubled, politically committed, and a man committed to recovery. He is a role model, a hero, a Spokane Indian, but an individual Spokane Indian (definitely not a spokesperson). Dreams helped lift him from what he had become in college: "a case-of-beer, fifth-of-tequila drunk: I knew who I was going to be. I knew this is where I would end up. I didn't want to be another public-figure Indian who would break the hearts of other Indian kids by being drunk."[19]

In addition to his performances, Alexie has created interest in his work through dozens of interviews. These interviews not only fashion his authorial persona; they also provide him with a bully pulpit, a soapbox to sound off about the state of Native America, Native literary studies, and the sometimes-exasperating experience of being a Native author. For example, in a 1997 interview with John Purdy, Alexie claims that he wants to reach twelve-year-olds living on the reservation; he yearns to take Indian literature from what it "is now"; he says readers and scholars should ask, "What does Indian literature mean?"; he criticizes Native critics for expecting Native writers to focus on tradition; he condemns Native writers for selling out their culture, saying they are doing what no other Indian people would do: "No Indian will stand on the roadside singing traditional songs for money—this is what writers do when they put it in a book and sell it."[20]

Most obviously, interviews give Alexie the opportunity to discuss his new publications—including their inspiration—and the way he hopes readers will value and interpret his writing. The work of an interview is often discursive, too, as topics make their way into and back out of fictional works. Just as Alexie commented in 1997 about not selling out his culture, his poetic and film meditations on authorship have returned to this authorial double bind, something the last essay in this collection focuses on specifically. When asked, in March 2003 in an identitytheory.com interview, if he had "sold out" his own people, Alexie responded,

> No, well, I've made mistakes about subject matter, things I probably shouldn't have written about. I wrote about events I shouldn't have written about. And that was a personal moral choice to stop writing about those events. . . . You know, as an artist, it's not my job to fit in; it's not to belong. I'm not a social worker; I'm not a therapist. It's my job to beat the shit out of the world. I'm not here to make people feel good.[21]

I propose that seeing his extraliterary interviews as part of the continuum of his creative expression—rhetorically sophisticated efforts in their own right—enables critics to examine returned-to themes and issues. To give but one example, using his interviews as discursive essays on authorship and appropriation puts them in dialogue with his poems "The Business of Fancydancing," "Open Books," and "How to Write the Great American Indian Novel"; the novel *Indian Killer* (1996); the short story "Search Engine"; his essay "The Unauthorized Autobiography of Me";

and the film *The Business of Fancydancing*. In this way, the interrelationship among and the inseparability of so many of Alexie's texts, as well as his continuing negotiation of and metacommentary on the experiences of being an author, become clear.

Alexie's readers look forward to his innovations, extensions, and reworkings of familiar themes and characters, mirroring his enthusiasm for the whole universe of critical responses. These reworkings often represent work across genres. The short story "One Good Man" from *The Toughest Indian in the World* becomes richer after reading the poem "Sugar Town" from *One Stick Song* (2000), "The Father and Son Road Show" from *Dangerous Astronomy,* "Diabetes" and "Father and Farther" from *The Summer of Black Widows* (1996), and "At the Diabetic River" from *The Man Who Loves Salmon* (1998). And the ending of "The Toughest Indian in the World" from the eponymous collection is enriched by considering the culturally significant motif of salmon in *Smoke Signals,* "Exact Drums" from *Water Flowing Home* (1996), the entire chapbook of *The Man Who Loves Salmon,* and "That Place Where Ghosts of Salmon Jump" from *The Summer of Black Widows.*

One extended example of thematic and topical reworking involves his novels *Flight* and *Indian Killer*. It's intriguing that Alexie *considers Flight* to be his antidotal response to *Indian Killer,* a novel he has largely disowned since 2001 because of its fundamentalism and dangerously narrow view of tribalism.[22] *Indian Killer,* no matter how Alexie feels about it, has been compared to such twentieth-century classics as Richard Wright's *Native Son* and Ralph Ellison's *Invisible Man.* These comparisons likely stem from the parallels between John Smith, the novel's protagonist, and Ellison's narrator and Wright's Bigger Thomas. Smith, who is Native and adopted by white parents, is a "lost bird," disenfranchised, spiritually and emotionally bereft. The novel traces his difficulty in finding a way to belong. His growing dis-ease, as a post-high-school graduate, coincides with a string of brutal murders. While the identity of the murderer is never revealed, readers are led by possibly culturally biased assumptions to think that either Smith's psychological problems have incited him to kill, or a non-Native killer is capitalizing on the racist ideologies fomented by a talk-radio disc jockey. The end of the novel suggests that the murders may be related to a contemporary Ghost Dance and the work of many individuals.

By contrast, *Flight,* featuring a first-person teenage narrator named Zits, encompasses a much broader sweep of history—from the 1890 Ghost Dance to the present—with time-travel stopovers in the early 1970s during an American Indian Movement–style episode and sometime around 9/11, when a would-be terrorist is in flight training. Zits (named for his acne-covered face) is mixed blood, has been the victim of sexual abuse, and, like John Smith, is an orphan. Unlike Smith, though, Zits is shuffled from one foster home to another. He abuses drugs and is nihilistically violent (shades of the Columbine High tragedy), yet is an autodidact who loves to read and yearns for love and understanding. A violent, would-be armed robbery is interrupted when Zits finds himself physically transported through time into different bodies: from a white FBI agent in the 1970s, to a white "Indian tracker" in the nineteenth century, to a white flight-school trainer, to a Native homeless man who is alcoholic (his biological father). In each episode, Zits is confronted with a different set of ethical obligations, several of which have explicit political implications. Alexie's alternative histories for Zits—who is a contemporary version of the biblical and Melvillian Ishmaels (the novel opens with "Call me Zits") or Ellison's invisible man—require him to be a subject in and through history. When his personal traumas are clearly integrated with larger historical ones, Zits is led away from nihilism and self-destruction to realize that "revenge is a circle inside of a circle inside of a circle" (*Flight,* 77). To end violence, one must get outside it.

Most of us [Indian writers] are outcasts. We don't really fit within the Indian community, so we write to try to fit in and sound Indian. So it's ironic that we become spokespeople for Indian country, that we are supposed to be representative of our tribes.

—Sherman Alexie, "Fancy Dancer: A Profile of Sherman Alexie"[23]

*I'm the first practitioner of the Brady Bunch-school
of Native American literature. I'm a twenty-first-century Indian
who believes in the twenty-first-century.*

—SHERMAN ALEXIE, "TRIBAL VISIONS"[24]

Alexie's character Thomas Builds-the-Fire is known for his ability to tell stories, but Alexie has bristled when he is described as a storyteller, connecting it to stereotypical proscriptions forced upon Native writers. Alexie is quite aware of writing in the face of such assumptions:

> [It's] that whole "corn pollen, four directions, Mother Earth, Father Sky" Indian thing where everybody starts speaking slowly, and their vocabulary shrinks down until they sound like Dick and Jane. And it's all about spirituality, and it's all about politics. So I try to write about everyday Indians, the kind of Indian I am who is just as influenced by the Brady Bunch as I am by my tribal traditions, who spends as much time going to the movies as I do going to ceremonies.[25]

Consequently, literary and pop-culture references abound in Alexie's writing. Undoubtedly the contemporary echoes in Alexie's work—from mass popular culture, in particular—account for his appeal to diverse audiences. In a number of instances, in fact, popular entertainment becomes a substitute for ritual and shared communal meaning. For example, his narrator in "The Ballad of Paul Nonetheless" from *War Dances* wonders,

> Hadn't pop music created a new and invisible organ, a pituitary gland of the soul, in the American body? Could one honestly say that Elvis is a more important figure in American history than Einstein? Could one posit that Aretha Franklin's version of "Respect" was more kinetic and relevant to American life than Dwight D. Eisenhower's 1961 speech that warned us about the dangers of a military-industrial complex? Could a reasonable person think that Madonna's "Like a Prayer" was as integral and

universal to everyday life as the fork or wheel? Paul believed all these heresies about pop music but would never say them aloud for fear of being viewed as a less-than-serious person. (*WD*, 118–19)

Readers familiar with Alexie's writing aren't surprised to see allusions to mass culture mixed in with so-called highbrow literary references: *Invisible Man,* Allen Ginsberg's *Howl,* Emily Dickinson's poems, Tim O'Brien's *The Things They Carried,* Miguel de Cervantes's *Don Quixote,* Leslie Marmon Silko's *Ceremony,* Joy Harjo's *She Had Some Horses,* James Wright's *The Branch Will Not Break,* John Steinbeck's *The Grapes of Wrath,* and Toni Morrison's *Beloved* alongside John Wayne, Jimi Hendrix, Marilyn Monroe, Eminem, Curt Cobain, Steve Nash, Patsy Cline, the White Stripes, Hank Williams, Julius Irving, Hitchcock's *North by Northwest,* John Ford's *The Searchers,* and infomercials for acne treatments featuring Jessica Simpson and P. Diddy.

Nonetheless, he knows that he will always be labeled an "Indian writer," no matter what his focus is. Instead of worrying about limits imposed from without, including the critique that he is obsessed with popular culture, Alexie parodies the expectations of Native writers in poems such as "How to Write the Great American Indian Novel" and his essay/memoir "The Unauthorized Autobiography of Me," and through characters like Jack Wilson in the novel *Indian Killer.* In later works such as "The Search Engine" from *Ten Little Indians* and his film *The Business of Fancydancing,* he continues to question expectations placed on Indigenous writers, something considered explicitly in my essay, "The Business of Writing: Sherman Alexie's Meditations on Authorship," included in this collection.

In most of his writing, Alexie reshapes readers' attitudes about Native people, particularly notions based on stereotypes and misinformation. Taking on all the wannabe Indians out there, the Hollywood stereotypes, and the pop-culture heroes, he has the narrator of the first poem in his first collection of poems, *I Would Steal Horses,* declare to the world: "I got eyes, Jack,"[26] eyes that can see and a voice that can decry five hundred years of injustice. More recently, his poetry and fiction dismantle stereotypes by their subject matter—subject matter that has no overt, stereotypical, or exclusive connection to Indigenous culture—whether it be the father-son relationship in "The Senator's Son," or the ethnically unidentified owner of a lucrative used-clothing business who is a serial adulterer in "The Ballad of Paul Nonetheless," or the poems dedicated to now-antiquated fixations of the poet's young adulthood in the 1980s: "An Ode to Pay Phones" or "Ode to Mixed Tapes," all in *War Dances.*

Over the years, scholars such as Elizabeth Cook-Lynn (Dakota), who is often the target of Alexie's critique of the contemporary state of academia, have criticized him for not appropriately focusing on issues related to Native sovereignty. Alexie continues to confront such critiques directly and indirectly by finding a unique way to view subjects that compel him as an Indian man, an artist, a U.S. citizen living in the media-saturated early twenty-first century and discovering what may be called the "sovereignty of self": "My sobriety does give me sovereignty. Most Indians use 'sovereignty' to refer to the collective and tribal desire for political, cultural and economic independence. But I am using it here to mean 'the individual Indian artist's basic right to be an eccentric bastard'" (*Face,* 79). He suggests that the critics who chastise him for not writing in the service of sovereign nationalism—and he includes Cook-Lynn in this group—are "dying of nostalgia. She had taken nostalgia as her false idol—her thin blanket—and it was murdering her" (*WD,* 36–37).

While Alexie's characters and subject matter are most often rooted in lives that have been influenced by the Spokane or Coeur d'Alene cultural experience, on the reservation or off, his artistic reach is pan-tribal. For example, his repeated references to Crazy Horse, the Ghost Dance, Sand Creek, or Wounded Knee—to name several associations—assert a shared history among Native peoples across space and time. For example, the speaker—perhaps Alexie himself in "Looking Glass" from *War Dances*—represents the well-known Nez Perce leader, Chief Joseph, as a family familiar, one of his grandmother's favorite babysitters, and a loving man whose famous words of surrender were taken out of context. And, in the same collection, Alexie offers a correction to American history's remembrance of the Lincoln who signed the Emancipation Proclamation: a year before in 1862, he had approved "the largest public execution" in United States history; "Another Proc-lamation" remembers the thirty-seven Sioux hung in Minnesota and vividly calls on readers to imagine the "cacophony of thirty-seven dif-ferent death songs" (*WD,* 106). Alexie—being Alexie—asks us to imag-ine the one pardoned survivor's mourning song and poses the question, "If he taught you the words, do you think you would sing along?" (*WD,* 106). In other words, will you honor his memory and sense of injustice, or will you sustain the historical fiction and comfortable myths about a leader such as Lincoln?

Alexie acknowledges a responsibility to other American Indian peo-ple to build a better, less-factionalized America, but he's not interested in making his readers feel comfortable or complacent or fulfilling any-one's expectations. He knows that even poets suffer from illusions about possibility: "Why do poets think / They can change the world?" Alexie's speaker asks at the outset of his twenty-first book (*WD,* 2). If anything, he works to frustrate complacency, even in his view about the role of writ-ing and art: "The only life I can save / Is my own" (*WD,* 2). His series of poems—"The Alcoholic Love Poems"—from *First Indian on the Moon* (1993) is just one example of the way his writing confronts readers with-out pretense. Readers see the poet trying to come to terms with his fam-ily legacies, his own personal demons, and internal conflicts difficult to resolve easily. In "Shoes" from his book *Old Shirts and New Skins* (1993), Alexie asks, "How do you explain the survival of all of us who were never meant to survive?"[27]

In other contexts, Alexie offers a personal answer to this rhetorical question. For example, in "Imagining the Reservation" from *The Lone Ranger and Tonto Fistfight in Heaven,* he writes, "Survival = Anger × Imagination. Imagination is the only weapon on the reservation."[28] By the time "The Unauthorized Autobiography of Me" was published in *One Stick Song,* this formula had been transformed into "Poetry = Anger x Imagination,"[29] leading to the conclusion that "Survival = Poetry." Anger is a likely reaction to deep economic, social, and political inequities, but it is a self-destructive force if left to fester. If mediated through the cre-ative process of poetry making, though, anger can be transformed into survival.

How can we imagine a new language when the language of the enemy keeps our dismembered tongues tied to his belt?

—SHERMAN ALEXIE, "IMAGINING THE RESERVATION,"
THE LONE RANGER AND TONTO FISTFIGHT IN HEAVEN

Sherman Alexie's transformative imagination and the vivid contrasts in the range of his writing to date have kept scholars and teachers racing to keep pace with his literary output. Anyone who has taught Alexie's writing knows that it energizes students and provokes deep thought about complex subjects. His work appeals to readers who are interested in mining the dimensions of our human experiences, but it also demands a different kind of literary analysis than that currently practiced in the academy. Over the years, Alexie has criticized how out of sync contemporary criticism is from the real world that readers—Native and non-Native alike—inhabit. This collection asks readers to rise to the challenge of finding a meaningful intersection with Alexie's writing through the various scholarly points of entry into the world of his characters and poetic vision.

In selecting these essays, Jan Roush and I have had the good fortune of collaborating with some of the best scholars on Sherman Alexie within the field of American Indian literary studies who teach, publish, and present at conferences. Our editorial collaboration grew out of a Western Literature Association panel in Tucson, Arizona. Many of the writers whose work appears in this collection have been in the audience during each other's presentations at MELUS, the Native American Literature Symposium, American Studies Association, Popular Culture Association, and Native American and Indigenous Studies Association, among others.

In addition to collecting the best scholarship on Alexie, this volume also offers readers the first comprehensive bibliography of secondary criticism of his work published in the last fifteen years. Its eclectic list of primary works assembles published books, interviews, uncollected essays and poems, video pieces, and album contributions that will enable readers to find an entry point into the ever-ranging, energetic oeuvre of one of the twenty-first century's most provocative talents. Given the rapid pace of Alexie's career—fueled by his bottle-rocket imagination that never seems to burn out—we predict that these resource lists will only lengthen as critics keep pace with his prolific output.

In selecting these essays, we were interested in sharing fresh approaches to a wide range of Alexie's works. Not surprisingly, many of them focus on multiple texts and genres. While this approach seems logical and necessary because of Alexie's imaginative output, it presents some logistical and organizational challenges. Based on the essays' primary emphases, we have roughly organized this collection following the chronology of Alexie's career.

In the first essay, "Dancing That Way, Things Began to Change: The Ghost Dance as Pantribal Metaphor in Sherman Alexie's Writing," Lisa Tatonetti analyzes a recurring motif in much of Alexie's writing: the 1890 Lakota Ghost Dance and the Wounded Knee Massacre. She focuses readers' attention on moments in *Old Shirts & New Skins, First Indian on the Moon, The Lone Ranger and Tonto Fistfight in Heaven, Reservation Blues, The Summer of Black Widows,* and *Indian Killer.* By constructing this intertextual series of readings about a significant event in Native American and United States history—something Tatonetti has done elsewhere with Alexie's repeated references to salmon—she demonstrates the way Alexie sustains an argument for Native resistance and the potential of Indigenous coalition building.

Philip Heldrich's essay, "Survival = Anger × Imagination: Sherman Alexie's Dark Humor," offers readers a way to understand the comic elements in Alexie's fiction, particularly their intermixture with tragedy and trauma. Heldrich examines *The Lone Ranger and Tonto Fistfight in Heaven, Old Shirts & New Skins, Reservation Blues,* and *The Toughest Indian in the World* and contextualizes Alexie's writing within both European and Native American tragicomical traditions. He suggests that these dark comic moments open a dialogue with readers, in a liberating manner, and enable "self-actualization and social action, [by] providing a means of survival amid often-bewildering and absurd conditions."[30] Heldrich's essay reminds readers of what eminent intellectual Vine Deloria Jr. had to say about Indian humor in *Custer Died for Your Sins*: "The more desperate the problem, the more humor is directed to describe it.

Satirical remarks often circumscribe problems so that possible solutions are drawn from the circumstances that would not make sense if presented in other than a humorous form."[31]

In "'An Extreme Need to Tell the Truth': Silence and Language in Sherman Alexie's 'The Trial of Thomas Builds-the-Fire,'" Elizabeth Archuleta (Yaqui) offers a dense reading of one short story from *The Lone Ranger and Tonto Fistfight in Heaven.* Thomas Builds-the Fire, who appears elsewhere in this short-story collection, the film *Smoke Signals,* and the novel *Reservation Blues,* usually talks a blue streak. His unusual silence in this story, thus, is notable. Using the lenses of testimony and witnessing as well as critical legal theory, Archuleta analyzes the buried, yet politically and historically resonant, aspects of this story to demonstrate the way Thomas's silence is a powerful "voiced" reaction to what he sees as troubling shifts in tribal power, orchestrated by the Bureau of Indian Affairs.

We are pleased to include an updated version of one of the earliest essays on Sherman Alexie's novels. In "Rock and Roll, Redskins, and Blues in Sherman Alexie's Work," P. Jane Hafen (Taos Pueblo) examines the author's use of music—in particular the subversive tradition of blues and rock and roll—in *Reservation Blues.* Hafen provocatively suggests that the variety of musical expressions in this novel acts as a "mediator" that compels readers to reconsider popular-culture imagery. This revised essay includes a consideration of Alexie's collaboration with Jim Boyd (Colville) to produce a sound track, *Reservation Blues.* It was well known that Alexie was working on a screenplay for this novel, but quite remarkably this 1995 album predates any likely film. Hafen notes the clear intersections between the novel and album tracks, suggesting an interesting avenue for further research.

Perhaps Hafen's greatest contribution to this volume and the body of critical responses to Alexie's work, however, is her meditation on the personal meaning of this novel. In contrast to Gloria Bird's characterization of Alexie's exaggerations of reality, Hafen issues this important reminder: "As a scholar, I hope Alexie's writings will challenge critics to recognize that Native American literature is not simply an exercise in literary theory.... The greater critical challenge is acknowledging that Alexie's work depicts real contemporary people who are not historical artifacts, anthropological phenomena, objects of literary theories, or simply Earth's children."[32]

This collection features two previously unpublished essays on Alexie's film *Smoke Signals,* undoubtedly the most influential work connected to his diverse writing career. James H. Cox's "This Is What It Means to Say Reservation Cinema: Making Cinematic Indians in *Smoke Signals*" examines the way Sherman Alexie's screenplay and Chris Eyre's directorial decisions create a different image of Indian people in film. For the better part of the twentieth century, European Americans were (and still are) the primary producers of these Indian stereotypes and the attendant definitions of "Indianness" in film and fiction, as well as anthropological, ethnographic, and historical texts. Cox, who has written about Alexie's confrontations with popular culture in *Muting White Noise: Native American and European Novel Traditions,* emphasizes the way that *Smoke Signals,* adapted from stories in *The Lone Ranger and Tonto Fistfight in Heaven,* establishes new terminology and points of reference for establishing characters' tribal and Indigenous identities. Undoubtedly the film evokes comparisons to previous cinematic images, most obviously when Thomas Builds-the-Fire jokes, "The only thing more pathetic than watching Indians on TV is Indians watching Indians on TV."

In "Native Sensibility and the Significance of Women in *Smoke Signals,*" Angelica Lawson (Northern Arapaho) takes a fresh look at the film. In contrast to views that women play a minor part in the film, Lawson contends that their roles are deeply significant if Victor and Arnold's story is considered within the richer context of canons of Native oratory. Not denying that the film appropriates the Hollywood genres of the buddy and road-trip films, Lawson adds depth to the film by considering a generally unnoticed narrative framework: the quest of hero twins, an archetypal tale common to many tribes. Within the framework of this tale, women in the film become much more significant as they assume the important roles of advisors, guides, and catalysts for the development of self-understanding.

Susan Brill de Ramírez's essay, "The Distinctive Sonority of Sherman Alexie's Indigenous Poetics," challenges us to consider generic and formal elements of Alexie's poetry. Brill de Ramírez, who has written about

Alexie for the *Dictionary of Literary Biography* and elsewhere, notes that his complex metrics and intricate poetic forms are too often ignored by readers. Heeding a call by scholars in Indigenous literary studies, Brill de Ramírez offers readers a close analysis of a series of thematically linked poems whose meaning is deepened by their intricate connection to sonorous language and sophisticated, purposeful metrics.

We are pleased to include Nancy Peterson's nuanced and challenging reading of Alexie's complex collection of poetry, *The Summer of Black Widows,* in this collection. Peterson, who edited the first comprehensive collection of interviews with Alexie, analyzes the way the thematic and formal tensions in his poetry intersect with the pull between "Alexie's tribalist, reservation roots and the writer's engagement with non-Native and multicultural materials associated with the world beyond the reservation."[33] Peterson notes a unique, unexpected dynamic: as Alexie's poems topically, geographically, and formally move away from his cultural homeland, they become more clearly "rooted in tribalism." Notably, Peterson argues, Alexie's exploration of poetic forms forces readers to change their assumptions about power and begin to consider European genres such as the sonnet as an *Indigenous* form.

In "Sherman Alexie's Challenge to the Academy's Teaching of Native American Literature, Non-Native Writers, and Critics," previously published in *Studies in American Indian Literatures,* Patrice Hollrah explores Alexie's criticism of the university's historical treatment of Indigenous people in the areas of research and curricula. Hollrah focuses on Marie Polatkin's critiques of educators in the novel *Indian Killer* and Etta Joseph's humorous deconstruction of anthropology in "Dear John Wayne," as well as "One Good Man"'s depiction of professors who insist on defining what it means to be Indian, even to Native people. Hollrah's analysis of these stories—included in *The Toughest Indian in the World*—as well as "The Unauthorized Autobiography of Me" from *One Stick Song* introduces readers to crucial debates in contemporary American Indian studies and uses the scholarship of Robert Warrior, Craig Womack, Elizabeth Cook-Lynn, Waziyatawin Angela Wilson, Devon Mihesuah, and Duane Champagne to inspire non-Native critics and educators to find their culturally appropriate—meaning nonappropriative—role within that field.

In "'Indians Do Not Live in Cities, They Only Reside There': Captivity and the Urban Wilderness in *Indian Killer*," Meredith James places Alexie's *Indian Killer* within the context of captivity narratives, rather than in the murder-mystery genre to which many critics and reviewers have relegated it. Considering the novel within this broader framework of American literature—beginning with the captivity narrative of Mary Rowlandson but focusing especially on what James terms the "reverse captivity narrative" of Gertrude Simmons Bonnin, aka Zitkala-Ša, the well-known late-nineteenth-century Yankton Sioux author—James analyzes the way Alexie similarly allows his protagonist, John Smith, to comment on the inherent problems such "Lost Birds" encounter when captured and forced to comply with policies propagated by the dominant culture—no matter how well intentioned. By doing so, James contends, Alexie moves the novel well beyond the formulaic detective story, instead allowing it to highlight and comment on the complex challenge of modern, urban Indians achieving identity within the cultural context of captivity.

Stephen F. Evans's essay, "Indigenous Liaisons: Sex-Gender Variability, Indianness, and Intimacy in Sherman Alexie's *The Toughest Indian in the World*," analyzes characters whose sense of Indian identity is conflicted. In a significant number of stories, Evans notes, this identity crisis is framed by the parameters of sexuality. Evans explains that by writing against homophobia and other forms of sexual prejudice, Alexie delegitimizes heteronormativity. Readers may recognize Evans's critical strategies from "'Open Containers,'" his well-known essay on Alexie's representations of alcoholism. Rather than a unified view of the situation, Evans notes the multiple ways that different characters "subvert, adopt, or manipulate stereotypes" as either an unconscious or conscious expression of anxieties about sexuality and race, notions shaped within Indigenous communities by the forces of colonialism, including religion. The focus on *The Toughest Indian in the World* also applies to other works, including the film *The Business of Fancydancing*, where Alexie continues—as he has done through most of his career—to construct characters whose identities and experiences range along the entire sexual continuum.

In "Sherman Alexie's Transformations of 'Ten Little Indians,'" Margaret O'Shaughnessy analyzes Alexie's use of the familiar nursery rhyme to reveal that the negative depiction of Indians being counted down to total destruction becomes, in his hand, a positive representation of Indian survival in the face of overwhelming odds. Ranging across the prolific body of Alexie's works for representative examples, O'Shaughnessy makes a convincing case for this inversion.

Jan Johnson's essay, "Healing the Soul Wound in *Flight* and *The Absolutely True Diary of a Part-Time Indian,*" explores intergenerational trauma. She considers the way each of Alexie's two most recent novels—the second written for young adults—imagines a healing journey, a movement beyond the cycle of trauma. In particular Johnson examines Alexie's portrayal of fathers and compares the consequences of the absence of a good Indian father in *Flight* to the presence of a caring one in *The Absolutely True Diary of a Part-Time Indian.*

In the concluding essay in this collection, "The Business of Writing: Sherman Alexie's Meditations on Authorship," I consider his creation of author characters in his film *The Business of Fancydancing* and short story "The Search Engine" from *Ten Little Indians.* My analysis includes the critiques, claims, needs, and desires that run along the circuit of culture-writer-reader-culture. Through his fictional authors and readers, Alexie advances multiple views of the pressures facing Indigenous authors while simultaneously honoring and investigating the merit of readerly claims. I position these meditations within the broader trends of American Indian literary scholarship, suggesting that Alexie's fictional and poetic works provide readers with theoretical insights on reading and methodology.

Trust me. The whole damn universe of response to your art,
to your tiny little creation, is a beautiful, amazing thing.

—SHERMAN ALEXIE, PREFACE TO *THE BUSINESS OF FANCYDANCING*

In the preface to his published screenplay for *The Business of Fancydancing,* Alexie notes seven discoveries he made while making his film; the most significant to this discussion is that "art is kinetic," and the

> following are all good things: the ecstatic and disdainful
> reviews; the enraptured and bored audiences; the fans and

the enemies...the puzzled, confused, enlightened, and chal-
lenged...when Ally Sheedy gives you a hug and kiss for making
a movie about Indians; when Harvey Weinstein ignores you for
making another movie about Indians; when Indians love you and
hate you for making a movie about Indians; and so on and so on.
Trust me. The whole damn universe of response to your art, to
your tiny little creation, is a beautiful, amazing thing.[34]

Alexie made this statement after completing a highly collaborative
production—his directorial debut of his own screenplay—and near the
end of his first decade of publishing. He has obviously received plenty of
feedback from readers. His work continues to evoke strong reactions, and
he remains engaged with those who critique his work: in some respects,
his fiction and poetry continue to evolve because of these challenges; in
other cases, he sharpens his own arguments, refusing to write according
to anyone else's proscriptions.

I read his work for many reasons but mainly because I enjoy participating in this ongoing conversation and exploration. I know that one of the
great pleasures of reading is discovering new insights: about the world,
about ourselves, and about the combination of talent and vision that is
masterfully encoded in language. Of course, the meaning and value of a
literary work are always contested. For many, including me, that is the
real pleasure of great literature: debating, arguing, probing more deeply
into a literary work through shared conversations. Alexie's comments
about his characters, intended meanings, and hopes for and critiques of
scholar readers are only one part of the shared conversation at the heart
of this book. His stories, poems, and novels now have a life independent
of their creator.

In Alexie's first widely read short-story collection—*The Lone Ranger
and Tonto Fistfight in Heaven*—the narrator wonders how the burden of
history, of genocide, can ever be overcome and if a voice can be reclaimed
from the colonizers: "How can we imagine a new language when the language of the enemy keeps our dismembered tongues tied to his belt?"
(*LRT,* 152). I invite readers to consider all of the ways that Alexie claims a
new voice, loosening the tongues that colonialism tied up. Do you think
the scholarship here, in concert with Alexie's writing, helps create a new

language, or is it simply the enemy's language of yesteryear in a new guise? Your voice is essential to this dialogue. Pull a chair up to our circle and join our conversation. Find a way to enter into a world of fiction and poetry that we believe fiercely resonates today. You'll learn that while Alexie's writing has deep roots in a too-often-neglected past, it is involved in creating an unflinching forward-looking view of the world that awaits us in our shared futures.

NOTES

1. Rick Margolis, "Song of Myself: Interview with Sherman Alexie," 29.
2. Ibid.
3. This phrase is a repeated line in Adrian C. Louis's poem "Elegy for the Forgotten Oldsmobile" in *Fire Water World*. Alexie has noted that this poem profoundly inspired him as a young writer. From an interview with Tomson Highway, "Spokane Words: Tomson Highway Raps with Sherman Alexie."
4. Sherman Alexie, "Superman and Me."
5. "Up All Night," *Now with Bill Moyers*.
6. Sherman Alexie, *Flight,* 12 (hereafter cited in the text).
7. Sherman Alexie, *The Absolutely True Diary of a Part-Time Indian,* 11 (hereafter cited in the text as *ATD*).
8. Russ Spencer, "What It Means to Be Sherman Alexie."
9. John Purdy, "Crossroads: A Conversation with Sherman Alexie," 7.
10. Robert Capriccioso, "Sherman Alexie: American Indian Filmmaker/Writer Talks with Robert Capriccioso."
11. P. Jane Hafen, "Rock and Roll, Redskins, and Blues in Sherman Alexie's Work," in *Sherman Alexie: A Collection of Critical Essays,* 62.
12. Diane Thiel, "A Conversation with Sherman Alexie."
13. Sherman Alexie, *War Dances,* 63 (hereafter cited in the text as *WD*).
14. Sherman Alexie, *Face,* 115 (hereafter cited in the text).
15. Highway, "Spokane Words."
16. Duncan Campbell, "Voice of the New Tribes."
17. "The Toughest Indian in the World," *Sixty Minutes II*.
18. Thiel, "A Conversation."
19. "The Toughest Indian."
20. Purdy, "Crossroads," 16.
21. Capriccioso, "Sherman Alexie: American Indian Filmmaker."
22. Sarah T. Williams, "Man of Many Tribes."
23. Susan Berry Brill de Ramírez, "Fancy Dancer: A Profile of Sherman Alexie," 57.
24. Kelley Blewster, "Tribal Visions," 22.

25. "The Toughest Indian," *Sixty Minutes II.*

26. Sherman Alexie, *I Would Steal Horses.*

27. Sherman Alexie, *Old Shirts & New Skins,* 90.

28. Sherman Alexie, *The Lone Ranger and Tonto Fistfight in Heaven,* 150 (hereafter cited in the text as *LRT*).

29. Sherman Alexie, *One Stick Song,* 20.

30. Philip Heldrich, "Survival = Anger × Imagination: Sherman Alexie's Dark Humor," in *Sherman Alexie: A Collection of Critical Essays,* 25.

31. Vine Deloria Jr., *Custer Died for Your Sins: An Indian Manifesto,* 147 (page reference is to the 1969 edition).

32. Hafen, "Rock and Roll, Redskins, and Blues," 71–72

33. Nancy J. Peterson, "The Poetics of Tribalism in Sherman Alexie's *The Summer of Black Widows,*" in *Sherman Alexie: A Collection of Critical Essays,* 134–135.

34. Sherman Alexie, "What I've Learned as a Filmmaker," preface to *The Business of Fancydancing: The Screenplay,* 8.

■ *Lisa Tatonetti*

CHAPTER I

Dancing That Way, Things Began to Change

The Ghost Dance as Pantribal Metaphor in Sherman Alexie's Writing

Sherman Alexie is a Spokane/Coeur d'Alene Indian born into a Salish-speaking tribe that historically fished for salmon, hunted elk, and dug camas bulbs for sustenance. The 155,997-acre Spokane Reservation, covered with basalt and pine forests, is a far remove from South Dakota and, particularly, the arid country where the Lakota make their home. But for brief moments—in the haunting refrains of Alexie's work—the two come together in allusions to the 1890 Lakota Ghost Dance and the Wounded Knee massacre.[1] Alexie uses Ghost Dance and Wounded Knee references in a myriad of ways, ranging from the succinct, tongue-in-cheek word-play in *Old Shirts & New Skins*—"You can always find me mumbling here / about how I wounded my knee"—to the revisionary plotline in *Indian Killer,* which suggests that "maybe this Indian Killer is a product of the Ghost Dance. Maybe ten Indians are Ghost Dancing. Maybe a hundred.... Maybe this is how the Ghost Dance works."[2]

In this essay, I analyze a number of these moments in *Old Shirts & New Skins, First Indian on the Moon, The Lone Ranger and Tonto Fistfight in Heaven, Reservation Blues, The Summer of Black Widows,* and, finally, *Indian Killer,* examining how and to what end Alexie employs images of the 1890 Lakota Ghost Dance and the Wounded Knee massacre. The body of these images, I argue, suggests a trajectory in which Alexie's Ghost Dance and Wounded Knee references progress from historical allusions and personal metaphors to politically charged sites of resistance. By analyzing representative pieces from Sherman Alexie's poetry and fiction, I investigate the way Alexie—whose ancestors did not participate in the Ghost Dance—uses it as an explicit metaphor for Native resistance. Ultimately, I contend that Alexie capitalizes on the iconic power of the Ghost Dance, which has historically flattened and contained Native identities, by depicting it as a potential impetus for Indigenous coalition.

In light of the significance of Ghost Dance and Wounded Knee images in Alexie's later work, it is interesting—and rather surprising—that his first book, *The Business of Fancydancing,* contains allusions to neither. Instead, this eclectic combination of prose and poetry works its magic using images of Crazy Horse in 7-Eleven, commodity cans, and reservation boys with basketball dreams. In 1993, the year after the acclaimed debut of this first book, Alexie published two volumes of his already-signature blend of flash fiction and poetry—*Old Shirts & New Skins* and *First Indian on the Moon*—and one book of short stories—*The Lone Ranger and Tonto Fistfight in Heaven.* While these three books return to the themes and characters of the first, they also include recurrent allusions to the Ghost Dance and Wounded Knee in their barrage of rapid-fire images.

Old Shirts & New Skins, Alexie's first book published in 1993, is also the first of any of his texts to include Ghost Dance and Wounded Knee imagery. And while Alexie's allusions to these two events have slightly less revolutionary potential impact than in some of his later books, these references still unsettle prevailing readings of either event. In the prose poem "Vision (2)" (*OSNS,* 27), for example, the speaker compares America, where "progress or Manifest Destiny" are snake-entwined poles, to "*my* country," the Spokane Reservation where Alexie grew up. After juxtaposing the two worlds, the speaker comments: "Then again, who am I to talk? In the local newspaper I read this morning that my tribe escaped many of the hardships other Native Americans suffered. By the time the 20th century reached this far west, the war was over. Crazy Horse was gone and the Ghost Dancers were only ghosts. Christopher Columbus was 500 years and 3,000 miles away, fresh from a starring role in the Great American Movie." (*OSNS,* 27)

In many ways, the allusion to the Ghost Dance—in tandem with words like "over," "gone," and "ghosts,"—reiterates the classic iconography where the dance marks the mythical end of Native culture. And although it's not explicit, Wounded Knee is, nevertheless, invoked with the Ghost Dance since the dancers who become ghosts are undoubtedly the Minniconjou killed at Wounded Knee Creek. The passage's somewhat vague wording, however, leaves unresolved whether the newspaper reporter or the narrator is responsible for this stereotypical conflation. The biting "who am I to talk?" suggests the former, but in either case, this repetition of dominant stories about the Ghost Dance and Wounded Knee is an ironic backdrop for the paper's inaccurate version of Spokane history that we see in the poem's final passage.

The last verses leave the nineteenth century behind, leaping from the Ghost Dance to Christopher Columbus and a commentary about the way the Columbus story circulates in the U.S. imagination: "I've seen that film at the reservation drive-in. If you look closely, you/can see an Indian leaning against the back wall. You won't find his name/among the end credits; you can't hear his voice or his song./Extras, we're all extras" (*OSNS,* 27). The film, which the narrator earlier called the "Great American Movie," is the dominant version of U.S. history. I have seen this edited-for-TV drama several times. It goes something like this: *Front stage:* America is "discovered!"; *Backstage:* Indians, dispossessed of land and voice, are pushed to the outskirts, relegated to the "back walls" of their own countries; *Front stage left:* It's *The Last of the Mohicans,* and Natty Bumppo is sad, sad, sad; *Front stage right:* The Indians dance, "wild and crazy"; (Cue cavalry; swell strings); *Center stage:* The Indians die. As the credits roll, a voice-over in broken English—*the nation's hoop is broken and scattered. There is no center any longer, and the sacred tree is dead*—and the last words that Black Elk never spoke erroneously become the single version of Native "history" into which all Native pasts are subsumed. Pretty soon the whole damn thing is the only film on the all-day History Channel movie marathon.

And so it is with Alexie's Spokane narrator, who, with "no money for lunch," opens the paper only to discover that the history and hardships of his own tribe have apparently been buried at Wounded Knee. In this vignette, then, Alexie's explicit allusion to the Ghost Dance and implicit one to Wounded Knee superimpose the history of the Plains Indians over that of the Spokane. The resulting conjunction highlights the inaccuracy of prevailing accounts of Native history, where the conflated image of the Ghost Dance and Wounded Knee becomes a metonym for all Native history.

Specific allusions to Wounded Knee also appear in *Old Shirts & New Skins*. "Custer Speaks," for instance, features a monologue where the (in)-famous General George Armstrong Custer, who died in the 1876 Battle of Little Bighorn (Greasy Grass), tells his side of the story. The poem is divided into seven sections in which events from Custer's life are interspersed with his postmortem commentary. In the third stanza, Custer says:

> I see by your eyes what you think of me, of my surprise ride into
> Black Kettle's camp on the Washita River. It's easy
> to blame me, to call it a massacre. But it was no Sand Creek, no
> Wounded Knee. Still, call me what you need to call me:
> . . . .
> It doesn't change anything, make the fight mean less.
> Just because Black Kettle's camp was on the reservation doesn't
>   allow it
> to be called anything short of victory.
> They had to be removed to make Kansas, the West, safe. They were
>   barriers
> to progress. You call it genocide; I call it economics. (*OSNS*, 36–37)

This offhand reference to Wounded Knee is embedded in Custer's reminiscence about Black Kettle and the cavalry massacre that led to the Southern Cheyenne peace chief's death on November 27, 1868. At the time, Custer headed a U.S. cavalry strike force for General Philip Sheridan, and in this "battle"—just as in the Sand Creek massacre that Custer mentions with Wounded Knee—the cavalry attacked an unsuspecting village in the early hours of the morning, killing men, women, and children as a white flag of truce waved above.[3] I argue that Custer's (Alexie's) narrative juxtaposition—setting Wounded Knee next to the 1868 cavalry attack on Black Kettle's Washita River encampment, and both of those attacks alongside the 1864 Sand Creek massacre—effectively changes the way that we read Wounded Knee: although still a violent, horrifying event, Wounded Knee, when contextualized, is shown to be one in a long line of attacks, rather than the *only* massacre and single defining event in Native history.

In "Custer Speaks," then, Wounded Knee, while only an aside, is historicized and thus removed from the realm of a tragic, inevitable aberration. In the case of both these poems—"Vision (2)" or "Custer Speaks"—allusions to the Ghost Dance and Wounded Knee reiterate and revise dominant images of these historical events: in "Vision (2)," Alexie reproduces, albeit ironically, the ubiquitous rhetoric of Lakota annihilation as a commentary on the media's inaccurate representation of Spokane tribal history, while in "Custer Speaks," he highlights the layered reality of Native history, juxtaposing Wounded Knee against two other U.S. Army massacres of Native people to emphasize the genocidal nature of all these attacks. While these two examples function very differently, both employ the iconographic images of the Ghost Dance and Wounded Knee in new ways. Thus, one of Alexie's earliest published texts already contains the seeds of his later, more radical interpretations of these overdetermined images.

Describing the way these images function in Alexie's work, Taos Pueblo scholar P. Jane Hafen maintains, "Alexie's people were not at Sand Creek or Wounded Knee; neither are the Spokane related to Crazy Horse. Yet these are events and figures that have impact upon all Native peoples."[4] As opposed to critics like Gloria Bird, who suggest Alexie's comparisons inevitably distort and compress Native cultures into a false conglomerate, Hafen effectively asserts the common ground that such allusions implicitly posit.[5] And although Hafen's analysis centers on *Old Shirts & New Skins*, her contention is equally valid for any of Alexie's texts since each one alludes to a non-Spokane tribal history at one point or another.

Matt Herman alleges that such questions of authenticity, while often couched as cultural protection, can "leave behind [their] important capacity as guardian[s] of cultural and ethnic propriety" and become a form of "cultural hegemony" that "elides attention to social and material conditions."[6] While Herman leaves these conditions unspecified, I argue that in Alexie's work they are, on one hand, the similar material conditions of poverty and oppression that characterize many reservations across the country and, on the other, the rise of various kinds of pan-Indianism: manifestations of the shared, Plains-influenced culture that has arisen as a result of boarding schools, termination and relocation policies, the steady growth of powwows, and the rise of urban Indian centers. Although poverty is not universal among Native nations in the U.S. and pan-Indianism is by no means uniformly accepted by all Native people, these material and social conditions do—perhaps more than any others—routinely cross tribal boundaries.

Therefore, whether such common ties are dismissed as cultural distortions, as they are by Bird, or accepted as cultural realities, as they are by Hafen, pan-Indian practices and metaphors are undeniably present within the majority of Indian communities. And that common ground underlies and, in many ways, authorizes Alexie's use of Ghost Dance and Wounded Knee allusions since—as Hafen points out—there is, on some level, a common Native history where events from one specific tribe have meaning for contemporary Native people from many different tribes. Thus, when Alexie employs and historically weights images of Wounded Knee and the Ghost Dance, he both draws upon and constructs a pan-Indian aesthetic.

In *First Indian on the Moon*, Alexie's second 1993 book, Ghost Dance and Wounded Knee metaphors seem, at first glance, to move away from globalization and become, instead, intensely personal. Rather than signifying intertribal connection, these images reflect the speaker's inner conflicts as "Reservation Mathematics" vividly illustrates: "Mixed-up and mixed-blood...I belong to both tribes. It's my personal Wounded Knee, my own Little Bighorn."[7] Grappling with the difficulties of being mixed blood in the equally striated worlds of the reservation and dominant U.S. society, the speaker struggles with a personal conflict rooted in a specific political history: the long and troubled narrative of Indian-white relations in the U.S. In many ways, this conflict is epitomized by the rhetoric of blood quantum, an attempt by the U.S. government to codify (and thus limit) tribal membership, regulate Native identities and bodies, and, ultimately, control Native lands by legislating indigeneity into ever-diminishing fractions.[8] It is this layered and difficult history that the speaker invokes, then, when he voices the need for a space of mediation, "a life between / the 3/16 that names me white / and the 13/16 / that names me Indian" (*FIM,* 43).[9] Experiencing what W. E. B. Du Bois first called "twoness" and postcolonial theorists have termed "hybridity," the speaker finally claims liminality—"I belong to both tribes." But that liminality is more mournful than celebratory, more fault line than foundation, as evidenced by the metaphors that the speaker uses to describe his background: the 1876 Battle of Little Bighorn and the 1890 Wounded Knee massacre.

Little Big Horn and Wounded Knee are two historical moments that represent the extreme ends of Indian-white conflicts. In the Battle of Little Big Horn, General George Armstrong Custer and the 215 men in his cavalry regiment were killed after they attacked the peaceful summer encampment of more than two thousand Lakota and Cheyenne, while in the Wounded Knee massacre, U.S. soldiers slaughtered nearly three hundred unarmed Lakota after they surrendered to Custer's old unit, the Seventh Cavalry. Both battles intensified the already-fraught relationship between Indians and whites in the U.S. As Alexie no doubt intends, these metaphors remind readers of the long and bitter history that invariably complicates the speaker's claim to "belong to both tribes." In this analogy, Wounded Knee becomes the symbol of all wrongs that whites have wrought on Native people, and the speaker's personal history, a metaphor for the entire canvas of Native-white relations. Rather than erasing Native histories as it did in "Visions (2)," the Wounded Knee allusion in "Reservation Mathematics" becomes a key image through which the speaker understands and describes personal history.

If "Reservation Mathematics" moves the massacre from the larger context of American Indian history to a narrower, personal level, "Apologies," another poem from *First Indian on the Moon,* reverses that pattern, extending the image of Wounded Knee from local U.S. history to global world history and changing the massacre's meaning. Although their conclusions diverge, "Apologies," like "Reservation Mathematics," embeds its allusion to the Wounded Knee massacre in a personal dilemma: an Indian man in love with a white woman tries to reconcile his history and emotions with the racist hatred and pain her white father has "been growing since World War II" (*FIM*, 59). When the father "curses the suggestion that we owe Japan / an apology for Nagasaki and Hiroshima" (*FIM*, 59), the poet asks how pain, anger, and fear justify war. The speaker turns to two pictures for answers: "the photograph / of a mummified Vietnamese soldier's skull / perched like a crazy ass scarecrow / on an American tank in '66 or '67 / or whenever," and the picture "of another dark-skinned enemy, Bigfoot / the Minniconjou chief, frozen solid/in the snow at Wounded Knee, one hand / reaching toward the camera, a gesture / that would have looked staged today / but in 1876 it meant he died / with questions" (*FIM*, 59).

Alexie's juxtaposition of the mummified head and frozen body of these two U.S. "enemies" is a powerful commentary on the imperialist nature of U.S. history. These images point to the dehumanizing effects of war and the fact that dark-skinned people are often on the wrong end of both the gun and the camera in these horrifying situations. As a result, Alexie's most vivid description of Wounded Knee—the detailed picture of Big Foot—represents his most all-encompassing commentary about the massacre: the picture symbolizes the horror and racism of *all* war, *all* hatred, rather than acting as a specific commentary on Native history or the events of 1890.

The universal function of the famous photograph is further emphasized by the fact that Alexie incorrectly attributes Big Foot's picture and death to 1876.[10] Such generalizations, while important as commentaries, are somewhat troubling because they duplicate what they criticize: suggesting that all oppression, all war, all people of color are somehow interchangeable. As Latina author Cherríe Moraga writes, "The danger lies in ranking the oppressions. *The danger lies in failing to acknowledge the specificity of the oppressions.*"[11] Alexie's collapse of one significant date in American Indian history into another—his "fail[ure] to acknowledge the specificity"—is troubling because of the cultural baggage attached to this particular picture. This haunting photograph is one of the most frequently reproduced images of the massacre, and that repetition brings the danger of eventual meaninglessness. The camera snaps, a moment is frozen in time, and Big Foot the man, the Minneconjou leader, disappears. Like the pictures of Geronimo in Leslie Silko's *Almanac of the Dead,* Big Foot's pictures proliferate, none of them accurate, none of them holding the "truth" about the man or the massacre. A twisted body in the snow, Big Foot is not located in time, nor tribal history, nor geography, sacred or otherwise. And although he has a name, the dead figure Alexie describes "reaching toward the camera" has no more resonance than the nameless skull that serves—for the soldiers in the photograph—as the paradigmatic symbol for all Vietnamese: each photo represents death, each photo represents racism, and each photo represents the horrors and inhumanity of war.

I argue, then, that in this 1890 picture—and again in Alexie's poem—the real Big Foot is subsumed by the image of his death, caught in what Anishinaabe theorist Gerald Vizenor calls "the tragic in the ruins of representation."[12] Thus, the Wounded Knee reference in "Apologies"—while it first appears to critique the ways images circulate and desensitize—ultimately reinforces, rather than revises, the loss historically associated with well-known images of the massacre.

In *The Lone Ranger and Tonto Fistfight in Heaven,* Alexie's first collection of short stories and the last of his 1993 publications, the image of Wounded Knee falls away. Instead, the Ghost Dance becomes prominent and is, for the first time, imagined as a site of future possibility, rather than historical loss. This shift is most obvious in the second story of the collection, "A Drug Called Tradition," which begins at the house of the Spokane Reservation's misfit, tribal storyteller—Thomas-Builds-the-Fire—during "the second-largest party in reservation history."[13] At the party, Victor Joseph, the narrator, and his best friend, Junior Polatkin, have a whispered conversation about Victor's new drug. They leave to try the drug and are joined a short while later by Thomas, whom Victor invites with the laughing comment, "We're going out to Benjamin Lake to do this new drug I got. It'll be very fucking Indian. Spiritual shit, you know?" (*LRT,* 14). The boys take the drug and begin to tell stories about each other, seeing, as the narrator explains, "through some hole in the wall into another world. A better world" (*LRT,* 14).

The second story the boys tell begins with Junior's exclamation, "Oh, shit,...I can see Thomas dancing" (*LRT,* 14). And despite the fact that Thomas states flatly, "I don't dance," the narrative moves from Junior's vision into Thomas's description of his dance, which—like so much of Alexie's prose—is both painful and beautiful:

> *They're all gone, my tribe is gone.* Those blankets they gave us, infected with smallpox, have killed us. I'm the last, the very last, and I'm sick, too.... I'll dance a Ghost Dance. I'll bring them back.... I dance one step and my sister rises from the ash. I dance another and a buffalo crashes down from the sky onto a log cabin in Nebraska. With every step, an Indian rises. With every other step, a buffalo falls....
>
> We dance in circles growing larger and larger until we are standing at the shore, watching all the ships returning to Europe. All the white hands are waving good-bye and we continue to dance, dance until the ships fall off the horizon, dance until we are so tall and strong that the sun is nearly jealous. *We dance that way.* (*LRT,* 17; italics in original)

There is tremendous movement in Thomas's vision, which begins with the classic tragic rhetoric of the vanishing Indian and ends in a Native utopia. The disease-infested blankets and Ghost Dance at the beginning suggest that Thomas's dance occurs sometime in the nineteenth century when several smallpox epidemics swept through the Native population on the Plains.[14] On the reservation of Thomas's imagination, his tribe has been reduced by half, and half, and half again until its members have dwindled down to him. Though some may feel that Thomas's hopeless cry—"I'm the last, the very last"—reiterates the dominant image of Indian annihilation too strongly, the refrain is only momentarily true. Thomas moves past this moment of despair and takes decisive action, ultimately changing the course of history with his dance. And although the Ghost Dance occurs in a fleeting hallucination, rather than present time, the revolutionary potential of the dance is apparent—the whites disappear, the Indian people grow strong—and the boys' next vision initiates an alternative history.

Junior's vision, like Thomas's, is introduced by another character (in this case, Victor) before Junior's voice picks up the story. Wearing a ribbon shirt and carrying a guitar, Junior leads readers into a world where Indians get all the best seats and "white folks...have to sit in the back of the theater" (*LRT,* 18). He tells us, "Even the President of the United States, Mr. Edgar Crazy Horse himself, came to hear me once. I played a song I wrote for his great-grandfather, the famous Lakota warrior who helped us win the war against the whites" (*LRT,* 18). In Junior's United States, the potential of Thomas's Ghost Dance has come to fruition, the racial balance and population statistics are reversed, and Crazy Horse is firmly ensconced as the nation's culture hero. This new order seems—as Junior says at the close of his vision—*"like a thousand promises come true"* (*LRT,* 19; italics in original). According to James H. Cox, in vignettes such as this, Alexie

> suggests that imagining alternatives to the dominant culture's narratives of conquest (Columbus' voyage; the Manifest Destiny conferred by the Christian God on Europe's children) is a powerful weapon. Imagining alternative histories might not change the present . . . but conceiving of other possibilities, revisioning a history in which Native Americans write Native Americans back into the landscape, will influence the future. As Alexie explains, imagination is one part of the equation for survival.[15]

In "A Drug Called Tradition," we see such revisioning taking place. Even the story's title underlines the generative powers of the mind by implying that the "spiritual shit" of Victor's drug is just that: the spirit, practices, and beliefs of his people. When absorbed by the boys' bodies, the heady stuff of tradition expands their understanding. And while their experiences are temporary, Thomas's final narrative—which, significantly, is not drug induced but a story like those he tells every day—brings new possibilities from the realm of vision into ordinary life. Thomas says,

> *It is now.* Three Indian boys are drinking Diet Pepsi and talking out by Benjamin Lake. . . . The Indian boys have decided to be real Indians tonight. . . . The boys sit by the fire and breathe, their visions arrive. They are all carried away to the past, to the moment before any of them took their first drink of alcohol. The boy Thomas throws the beer he is offered into the garbage. The boy Junior throws his whiskey through a window. The boy Victor spills his vodka down the drain.

Then the boys sing. They sing and dance and drum. They steal
horses. I can see them. *They steal horses.* (*LRT,* 20–21; italics in
original)

When Thomas finishes his story, Victor asks, "You don't really believe
that shit?" (*LRT,* 21). Thomas's answer—"Don't need to believe anything. It just is." (*LRT,* 21)—provides a commentary on the entire narrative by dissolving the thin veil between story and vision, vision and truth,
and truth and tradition. Without this controlling veil—which discredits
Native beliefs with Western, scientific skepticism (e.g., "You don't really
believe that shit?")—the connections between tradition and personal
regeneration can emerge, as they do in Thomas's final story. These ties
are especially apparent in Thomas's vision of the Ghost Dance, where the
performance of a traditional ceremony—the act of dance—engenders a
whole new world. And much as Thomas's vision becomes the center of
Alexie's story, so the underlying metaphor of the Ghost Dance serves as
the foundation for the entire collection.

In *The Lone Ranger and Tonto Fistfight in Heaven,* the Ghost Dance
testifies to the regenerative power of Native cosmologies, which—as
Thomas points out—have more power than belief. Like Thomas's decision to dance, the boys' determination "to be real Indians" (*LRT,* 20)
locates power not in the degree of belief, which is clearly incomplete—
they initially think "*Maybe* they'll see it in the flames," "*Maybe* the smoke
will talk" (*LRT,* 20; italics added)—but in the way they see themselves.
Much as in N. Scott Momaday's landmark essay "Man Made of Words,"
knowledge, strength, and, thus, the true potential for transformation
lie in vision and imagination: the choice to be, even if only for a night,
a "real Indian." Whereas in Alexie's previous work, his Ghost Dance and
Wounded Knee references signified loss, the Ghost Dance allusions in *The
Lone Ranger and Tonto Fistfight in Heaven* take on an entirely new meaning, situating Native survivance in imaginative acts.[16]

Alexie's first novel, *Reservation Blues,* published in 1995, follows the
formation, short-lived success, and eventual disintegration of an all-
Indian rock group known as Coyote Springs. A barrage of rapid-fire allusions punctuates the band's interactions; there are references to movies

and film stars, TV shows and comics, and—as always in Alexie's work—
history. While many of the historical allusions come from Spokane history, Alexie also continues to incorporate images of the Ghost Dance and
Wounded Knee. Perhaps the most significant reference occurs during a
conversation between Chess Warm Water, one of Coyote Springs's singers
and keyboard players, and Thomas Builds-the-Fire, the bass player and
lead singer; here, for the first time, Wounded Knee is not just an aside or
brief allusion but a fully articulated story.

The conversation takes place as Coyote Springs returns to the Spokane
Reservation after winning Seattle's tenth annual Battle of the Bands.
During the drive, Chess and Thomas discuss the upcoming week: "'So,'
Chess asked Thomas as the blue van crossed the reservation border, 'are
you coming to church on Sunday?'"[17] Thomas avoids answering until
pressed, when he asks, "How can you go to a church that killed so many
Indians?" (RB, 166). Chess, a devout Catholic, argues for the existence of
God and the humanity of Christianity despite the fact that, as she admits,
"the church does have a lot to atone for" (RB, 166). In response,

> Thomas closed his eyes and told Chess this story: "We were both
> at Wounded Knee when the Ghost Dancers were slaughtered. We
> were slaughtered at Wounded Knee. I know there were whole
> different tribes there, no Spokanes or Flatheads, but we were
> still somehow there. There was a part of every Indian bleeding
> in the snow. All those soldiers killed us in the name of God, enit?
> They shouted 'Jesus Christ' as they ran their swords through our
> bellies. Can you feel the pain still, late at night, when you're try-
> ing to sleep, when you're praying to a God whose name was used
> to justify the slaughter?
>
> "I can see you running like a shadow, just outside the body
> of an Indian woman who looks like you, until she was shot by
> an eighteen-year-old white kid from Missouri. He jumps off the
> horse, falls on her and you, the Indian, the shadow. He cuts and
> tears with his sword, his hands, his teeth. He ate you both up like
> he was a coyote. They all ate us like we were mice, rabbits, flight-
> less birds. They ate us whole." (RB, 167–68)

Thomas's description of Wounded Knee is most obviously a scathing critique of Christianity's colonial history, where Christian dogma has been used to justify genocide again and again. Most interesting for this essay, though, is the way Wounded Knee becomes a shared experience for all Native people and, thus, a universal signifier of Native identity. This particular moment becomes one of the clearest articulations of the pan-Indian aesthetic that underlies so much of Alexie's work.

To examine the way such pan-Indianism functions in *Reservation Blues*, I need to reiterate an idea central to this essay: stories in the dominant culture about Native people often elide Native voices and identities, substituting monolithic representations that ultimately have little or nothing to do with the cultures they supposedly represent. Such is the case with the narratives surrounding Wounded Knee, a historical event that has long been situated as the dying gasp of all Native people. In many ways—rather than being circumscribed by such limitations— Thomas's depiction of Wounded Knee relies on this prevailing image: his contention can be made precisely because of the way Ghost Dance and Wounded Knee narratives have functioned in the dominant culture. When Thomas tells Chess, "There was a part of every Indian bleeding in the snow," he—and I argue Alexie—stakes a claim for pan-Indianism, one based on the assertion of a communal Native history, a psychological and physical connection among Native people.

Thomas's description of the cavalry soldier's attack highlights this connection: "He jumps off the horse, falls on her and you, the Indian, the shadow. He cuts and tears with his sword, his hands, his teeth" (*RB*, 168). A closer look at this passage reveals that when the soldier assaults the Lakota woman and, simultaneously, Chess, he attacks not a person but "an Indian," a one-dimensional, static product of the U.S. imagination. And though he kills the woman, the image persists.

Instead of contradicting this impossibly entrenched rhetoric of loss, Thomas builds his story upon it. Moreover, since the cultural mythology surrounding Wounded Knee *already* depends on the image of a unified Indian past, it actually enables Thomas to transform Wounded Knee from a site of irreparable loss to one of coalition. The prevailing images of these stories, then, become the weakness that Alexie exploits. In *Reservation Blues,* through the voice of Thomas-Builds-the-Fire, he offers a

Wounded Knee narrative with revolutionary possibilities for contemporary Native people. And, while the outcome of Thomas's story is grim—like the massacre—the door that it opens for pantribal coalition is undeniable.

In many ways, Alexie's 1996 book of poetry, *The Summer of Black Widows,* segues between the possibilities implicit in *Reservation Blues*'s depiction of Wounded Knee and their radical manifestation in Alexie's treatment of the Ghost Dance in his second novel, *Indian Killer.* Like *The Lone Ranger and Tonto Fistfight in Heaven, The Summer of Black Widows* contains far more images of the Ghost Dance than of Wounded Knee. Two of these images, in particular, show the way Alexie's attitudes about Native identity continue to change in each text. The initial shift occurs in a poem called "The First and Last Ghost Dance of Lester FallsApart," where "it rain[s] buffalo" who wander "confused," "homeless," "but otherwise free / of injury."[18] Although not stated in the text, the poem's title implies that one of Alexie's recurring characters—the alcoholic, but loveable, reservation philosopher Lester FallsApart—has danced the Ghost Dance. And, like Thomas in *The Lone Ranger and Tonto Fistfight in Heaven,* Lester is successful in his endeavor.

But while Thomas's Ghost Dance results in the whites' disappearance, Lester's causes a sort of intermediate moment where buffalo pose an as-yet-unrealized threat to the white tourists at the Spokane Zoo. This diminished effect is best explained by the contrasting historical setting of the two dances: while Thomas clearly dances in the nineteenth century, Lester dances in the uncertain present, where freely wandering buffalo no longer have anywhere to go, thus comically complicating the fulfillment of the Ghost Dance prophecy.

Alexie's tongue-in-cheek description of a present-day Ghost Dance turns serious in "Bob's Coney Island," the last poem of *The Summer of Black Widows,* where he answers the grim question posed by "Inside Dachau," where the narrator repeatedly asks of "the great-grandchildren of Sand Creek and Wounded Knee": "What do we indigenous people want from our country?" (*SBW,* 119–20). Although it occurs six poems later, the first stanza of "Bob's Coney Island" seamlessly responds to the repeated refrain:

> Let's begin with this: America.
> I want it all back
> now, acre by acre, tonight. I want
> some Indian to finally learn to dance the Ghost Dance right
> so that all of the salmon and buffalo return
> and the white men are sent back home
> to their favorite European cities. (*SBW,* 138)

This final demand shifts Alexie's depiction of the Ghost Dance from the comic to the serious, no longer a parody but a possibility. He also— for the first time—revises the prophecy so it promises the return of a culturally significant Spokane symbol—salmon—along with the Plains buffalo. This addition recalls the adaptable spirit of the 1890 Ghost Dance, which often melded with the beliefs of those who adopted the religion. For example, the Lakota revised Wovoka's prophecy to include Ghost Dance shirts and the demise of the whites, which reflected the warrior traditions central to their cosmology. But while the Lakota Ghost Dance was only one of the many variations, that single interpretation has dominated the narratives surrounding the Wounded Knee massacre. By expanding the Ghost Dance to meet the needs of the Spokane, Alexie frees the religion from the frozen annals of history and renews it, paving the way for his next novel, *Indian Killer.*

If the present-day possibilities for the Ghost Dance in *The Summer of Black Widows* were combined with the proposed coalition politics of *Reservation Blues,* the result would be Alexie's 1996 novel, *Indian Killer,* where the Ghost Dance becomes a metaphor for Indigenous revolution. The plot of Alexie's second novel follows the grim life of a Native boy who is adopted by a white couple and named, ironically, John Smith. While the agent assures his adoptive parents that "this child will be saved a lot of pain by growing up in a white family" (*IK,* 10), John's anguish shows otherwise. With odd patterns of behavior and a burning, submerged anger, the twenty-seven-year-old John becomes a prime suspect in the rash of serial killings taking place in Seattle. White men are being murdered, found stabbed with eyes torn out and two white owl feathers left as a cryptic calling card by the person talk-radio host Truck Schultz, the voice of racial hatred in the novel, dubs the "Indian killer."

While the plot of *Indian Killer* is driven by the classic question "who-dunit?", its underlying themes reveal and critique the ongoing legacy of settler colonialism in the U.S. And it is within the cross sections of these explorations that Alexie situates his allusions to the Ghost Dance, which is the central metaphor for Native resistance in the novel. The first reference occurs at a white-owned Indian bar called Big Heart's, where Jack Wilson, a white man who spent his childhood in a series of abusive foster homes where he "read about Indians and recreated himself in the image he found inside those books" (*IK*, 157), goes to drink and fraternize with his Indian "brothers." During one visit, Wilson has a conversation with Reggie Polatkin and Reggie's friends Harley and Ty Wilson; he tries to win points with the three Indian men by sharing the as-yet-unannounced news of the Indian killer. He says enthusiastically, "Hey,...I heard something crazy.... I heard a white guy was scalped" (*IK*, 183). Conversation comes to a grinding halt, and after informing Wilson that "there are lots of real Indian men out there with plenty enough reasons to kill a white man" (*IK*, 184), Reggie and his friends leave the table. Before he reaches the door, however, Reggie delivers this warning:

> "You know about Bigfoot? That Sioux Indian?"
> "Yeah," said Wilson. "He died at the Wounded Knee massacre in 1890. He was Minneconjou Sioux, I think. He was killed because he was leading the Ghost Dance. . . ."
> "Yeah, and who killed Bigfoot? . . ."
> "Some soldier, I guess. Nobody knows for sure."
> "You're not paying attention. What color was the man who killed Bigfoot?"
> "He would've been white."
> "Exactly, Casper. Think about that." (*IK*, 185)

By using Wounded Knee to remind Wilson, who shares the Ghost Dance prophet Wovoka's white name, that his skin color implicates him in the legacy of settler colonialism in the United States, Reggie constructs history and, specifically, the Wounded Knee massacre as the potential rationale for the murders. But it is not the stagnant image of Wounded Knee but the rebellious echo of the Ghost Dance that resonates after the two men's conversation, as becomes clear when the narrator describes the speedy dissemination of Wilson's news: "Within a few hours, nearly every Indian in Seattle knew about the scalping. Most Indians believed it was all just racist paranoia, but a few felt a strange combination of relief and fear, as if an apocalyptic prophecy was just beginning to come true" (*IK,* 185). This apocalyptic prophecy—undoubtedly of the Ghost Dance — excites more interest within the Seattle Indian community as the novel unfolds.

In the following chapter, "Testimony," word has spread as we see when Arthur Two Leaf, a Makah Indian, gives the police a statement about being attacked by three white men. Arthur testifies not only to the crime but also to the possibility of a burgeoning underground revolution, much like the one imagined in Leslie Silko's *Almanac of the Dead,* where Indigenous people from across tribal and national boundaries band together and march from Mexico to the United States.[19] Arthur explains, "Indians are outnumbered, Officer. Those three guys scared me bad....I've been hearing rumors, you know?...Indians are organizing, they're looking to get revenge" (*IK,* 188). For many of the characters in Alexie's novel, the image of the Indian killer embodies this growing possibility. A comment made by Boo, one of the homeless Native people whom Reggie's cousin, Marie Polatkin, helps feed, illustrates this point. Boo compares the Indian killer to a series of significant Indian leaders: "This Indian Killer, you see, he's got Crazy Horse's magic. He's got Chief Joseph's brains. He's got Geronimo's heart. He's got Wovoka's vision. He's all those badass Indians rolled into one" (*IK,* 219).

The brief glimpse we get into the killer's psyche reinforces this suggestion that the murders have symbolic meaning. After kidnapping the white child, Mark Jones, the unnamed killer looks at the boy's sleeping body and recognizes the abduction as "the true beginning, the first song, the first dance of a powerful ceremony that would change the world" (*IK,* 192). The Indian killer, then, becomes the catalyst for retribution, and his acts are, in many ways, the initial steps in the fulfillment of the Ghost Dance prophecy with which the novel ends.

If the Indian killer is the instrument to fulfill the Ghost Dance prophecy, the question of whodunit no longer matters since meaning lies in the outcome of the killer's actions, rather than his or her identity. So, while the final chapters of *Indian Killer* strongly suggest that Jack Wilson, the wannabe Indian author, commits the crimes, the most significant question by then is not who, but why? Marie Polatkin provides a compelling answer when she challenges her professor, Dr. Mather, who teaches a whitewashed version of Native American literature and romantically admires the Indian killer as "an inevitable creation of capitalism, . . . a revolutionary construct" (*IK,* 245). She offers this explanation for the novel's serial murders:

> You just love Indians so much . . . you think you're excluded from our hatred. Don't you see? If the Ghost Dance had worked, you wouldn't be here. You'd be dust.
>
> So maybe this Indian Killer is a product of the Ghost Dance. Maybe ten Indians are Ghost Dancing. Maybe a hundred. It's just a theory. How many Indians would have to dance to create the Indian Killer? A thousand? Ten thousand? Maybe this is how the Ghost Dance works.
>
> If the Ghost Dance worked, there would be no exceptions. All you white people would disappear. All of you. If those dead Indians came back to life, they wouldn't crawl into a sweathouse with you. . . . They'd gut you and eat your heart. (*IK,* 313–14)

While Marie initially configures the contemporary Ghost Dance as speculation—e.g., "*maybe* this Indian Killer is a product of the Ghost Dance," "*Maybe* ten Indians are Ghost Dancing," "*if* the Ghost Dance worked" (italics added)—in her final speech and the penultimate moment in the novel, she states it as fact. Like Arthur Two Leaf's police report, Marie's claim is testimony. In this case, that testimony is given during a police interview about John's attack on Wilson and subsequent suicide, which the authorities believe solve the mystery of the Indian killer: "I know then John Smith didn't kill anybody except himself. And if some Indian is killing white guys, then it's a credit to us that it took over five hundred years for it to happen. And there's more. . . . The Indians are dancing now and I don't think they're going to stop" (*IK,* 418).

Marie ultimately contends, then, that the Indian killer is a product of an ongoing Ghost Dance with revolutionary potential for Native people.

And like Wounded Knee in *Reservation Blues,* the Ghost Dance becomes the site of Indigenous coalition in *Indian Killer.* But while Alexie's stories about Wounded Knee build that coalition on the dominant culture's tragic representations of Indians, his depictions of the Ghost Dance ultimately identify Native survivance as a pan-Indian phenomenon set within current cultural practices.

Ranging through Alexie's work, we can clearly see both the importance and diversity of Ghost Dance and Wounded Knee metaphors. Through appropriating or resignifying them, Alexie retrieves Ghost Dance and Wounded Knee images from the annals of prevailing historical accounts and transforms them into provocative commentaries on past and present American Indian life. In *Old Shirts & New Skins*, the Ghost Dance appears as the dominant signifier of Native loss to highlight the inaccuracies of master narratives of Native history, and then Custer, one of the central figures in nineteenth-century Indian-white relations, writes the story differently. In *First Indian on the Moon,* Alexie uses Wounded Knee to depict mixed-blood identity as conflicted and also appropriates one of the most popular images of the massacre—Big Foot's photograph—to condemn the way such racial hierarchies lead to war and violent death. In *The Lone Ranger and Tonto Fistfight in Heaven,* Alexie's literal and metaphorical evocations of the Ghost Dance situate the Native future in imaginative acts of survivance. These attempts to define identity are also significant in Alexie's first novel, *Reservation Blues,* where Wounded Knee becomes the location for pantribal coalition, and *Indian Killer*, where the Ghost Dance becomes a pan-Indian symbol for Native resistance.

While Alexie's commentaries are by no means the same in each case, they do, when examined together, shed light on his argument about American Indian identities, about how such identities became the site of dominant misrepresentations, of internal conflict, and later, of hope and resistance. I began this essay by arguing that an overarching trajectory exists in Alexie's work, moving his Ghost Dance and Wounded Knee references from historical allusions and personal metaphors to politically charged sites for resistance. I conclude by suggesting that the Ghost Dance image transforms from tragic iteration to triumphant sign, ultimately identifying the imaginative spirit of the dance as the hope for the next generation of American Indian people.

Clearly Alexie responds to dominant narratives of the Ghost Dance and Wounded Knee by appropriating, revising, and rejecting them throughout his work.[20] But his depiction of these images, and especially their pan-Indian potential, is intimately tied to his own subjective position: he is a Spokane author reworking images from Lakota history. The particular historical moments that Alexie emphasizes—as P. Jane Hafen points out—hold great significance for all Indian people. But these images become pantribal metaphors at a price, which is the loss of their cultural specificity. Alexie's appropriation of Big Foot's photograph is one example where a specific historical moment and document become a decontextualized symbol. And while that symbol may still speak for social justice, as Alexie's Big Foot image does, it nevertheless loses tribal specificity to enable it to function as an abstract signifier.

With this in mind, I pose some final questions: if abstraction is the price of some pantribal metaphors, what are the benefits of embracing a pan-Indian aesthetic? How should metaphors like Alexie's depictions of the Ghost Dance and Wounded Knee be understood, and what do they mean to Native studies? The question is significant because these images are so widespread in contemporary American Indian literature. For example, novels by three prominent American Indian authors, published after the Alexie texts discussed here—Leslie Marmon Silko's (Laguna) *Gardens in the Dunes* (1999), James Welch's (Blackfoot) *The Heartsong of Charging Elk* (2000), and Louise Erdrich's (Anishinaabe) *The Master Butcher's Singing Club* (2003)—all adopt the Ghost Dance and/or Wounded Knee massacre as central metaphors for Indian identity despite each author's different tribal affiliation and each book's radical difference in era, geographical location, and subject matter. Moreover, all three novels employ pantribal images of the Ghost Dance and Wounded Knee to reclaim Indigenous traditions as sites of survival and revitalization for tribally connected characters. Ultimately, the continued significance of pan-tribal images among American Indian authors reinforces the importance of such investigations to Native America and Indigenous studies. As Alexie's work recognizes, commonalities exist among Native peoples, nations, and literatures, and those ties strengthen, rather than threaten, tribal identity, thereby highlighting the way pan-Indian metaphors can be employed to construct tribally specific realities in the twenty-first century.

NOTES

1. In 1890 the Paiute prophet Wovoka described a new religion that included specific performances of dance and prayer that would bring about the whites' disappearance, the return of the dancers' dead relatives, and the restoration of decimated buffalo herds. The religion—later called the Ghost Dance—gained adherents from members of many different Native nations, among them the Lakota, to whom such a promise sounded especially appealing in the wake of the disease, drought, and widespread starvation that had plagued them in recent years. An increasing number of Lakota embraced Wovoka's teachings in the summer and fall of 1890, and performances of Ghost Dance ceremonies proliferated. These gatherings of Native people terrified several inexperienced government agents, including Pine Ridge Reservation Agent Daniel Royer, whose panicked missives to Washington were, in part, responsible for the subsequent congregation of the largest number of troops since the Civil War. On December 29, 1890, this escalation of panic culminated in the Wounded Knee massacre in South Dakota. During the attack, more than three hundred Lakota were killed by U.S. troops. A large number of books offer in-depth studies of the Ghost Dance and the Wounded Knee massacre. Among them are Michael Hittman's biography of the Ghost Dance prophet, *Wovoka and the Ghost Dance;* Richard Jenson, R. Eli Paul, and John E. Carter's *Eyewitness at Wounded Knee;* Alice Beck Kehoe's *The Ghost Dance: Ethnohistory and Revitalization;* James H. McGregor's *The Wounded Knee Massacre from the Viewpoint of the Sioux,* which contains some lesser-known eyewitness accounts; James Mooney's seminal text, *The Ghost Dance Religion and the Sioux Outbreak of 1890,* a detailed ethnographic government report written just after the massacre; and, most recently, William E. Coleman's *The Voices of Wounded Knee,* an excellent compilation of the textual sources on the events of the period.

    Historians most often recognize at least two Ghost Dance religions: the 1870 Ghost Dance and the better-known 1890 Ghost Dance, which the Lakota adopted in the months before the Wounded Knee massacre. Both of these movements originated among the Paiute on the Walker River Reservation in Nevada, where two different Paiute healers—Wodziwob (Fish Lake Joe, who died about 1920) in the late 1860s and Wovoka (Jack Wilson, ca.1858–1932) in 1889—had visions where they were instructed to bring dance ceremonies back to their people. The 1890 Ghost Dance has attracted a great deal more attention than the 1870 movement. While this dearth of critical notice may be due, in part, to the lack of documentation about the 1870 dances, it is also undoubtedly connected to the false melding of the 1890 Ghost Dance and the Wounded Knee massacre.

2.   Sherman Alexie, *Old Shirts & New Skins,* 77 (hereafter cited in the text as *OSNS*); Sherman Alexie, *Indian Killer,* 313 (hereafter cited in the text as *IK*).

3.   See Robert Utley's *The Indian Frontier of the American West, 1846–1890* for more on the attack.

4.   P. Jane Hafen, "Rock and Roll, Redskins, and Blues in Sherman Alexie's Work," 73.

5.   Elsewhere in her article, though, Hafen is quick to point out that this interpretation in no way supersedes or negates specific tribal histories. And, in fact, she concludes her analysis of *Reservation Blues* by contending that Alexie situates the possibility of redemption firmly in a Spokane context at the end of his novel.

6.   Matt Herman, "Authenticity Reconsidered: Toward an Understanding of a Culturalist Reading Paradigm," 126–27.

7.   Sherman Alexie, *First Indian on the Moon,* 43 (hereafter cited in the text as *FIM*).

8.   While the federal government preferred all tribes to use blood quantum as enrollment criteria, many nations did not, and it's important to note that these criteria are tribally determined. See Kimberly TallBear's "DNA, Blood and Racializing the Tribe," 81–107; and Chadwick Allen's "Blood (and) Memory," 93–116; and "Postcolonial Theory and the Discourse of Treaties," 59–89) for three excellent discussions of Native responses to this attempt.

9.   I identify the speaker as male because it seems disingenuous to do otherwise when the poem specifically details Alexie's own blood quantum. But making that correlation in this case does not imply that Alexie's work is non-fiction or his narrators have a one-to-one correlation with their creator.

10.   This error can be a simple mistake or an example of artistic license since 1876—the year of Little Bighorn—provides a neater parallel to the [19]'66 or '67 of the Vietnam War than does 1890. The error may also mirror the "or whenever" that follows the possible dates of the later picture, a phrase that focuses not on the year but the repetition of the racist and violent action.

11.   Cherríe Moraga, *Loving in the War Years: Lo Que Nunca Pasó por Sus Labios,* 52; italics in original.

12.   Gerald Vizenor, *Manifest Manners: Postindian Warriors of Survivance,* 83. Vizenor coins the term *survivance,* a combination of survival and endurance, to describe the active process of resistance, recovery, and renewal for Native people and communities.

13.   Sherman Alexie, *The Lone Ranger and Tonto Fistfight in Heaven,* 12 (hereafter cited in the text as *LRT*).

14.   During the nineteenth century, smallpox, like so many other viruses before it, spread like wildfire among Indian people, who had no previous exposure and hence no immunity. When Alexie's tribe confronted their worst episode

of smallpox in 1782, for example, the disease reduced the population by half. Robert H. Ruby and John A. Brown. *The Spokane Indians: Children of the Sun,* 29.

15. James H. Cox, "Muting White Noise: The Subversion of Popular Culture Narratives of Conquest in Sherman Alexie's Fiction," 58.

16. The constraints of this essay have limited my analysis to only one of the short stories in *The Lone Ranger and Tonto Fistfight in Heaven.* Another important story is "Distances," which is set in what appears to be the aftermath of a nuclear war. The piece begins with a paraphrase of Wovoka's prophecy and suggests that either "Custer could have, must have, pressed the button. . . . Or maybe it was because the Ghost Dance finally worked" (*LRT,* 105). The ensuing narrative is a commentary on the divisions between urban and reservation Indian identities where the ghosts of dead Indians return as strange and sometimes frightening Others. Much as in "Apologies," where the Wounded Knee allusion is conflicted, "Distances" reveals that Alexie's Wounded Knee and Ghost Dance images never entirely fit within a single argument.

17. Sherman Alexie, *Reservation Blues,* 166 (hereafter cited in the text as *RB*).

18. Sherman Alexie, *The Summer of Black Widows,* 18 (hereafter cited in the text as *SBW*).

19. Alexie addresses this connection in an interview, saying, "I think *Indian Killer* is the first step and *Almanac* is the last step in the time line of a fictional revolution." Susan Berry Brill de Ramírez, "Fancy Dancer: A Profile of Sherman Alexie," 56.

20. An overview of the first decade of Alexie's work reveals that two of his early-twenty-first-century collections of short stories—*The Toughest Indian in the World* (2000) and *Ten Little Indians* (2003)—contain almost no references to Wounded Knee and the Ghost Dance. One of his 2003 short stories, however, is entitled "Ghost Dance." "Ghost Dance," *McSweeney's,* 350–64. This piece features a fifties-style, *Night of the Living Dead* commemoration of the Custer battle where two racist white police officers—who, according to the accompanying picture, are modeled on the Lone Ranger—murder two Indian men on the grounds of the Custer Memorial cemetery. When the blood of the fallen men soaks into the ground, the soldiers of the Seventh Cavalry rise from the dead in a cannibalistic frenzy. The 256 ghouls eat the two officers alive before they split up and embark across the country to search for more victims. In this case, Alexie overturns the image of the Ghost Dance as *whites* rise from the dead. The story mirrors many of Alexie's previous Ghost Dance and Wounded Knee references because it, too, is a scathing commentary on the rapacious nature of racism. Most recently, in Alexie's 2007 novel *Flight,* the adolescent protagonist, Zits, is seduced into opening fire on unsuspecting bank customers by a homeless white boy named Justice, who repeatedly invokes the Ghost Dance as a way to incite him to violence.

■ *Philip Heldrich*

CHAPTER 2

"Survival = Anger × Imagination"

Sherman Alexie's Dark Humor

Humor in the face of dire circumstances is perhaps the most fundamental characteristic shared by Sherman Alexie's first and second collections of short fiction—*The Lone Ranger and Tonto Fistfight in Heaven* (1993) and *The Toughest Indian in the World* (2000).[1] Combining laughter and the trenchant irony such comedy often produces, Alexie's use of humor or, more particularly, dark humor addresses absurdity predicated upon such problems as unemployment, poverty, alcoholism, drug abuse, diabetes, the uncertain future, and eroded cultural traditions. For Alexie dark humor and irony, formed partly by such techniques as parody, satire, burlesque, hyperbole, and farce, are an effective strategy to point out historical and present conditions of inequality created by white hegemony and convey conflicts generated by assimilation. Such tragicomic laughter exposes the false ideologies and empty promises of the dominant culture as it opens a dialogue with readers about difficult issues and stereotypes. Such edgy, disruptive, even liberating humor also promotes self-actualization and social action, providing a means of survival amid often-bewildering and absurd conditions.

Dark humor is nothing novel, and Alexie's use of it reflects literary traditions with both European and Native American roots.[2] Alan R. Pratt credits French surrealist poet and critic André Breton with having coined the term *humor noir* (dark or black humor) in the late 1930s.[3] Pratt further notes—in relation to the Western literary tradition—that humor noir describes writing by such disparate figures as "Aristophanes, Juvenal, Petronius, Erasmus, Shakespeare, Cervantes, Rabelais, de Sade, Swift, and Voltaire."[4]

More contemporarily, American black humorists of the 1950s through 1970s used this tragicomic technique to respond to a perceived, bewildering condition of absurdity created by the postmodern, post-Holocaust, postatomic world.[5] "The novelist-satirist, with no real territory to roam," wrote Bruce Friedman in 1965, "has had to discover new land, invent a new currency, a new set of filters, has had to sail into darker waters somewhere out beyond satire."[6] The same can be said for Alexie, who employs dark humor to navigate the absurdities of cultural inequality, the breakup of community, and a loss of myth and ritual. The novelist in a time of crisis, John Aldridge notes, uses dark humor to go beyond "social appearances and surfaces...to take into account the chaotic multiplicity of meanings...both above and beneath the surfaces."[7] Similarly the tragicomedy of Alexie's work deepens cultural awareness by effectively deconstructing dominant ideologies.[8] Alexie takes full advantage of the irony, the humorous incongruities, and the doublespeak dark humor produces. In subverting his subject, Alexie creates a dialogue outside the dominant discourse to address the very real problems facing Indians on and off the reservation.[9]

Alexie's dark humor reflects the general strategies used by black humorists, where "no subject is sacrosanct; myths, taboos, theologies, philosophies, and ideologies are twisted, blasphemed, or lampooned."[10] These blasphemed myths, taboos, theologies, philosophies, and ideologies are, for Alexie, often those of the dominant culture, though he is also critical of his own community, especially people who have adopted or fallen victim to the stereotypes posed by these ideologies. However, his comedy purposefully undermines the stereotypes he depicts to examine their origin and draw attention to the problems they create. In other words, Alexie's dark humor asks those in his community to recognize the way the dominant culture has stereotyped and eroded culturally specific rituals and traditions. His multilayered humor continually draws attention to the relationships between center and margin, inside and outside, white and red.

From his poetry to his fiction, humor has always been a central part of Alexie's work. Jennifer Gillan notes the tragicomic aspect of poems in *Old Shirts & New Skins* and the way this humor plays a role in both the songs and the band's stories in *Reservation Blues*.[11] Kenneth Lincoln likens Alexie's poetry to "stand-up comedy on the edge of despair."[12] Similarly Alexie's short fiction contains what Darby Li Po Price describes as a more general aim of contemporary Indian humor: "revealing the shortcomings, errors, and contradictions of the dominant culture."[13] Such Indian comedy contrasts with "the humorless, stoic, tragic 'Indian,'" which Price points out "is the overriding image in literary, film, and television depictions of Native Americans."[14] Lincoln, in his extensive study *Indi'n Humor,* identifies the drama of Hanay Geiogamah as reflecting the intrinsic importance of joking to Indian culture. As Geiogamah tells Lincoln, "I see the Indi'n capacity for humor as a blessing. And I see it as one of the fundamental miracles of our lives. It's a miraculous thing that's pulled us through so much. It's a force that's part of religion."[15]

Geiogamah is not alone in clarifying humor's role in Indian life. Paula Gunn Allen—responding to Lincoln about Indian joking—noted, "Not to make too much of it, but humor is the best and sharpest weapon we've always had against the ravages of conquest and assimilation."[16] In relation to other contemporary Native American writing, Alexie's dark humor most closely recalls James Welch's *Winter in the Blood*. Like the unnamed narrator in Welch's novel, Alexie's characters face bewildering conditions portrayed through tragicomic humor fueled with irony.[17]

Lincoln seems to have anticipated Alexie when he wrote, "As expressed by survivors of tragedy, nonvanishing Native Americans, this humor transcends the void, questions of fatalism, and outlasts suffering.... At cultural ground zero, it [Indi'n humor] means that Indians are still here, laughing to survive."[18] More specifically, in Alexie's *Lone Ranger,* dark humor addresses difficult issues faced by those living on the Spokane Reservation, problems often created by conflicting ideologies generated from the opposition between the reservation and the dominant culture;

in *Toughest Indian,* on the other hand, Alexie's tragicomedy moves off the reservation to explore the contradictions generated by cultural exchange or presumptions related to assimilation.

Created by the juxtaposition of an incongruous relationship, the humorous title of Alexie's acclaimed first collection, *The Lone Ranger and Tonto Fistfight in Heaven,* establishes the book's fundamental comedic approach. The humorous titles of the individual stories, which read like tabloid headlines, evoke both laughter and pathos: "The Only Traffic Signal on the Reservation Doesn't Flash Red Anymore," "Jesus Christ's Half-Brother Is Alive and Well on the Spokane Indian Reservation," "The Approximate Size of My Favorite Tumor," or "Somebody Kept Saying Powwow." Such stories—loosely linked by recurring narrators, characters, and themes—depict absurd circumstances with characters limited in their ability to affect change. Unlike many texts by Native American Renaissance writers, who opened paths for a second generation of authors such as Alexie, the focus of *Lone Ranger* is not on tribal traditions or the way tribal ritual can structure daily life. For Alexie's characters, such traditions and rituals seem largely inaccessible or irrelevant, eroded by the absurdity of contemporary reservation life.

As the book's initial story, "Every Little Hurricane," suggests through its storm metaphor, whatever once existed on the reservation has been seemingly wiped out for the present generation: "Houses were flattened, their contents thrown in every direction. Memories not destroyed, but forever changed and damaged."[19] Afflicted by continual cultural assault, this current generation at the end of the twentieth century has had to adopt different survival strategies from previous ones: "This was the generation of HUD house, of car wreck and cancer, of commodity cheese and beef. These were the children," Alexie notes in "A Good Story," "who carried dreams in the back pockets of their blue jeans, pulled them out easily, traded back and forth" (*LRT,* 142). Such a reservation differs markedly from the close-knit world defined by tribal traditions portrayed in Momaday's *House Made of Dawn* or Silko's *Ceremony*; on Alexie's imagined reservation, ritual-defined living no longer seems to shape daily life.

"The Only Traffic Signal on the Reservation Doesn't Flash Red Anymore" is a typical story from the collection where Alexie's dark situational comedy addresses real problems on the reservation, in this case, suicide and alcoholism. This humor becomes a way to approach the unapproachable and mock the stereotypical to speak about the unspeakable, as in the story's initial scene between Victor and Adrian, who burlesque Russian roulette, tragic as the allusions may be:

> Adrian took the pistol, put the barrel in his mouth, smiled around the metal, and pulled the trigger. Then he cussed wildly, laughed, and spit out the BB.
>   "Are you dead yet?" I asked.
>   "Nope," he said. "Not yet. Give me another beer."
>   "Hey, we don't drink no more, remember? How about a Diet Pepsi?" (*LRT*, 43–44).

BBs and Diet Pepsi mock real bullets and alcohol abuse. Through its tragicomedy, the scene draws attention to the problems that plague young people such as Julius Windmaker, "the best basketball player on the reservation" (*LRT*, 45). These images of reservation life go beyond stereotypes and what Louis Owens describes as "sensationalized alcoholism and cultural impotence."[20] In this scene and others, Alexie creates an ethical undercurrent that addresses tribal youth in terms they can understand.

The real problems of alcohol abuse and suicide receive further attention through the subsequent narrative concerning basketball,[21] which acts as a tragicomic metaphor that humorously speaks to those on the reservation about serious problems: "There's a definite history of reservation heroes who never finish high school, who never finish basketball seasons" (*LRT*, 47). Basketball, as the story continues, assumes ethical importance. According to Peter Donahue, basketball has an important "reshaping influence" that promotes "healing qualities" by creating "Indian identity, pride, and resistance."[22] Basketball lore becomes the stuff of myth when the past seems inaccessible, something that binds together the tribe, as with Adrian's admiration for Silas Sirius: "I was there when he grabbed that defensive rebound, took a step, and flew the length of the court, did a full spin in midair, and then dunked that fucking ball" (*LRT*, 47). Such moments—shared legends of great feats and failures in the face of dire circumstance—create a means of survival through laughter. "I laughed," says Victor, "...because it was the right thing to do" (*LRT,* 47). According to Mikhail Bakhtin, subversive humor undermines stereotype: "laughter [has] a deep philosophical meaning... [as] one of the essential forms of the truth concerning the world as a whole.... The world is seen anew, no less (and perhaps more) profoundly than when seen from the serious standpoint.... Certain essential aspects of the world are accessible only to laughter."[23]

For Victor, laughing may also be the only thing that he can do, given his bewildering situation, the tragic side of the comic:

> It's hard to be optimistic on the reservation. When a glass sits on a table here, people don't wonder if it's half filled or half empty. They just hope it's good beer. Still, Indians have a way of surviving. But it's almost like Indians can easily survive the big stuff. Mass murder, loss of language and land rights. It's the small things that hurt the most. The white waitress who wouldn't take an order, Tonto, the Washington Redskins.
>
> And, just like everybody else, Indians need heroes to help them learn how to survive. But what happens when our heroes don't even know how to pay their bills? (*LRT,* 49)

Julius Windmaker represents this fallen hero. To make it, Windmaker has to rise above difficult circumstances such as alcoholism that first threaten, then keep him from becoming "the best ever" (*LRT,* 46). Victor knows such problems firsthand because he was once such a hero, but he played ball drunk and became "disconnected" (*LRT,* 51). Basketball players, as Victor makes clear, have the status of "saviors," so when heroic players such as Julius Windmaker fail because of alcoholism, "it hurts" (*LRT,* 52). Such losses jeopardize the tribe. "Whatever happened to the tribal ties, the sense of community?" Victor asks in "This Is What It Means to Say Phoenix, Arizona." "The only real thing...shared with anybody was a bottle and broken dreams" (*LRT,* 74). For Victor's and Julius Windmaker's generations, the past has become mute and the future uncertain, an existential condition of absurdity once similarly articulated—though the causes were different—by black humorists of the late 1950s and 1960s, who were struggling to understand the Holocaust and the atrocities of World War II. However, comedic stories about basketball and its potential heroes create a dialogue to address the severe conditions facing those on the reservation.

For Alexie conditions forced upon Indian people by the white world—"For hundreds of years, Indians were witnesses to crime of an epic scale" (*LRT*, 3)—are in part responsible for the hardships of contemporary reservation life. "The Trial of Thomas Builds-the-Fire,"—with typical Alexie dark humor—details this history.[24] Like something out of a Kafka story (to which the epigraph alludes), Thomas Builds-the-Fire finds himself senselessly arrested for holding "the reservation postmaster hostage for eight hours with the idea of a gun" (*LRT*, 93). After "surrender[ing] voluntarily" and "agree[ing] to remain silent" for what becomes twenty years, Builds-the-Fire breaks his silence with an absurd madness: "small noises...syllables that contained more emotion and meaning than entire sentences constructed by the BIA" (*LRT*, 94).

Again Alexie's humor—one-liner punches at the BIA and government policy—makes it possible to address a serious situation. Through Builds-the-Fire's mad speech—with a humor that Joseph Coulombe states "reveal[s] injustice,"[25] Alexie addresses atrocities committed by Col. George Wright's slaughter of eight hundred Spokane horses. Builds-the-Fire also alludes to Wright's hanging of Qualchan and "six other Indians" (*LRT*, 99). Ironically and tragicomically, Qualchan, as Builds-the-Fire notes, is the name of a golf course under construction in the city of Spokane.

While dark humor criticizes present and historical atrocities, the absurdity generated by coping with adversity represents a real condition of existence. In "A Train Is an Order of Occurrence Designed to Lead to Some Result," individuals like Samuel Builds-the-Fire have been robbed of their pasts and left with uncertain futures. As Samuel realizes on his birthday—the day he quits his job as housekeeper at a cheap motel and takes up drink for his first time—"At the halfway point of any drunken night, there is a moment when an Indian realizes he cannot turn back toward tradition and that he has no map to guide him toward the future" (*LRT*, 134). Unlike Momaday's Abel or Silko's Tayo, Alexie's Samuel and characters like him have no guides and live bereft of tradition. Samuel's life symbolizes such loss and isolation. He "lived on the reservation, alone, for as long as he could, without money or company. All his friends had died and all the younger people on the reservation had no time for stories" (*LRT,* 135). Samuel witnesses countless Indian lives on and off the reservation reduced to prostitution and drug abuse: "His brothers and sisters, most of his tribe, fall into alcoholism and surrendered dreams" (*LRT,* 133). His own life ends tragically and absurdly when, drunk for the very first time, Samuel stumbles onto the railroad tracks.

In revealing absurd, extreme circumstances that often fuel rage, Alexie's dark humor resembles the approach of the Indian stand-up comedian, who uses humor, according to Price, to "expand conceptions of Indianness, undermine expectations, and reveal dominant truths to be fictions."[26] "Imagining the Reservation" exemplifies this strategy; its narrator plays the role of a stand-up, punning his way through biting commentary: "I am in the 7-11 of my dreams, surrounded by five hundred years of convenient lies" (*LRT,* 150). Robbed of tradition or a future, "left...for rescue between the expired milk and broken eggs" (*LRT,* 150), characters like the narrator must seek alternative ways—as with the example of basketball—to replace the lost rituals that once structured their lives. They must invent a new means to survive. For these characters, then, "Survival = Anger × Imagination. Imagination is the only weapon on the reservation" (*LRT,* 150). With imagination grounded in humor, characters can resist the dominant culture's fictions: "Does every Indian depend on Hollywood for a twentieth-century vision?" (*LRT,* 151). The outside, primarily white world mostly offers false hope, opportunity unavailable to those on the reservation.

Alexie sees this problem of defining Indian life as partly a result of colonized language: "How can we imagine a new language when the language of the enemy keeps our dismembered tongues tied to his belt? How can we imagine a new alphabet when the old jumps off billboards down into our stomachs?" (*LRT,* 152). Alexie expresses a paradox that seems only resolvable through subversive humor, comedic language that undermines, resists, levels, and liberates. In Alexie's hands, dark humor becomes a weapon enabling survival "in hunger, in anger, in laughter, in prayer...Jesus, we all want to survive" (*LRT,* 198).

Laughter for Alexie also has important political and social power. "Imagine every Indian is a video game with braids," he writes. "Do you believe laughter can save us? All I know is that I count coyotes to help me sleep. Didn't you know? Imagination is the politics of dreams; imagination turns every word into a bottle rocket" (*LRT,* 152).[27] In addition to permitting disruptive language, laughter also consoles. Perhaps James Many Horses in "The Approximate Size of My Favorite Tumor" best defines Alexie's complex use of dark humor: "You have to realize that laughter saved Norma and me from pain, too. Humor was an antiseptic that cleaned the deepest of personal wounds" (*LRT,* 164).

While dark humor in *Lone Ranger* most often addresses reservation life, *Toughest Indian* expands Alexie's vision of absurdity to include the struggles of Indians in confronting predominantly urban Northwest white culture. In this book, Alexie again uses humor as a way to approach the difficult, the unspeakable, and the tragic. In *Toughest Indian,* absurdity and its accompanying confusion result largely from the opposition between the forces of assimilation and the challenges of retaining a cultural knowledge of self, especially when separated from the tribe. Despite their critical disagreements, I contend that Alexie's collection shares what Louis Owens identifies as a central theme of Native American novels: "the problem of internalized transculturation."[28] Alexie dramatizes this problem of self-knowledge most frequently through the collection's stories involving interracial relationships, which represent, Stephen F. Evans contends, "the author's most mature handling of the themes of racial essence."[29] *Toughest Indian,* perhaps more than *Lone Ranger,* also articulates by its end a greater ethos of self-actualization, enabled through humor that defines an individual's relationship to family and tribe.

"Assimilation," the first story of *Toughest Indian,* establishes the collection's thematic focus. In this piece, Mary Lynn, a "Coeur d'Alene Indian married to a white man," desires to sleep with an Indian man "only because he was Indian."[30] Alexie expresses Mary Lynn's crisis of assimilation and identity through the joking and exaggerated politicization of her sexual experiences, likening them to "a carnal form of affirmative action...her infidelity was a political act! Rebellion, resistance, revolution!" (*TIW,* 4). For Mary Lynn, it is as if sleeping with an Indian can help her recover her cultural self, which has been steadily eroding all her life, and more so in the years since she moved off her reservation. Her

reasons for leaving the tribe are rooted in the very conditions of the reservation. She compares the memories of growing up on the reservation
to "Nazi death camps," where "the best...did not survive the camps"
(*TIW,* 5). Even the Indian men in her life have played a role in the reasons
she desires to assimilate into the white world: "God, she hated to admit
it, but white men—her teachers, coaches, bosses, and lovers—had always
been more dependable than the Indian men in her life" (*TIW,* 5). In seeking stability, Mary Lynn forsakes passion and her culture, which leaves
her unfulfilled: "White men had rarely disappointed her, but they'd never
surprised her either. White men were neutral, she thought, just like Bel-
gium!" (*TIW,* 5).

However, Mary Lynn's tragicomic affair does little to help her. Again,
for another of Alexie's characters, the past, once lost, seems largely unrecoverable, not even a one-night stand with an Indian can adequately
abate her cultural longing. Tragically, it becomes clear that Mary Lynn
will always be plagued by questions prompted by her assimilation, conflicts manifested in her children's skin color or "race as a concept, as a foreign country they [her family] occasionally visited, or as an enemy that
existed outside their house, as a destructive force they could fight against
as a couple, as a family" (*TIW,* 14). Questions about race, which Alexie
presents with a touch of parodic melodrama, even color Mary Lynn's love
for her husband: "Oh, God, she loved him, sometimes because he was
white and often despite his whiteness" (*TIW,* 19). As far as her love for her
husband goes, there is always an accompanying, unbreachable "distance"
generated by their racial difference (*TIW,* 20).

"Class," another story in *Toughest Indian,* similarly examines the issue
of assimilation, though this time from the perspective of a young urban
attorney whose white wife cuckolds him. As with Mary Lynn, Edgar Eagle
Runner has mixed feelings about his race that began in his youth with a
struggle to survive reservation life:

> As for me, I'd told any number of white women that I was part
> Aztec and I'd told a few that I was completely Aztec. That gave
> me some mystery, some ethnic weight, a history of glorious color
> and mass executions. Strangely enough, there were aphrodisi-
> acal benefits to claiming to be descended from ritual cannibals.

In any event, pretending to be an Aztec warrior was a lot more impressive than revealing I was just some bright kid who'd fought his way off the Spokane Indian Reservation in Washington State and now was a corporate lawyer in Seattle who pretended to have a lot more money than he did. (*TIW*, 40)

Alexie's dark humor, couched in Eagle Runner's ridiculous lies that mask the truth about him, articulates the character's conflicted feelings of racial pride and his struggle to make it off the reservation. Like Mary Lynn, Eagle Runner believes sleeping with an Indian may help ease his troubled emotions, but the comic, faux-Indian prostitute, Tawny Feather, "a white woman wearing a black wig over her short blond hair" (*TIW*, 45), brings him no salvation.

The tragic death of his mixed-blood child, followed by the growing gulf between him and his wife, triggers more depression. Eagle Runner soon finds himself in an Indian bar seeking respite "from emotional obligations and beautiful white women, even the kind of white woman who might be the tenth most attractive in any room in the world" (*TIW*, 47). Yet again, Alexie's comic riff is not without its tragic side: the assimilated attorney in a lower-class Indian bar finds himself drawn into a fight. "I'm sick of little shits like you," a tough-talking big Indian, Junior, accuses him. "Fucking urban Indians in your fancy fucking clothes. Fuck you. Fuck you.... Just drive back to your fucking mansion...or whatever white fucking neighborhood you live in. Drive back to your white wife" (*TIW*, 50). The largely one-sided exchange accentuating the dilemma of his assimilation leaves Eagle Runner with a broken nose. His profession, wealth, and marriage have separated him from his heritage.

Perhaps Eagle Runner's greatest fault is turning away from the real needs of his people, as others make clear to him: "Yeah, we're Indians. You, me, Junior. But we live in this world and you live in your world," Sissy, the bartender, tells him (*TIW*, 55). "We have to worry about having enough to eat," she continues. "What do you have to worry about? That you're lonely? That you have a mortgage? That your wife doesn't love you? Fuck you. Fuck you. *I have to worry about having enough to eat*" (*TIW*, 56; italics in original). At the story's end, there is no easy resolution. The disconnected Eagle Runner returns to his urban home without a solution or appeasement of his condition, though there is a sense he experiences regret and resignation in the wake of his encounters.

"Indian Country" is yet another story in *Toughest Indian* that examines life lived off the reservation. Low Man Smith, a successful Indian mystery writer from Seattle, finds himself in Missoula, Montana, for a rendezvous with Carlotta, a Navajo poet who teaches on the Flathead Indian Reservation. Like most of the protagonists in *Toughest Indian,* Smith is an assimilated, mixed-blood Indian: "He was a Coeur d'Alene Indian, even though his mother was white. He'd been born and raised in Seattle, didn't speak his own tribal language, and had visited his home reservation only six times in his life. His mother had often tried to push Low Man toward the reservation, toward his cousins, aunts, and uncles—all of those who had survived one war or another—but Low Man just wasn't interested" (*TIW*, 121). Smith has little regard for his cultural past and the living relatives who represent it. He sees the reservation satirically as a "monotonous place—a wet kind of monotony that white tourists saw as spiritual and magic" (*TIW*, 122).

However, Smith has the ability—unlike Eagle Runner from "Class"— to recognize problems faced by those on the reservation: how a smoldering rage eventually leads to shootings and violence; how "one man would eventually pull a pistol from a secret place and shoot another man in the face"; how "a group of women would drag another woman out of her house and beat her left eye clean out of her skull" (*TIW*, 122). Smith wonders if such "dangerous" conditions also exist on the Flathead Reservation, where Carlota teaches (*TIW*, 122). However, he will never know.

Jilted in Missoula, alone at the airport with a broken heart, Smith finds himself on the verge of a nervous breakdown. As do most of Alexie's characters, he faces the absurdity of his predicament with laughter, "softly at first, but then with a full-throated roar that echoed off the walls. He laughed until tears ran down his face, until his stomach cramped, until he retched and threw up in a water fountain" (*TIW*, 125). After being "escort[ed]...out of the airport" (*TIW*, 125), Smith soon finds himself in a phone booth outside a local 7-Eleven—a scene ironically reminiscent of "Imagining the Reservation" in *Lone Ranger*—where he comes to the realization that "whites and Indians laughed at most of the same jokes, but they laughed for different reasons" (*TIW*, 125–26).

He defines this difference in the light of the white world of "rules" and "order" that governs the life of the teenage clerk (*TIW*, 128). He feels the difference also includes his ability to carry on with laughter despite the absurdities of his life and the situations where he finds himself.

Smith soon frees himself from his material possessions—his suitcase and computer—burdens connected to his professional life as a writer. Escorted to the police station from the Missoula Barnes & Noble bookstore by two officers, Smith, who gives his name as Crazy Horse (*TIW*, 134), calls Tracy, an old college friend, who is soon to be married to her lesbian lover, Sara Polatkin, a Spokane Indian. He then eats dinner with Tracy, Sara, and Sara's Indian parents, who are lesbian-hating Mormons who have just come to Missoula from the Spokane Reservation to try to stop their daughter's marriage. When conversation between Smith and the parents breaks down, Tracy believes that laughter may be the only remedy to repair the rift: "'Hey,' she thought, 'everybody should laugh. Ha, ha, ha, ha, ha! Let's all clap hands and sing!'" (*TIW*, 140).

Alexie's dark humor, expressed in the farce of this situational comedy, characteristically acquires a more tragic tone. Smith and Sid, Sara's father, cannot stop their heated arguing. "You think everything is funny," Sid accuses Smith, and he's mostly correct. For Smith, who accepts the absurdities of his life, "everything was funny. Homophobia? Funny! Genocide? Hilarious! Political assassination? Side-splitting! Love? Ha, Ha, Ha!" (*TIW*, 144). Unlike Sid, what Smith understands is that laughter "overcomes fear."[31] It makes the unspeakable and the difficult approachable, as in the case of Tracy and Sara's love, the loss of Carlota, his ambivalent feelings for the reservation, and his uncertain future. However, nobody takes Tracy's advice, the Polatkins fail to recognize their daughter's love for Tracy, and the dinner comes to a violent end when Sid slaps Sara. At the end of the story, ironically and humorously, the once-manic Smith—now playing the comedic role of straight man—seems the most sensible person involved.

In *Toughest Indian*'s final story, "One Good Man," Alexie once again addresses the question of Indian identity, making as well a more overt response to critics who say that his work lacks a tribally centered, ethical agenda. "One Good Man" is a masterful piece concerning a son's return home to his reservation to care for his dying, diabetic father. Throughout

much of the story, Atticus, the narrating son, raises the issue of identity—*"What is an Indian?"* (*TIW,* 218; italics in original)—that initiates
an exploration that only he can properly understand based on both his
return to the reservation and his relationship with his father. "One Good
Man" is quintessential Alexie, a story where dark humor—generated here
by hyperbole and satire—undermines stereotypes and plays a central
role in orchestrating the tone as a mix of laughter and compassion that
prompts the ending's clarity and understanding.

After returning home, Atticus's first task in caring for his diabetic
father is to eliminate sugar from the house. With humorous hyperbole,
Alexie describes the challenge Atticus is taking on:

> I poured out ten pounds of Hershey's chocolate kisses one by one
> from an aluminum gas can. In the attic, I wore gloves and long
> sleeves when I pulled seven Payday peanut bars from between
> layers of fiberglass insulation. I flipped through fifty-two west-
> erns, twelve mysteries, and nine true-crime books, and dis-
> covered one hundred and twelve fruit wraps pressed tightly
> between the pages. Inside the doghouse, a Tupperware con-
> tainer filled with Oreo cookies was duct-taped to the ceiling.
> I gathered all of it, all of those things that my father stupidly
> loved, and filled seven shopping bags. (*TIW,* 214)

This laundry list of candies represents much more than what the son
faces or the father's helpless addiction. Even the father's reading—sugary
genre fiction—lacks substance. What he needs is something substantial,
something nourishing no food or medicine can provide.

Atticus's new role as caregiver and his return to the reservation prompt
his recurrent question, "What is an Indian?" and Alexie responds with satire: "I'd left the reservation when I was eighteen years old, leaving with
the full intention of coming back after I'd finished college. I had never
wanted to contribute to the brain drain, to be yet another of the best and
brightest Indians to abandon his or her tribe to the Indian leaders who
couldn't spell the word *sovereignty*. Yet no matter my idealistic notions, I
have never again lived with my tribe" (*TIW,* 220; italics in original). Atticus realizes that being an Indian is not simply growing up on a reservation,

nor is it defined by being "in three car wrecks" or knowing the "secret names of every dog that had lived on my reservation during the last twenty years" (*TIW*, 225).

For Atticus his self-definition—"a man who keeps promises"—comes from the selfless act of caring for his father (*TIW*, 229). Through self-denial, Atticus finds self-actualization, that "Indian was the best thing to be!" (*TIW*, 227). What he comes to understand about himself through his family and tribe, his values and obligations, is what most of the other characters throughout *Toughest Indian* are seeking. Unlike these other characters in absurd or tragic circumstances, Atticus—stranded with his father both literally and metaphorically at the U.S./Mexican border—achieves through shared laughter what they do not: "We laughed. We waited for hours for somebody to help us. *What is an Indian?* I lifted my father and carried him across every border" (*TIW*, 238; italics in original). Self-definition involves self-action.

The humor at the end of the story loses much of its dark edge and takes on a compassion that Geiogamah describes as "respect and caring for each other."[32] Atticus's actions—in coming home to care for his father, returning to the reservation, recognizing his own legacy in the life of his father and deciding to carry it with him—give him some answers to his question. He recognizes what Etta Joseph from "Dear John Wayne" understands when she remarks, "You're not required to respect elders. After all, most people are idiots, regardless of age. In tribal cultures, we just make sure that elders remain an active part of the culture, even if they're idiots. Especially if they're idiots. You can't just abandon your old people, even if they have nothing intelligent to say. Even if they're crazy" (*TIW*, 205).

Atticus likewise discovers that his identity is rooted in the continuity between generations, even when traditions seem largely unrecoverable and the future uncertain. He also understands that he must do the "lifting"—taking action with humor—against the problems and absurdities that challenge him.

In both *Lone Ranger* and *Toughest Indian,* Alexie's characters, living both on and off the reservation, struggle over retaining a sense of self amid the absurd conditions of their existence and their difference from the dominant culture. With dark humor's ironic laughter, Alexie can subvert dominant ideologies, undermine ridiculousness or stupidity, and address such problems as alcoholism, drug abuse, and violence.

While dark humor is a trenchant and fundamental element in these collections of short fiction, it also plays an important part in Alexie's poetry, novels, public performances, and films. *Reservation Blues* (1995)—though it incorporates magic realism and is structured as a blues novel—uses dark humor in its often-satirical descriptions of the Spokane Reservation, for example: "Thomas smiled and walked into the Trading Post, one of the few lucrative businesses on the reservation. Its shelves were stocked with reservation staples: Diet Pepsi, Spam, Wonder bread, and a cornucopia of various carbohydrates, none of them complex."[33] Many other scenes in *Reservation Blues* have a darkly humorous tone, creating an ethical imperative not dissimilar from the approach in stories such as "The Only Traffic Signal on the Reservation Doesn't Flash Red Anymore" and "One Good Man."

Alexie's public appearances, which often take the form of stand-up comedy, also use dark humor to address race, class, and political issues within mainstream and/or Indian culture. Speaking in Lawrence, Kansas, as part of the Hall Center Humanities Lecture Series, Alexie described a Seattle run-in with a local bigot, who in a post-9/11 rage yelled from his "big phallic car" for him "to go back to [his] country." "It wasn't so much a hate crime," Alexie told the audience, "but a crime of irony."[34]

It is precisely such irony created by dark humor that structures so much of Alexie's work. To understand him—whether as a novelist, short-story writer, poet, speaker, or filmmaker—is to recognize the importance of this hard-edged humor. This flippant hilarity does a rope-a-dope around mainstream attitudes and provides release and relief, proving that survival really does depend upon a good laugh.

NOTES

1. The ideas here on Alexie's use of dark humor advance beyond those in my earlier article, "Black Humor and the New Ethnic Writing of Tony Diaz and Sherman Alexie," 47–58; that article explored the role tragicomic humor plays in creating new customs and tradition. Portions of that work are reexamined, represented, or adapted here to provide a more comprehensive exploration of dark humor as a fundamental element in Alexie's treatment

of life on and off the reservation in *The Lone Ranger and Tonto Fistfight in Heaven* and *The Toughest Indian in the World.* This essay uses the term *Native American* when referring to the literary tradition; *Indian* is used otherwise to remain consistent with Alexie.

2. Readers familiar with Native American literature should recall humor's important role in the trickster story in various tribal cultures. While a direct comparison between Alexie's dark humor and this tradition might be interesting, his comedic strategies seem more focused on addressing the absurdity created by bewildering circumstances and differ in many ways from the humor of the trickster tradition. Perhaps Etta Joseph, the 118- year-old Spokane woman who sleeps with Marion Morrison (aka John Wayne) in "Dear John Wayne," voices a position closest to Alexie's: "Don't give me that oral tradition garbage. It's so primitive. It makes it sound like Indians sit around naked and grunt stories at each other." *The Toughest Indian in the World,* 193.

3. Alan R. Pratt, introduction to *Black Humor: Critical Essays,* xx.

4. Ibid., xxi.

5. Most contemporary studies of black humor address the work of a core group of postmodern writers including, but not limited to, Heller, Vonnegut, Barth, Coover, Pynchon, and Barthelme. The most extensive collection of readings on the subject's theory and history is Pratt's *Black Humor: Critical Essays;* in many ways, it supersedes Bruce Friedman's earlier *Black Humor.* I use the term *dark humor* when discussing aesthetic practice and *black humor* when referring to those authors working in the 1950s–1970s identified by Pratt and Friedman as black humorists. This shift represents a move toward greater specificity as well as a revision of terminology in my earlier article. Foreword to *Black Humor,* vii–xi.

6. Ibid., x–xi.

7. John W. Aldridge, *Time to Murder and Create: The Contemporary Novel in Crisis,* 145.

8. Scholars critical of Alexie's work—particularly Kenneth Lincoln, Louis Owens, and Elizabeth Cook-Lynn—have been concerned with whether his stylized writing has an ethical purpose beyond a good laugh. Lincoln— focusing on the comedic elements in Alexie's poetry—describes such writing having "more attitude than art, more schtick than aesthetic," though Lincoln does concede it "open[s] the talk." Kenneth Lincoln, "Futuristic Hip Indian: Alexie," in *Sing with the Heart of the Bear: Fusions of Native American Poetry,* 1890–1999, 271. Owens says Alexie too easily "reinforces all of the stereotypes desired by white readers...offering Indian readers plenty of anger but no ground upon which to make a cultural stand." Louis Owens, *Mixedblood Messages: Literature, Family, Film, Place,* 79, 81. Similarly Cook-Lynn admonishes Alexie, and other mixed-blood Indian writers, for not adopting an "ethical endeavor" to defend first nationhood. Elizabeth Cook-Lynn, "American Indian Intellectualism and the New Indian Story,"

in *Natives and Academics: Researching and Writing about American Indians,* 126. However, Joseph L. Coulombe and Stephen F. Evans defend Alexie's approach. "Throughout his fiction," Coulombe contends, "Alexie emphasizes the need for a revaluation of personal morality and social ethics." Joseph L. Coulombe, "The Approximate Size of His Favorite Humor: Sherman Alexie's Comic Connections and Disconnections in *The Lone Ranger and Tonto Fistfight in Heaven,*" 103. Evans thinks that Alexie is a "consciously moral satirist" who "uses the meliorative social and moral values inherent in irony and satire," especially with regard to Indian stereotypes such as alcoholism. Stephen F. Evans, "'Open Containers': Sherman Alexie's Drunken Indians," 48. I argue that understanding Alexie's dark humor is essential to understanding the absurdity his work addresses through that humor.

9.   Coulombe, whose article appeared not long after my earlier study that partially considered Alexie's dark humor, concurs that humor opens a "dialogue" ("Approximate Size of His Favorite Humor," 95) and plays a crucial role in the ability to "re-evaluate past and present ideologies" (Ibid., 96). I further assert that what's essential in creating this dialogue is the way Alexie takes particular advantage of dark humor to generate the necessary irony. In "Dear John Wayne," Spencer Cox, the lampooned anthropologist, remarks, "Irony, a hallmark of the contemporary indigenous American" (*Toughest Indian,* 190). While the irony partly focuses on Cox—a white cultural anthropologist from Harvard, "author of seventeen books, texts, focusing on mid- to late-twentieth-century Native American culture," who speaks with an unerring authority on all things Indian (Ibid.)—Alexie also suggests that irony—true to its own doublespeak—seems to be an important rhetorical approach to contemporary situations where Indians live.

10.   Pratt, introduction to *Black Humor,* xxi.

11.   Jennifer Gillan, "Reservation Home Movies: Sherman Alexie's Poetry," 91–110.

12.   Lincoln, "Futuristic Hip Indian," 271.

13.   Darby Li Po Price, "Laughing without Reservation: Indian Standup Comedians," 263.

14.   Ibid., 269. Price's ideas contrast with those of Gerald Vizenor, who has noted that Indian stereotypes, including "idiotism and 'genetic code' alcoholism, are *hypotragic* impositions that deny a comic world view." *Manifest Manners: Postindian Warriors of Survivance,* 11; italics in original. Rather than perpetuating stereotypes, as Cook-Lynn and Owen have accused him, Alexie subverts them by acknowledging their existence and undermining them with dark humor.

15.   Kenneth Lincoln, *Indi'n Humor: Bicultural Play in Native America,* 328, 336. Lincoln refers largely to the comedy in Geiogamah's play *Body Indian;* however, humor also plays an important role in his *Foghorn.*

16.   Ibid., 7.

17. Several critics have studied the comedic strategies in Welch's *Winter in the Blood*. Andrew Horton places Welch's humor in the tradition of Indian humor from "comic ceremony-dramas" with "laughter as a liberating force" to trickster stories (131); he also sees Welch as a black humorist who makes use of absurdist humor (132). "The Bitter Humor of *Winter in the Blood*," 131–39. Kate Vangen finds *Winter in the Blood* similar to the work of other Native writers, where "defiance and humour blend in Native literature to mediate an otherwise tragic vision and to provide hope for further struggles against oppression" (189). "Masking Faces: Defiance and Humour in Campbell's *Halfbreed* and Welch's *Winter in the Blood*," in *The Native in Literature*, 188–205. Alan Velie focuses on Welch's management of tone through such techniques as farce and satire, placing him, as did Horton, among black humorists (191). "*Winter in the Blood* as Comic Novel," in *Critical Perspectives on Native American Fiction*, 189–94. Lincoln, writing in *Indi'n Humor* on the way humor is an intrinsic aspect of Native American culture, story, and language, notes, "Laughter in the novel *[Winter in the Blood]* can be taken as an absurdist cry for survival" (274).

18. Lincoln, *Indi'n Humor*, 45–46.

19. Sherman Alexie, *The Lone Ranger and Tonto Fistfight in Heaven*, 4 (hereafter cited in the text as *LRT*).

20. Owens, *Mixedblood Messages*, 72.

21. For those interested in Alexie's descriptions of alcohol abuse in his fiction, see Evans, "'Open Containers.'"

22. Peter Donahue, "New Warriors, New Legends: Basketball in Three Native American Works of Fiction," 44, 52, 55.

23. Mikhail Bakhtin, *Rabelais and His World*, 66.

24. For a discussion of "The Trial of Thomas Builds-the-Fire," see Elizabeth Archuleta's essay in this collection as well as chapter four in James H. Cox's *Muting White Noise: Native American and European Novel Traditions*.

25. Coulombe, "Approximate Size of His Favorite Humor," 94.

26. Price, "Laughing without Reservation," 269.

27. Amiri Baraka in "Black Art" calls for "'poems that kill.'/Assassin poems, Poems that shoot/guns." Baraka, "Black Art," in *Transbluesency: The Selected Poems of Amiri Baraka/LeRoi Jones* (1961–1995), 142. This sounds similar to what Louis Owens terms "literary terrorism" (*Mixedblood Messages*, 46). Alexie seems to be humoring the overt militancy of such authors as Owens and Baraka with his facetious "bottle rocket" (*LRT*, 152).

28. Owens, *Mixedblood Messages*, 46.

29. Evans, "'Open Containers,'" 66.

30. Alexie, *Toughest Indian in the World*, 1 (hereafter cited in the text as *TIW*).

31. Bakhtin, *Rabelais and His World*, 90

32. Lincoln, *Indi'n Humor*, 336.

33. Sherman Alexie, *Reservation Blues*, 12.

34. Sherman Alexie, "Killing Indians: Myths, Lies, Exaggerations."

■ *Elizabeth Archuleta*

Chapter 3

"An Extreme Need to Tell the Truth"

Silence and Language in Sherman Alexie's
"The Trial of Thomas Builds-the-Fire"

In Sherman Alexie's short story, "The Trial of Thomas Builds-the-Fire," Thomas breaks a vow of silence he took twenty years earlier.[1] Breaking this vow results in his arrest and a trial where he faces undisclosed charges. Thomas chooses to represent himself in court and appear as his first and only witness. Assuming the role of lawyer, defendant, and witness, he engages in a process of storytelling, challenging so-called Indian crimes and providing evidence for Euro-American crimes silenced in official Washington state histories.

In the three historical narratives he relates, Thomas collapses time when he becomes the voice for the figure telling each story. His first story, told from the perspective of a young pony, focuses on the eight hundred horses that Colonel George Wright ordered his soldiers to slaughter. The pony escapes, living to tell, through Thomas, its emotional and defiant response to witnessing the soldiers shooting, clubbing, and killing its companions over the course of two days.[2] By labeling the theft and slaughter of horses a crime, the pony incriminates Wright for his involvement in what was once an unlawful activity. The Yakima warrior, Qualchan, tells the second story. After initial promises of peace meant to lure

Qualchan to his camp, Wright orders him to be hung, committing another act of betrayal. Wild Coyote tells the final story. His people defeated Lieutenant Colonel Edward J. Steptoe, which led to Wright's engaging in a punitive military expedition against the Yakama, Spokane, Palouse, and Coeur d'Alene tribes in May 1858.[3]

The silence surrounding these histories becomes deafening when you learn about a Web site for a Spokane business called Sullivan Homes.[4] Its Web site lists several neighborhoods where potential buyers can build their dream homes. One neighborhood, called Overlook at Qualchan, is described as "a private community in the Qualchan Hills" and includes "beautiful views of the Hangman Valley." "If you love golfing," it goes on to say, "you will be happy to know your new home is conveniently close to Qualchan, Hangman and Indian Canyon golf courses." The name of the neighborhood and its nearby recreational areas partially exposes the violent histories that Thomas describes during his trial. Coincidentally the publication date of *The Lone Ranger and Tonto Fistfight in Heaven*, the collection where this story appears, corresponds with the opening of Qualchan Golf Course: 1993.

While golf enthusiasts undoubtedly celebrated the opening of another course, Alexie—through Thomas—commemorates the memory of those who died trying to protect the land it now occupies. Indeed, Thomas tells the judge that this is the whole point for his legal storytelling—to honor the memory of warriors defending their homeland who have been forgotten in local Washington and United States histories. Moreover, he breaks his silence in the courtroom to implicate Colonel Wright for crimes that have gone unpunished; therefore, Thomas transforms the sacred space of law into a place where people inhabiting elite neighborhoods and recreation areas become aware of the violent histories underlying their landscape.

While the liberating rhetoric of social-justice movements advocates the importance of speaking out against oppression, injustice, or historical amnesia and giving voice to silences that consent to subjugation, knowing that Thomas's silence is self-imposed challenges the notion that speechlessness is necessarily antithetical to freedom.[5] At the same time, Thomas's decision to speak out in a courtroom and during a trial where rules constrain language also compels us to reconsider the way language and silence operate in the world of law. Clearly there are qualitative differences between being silent and being silenced and different processes involved in being quiet and being unheard.

This essay examines "The Trial of Thomas Builds-the-Fire" with its parodies of law, its consistent rupturing of dominant-culture narratives, and its critique of historical and legal translations, which force readers to consider the parameters of language and silence. Homi Bhabha's concept of *hybridity*—or a "third space"—defines "the hybrid moment of political change. Here the transformational value of change lies in the re-articulation, or translation, of elements that are neither the One...nor the Other...but something else besides, which contests the terms and territories of both."[6] Thomas's critical control of speech and silence in social and legal settings creates a third space for language to interrogate the foundational dualisms that underpin the split between law and society and legal and social expression.

Linguists are still decoding the language and rhythms of silence in different communities, so its nature remains ambiguous, especially when encountered in cross-cultural situations. In *Unspoken: A Rhetoric of Silence,* Cheryl Glenn observes that Western culture incorrectly interprets silence as passive agreement; yet research indicates that American Indians use silence as a rhetorical device.[7] Keith Basso's work among Western Apaches leads him to conclude that relationships determine when one should speak. He also finds that "keeping silent...is a response to uncertainty and unpredictability in social relations," and he notes that this tendency extends to other tribes.[8]

Therefore, we can read Thomas's silence as a reaction to the anxiety he feels about his role within his community—he is a misfit storyteller who usually remains unheard and misconstrued. His silence may also be a response to shifts in tribal power that he finds problematic. For instance, when Bureau of Indian Affairs (BIA) officials accuse Thomas of nearly causing a crisis two decades earlier, he reacts to the unpredictability of his situation by employing silence to defuse, defer, and defeat the power of United States dominant-culture narratives espoused by these officials.

Twenty years before, Thomas used language as a weapon to confront the voice of mainstream authority that the BIA and tribal officials had substituted for the tribal community's vision and values. Thomas realized that this collective voice of the dominant culture threatened to over-shadow and eclipse the Native community. The U.S. Constitution's Pre-amble, which begins with "We the People," as well as the Declaration of Independence, which declares, "We hold these truths to be self-evident," incorporates a disembodied voice that addresses a universal audience through words that create and maintain a myth of the nation as unitary, homogeneous, and stable. Nevertheless, these documents contain at their borders the silenced voices of those historically excluded from the designated "we," thus maintaining voicelessness among the powerless and preserving the status quo. Ironically, the universal and disembodied voice of dominant-culture narratives relies on silence because it retains its power "only as long as contradictory voices remain silenced."[9] Even the self-evident nature of these truths requires the consent of the people to make them legitimate.

When Thomas witnesses the BIA and tribal police participating in the dominant culture's silencing of American Indians through their accep-tance of a nontribal voice and sense of self, he holds "the reservation postmaster hostage for eight hours with the idea of a gun" (*LRT,* 93) and "threaten[s] to make significant changes in the tribal vision" (*LRT,* 93) or, as he sees it, the nontribal vision. In effect Thomas's action suggests that nontribal documents and ideas are holding his tribe hostage, a threat he mimics when he takes hostage Eve Ford, a representative of an institution that facilitates long-distance communication.

As a result of this past act, Thomas sits in a holding cell when the story opens while BIA officials consider his circumstances. Reflecting on Thom-as's past, one official reminds the others, "Builds-the-Fire has a history of this kind of behavior.... A storytelling fetish accompanied by an extreme need to tell the truth" (*LRT,* 93). The official ends by describing Thom-as's behavior as "dangerous" (*LRT,* 93). When his penchant for storytell-ing and testifying to the truth threatened to cause a crisis in the past, "Thomas surrender[ed] voluntarily and agree[d] to remain silent" (*LRT,* 94). For twenty years, he refused to engage in any form of communica-tion; he did "not even send letters or Christmas cards" (*LRT,* 94). Seeing the extent of Thomas's silence, how do we interpret his refusal to speak? Should we define it as an attempt to communicate resistance and oppo-sition to those who marginalize him by defining him as dangerous, or do we interpret his silence in more complex and varied ways because of the story's numerous references to language, communication, and the significance of words?

Because Thomas's silence anticipates some level of audience interaction, it makes a statement in two ways. First, his silence is out of character, making everyone conscious of the fact that he is communicating but doing so without words. The community remarks on his silence. Thus, it is deliberate and calculated, designed to seize attention. Second, Thomas's silence positions him to challenge the authority of BIA officials and tribal police in the future. In other words, if and when he does speak again, they will notice because, twenty years earlier, they labeled his use of language as dangerous. Consequently, they can also characterize his return to speech as potentially threatening. We can also interpret Thomas's silence as ambiguous because the story suggests that his community misunderstood both his period of silence and the so-called threatening words that preceded it.

United States documents that maintain the status quo silence opposition from voices that threaten Americans and American identity. Nevertheless, Thomas initially refused to stand by silently while BIA officials and tribal police took over the dominant culture's role of silencing tribal voices that questioned the existing state of affairs. He became the lone, contradictory voice that opposed the nontribal, disembodied voice imposed on his people. When Thomas's language became a weapon threatening to destabilize the myth of tribal unity and its passive acceptance of BIA authority, his words unsettled the linguistic hegemony that had shaped the relationship between the mainstream majority and the presumed leaders of tribal communities.

Like their federal counterparts, the BIA and tribal officials are aware of the potential threat that language poses to power. They consider words more threatening than weapons. Consequently, when Thomas holds the postmaster hostage, the community's silence indicates its apprehension about his efforts to overturn linguistic hegemony through alternative storytelling. As a result, he chooses silence over being silenced. Thomas's silence is his effort to resist engaging in the colonized language that governs punitive or legal actions, which emphasize retribution over reconciliation. Until Thomas can create something akin to Bhabha's third space, his silence is complete.[10] With his reputation for opposition, Thomas knows that any word he utters may be construed as threatening, which is precisely what happens when he finally breaks his silence.

When Thomas begins making noise and "form[ing] syllables that contained more emotion and meaning than entire sentences constructed by the BIA" (LRT, 94), the agents incarcerate him, possibly to enforce his voluntary silence. Tribal police place him in a holding cell with the hope of sending him to prison. The BIA thus demonstrates its willingness to eliminate from its vision of "we the people" individuals who threaten to undo the false sense of homogeneity or stability that veils their community. The instability that Thomas's speech threatens becomes real when Esther WalksAlong finds the courage to leave her husband, tribal chairman David WalksAlong, after hearing Thomas make a noise that sounds like rain to her.

Unable to interpret the meaning of Thomas's utterance, the BIA agents deem him dangerous, stating, "We don't need his kind around here anymore" (LRT, 94; italics added). In other words, they do not want individuals whose words appear to challenge them. To preserve their authority, they place Thomas in jail and wonder what charges they can bring against him: "Inciting a riot? Kidnapping? Extortion? Maybe murder?" (LRT, 94). While he sits in his holding cell, Thomas does admit guilt for some past act, but he does not specify the crime. Based on his past, we can surmise that his self-imposed guilty verdict stems from his penchant for storytelling, his use of language and silence, or his need to tell the truth, all of which he knows are powerful.

Silence is not merely the absence of speech; it is a different way of saying. In Woman, Native, Other, Trinh T. Minh-ha suggests that "silence as a refusal to partake in the story does sometimes provide us with a means to gain a hearing. It is a voice, a mode of uttering, and a response in its own right."[11] Thus, Thomas's silence becomes a response to the disembodied, unitary voice adopted by the BIA as the tribal voice, a way of refusing to authorize the dominant culture's stories. When he then decides to speak, Thomas faces the possibility of the BIA charging him with using language that empowers, rather than dehumanizes, American Indians and telling stories that may replace mainstream narratives. He realizes that tribal representatives have internalized dominating language so fully that David WalksAlong calls his wife, Esther, a "savage in polyester pants" (*LRT,* 94). Thomas understands the ability of language to imprison people through terms that maintain the power structure. Therefore, he returns to speech as empowerment.

Evidence that his speaking effects change comes when Esther gains the courage to reject her husband's caricaturization and dehumanization: "The day after she listened to Thomas speak" (*LRT,* 94), Esther packed her bags and left her husband. Thomas communicates with Esther through sound, which the BIA perceives as ambiguous and therefore threatening. Undoubtedly they judge his sound as ominous because Esther can determine its meaning. Esther's freedom to establish the import of Thomas's utterance contrasts sharply from the way Western law practitioners construct and use legal discourse, rendering it unchallenged and unchanged because it is somehow exalted.

In the same way that Thomas's speechlessness makes us reexamine assumptions that equate silence with oppression, his return to language compels us to reconsider traditional notions about speech and subjectivity. In her examination of silence in Asian American women's writing, Patti Duncan questions the attitude that speech ensures democratic representation.[12] She quotes Kyo Maclear's equation "located in the Western philosophical tradition that posits…'speech = agency = freedom.'" Maclear and Duncan do not accord the same privilege and power to speech as Westerners. They both recognize that language is limited and constrained, noting that "even speech is structured by always already existent relations of power."[13]

For example, if one is accused of a crime, the legal system demands a confession of guilt, which Michel Foucault interprets as a method of searching for "truth" by those in power. In the *History of Sexuality,* he describes the early Christian ritual of confession, later embraced by psychoanalysts, as an obligation to speak the truth:

> The confession is a ritual of discourse in which the speaking subject is also the subject of the statement; it is also a ritual that unfolds within a power relationship, for one does not confess without the presence (or virtual presence) of a partner who is not simply the interlocutor but the authority who requires the

confession, prescribes and appreciates it, and intervenes in order to judge, punish, forgive, console, and reconcile.[14]

Confession as a ritual discourse is implicit in law; it is perceived as an uncovering of truth but belies the mechanisms of power that generate truth and their processes—(e.g., violence, coercion, force, or threat of punishment). In a legal context, then, speech does not always lead to freedom and is tightly controlled and regulated. Indeed, "free" speech does not prevail in the court of law.

Recognizing this, Alexie underlies his story with a suspicion of legal institutions by imaginatively depicting the trial as the law's principal process and ironically alluding to its major idiom—rights—and controlling value—justice. Thomas's trial challenges orthodox legal practice and theory that lead mainstream practitioners to assume that law—as a set of norms, practices, and rules—is a system closed to politics and societal influence. They feel the law makes sense as a closed system because it is structured through logic, rationality, and regulation, rather than being irrational or random. They also perceive law as balanced, fair, and consistent with what is right and a practical way to help individuals maneuver through their rights and duties as citizens. As a result, law must differentiate itself by boundaries that isolate legal speech from other types.

Despite attempts to keep legal and social discourse apart, however, the law's need for stories keeps them together. From judicial opinions, court transcripts, and legal texts to the stories clients tell lawyers, witnesses tell courtroom audiences, and lawyers tell juries, stories permeate the legal world whether it is acknowledged or not.[15] As these examples indicate, legal storytelling occurs in specific contexts that affect its telling, meaning, and outcome. These stories are also constrained by rules that shape performance and content by defining what is appropriate and necessary.

John Conley and William O'Barr describe courtroom narratives as falling somewhere between "rule orientation" and "relational orientation."[16] Rule-oriented accounts invoke legal rules and rights, construct stories linearly, and identify a human agent. Relational accounts wander, introduce a great deal of context, and assume that the audience shares background information. Rule-oriented accounts typically fare better in courtrooms, which treat relational accounts as irrelevant and inappropriate, indicating that the law privileges certain modes of story-telling and speech over others. In *Just Words: Law, Language, and Power,* Conley and O'Barr conclude that legal discourse is more than "just words" because it perpetuates unequal power relations, an act they iden-tify as unjust,[17] even though the law promises equality.

Legal language operates on the assumption that "we the people" have already consented to the "rule of law" because it is fair and just. Mean-ing is precise and strictly enforced by legal representatives who wish to appear objective and neutral, rather than biased and subjective. They transform the courtroom into a space that limits language to an author-itarian and coercive voice. As the trial begins, the judge residing over Thomas's trial utilizes a disembodied, authoritative voice to appear neu-tral: "'Mr. Builds-the-Fire,' the judge said to Thomas. 'Before *we* can begin this trial, *the court* must be certain that you understand the charges against you.' 'Your Honor,' he said, 'I don't believe that the exact nature of any charges against me have been revealed, let alone detailed. . . .' There was a hush in the crowd followed by exclamations of joy, sadness, etc." (*LRT,* 95; italics added).

The judge denies Thomas a fair trial by refusing to outline the charges against him. He interacts with Thomas as if he were an object, rather than a person whose life the law has the power to change by speaking in the third person as "the court," an entity whose hands are on the levers of power. Thomas challenges this authority as well as the status quo when he contradicts the judge, an act that stuns the courtroom crowd. More-over, Thomas insists that the judge use more specific words to describe his crime, but the judge continues to talk past him:

> "Well, Mr. Builds-the-Fire," the judge said, "I can only infer by your sudden willingness to communicate that you do in fact understand the purpose of this trial."
> "That's not true."
> "Are you accusing this court of dishonesty, Mr. Builds-the-Fire?"
> Thomas sat down to regain his silence for a few moments.
> (*LRT,* 95)

In this linguistic interchange, the court, the judge, and Thomas engage in dialogue shaped by predetermined rules and practices that power and the law maintain. Legal critics have revealed the persistence of hierarchies in the United States' legal system that allow the judge to talk to, rather than with, Thomas. For instance, according to Robert Yazzie, chief justice of the Navajo Nation, the legal system is a vertical one shaped by "written rules which are enforced by authority figures" such as the judge.[18] Robert Cover describes the power of law and legal interpretation this way: "Legal interpretation takes place in a field of pain and death....Legal interpretive acts signal and occasion the imposition of violence upon others: A judge articulates her understanding of a text, and as a result, somebody loses his freedom, his property, his children, even his life."[19]

The judge attempts to silence Thomas through such a display of coercive power. He asks a question in a yes-or-no format that highlights the adversarial nature of American law. Answering would place Thomas in a no-win situation: yes indicates that he does understand the trial's purpose and is merely being combative; no may lead to a charge of contempt; thus, he remains silent.

When Thomas refutes the judge and resorts to silence, he confronts the principle of certitude that governs the legal system. His silence should not be interpreted as acquiescence, however. The judge's rank and power do not impress or instill fear in Thomas, which challenges the notion of the trial and renders courtroom communication and law's authority suspect. Thomas can either accept or reject that authority, but for law to retain its power, he must acquiesce, which he refuses to do. For the past twenty years, Thomas has adopted alternative modes of speaking to overcome univocal, monologic utterances like these.

The judge misreads Thomas's silence as obedience to the law, a presumption that Mikhail Bakhtin characterizes as the law's tendency toward authoritative speech: "The authoritative word demands that we acknowledge it, that we make it our own;...we encounter it with its authority already fused to it.... It is, so to speak, the word of the fathers."[20]

However, Thomas does not acknowledge the authoritative word of law nor has he made it his own. He has chosen other modes of communicating that better serve his needs, and his presence in a courtroom will not change his approach to language.

Because American law is primarily adversarial, exercised partially by controlling language, trials cannot be measured by standards of fairness. The goal of the adjudication process is to punish wrongdoers, which creates winners and losers: those who are right and others who are wrong. Therefore, determining truth is the most significant feature of adversarial law, and competition results when different versions of the same story struggle for validation. When Thomas's stories contest legal practice, they become a centrifugal force that has the potential to destabilize power and privilege, demonstrating that law is and always has been contingent, political, and contestable.

In addition to challenging the authority and power of law and legal language, Thomas's testimony introduces competing laws, truths, and histories. In effect, by introducing historical narratives into a legal setting, Thomas puts the notion of truth on trial and forces the courtroom to question whether the litigation process can ever establish an objective truth. As the judge swears him in, Thomas again challenges the accepted definitions of truth and justice in legal settings. The judge tells Thomas, "'Raise your right hand and promise me you'll tell the whole truth and nothing but the truth.' 'Honesty is all I have left,' Thomas said" (*LRT,* 96).

In his response, Thomas juxtaposes *truth* and *honesty,* pointing to their divergent meanings, especially in a legal setting. Honesty suggests that sincerity and integrity are relative, but still important, yet they are not the facts that trials require witnesses to provide. Thomas realizes that the truth trials seek is really a struggle over stories where only one side can win, so he renounces the practice that courts demand a single truth that will enable one version of a narrative to become the means to punish someone such as himself of a crime.

Although adversarial law is preoccupied with establishing truth, Thomas is more concerned with problem solving, an approach analogous to a horizontal system of justice where everyone is truly equal. Yazzie describes this system as one that "permits anyone to say anything during the course of a dispute." It is "a system in which no authority figure has to determine what is 'true.'" Finally, it is "a system with an end goal of

restorative justice which uses equality and the full participation of dispu-
tants in a final decision."²¹

Thomas bypasses the rules of a vertical system that constrain and
shape legal storytelling and instead adopts a horizontal system that recognizes the equality of all living beings. Indeed, his testimony begins by
blending history and narrative through the voice of a pony: "It all started
on September 8, 1858. I was a young pony, strong and quick in every
movement. I remember this. Still, there was so much to fear on that day-
when Colonel George Wright took me and 799 of my brothers captive.
Imagine, 800 beautiful ponies stolen at once. It was the worst kind of war
crime" (*LRT,* 96).

It is not enough that the pony calls Wright's theft of eight hundred
horses a crime, thus implicating him and his soldiers in legal wrong-
doing; Thomas also creates a space for the pony to participate fully in
legal proceedings and the act of confession demanded by trial courts.
For many readers, Alexie may be pushing the limits of equality, but the
pathos of the pony's story leaves us unable to discount what he tells us
about a horrific moment in Washington's history.

Traditionally, testimony disallows language that veers away from facts
and focuses on relational accounts, but the pony's story intertwines violence and language in a way that is meant to incite emotion in his chosen audience—the Indians in the courtroom. Therefore, in addition to
Wright's letter, the pony includes graphic details of not only the horses'
capture but also their slaughter: "It was a nightmare to witness. They
were rounded into a corral and then lassoed, one by one, and dragged
out to be shot in the head. This lasted for hours, and all that dark night
mothers cried for their dead children. The next day, the survivors were
rounded into a single mass and slaughtered by continuous rifle fire"
(*LRT,* 97).

The pony's story begs the question, "Who is really the animal?"
because—in spite of an act that horrified both Indians and non-Indians—the legal system failed to identify Wright's acts as criminal. Wright
attempts to justify his theft and murder of the eight hundred horses in
a letter that the pony presents as part of his evidence: "Dear Sir: As I
reported in my communication of yesterday the capture of 800 horses
on the 8th instant, I have now to add that this large band of horses

composed the entire wealth of the Spokane chief Til-co-ax" (*LRT,* 96). Wright accused the chief of hostilities against whites to legitimize the horses' capture and subsequent slaughter as a form of punishment: "Retributive justice has now overtaken [the chief]; the blow has been severe but well merited" (*LRT,* 96–97). The horses paid for the chief's perceived crimes, yet it took more than a century before the horses had "their day in court" to present their version of events.

The pony repeats nearly verbatim Wright's September 10 missive to Father Joset of the Coeur d'Alene Mission, blurring the line between history and narrative.[22] Furthermore, by including Wright's version of events, the pony allows us to question his actions through his questionable choice of words; he states that he "captured," rather than "stole," the horses. His terminology reflects the customary way legal and historical narratives portray white/Indian relations: they rarely characterize non-Indians' actions as criminal but nearly always describe Indians' actions as criminal as well as immoral, an attitude that continues into the present.[23]

The pony includes the letter to illustrate Wright's complete disregard for life. Wright confesses that the horses were an "embarrassment." Since he could not see himself traveling with such a number—many of them wild—he "determined to kill them all, save a few in service in the quartermaster's department and to replace broken-down animals." He also confesses deep regret for killing them, "but a dire necessity drove [him] to it" (*LRT,* 97). By inserting the pony's interpretation of events as another truth that competes with Wright's account, Thomas reveals the way legal language reinforces a Western worldview that has the power to suppress alternative ways of speaking and describing events.

The purpose of storytelling is different from orthodox legal practice. Narrative is interactive, allowing the storyteller to respond to the audience, so when "Thomas opened his eyes and found that most of the Indians in the courtroom wept and wanted to admit defeat" (*LRT,* 97), he allows the pony to conclude its narrative differently. Despite being captured, the pony declares, "I was not going to submit without a struggle" (*LRT,* 97). It affirms, "I would continue the war. At first I was passive, let one man saddle me and ride for a while. He laughed at the illusion of my weakness. But I suddenly rose up and bucked him off.... They could not break me" (*LRT,* 97–98). At this point, "Thomas opened his eyes and saw that the Indians in the courtroom sat up straight." (*LRT*, 97–98). The pony admits that many despised his arrogance while others respected his refusal to admit defeat, an ending that empowers the Indians whose actions mimic the horse's pride and dignity in the face of violence. Restorative justice seeks reconciliation, rather than retribution, and healing, rather than punishment, a goal that the pony's story begins to achieve.

By calling himself as his "first and only witness to all the crimes [of which he is] accused" and allowing the pony's narrative to become part of his testimony, Thomas introduces a horizontal system of justice. During a trial, lawyers call witnesses to present narratives that confess or interpret events, yet the law limits who can be a witness and restricts their stories to facts; they cannot make inferences or evaluations; neither can they introduce stories without a lawyer prompting them. In the court's monopoly of power, conversations are one way—based on examination and cross-examination—making speech anything but free. In the same way that he dismisses the judge's authority, Thomas also ignores trial dynamics. He will not engage in examination and cross-examination with the pony, nor will he work to uncover any hidden truths; he simply becomes a conduit for the pony's narrative.

When the judge asks Thomas if his testimony is complete, he replies, "There is much more I need to say" (*LRT*, 98) and continues with his counternarratives. Similar to the horses' treatment, Wright also betrays Qualchan, who believes the colonel's word. Despite Wright's promises of peace, he hangs Qualchan, but—like the pony's experience—Qualchan refuses to admit defeat even when the soldiers place him in chains: "It was then I saw the hangman's noose and made the fight to escape. My wife also fought beside me with a knife and wounded many soldiers before she was subdued. After I was beaten down, they dragged me to the noose and I was hanged with six other Indians, including Epseal, who had never raised a hand in anger to any white or Indian" (*LRT*, 98–99).

Failing to comprehend the significance of Thomas's testimony, the judge asks him to clarify his point. He tells the judge, "The City of Spokane is now building a golf course named after me, Qualchan, located in that valley where I was hanged" (*LRT*, 99). Upon hearing this, the courtroom "burst into motion and emotion" (*LRT*, 99), posing a threat to order that enrages the judge. The bailiff struggles to restrain Eve Ford, who yells to Thomas that everyone is listening to him (*LRT,* 99). In the meantime, she slugs the bailiff twice, knocks him to the ground, and stomps on his belly, only stopping after "two tribal policemen tackled her, handcuffed her, and led her away" (*LRT,* 99).

Language is also key to the horizontal system of law because words bind people together who share common values and emotions. Rather than punish individuals or rely on coercion to ensure good behavior, a horizontal system uses words to repair relationships among people and facilitate peacemaking. Through language Thomas mends his relationship with his community, which now listens to his stories. The narratives that he shares revitalize his community and reconnect its members with heroic figures from the past whose stories official histories have silenced and concealed behind upscale neighborhoods and golf courses.

The judge deems the purpose of these narratives dangerous because they encourage response to injustice in the same way that Thomas's sounds encouraged Esther to leave her abusive husband. Therefore, the judge refuses Thomas an audience by clearing the courtroom. Then he blithely states, "Now...we can go about the administration of justice," prompting Thomas to ask, "Is that real justice or the idea of justice?" (*LRT,* 100). Thomas's question refers back to his original crime: holding the postmaster hostage with the "idea of a gun." Just as the post office encourages a form of communication that keeps people apart, rather than bringing them together, the United States system of justice acts in a similar way. The court regulates and controls communication, which prevents Thomas and his audience from validating one another by forming a common bond.

The United States maintains a system of retributive justice that tries to determine which laws were broken and who broke them to punish the guilty. Thomas knows that justice in this system is tentative because the focus is on the perpetrator and the victim appears at the trial only as a witness. In contrast, restorative justice balances the interests of the offender, victim, and community to heal all the affected parties. In this system, everyone comes together to determine the way to manage the aftermath of conflict, its future repercussions. Restorative justice gives offenders the opportunity to acknowledge the impact of their actions and make reparation. More significantly, however, it affords victims the chance to have their losses acknowledged and receive amends from the offender.

In Thomas's eyes, his stories describe many historical crimes that have gone unacknowledged, not the least of which is naming a golf course after a warrior from a community irreparably harmed by Wright's actions and their repercussions. Thomas's counternarratives contrast with legal discourse that forces victim and offender to take opposing sides. His stories are communal and shared, and they establish relationships among himself, his courtroom audience, and the non-Indigenous community. Ultimately, Thomas creates in the courtroom a third space or dialogics that moves beyond the colonizer/colonized and oppressor/victimized dichotomies that typify historical relationships between Indians and non-Indians. His stories give American Indians parity with the invading military forces; they show both sides as defending homeland and people; they even make it possible for each side to express admiration and respect for the opposing one, even in battle; and they express admiration for the bravery and skill of the non-Indian soldiers.

In a space where truth and honesty are expected, where witnesses, facts, testimony, and evidence will indicate a truthful story as opposed to a lie, Thomas introduces several historical narratives. His testimony places in competition accepted narratives of United States heroes who reigned victorious over "savage" Indians with counternarratives of American Indians who were equally courageous. As he retells Spokane and Yakima history, Thomas highlights the tension between mainstream stories and counternarratives as both sides compete to monopolize language and imbue it with their own meaning. Thomas introduces contrasting narratives and paradigms of justice that challenge the United States' belief in itself as a just nation. Critical race scholars acknowledge that law is narrative, and that makes it subject to challenges that impact other types of discourse. Reading law documents as narrative reveals truths about the social world that traditional legal scholarship silences. Critical legal scholarship transforms legal settings into positive social and cultural places when those whom the legal system tries to silence insist on telling their stories. Thus, critical race scholars focus on the way counternarratives make subjugated knowledge, histories, and identities legitimate as well as defy legal orthodoxy and its claims to truth and justice.[24]

Alexie's story uncovers gaps that lie between the law's image of itself as fair and rational and individuals' understanding of law as it affects their lives. But he offers another form of justice that presents the chance for Indian and non-Indian communities to heal. If healing is the goal of restorative justice, then stories and the involvement of all parties are necessary, yet the American justice system rejects stories like Thomas's and prevents restorative justice from happening.

Notes

1. Sherman Alexie, "The Trial of Thomas Builds-the-Fire," in *The Lone Ranger and Tonto Fistfight in Heaven,* 94 (hereafter cited in the text as *LRT).*
2. Wright left the horses' bodies to decompose, which resulted in a mound of bones now called Horse Slaughter Camp near Aturdee, east of Spokane, Washington.
3. For more information on this history, see Robert M. Utley, *Frontiersmen in Blue, the United States Army and the Indian*, 1848–1865, 207–10; William Stimson, *A View of the Falls: An Illustrated History of Spokane*, 14–19; and Carl P. Schlicke, *General George Wright: Guardian of the Pacific Coast.*
4. The Web site has since changed its content, but the neighborhood retains the original names. See Sullivan Homes at http://www.sullivanhomes.com
5. Alexie also incorporates silence in his short story "Dear John Wayne," even indicating the length of each quiet moment. The story describes a Harvard anthropologist's interview of an elderly Spokane woman. Reversing the power relationship typical in these situations, the woman seizes control of the interview by asking the anthropologist questions and introducing moments of silence that unsettle him. *The Toughest Indian in the World,* 189–95.
6. Homi Bhabha, *The Location of Culture,* xix.
7. Cheryl Glenn, *Unspoken: A Rhetoric of Silence,* xi.
8. Keith Basso, "'To Give Up on Words': Silence in Western Apache Culture," in *Western Apache Language and Culture: Essays in Linguistic Anthropology,* 96.
9. Angela P. Harris, "Race and Essentialism in Feminist Legal Theory," in *Critical Race Theory: The Cutting Edge,* 262.
10. Bhabha, *Location of Culture,* 28.
11. Trinh T. Minh-ha, *Woman, Native, Other: Writing Postcoloniality and Feminism,* 83.
12. Patti Duncan, *Tell This Silence: Asian American Women Writers and the Politics of Speech,* 8.
13. Ibid., 13.

14. Michel Foucault, *The History of Sexuality,* vol 1: *An Introduction,* 61–62.

15. Nancy L. Cook, "Speaking in and about Stories," 95.

16. John Conley and William O'Barr, *Rules Versus Relationships: The Ethnography of Legal Discourse.*

17. John Conley and William O'Barr, *Just Words: Law, Language and Power,* 2, 129.

18. Robert Yazzie, "'Life Comes from It': Navajo Justice Concepts," 177–78.

19. Robert M. Cover, "Violence and the Word," 1601.

20. Mikhail Bakhtin, *The Dialogic Imagination,* 342.

21. Yazzie, "Life Comes from It," 180.

22. USGenNet, "History of the Pacific Northwest, Oregon and Washington, 1889."

23. The Washington secretary of state's "Washington Territorial Timeline" indicates the ongoing silencing of alternative voices. Nearly every event on the timeline depicts Indians as the aggressors: "1847, Whitman Massacre; 1847, Beginning of the Indian Wars; 1849, Fort Nisqually attacked by Indians; 1855, Indian Agent Andrew J. Bolon killed by Indians; 1855–56, Indian War has begun; 1856, Seattle besieged by Indians; 1856, Indians raid Columbia River settlements; 1856, 'Indians are acoming in'; 1856, Massacre in the Grand Ronde River in Oregon; 1876, the Nez Perce War." Unless Indians are signing treaties with whites or killing whites, or whites are killing Indians, Washington's Indigenous residents are conspicuously absent from this official state Web site.

24. Lucinda Finley, "Breaking Women's Silence in Law: The Dilemma of the Gendered Nature of Legal Reasoning," 904.

■ *P. Jane Hafen*

CHAPTER 4

Rock and Roll, Redskins, and Blues in Sherman Alexie's Work

As a Native woman responding to the writings of Sherman Alexie, my mind and heart, much like my heritage, go in diverse directions and create a tension not unlike the structure/antistructure inherent in blues music. Also I am aware of Alexie's scorn for academic dissection of his work. So I am going to follow a bit of both paths. I begin with a cultural analysis that originally had a colonized title: "'Reservation Blues': Sherman Alexie's Mediating Music." Then I conclude with some of my thoughts on the way I—as an Indian woman—personally respond to Alexie's writings.

The writings of Sherman Alexie are a fusion of historical sensibilities with the grim realism of contemporary Indian life on the Spokane Reservation. Amid the imagery of Crazy Horse, cavalry charges, "rez" rods, basketball, addictions to alcohol and Pepsi, and send-ups of Indian lovers, he makes a major turn with a repertoire of rock and roll and blues references. Each musical style, even when blended, represents what Houston Baker calls a "vernacular voice" that plays against the domination of the mainstream culture.[1] Additionally Angela Davis describes blues as "address[ing] urgent social issues and help[ing] to shape collective modes of black consciousness."[2] In her discussion of black feminism in the blues of Ma Rainey, Bessie Smith, and Billie Holiday, Davis acknowledges that "this music resides not only within but far beyond the borders of black culture."[3]

Neither the blues nor rock and roll is specific to Spokane culture, nor particularly American Indian for that matter, despite the number of early blues and jazz musicians with Indigenous heritage.[4] If anything, rock and roll started as American counterculture that has since become institutionalized. Both Davis and Baker place blues at the center of the Afro-American cultural matrix. Alexie has taken these tropes and reinscribed them for his own purposes of presenting an American Indian cultural and political view of subversion and resistance. On one hand, he is demonstrating a reality of reservation life. Young Indian people in his writings and those who really inhabit the rez embrace a variety of music from powwow tapes to rock, rap, and blues. On the other hand, Alexie may be using these forms of music as mediators—claimed and reclaimed expressions that, in the context of the cosmology in his writings, compel the reader to reconsider the popular imagery.

In current theoretical parlance, this mediation may be considered *hybridity:* a blending of mainstream culture with Indigenous traditions. However, the terminology of hybridity is troublesome because it raises inevitable questions of identity and authenticity. In other words, if hybridity is a phenomenon of assimilation or acculturation, then the origin must be somehow diluted. That assumption asserts a static position of Indigenousness, rather than acknowledging the adaptive survival strategies of Native peoples. Instead, as Philip Deloria points out, "Even as Indian mixed blood characters and critiques concern themselves with the interstice and the overlap,... in the end they are as likely to point powerfully to Indian distinctiveness (*even as* a mixture) as to the hybrid invention of the new" (italics in original).[5] That confluence of Indian perspectives with the reality of outside or dominant-culture influences is the way Alexie presents and filters popular culture and invites the reader to experience familiarity with new understanding.

Alexie addresses rock and roll in *The Lone Ranger and Tonto Fistfight in Heaven* (1993) in the chapter titled "Because My Father Always Said He Was the Only Indian Who Saw Jimi Hendrix Play 'The Star-Spangled

Banner' at Woodstock." The title becomes a narrative itself by creating a sense of character, place, time, and artistic allusion. In that celebrated performance, Jimi bends, twists, and screeches the national anthem, playing notes not on the staff and rhythms outside the meter. He is a rock-and-roll subversive icon colliding with a national icon at a legendary gathering of mostly indistinguishable nonconformists in the chaos of the late 1960s. Hendrix has since been mythologized and institutionalized in an ironic turn of the establishment culture he was playing to oppose.

In the first sentence of the short story, the narrator, Victor, identifies the unique role of Indians at the time: "During the sixties, my father was the perfect hippie, since all the hippies were trying to be Indians."[6] In a multilayered inversion, hippies represent a mainstream culture that appropriates images, not realities, of Indians. Rather than being a subversive gesture, hippie Indian imitations are merely another extension of colonialism.

By joining the hippie community at Woodstock, the father both plays into and reinterprets the image. He feels a deep affinity with the anti-image of Jimi, a fellow native from Washington state. Not only does the father capture this Woodstock moment, but he ritually relives it by playing and replaying Jimi's cassette tape. As the narrator describes:

> Jimi Hendrix and my father became drinking buddies. Jimi Hendrix waited for my father to come home after a long night of drinking. Here's how the ceremony worked:
>
> 1. I would lie awake all night and listen for the sounds of my father's pickup.
> 2. When I heard my father's pickup, I would run upstairs and throw Jimi's tape into the stereo.
> 3. Jimi would bend his guitar into the first note of "The Star-Spangled Banner" just as my father walked inside.
> 4. My father would weep, attempt to hum along with Jimi, and then pass out with his head on the kitchen table.
> 5. I would fall asleep under the table with my head near my father's feet.
> 6. We'd dream together until the sun came up.

The days after, my father would feel so guilty that he would tell
me stories as a means of apology. (*LRT,* 26)

The ritual inspires stories of reconciliation. Although this ritual is pro-
cedural, numerically linear, and orderly, it documents the randomness of
connecting lives through narrative and storytelling. This ritualized storytelling and music enable the child, Victor, to unite, however tenuously,
with his alcoholic father.

Victor and his father make a pilgrimage to Seattle to visit Jimi's grave,
where Victor observes that Jimi died at a younger age than Jesus Christ.
Indeed, rather than Christ, Jimi becomes the figure of atonement and
mediation. Through Victor and his father, we hear Jimi in a way we have
never heard him before, and we see—through these Spokane Indians—a
new dimension of subversion and resistance culture.

In Alexie's novel *Reservation Blues* (1995), Victor is the character who
inherits the guitar of blues legend and actual historic figure Robert Johnson. Johnson is the legendary guitarist who, according to folklore, sold
his soul to the devil in exchange for his prodigious musical skills. Alexie
also includes Robert Johnson as a character in the novel.

However, his first explorations of blues music and Robert Johnson
appear in "Red Blues," a series of short vignettes in *Old Shirts & New
Skins* (1993). In that work, the narrative voice repeats the question: "Can
you hear the music, Indian boy?" The music can be popular images of
7-Elevens, pay phones, cars, or little league. The music also resonates
through myth and history in the vignette numbered thirteen. Alexie plays
on the legend of a song that Johnson recorded but has never been found
and suggests that the music can be both specific and general, past and
present: "Robert Johnson, Robert Johnson, where is that missing song?
Someone told me it was hidden at Sand Creek. Someone told me it was
buried near Wounded Knee. Someone told me Crazy Horse never died;
he just picked up a slide guitar."[7]

He continues, "If you listen close, if you listen tight, you can hear
drums 24 hours a day. Someone told me once that a drum means *I love
you*; someone told me later it means *Tradition is repetition*" (*OSNS,* 87;
italics in original). Repetition of characters and images and a circular
narrative reinscribe Spokane traditions through Alexie's voice and his

Spokane characters. The blues become the means for the narrator to tell his collective history. His people were not at Sand Creek or Wounded Knee; neither are the Spokane related to Crazy Horse. Yet these are events and figures that have impacted all Native people. Contemporary knowledge of Robert Johnson—a major musical influence on Jimi Hendrix— allows mediation of the historical past with the present.

Blues, along with basketball, is a trope in the novel *Reservation Blues*. A blues lyric prefaces each chapter. In a thwarted heroic quest, Victor, Junior Polatkin, and Thomas Builds-the-Fire form a rock band called Coyote Springs. Along the way, they pick up and discard two white girls, Betty and Veronica, who ultimately succeed as musicians by passing themselves off as Indians. The band also picks up but keeps two Flathead girls, Chess and Checkers Warm Water. The composition of the band figuratively represents an ideal tribal community, where the whole is greater than the sum of the parts: singular voices harmonize with instruments, and melodies, harmonies, and rhythms assemble together. In addition to the specific, individual instruments, the band members represent wholeness by balancing points of view and gender.

The inspiration for the band comes from Robert Johnson and his emblematic guitar. Johnson has been led to Big Mom, the mythic Spokane woman who cooks the best fry bread in the world and instructs various musicians. The narrative that introduces Johnson to Big Mom also refers to the historical killing of over eight hundred Spokane horses:

> In 1992, Big Mom still watched for the return of those slaughtered horses and listened to their songs. With each successive generation, the horses arrived in different forms and with different songs, called themselves Janis Joplin, Jimi Hendrix, Marvin Gaye and so many other names. Those horses rose from everywhere and turned to Big Mom for rescue, but they all fell back into the earth again.
>
> For seven generations, Big Mom had received those horses and held them in her arms. Now on a bright summer day, she watched a black man walk onto the Spokane Indian Reservation.[8]

The Native American historical and numerical regenerative references are obvious. Less clear is Alexie's use of self-destructive rock musicians, or the murdered Robert Johnson. The tragedy of these real-life figures may tempt critics into finding parallels with the "vanishing American" or terminal ethnic policies. Indeed, Coyote Springs fails as a band, and Junior Polatkin blows his life away with a gun. Nevertheless, the resolution of the novel is positive with Big Mom instigating tribal and communal support for Thomas, Chess, and Checkers as they embark on a journey of survival.

Alexie focuses not on the tragedy but the survival and the means to attain it, which are tribal and specific: "Part of the success comes from the process, the journey itself.... Coyote Springs created a tribal music that scared and excited white people in the audience.... The audience reached for Coyote Springs with brown and white hands that begged for more music, hope and joy" (*RB*, 79–80).

Yet the band succumbs to hubris and seals its inevitable fate: "Coyote Springs felt powerful, fell in love with the power and courted it" (*RB*, 80). Victor and Junior are seduced not only by power but by Betty and Veronica. They transgress Alexie's fundamental opposition to interracial unions that lead to tribal dissolution. True survival comes through Thomas, the teller of traditional stories, who overcomes those temptations and remains with the Flathead Indian women.

However, with this mixture of tragedy and survival humor, Alexie recreates a universe where the blues hurt so good. Big Mom teaches the band a lost chord that resonates through the reservation, history, and its audience:

> Big Mom played the loneliest chord that the band had ever heard.... [She] walked out of the bedroom carrying a guitar made of a 1965 Malibu and the blood of a child killed at Wounded Knee in 1890.... Big Mom hit that chord over and over, until Coyote Springs had memorized its effects on the bodies. Junior had regained consciousness long enough to remember his failures, before the force of the music knocked him out again.... "All Indians can play that chord," Big Mom said. "It's the chord created especially for us."(*RB*, 206–7)

Big Mom's chord is the genetic memory that unites diverse Indian peoples. It is the narrative chord that escapes specific musicality yet resonates through regenerative storytelling. The chord has the particular contemporary overtones that reverberate through mythic time and Spokane sensibilities.

In conjunction with the novel, Alexie collaborated with Jim Boyd (Colville) to produce a sound track, *Reservation Blues*.[9] Ten of the fourteen tracks are settings to the lyrics that introduce the novel's chapters. Three of those tracks also appear in Alexie's film *Smoke Signals*: "Reservation Blues," "Treaties," and "Father and Farther." The final four tracks, "Old Man Singing," "Break and Keep," "99 Percent Alike," and "Prophecy," are independent from the novel.[10] While Boyd is the primary musical performer/singer, Alexie also speaks some of the lyrics.

Most of the songs have the standard twelve-bar blues structure—verse and chorus—with the usual tonalities and harmonic progressions. Boyd's acoustic guitar is clearly articulated to complement the lyrics. What distinguishes the songs is the incorporation of traditional Indigenous elements such as the vocables in the chorus of "Indian Boy Love Song" (track three) and the addition of cedar flute, rhythm rattles, and bells to the accompaniment. "Old Man Singing" is an Indigenous, traditional-style song.

The lyrics portray resistance to colonization, just as African American blues resists domination by the mainstream culture. "Treaties" connects the political with the personal: "Somebody breaks a hard promise / Somebody breaks your tired heart.... Treaties never remember / They give and take 'til they fall apart" (*RB*, 31). In "My God has Dark Skin," the speaker proclaims, "My braids were cut off in the name of Jesus / To make me look so white" (*RB*, 131). "Urban Indian Blues" is premised on policies of government relocation.

Other themes common in Alexie's writings are also echoed in the songs. For example, "Falling Down and Falling Apart" proclaims the strength of women: "But her medicine will never let her break" (*RB*, 171). The power of Big Mom and storytelling appears in her eponymous song: "And I hear Big Mom / Telling me another story / And I hear Big Mom / Singing me another song" (*RB*, 197).

The lyrics also detail the social trials in the novel—violence, heart-break, drinking, and destruction—familiar blues laments. Like the novel, the music celebrates survival. The double meaning of "wake" evokes both the ritual of mourning and awakening to hope: "I can't bury my grief/ Unless I bury my fear.... Wake alive, alive, wake alive, alive" (*RB,* 275–76). The verbal chord that Big Mom acknowledges in the novel is echoed by the musical chords on the sound track.

When I read Sherman Alexie, I know his work; I hear that musical chord. I recognize the circumstances and the characters. The reservation where I grew up was, like most, tribally ethnocentric. I and a handful of other Indians and mixed bloods were outsiders to both the tribe and the white community. We had to forge our own identities. I chose the academic route and became the token showpiece in the public-school system. One young man made a name for himself by playing basketball and running off with a white girl named Cherie. Some popular Navajos were also athletes and attracted to white girls. We were band geeks, too. One boy and I sat together and played baritones. He went on to form his own music group and company. He markets his music through a Web site.

We Indians were an odd collection that the white teachers and community recognized as Indian Others but did not distinguish from the major tribe. Those Indians—Ute Mountain Utes—did not generally include us. They were the hard-drinking, fast-driving traditionalists. White boys I knew got their weekend entertainment by rolling drunk Utes in the dark alleys of town. These Indians of my youth were much like the characters on the Spokane Reservation of Sherman Alexie. After high school, I heard stories of the way, one by one, young men followed the path of Junior Polatkin and took their own lives. Or, like Victor, they drifted in and out of alcoholic rehabilitation. My own sister lost her life in that struggle. While the gritty realities of Alexie's reservation life may serve as an outlet for white liberal guilt, they are all too familiar and personal to me.

I identify with Alexie's personal revelations because they uncover statistical trends in Native populations. He and I are part of this genetic inheritance he discusses in a poem from *The Summer of Black Widows* (1996):

Diabetes
Having learned sugar kills me
piece by piece, I have to eat
with more sense
than taste
so I travel alone in this
limited feast, choosing
the right place
and plate. [11]

The high incidence of diabetes among Native populations is well docu-
mented yet does not correspond with romantic notions of Indian people.
The introduction of milk sugar and other dietary changes into the lives of
Native peoples have led to major health crises not unlike the initial epidemic encounters. This historic factor creates a daily awareness of a disease I must live with.

Shortly after I wrote this paper in 1997, I took my two oldest sons—
aged twenty-one and nineteen—to our reservation. We drove our '96
sport-utility vehicle and mingled with the tourists. We played nickel slots
at the tribal casino, where my younger son could legally gamble. The
journey to place and family is one of regeneration. In *Reservation Blues,*
though, Alexie offers little compassion for mixed bloods like my children and grotesquely oversimplifies their interaction with their heritage.
Checkers Warm Water observes, "Those quarter-blood and eighth-blood
grandchildren will find out they're Indian and torment the rest of us real
Indians. They'll come out to the reservation, come to our powwows, in
their nice clothes and nice cars, and remind the real Indians how much
we don't have. Those quarter-bloods and eighth-bloods will get all the
Indian jobs, all the Indian chances, because they look white. Because
they're safer" (*RB,* 283).

Every time I return to the rez, I am aware of my economic and educational privileges. I rarely forget the life or the people I knew from my
childhood. When we went to the TCBY in town (where I could indulge in
a sugar-free dessert), we encountered two young Indian men who were
very drunk and trying to panhandle. I did not and do not know what I

can do to help those young men. Their suffering has not shaped my life, nor have my lucky turns of fortune led to their condition.

In the world of Indian-identity politics, Alexie is often uncomfortably essentialist. He raises significant questions, but his answers are uncompromising and not always consistent. My children, as privileged as they are, do not benefit from Indian preference or educational subsidies. We have tried to give them a traditional sense of who they are and where they come from. We have told them the stories of our people. However—as mixed bloods—they suffer indignities resulting from the ignorance and prejudices of others. For example, my second son—who does not "look Indian"—once wore his bead choker to school, where his high school English teacher ridiculed him for "playing Indian Joe." At college my older son—who does look Indian—has suffered violent and personal racist attacks.

Nevertheless, Alexie's sharp edge of essentialism and tribal awareness unmasks institutional and historical racism. As American Indians, we have the collective historical and genetic memory of Phillip Sheridan, Mr. Armstrong, and George Wright from *Reservations Blues*. We play with popular cultural images like those in *Lone Ranger*. Like the characters in *Indian Killer* (1996), we live with exploitative novelist wannabes like Jack Wilson, professors like Dr. Clarence Mather who fill our children and students with misdirected Noble Savage romanticism, and well-meaning individuals like Olivia and Daniel Smith, who want to possess us in the name of rescuing us.

As a scholar, I hope Alexie's writings will challenge critics to recognize that Native American literature is not simply an exercise in literary theory. He represents real life, and I believe his intended audience consists of real Indians, whoever they may be. It seems facile to apply techniques of poststructuralism, cultural studies, postcolonialism, or the amorphous postmodernism to his works, even as I have done in the first part of this chapter. These approaches illuminate the text and are often publishable. Nevertheless, I think it is a greater challenge for mainstream critics to assess his work in terms of tribal and intellectual sovereignty, as Robert Allen Warrior called for in *Tribal Secrets*.[12] The greater critical challenge is acknowledging that Alexie's work depicts real contemporary people who are not historical artifacts, anthropological phenomena, objects of literary theories, or simply Earth's children.

Finally, I like the writings of Sherman Alexie because they make me laugh. In the face of dismal reservation life and urban crises of self, community, and identity, he can make me laugh, often by inverting imagery and turning inside jokes. He helps make the pain bearable.

I would like to conclude with two short quotes from poems in *First Indian on the Moon* (1993). The first comes from "Seven Love Songs Which Include the Collected History of the United States of America" and depicts the paradoxical realism of his writings. The second, from "Song," recalls the musicality and timelessness of Alexie's voice:

> And we both laughed at the impossibility of all of it at the impossibility of *us*. Who would ever believe this story? If we translated our lives into every language could we find an audience that understood the irony?

> Believe me, the warriors are coming back
> to take their place beside you
> rising
> beyond the "just surviving"
> singing
> those new songs
> that sound
> exactly
> like the old ones.[13]

NOTES

1.   Houston Baker, "A Vernacular Theory," in *Blues, Ideology and Afro-American Literature,* quoted in Arthur P. Davis, J. Saunders Redding, and Joyce Ann Joyce, eds., *The New Cavalcade: African American Writing from 1760 to the Present,* 2:649.

2.   Angela Davis, *Blues Legacies and Black Feminism: Gertrude "Ma" Rainey, Bessie Smith and Billie Holiday,* xiv.

3.   Ibid., xviii.

4.   For example, Jim Pepper, Muscogee-Kaw tenor sax man (died in 1992). See Joy Harjo's poem "The Place the Musician Became a Bear: I Heard about

Jim Pepper..." in *The Woman Who Fell from the Sky,* 51. Jack Teagarden (1905–64), Choctaw, played trombone. Jesse Ed Davis (Kiowa) played guitar for blues band Taj Majal, Eric Clapton, and John Lee Hooker, among others. Clarence Williams (1898–1965), record producer and author of many early blues lyrics, was of Choctaw and Creole heritage. See the Web site http://www.redhotjazz.com/williams.html

5.   Philip J. Deloria (Standing Rock Dakota), "American Indians, American Studies, and the ASA," 673.

6.   Sherman Alexie, *The Lone Ranger and Tonto Fistfight in Heaven,* 24 (hereafter cited in the text as *LRT*).

7.   Sherman Alexie, *Old Shirts & New Skins,* 87 (hereafter cited in the text as *OSNS*).

8.   Sherman Alexie, *Reservation Blues,* 10 (hereafter cited in the text as *RB*).

9.   Jim Boyd (Colville), *Reservation Blues,* CD.

10. *Smoke Signals: Music from the Miramax Motion Picture,* CD. "Prophecy" is originally from Alexie's limited-edition work, *The Man Who Loves Salmon.*

11. Sherman Alexie, *The Summer of Black Widows,* 44.

12. Robert A. Warrior, *Tribal Secrets: Recovering American Indian Intellectual Traditions.*

13. Sherman Alexie, *First Indian on the Moon,* 65, 109.

■ *James H. Cox*

CHAPTER 5

This Is What It Means to Say Reservation Cinema

Making Cinematic Indians in Smoke Signals

I don't remember that fire. I only have the stories,
and in every one of those stories, I could fly.

—THOMAS BUILDS-THE-FIRE

From the earliest days of cinematic history in the United States, when Thomas Edison filmed performers in Buffalo Bill's Wild West show, films with Indian characters and themes have been popular and, at least for Hollywood studios and filmmakers, profitable.[1] The popularity and profitability of these films rest on the conventional plots that affirm European or European American superiority and the "savage" warriors, noble companions, wise sachems, and seductive "squaws" that populate them. With a monopoly on writing, directing, and acting—even in the Native roles—non-Indians controlled the construction of Native identity and culture for the first century of filmmaking in the United States. To construct cinematic Indians, non-Native filmmakers relied on visible ethnic markers, such as artificially browned skin, feathers, paint, and buckskin, that reduced Native identities and cultures to a code of signs easily translatable by a non-Native audience.[2] While Hollywood often promotes these cinematic Indians as authentic, Gerald Vizenor (Anishinaabe) calls them pure simulations that indicate "the absence of the tribal real."[3]

There was considerable excitement, therefore, for the premiere of *Smoke Signals* (1998) at the 1998 Sundance Film Festival. Screenwriter Sherman Alexie (Spokane and Coeur d'Alene) and director Chris Eyre (Cheyenne and Arapahoe) promoted *Smoke Signals* as "the first feature film written, directed, and co-produced by Indians to ever receive a major distribution deal."[4] One implication of this statement about the primarily Indian cast and crew is that the film contains neither a conventional Hollywood narrative about Indians nor conventional roles for the Indian characters.

Alexie, Eyre, and the actors in *Smoke Signals* challenge conventional Hollywood images of and narratives about Indians by avoiding depictions of specific cultural materials, beliefs, and practices that are frequently exoticized, romanticized, misrepresented, or otherwise exploited. There are no buckskin clothes, beaded moccasins, feathers, warbonnets, medicine bundles, peace pipes, or Coeur d'Alene religious ceremonies in *Smoke Signals*. Instead, Alexie, Eyre, and the actors create characters who remind each other and the audience that they are Indians and the film occurs in Indian time, Indian history, and an Indian cultural space where they laugh at Indian humor.[5]

In addition to eliminating cultural markers from the film, Alexie and Eyre make residing on the Coeur d'Alene Reservation an important part of the identity of the characters. There is a biographical motivation for Alexie to set the film there, but the decision to shoot on location also helped establish the Coeur d'Alene identity of the characters without exploiting the tribal nation's culture. As indicators of Coeur d'Alene identity, spatial or geographic markers connect the characters to a primarily Indian-owned and occupied landscape and allow the filmmakers to privilege familial and communal, or "communitist," rather than cultural, identities.[6] Alexie's focus in the screenplay on Thomas Builds-the-Fire's role also contributes to a Native cinematic presence that is communally informed, in this case, by the memory and imagination of the community's storyteller.

Alexie based the screenplay of *Smoke Signals* on stories in *The Lone Ranger and Tonto Fistfight in Heaven* (1993), in which, as the title indicates, his characters resist non-Native definitions of what constitutes an authentic Indian. In his early poetry, fiction, and essays, Alexie frequently acknowledges the power of popular culture to influence both non-Native perceptions of Natives and their self-perceptions.[7] In "Imagining the Reservation" from *The Lone Ranger,* for example, the narrator asks, "What do you believe in? Does every Indian depend on Hollywood for a twentieth-century vision?"[8] Alexie writes that Junior Polatkin, the drummer of Coyote Springs in *Reservation Blues* (1995), "always expected his visions to come true. Indians were *supposed* to have visions and receive messages from their dreams. All the Indians on television had visions that told them exactly what to do" (italics in original).[9] The band's lead guitarist, Victor Joseph, also wonders about television Indians: "most Indians never drink. Nobody notices the sober Indians. On television, the drunk Indians emote. In books, the drunk Indians philosophize" (*RB,* 151). In "All I Wanted to Do Was Dance," another story in *The Lone Ranger,* Joseph vomits immediately after viewing a commercial for a new candy bar. Television and film are literally dangerous to Alexie's characters.[10] "It is the small things that hurt the most. The white waitress who wouldn't take an order, Tonto, the Washington Redskins," Victor thinks in "The Only Traffic Signal on the Reservation Doesn't Flash Red Anymore" (*LRT,* 49). Alexie draws a direct correlation between these "small things" and the poverty, violence, and alcoholism on his fictional Spokane Reservation. Images and stories of archetypal Tontos colonize the reservation and the imaginations of its residents. Those residents who are dominated by these images and stories have great difficulty imagining and then creating a world different from the one where they live.

Billy Jack, the mixed-blood protagonist of three films in the 1970s, is one of those characters that occupied Alexie's imagination. Alexie's reflections on Billy Jack suggest that popular-culture images are seductive, yet the narratives that disseminate those images do not capture the challenges in the real Native world. In the introduction to the *Smoke Signals* screenplay, Alexie comments,

> I used to think movies were real. I mean, I thought, I truly believed, that every movie was actually a documentary. I believed this long past the age when it could be considered cute.

> Once, in Spokane, Washington, when I was eleven years old, an older, larger white kid called me a "dirty fucking Indian." And I jumped on him, despite his size, fully expecting to be rescued by Billy Jack, the half-breed Indian and Vietnam War veteran portrayed by Tom Laughlin in a series of pulp movies. (*SS*, x)

Alexie made the Billy Jack film a part of his eleven-year-old Spokane worldview, but the story put him in danger. Stories influence the way that we act in the world, yet there is little correlation between the world of an eleven-year-old Spokane boy and the stories controlled by non-Natives like Tom Laughlin, the writer, producer, director, and star of the Billy Jack films.[11] In "Billy Jack," a poem in *First Indian on the Moon* (1993), Alexie quotes the character's lines from a scene in an ice cream shop during which he saves a group of young Indians from several local white bullies. Alexie writes, "Oh, Billy Jack, I cheered then / just like all the other Indians / who ever saw your movies. I think / all Indians saw your movies, wanted you / to be real, wanted you to rise / and save the Indians from their sins. / But all these years later, we need more."[12] The more to which Alexie refers may be more accurate depictions of contemporary Native lives, but the issue is not necessarily the correlation between the real world and the story. Rather, Native audiences need films that nourish Native individuals and communities.[13]

The villainous savage stereotype was equally influential on Alexie's imagination. In "I Hated Tonto (Still Do)," a *Los Angeles Times* article that includes another homage to Billy Jack, Alexie writes, "I loved movies about Indians, loved them beyond all reasoning and saw no fault with any of them. I loved John Ford's *The Searchers*. I rooted for John Wayne as he searched for his niece for years and years. I rooted for John Wayne because I understood why he wanted to kill his niece. I hated those savage Indians just as much as John Wayne did."[14] The image of the cinematic savage, Alexie suggests, has the power to encourage Indian hating among non-Natives and self-loathing among Natives. At the same time, he hates the invention, not the real Indians.

Alexie also suggests that recognizing the image as a simulation is often not enough to prevent it from influencing the way one views the world. He notes, for example, that he hears iconographic ominous music when he walks in public, and he hates Tonto "because he was the only cinematic Indian who looked like me."[15] Whether hero or villain, and whether played by a Native or non-Native actor, cinematic Indians haunt him.

Smoke Signals appears as a corrective at a time in cinematic history when Hollywood studios were attempting to repackage these stereotypical cinematic Indians and reinvigorate traditional westerns. At the annual Academy of Motion Picture Arts and Sciences Awards in March 1991, *Dances With Wolves,* with a screenplay by Michael Blake based on his novel of the same name, won seven Academy Awards, including best picture, a best director honor for Kevin Costner, best cinematography, and best screenplay. The film's financial and mainstream critical success, and its role as an important nexus for discussions of conflict between the non-Native world and Native Americans, make *Dances With Wolves* an important indicator of the status of Indians in Hollywood in the early 1990s. The film, which Alexie critiques in the screenplay for *Smoke Signals,* forecloses on any future for the late-nineteenth-century Lakotas that it depicts.

The response of Native Americans to *Dances With Wolves* was not unanimous. Actors and actresses such as Floyd Red Crow Westerman (Dakota) and Tantoo Cardinal (Metis/Cree) praised the film as, Cardinal explains, "an immense breakthrough in Hollywood's perception of native people," though some Native scholars and cultural critics denounced it as a colonialist narrative.[16] Ward Churchill explains that the film perpetuates "the racist mythology so important to conventional justifications for America's 'winning of the West.'" Costner "holds closely to certain sympathetic stereotypes of Euroamerican behavior on the 'frontier,' at least insofar as he never quite explains how completely, systematically and persistently the invaders violated every conceivable standard of human decency in the process of conquest."[17] The film, in fact, almost completely ignores the colonial violence committed against Native Americans. Though the plot suggests an attack by the U.S. Army on the Lakotas is imminent, Costner ends the film before the battle occurs. By not depicting the violence that was committed against the Lakotas, Costner avoids condemnation of the United States and any serious discussion of who was responsible for the warfare that was so devastating to Native communities.

Louis Owens (Choctaw and Cherokee) also reads the film as a colonialist apology. He writes of the difficulty he has understanding the attraction of the wolf, Two Socks, to Dunbar:

> My guess is that Two Socks is an essential metaphor for the submission of natural America to the "white god"—as Blake repeatedly calls Lieutenant Dunbar—who has come to stake his colonial claim to the territory. In this role, Two Socks effectively foreshadows the submission of the Lakotas to the same white god, and together wolf and Indian serve to authorize the rightful role of the European invader in asserting his dominion over the continent and its occupants.[18]

Owens adds that *Dances With Wolves* is "the perfect, exquisite reenactment of the whole colonial enterprise in America, and it is the most insidious vehicle yet for this familiar message because it comes beautifully disguised as its opposite: a revisionist, politically correct western."[19] Blake and Costner change certain generic conventions of cinematic westerns: Native actors and actresses play Lakotas who speak their own language, rather than a monosyllabic pidgin English; the camera remains in Indian territory, rather than in a white settlement or military encampment; the narrative distinguishes Lakotas as individuals, rather than representatives of a singular, inflexible Indian identity.

However, the focus is still on a white hero, who in this film controls the construction both of the story and Native identity through his voice-over narration and the entries and sketches in his diary. The culmination of the plot shows this white hero/narrator returning to a white world with a white woman, Stands-With-a-Fist, whom he has recovered from a de facto captivity with the Lakotas. Civilization promises redemption for these white characters, but the end of the film implies doom for the Lakotas.

The audience learns in the postscript that, in spite of Dunbar's return to the white world with the recovered captive, the hero's promised social activism on behalf of the Lakotas does not change that white world's colonial intentions. The postscript reads, "Thirteen years later, their homes destroyed, their buffalo gone, the last band of free Sioux submitted to white authority at Fort Robinson, Nebraska. The great horse culture of the plains was gone and the American frontier was soon to pass into history."[20] In this brief narrative of conquest, the perpetrators of the violence are undefined, implied subjects of sentences in passive voice. Though the Sioux are apparently not passive witnesses to their conquest, the act that Blake and Costner allow "the last band of free Sioux" is submission to an invasive military and immigrant presence defined as an ambiguous "white authority." In addition, Blake and Costner efface contemporary Indians from the landscape—Siouan culture, the postscript explains, no longer exists.

Dances With Wolves did not exist in a cinematic or ideological vacuum but was the most visible of the films in the 1990s that addressed Native interaction with descendants of Europeans. Jacqueline Kilpatrick (Choctaw and Cherokee) traces the history of images of Native Americans from silent films to the 1990s and sees little change in them.[21] Films such as *The Last of the Mohicans* (1992), *Thunderheart* (1992), *Geronimo: An American Legend* (1993), *Last of the Dogmen* (1995), *Natural Born Killers* (1994), *The Scarlet Letter* (1995), *Pocahontas* (1995), *From Dusk Till Dawn* (1996), and *U-Turn* (1997) repackage narratives of conquest and rearticulate apologies for colonialism for a 1990s audience.[22] In a culture where people watch stories as often as they read them, these cinematic narratives influence non-Native perceptions of Native Americans in the same way as the magazines and newspapers in the nineteenth century that published frontier stories of bloodthirsty, drunken savages and treatises on the "noble savages" who yearned for civilization, Christianity, and democratic government.[23]

Resistance to stereotypical representations is a key component of Alexie's Indian characters in *Smoke Signals,* while the storytelling diverges dramatically from the plots of conventional westerns. The primary narrative movement in the film is the journey of Victor Joseph, played by Adam Beach (Ojibwa), and Thomas Builds-the-Fire, played by Evan Adams (Coast Salish), to Arizona to recover the ashes of Victor's long-absent father, Arnold Joseph, played by Gary Farmer (Cayuga). As they ride the bus south from the Coeur d'Alene Reservation in Idaho, Victor—who throughout the film responds with irritation to his friend's storytelling—asks Thomas, "You're always trying to sound like some damn medicine man or something. I mean, how many times have you seen *Dances With Wolves?* A hundred, maybe two hundred times?" After Thomas offers an embarrassed look as his response, Victor continues, "Oh, jeez, you have seen it that many times, haven't you? Man. Do you think that shit is for real? God. Don't you even know how to be a real Indian?" As the conversation continues, Victor tells Thomas he needs to look like a menacing, stoic warrior. But when Victor tells Thomas "to look like you just got back from killing buffalo," Thomas protests, "But our tribe never hunted buffalo. We were fishermen." Victor responds, "You want to look like you just came back from catching a fish? It ain't *Dances With Salmon,* you know?" Alexie mocks romanticized images of Indians as both stoic and savage warriors while also noting the way that these representations influence the self-images of individual Indians, in this case, Victor. In addition, he highlights European American culture's primary interest in Plains tribes as the source of cinematic Indians, a focus that ignores the majority of tribes and the vast cultural differences among them. The hypothetical film *Dances With Salmon* would not have been as commercially successful as *Dances With Wolves,* Alexie suggests, and ignoring tribes like the Spokane and Coeur d'Alene in the inland Pacific Northwest contributes to their effacement from history and the contemporary landscape.

Victor's comments to Thomas demonstrate that Hollywood has influenced his self-image, and in terms of Alexie and Eyre's construction of a cinematic Indian identity, the satire in this scene indicates primarily what his Indian characters are not. At a rest stop following the *Dances With Salmon* conversation, Thomas returns to the bus with his suit replaced by a T-shirt emblazoned with the words "Frybread Power," his hair loose, and a stern look on his face. Victor looks pleased with Thomas's new warrior identity, though Thomas emphasizes that it is a highly stylized performance by smiling broadly and putting on his thick glasses. Once on the bus, they discover that two men—whom Alexie describes in the screenplay as "white cowboys"—have appropriated their seats (*SS,* 64). When they refuse to relinquish the seats after a stare-down with Victor, Thomas says, "Jeez, Victor, I guess your warrior look doesn't work every time." Victor's Hollywood-referenced identity cannot function outside of a Hollywood narrative. The menacing warrior is a simulation that exists only in film, and though Victor can perform the stereotypical role, his attempt is as futile as Alexie's hope that Billy Jack would step from the screen and save him from a hostile Indian hater in Spokane.

In the scene immediately following the failure of his stereotypical pose and the loss of their seats, Victor discovers a different way to fulfill the promise of his name. He says to Thomas, "You know, in all those movies, you never saw John Wayne's teeth. Not once. I think there's something wrong when you don't see a guy's teeth." In the screenplay, Alexie writes that Victor is "pounding a powwow rhythm on the seat" (*SS,* 66), and he begins to sing a "49" called "John Wayne's Teeth." Alexie defines 49s in the short story "The Toughest Indian in the World" from the short story collection of the same name as "Indian blues . . . cross-cultural songs that combined Indian lyrics and rhythms with country-and-western and blues melodies."[24] The lyrics pose the following questions about John Wayne's teeth: "Are they false, are they real? Are they plastic, are they steel?" Though the cowboys appear to have defeated the Indians, Victor uses the 49 as an attack on a famous Hollywood Indian killer and an icon of European American masculinity and nationalistic pride. The song belittles John Wayne by reducing his identity to a single physical characteristic while the lyrics raise the question of the "reality" of John Wayne the film-studio product, who—as Alexie notes in the short story "Dear John Wayne"—changed his name from the conventionally feminine Marion Morrison (*TIW,* 196). Victor is not the only person in the scene giving a performance based on a Hollywood simulation, for John Wayne provides a culturally sanctioned source for the hostility and racism of the cowboys. The Hollywood cowboy, an image often constructed by such noncowboys as Ohio-born Roy Rogers, is as unreal, or as much a simulation, as the Hollywood Indian. Victor's 49 and powwow rhythm, which the filmmakers mix with increasing volume into a version of "John Wayne's Teeth" by the Eaglebear Singers, defeat the cowboys with humor and reclaim the bus as an Indian cultural space.

While his male characters are neither stoic warriors nor buffalo hunters, Alexie's main female characters are neither princesses nor squaws, the two prevailing identities that non-Natives impose on Native women. As Rayna Green (Cherokee) explains, the *princess* is a rescuer and helper of white men who "must defy her own people, exile herself from them, become white, and perhaps suffer death," whereas squaws are sexually available to white men and "share in the same vices attributed to Indian men—drunkenness, stupidity, thievery, venality of every kind."[25] Alexie defines two Coeur d'Alene women—Velma, played by Michelle St. John, and Lucy, played by Elaine Miles (Cayuse and Nez Perce)— by their sense of humor. The screenplay notes that they are "good-looking Indian women, although fairly goofy in their mismatched clothes and weird glasses" (SS, 34), and their attempts to be serious only elicit more laughter. They are also contemporary contraries, for they are driving their Chevy Malibu in reverse when they see Victor and Thomas walking on the road and offer to drive them to the bus station.[26] Arlene Joseph, played by Tantoo Cardinal, and Grandma Builds-the-Fire, played by Monique Mojica (Kuna/Rappahannock), are caring parents to Victor and Thomas, respectively, and Arlene is particularly well known for her fry bread. All four of these characters are definitively of the Coeur d'Alene Reservation: they are comfortable in the community and express no desire to leave, with or without white men.

Similarly to these four Coeur d'Alene characters, Suzy Song, played by Irene Bedard (Inupiat/Cree), is not defined by a relationship to a white man. She has moved from New York to Arizona—from East to West— where she works for Indian communities as an employee of the Indian Health Service. Her earlier life includes stealing from an old Indian woman at a powwow and, while in college, sleeping with her best friend's boyfriend, but these past transgressions humanize, rather than demonize, her. Suzy and Arnold "keep each other's secrets," as she explains, and this willingness to protect each other defines their relationship. A crucial part of the identities of Alexie's characters is that they care deeply about other Indians, even if they have just met. Though we know Suzy's tribal identification—Mohawk—she is Indian within the context of the film because she shares personal information about her life as an Indian with Arnold during their first meeting, then keeps his ashes safe for his son.

There are several scenes in the film during which the characters remind each other and the audience that they are Indians, as if their identities may be in doubt because they do not look, act, live, or talk like stereotypical cinematic Indians. At the beginning of the film, Thomas speaks in voice-over as an image of a house engulfed in flames brightens the night. Thomas establishes the context: "On the Fourth of July 1976, my mother and father celebrated white people's independence with the biggest house party in Coeur d'Alene tribal history." His statement underscores the distance between the characters in the film and any non-Native members of the audience. Indians, Thomas suggests, may still be waiting for a day to celebrate their independence. Additional examples of the construction of a cultural space distant from non-Natives include a scene with disc jockey Randy Peone, played by John Trudell (Santee Sioux), who speaks to his morning audience on the Fourth of July 1998. Peone tells his listeners, "And Coeur d'Alene people, our reservation is beautiful this morning. It's a good day to be indigenous." He adds, "It's 8:00, Indian time."

Eyre's filming of this scene emphasizes the beauty of the reservation, whereas a non-Native filmmaker might have focused more heavily on what Alexie calls in his scene notes "the poverty, the ugliness of reservations" (*SS*, 158). Peone's comments also remind viewers that some Indians may not subscribe to the same method of mechanical time keeping as other cultures. When Velma and Lucy finally drop Victor and Thomas at the bus station, Velma asks, "Do you guys got your passports? . . . You're leaving the rez and going into a whole different country, cousin." Thomas responds, "But it's the United States," and Lucy interjects, "Damn right it is. That's as foreign as it gets. I hope you two got your vaccinations."

Lucy's comments, in addition to the on-screen identification at the beginning of the film and a roadside sign at the end, establish the Coeur d'Alene Reservation as the privileged landscape and narrative center, just as the Spokane Reservation is the narrative center in Alexie's directorial debut, *The Business of Fancydancing* (2002).[27] In Alexie's film, the Indians, rather than immigrants or U.S. Army troops, cross an arbitrary border or frontier into a dangerous and foreign world. The storytelling traditions are also different in this alien world. When Thomas reminds a young woman that he and Victor are more like "Tonto and Tonto" than the Lone Ranger and Tonto, his statement reaffirms the shift Alexie facilitates between *Smoke Signals* and conventional Hollywood films about Indians. Though in jest, Thomas and Victor identify with Tonto as a hero—as the protagonist of the story—rather than the Lone Ranger.

Randy Peone's, Velma's, and Lucy's comments suggest that the term *reservation* is as important as the term *Indian* to a person's identity. His poetry, fiction, and nonfiction confirm Alexie's view of the reservation as a significant contributor to a resident's worldview. His short autobiography, "One Little Indian Boy," includes references to hydrocephalus, epileptic seizures, bed-wetting, and a suspicion that he might have been a fetal alcohol baby; Alexie explains, "I was a reservation Movie of the Week."[28] Poems where Alexie uses the term as an adjective include "Reservation Love Song" and "The Reservation Cab Driver" in *The Business of Fancydancing* (1992); "Reservation Graffiti" and "Reservation Stew" in *Old Shirts & New Skins* (1993); and "Reservation Drive-In," "A Reservation Table of the Elements," and "Reservation Mathematics" in *First Indian on the Moon* (1993). The three poems in *First Indian* illustrate Alexie's conception of the reservation as a force that influences a resident's perception of that which, like the periodic table and mathematics, may appear to have fixed meanings not subject to interpretation. In "A Reservation Table of the Elements," Alexie offers a reservation perspective on aluminum and oxygen as they relate to one alcoholic, who is trying to quit drinking, and another, Lester FallsApart, who drinks himself unconscious and stops breathing. A mixed-blood narrator in "Reservation Mathematics" discusses his life as the sum of two fractions while "Reservation Drive-In" is a lesson that most closely relates to Alexie's attempts in *Smoke Signals* to depict a contemporary reservation perspective. In the poem, Alexie presents the reservation responses to five Hollywood films, including *Star Wars,* which young Indian boys watch while they imagine their own battles with their fathers.

Reservation refers to a land base and community, rather than an ethnicity or culture, and by privileging this term in his poems, in fiction such as *Reservation Blues,* and in *Smoke Signals,* Alexie decreases the number of audience members who are cultural insiders. His strategy is exclusionary, and he chooses the reservation as the place least understood by most non-Natives; of least interest to most non-Native filmmakers, who prefer to make films set prior to the reservation era; and as the place generally maligned in the mainstream media when reservations are mentioned at all. Even when a mainstream book about a reservation appears, such as

Ian Frazier's *On the Rez,* Alexie argues, "Frazier's formal use of 'the rez' marks him as an outsider eager to portray himself as an insider."[29] Alexie's indignant response to Frazier's naïve and deceptive assumption of insider status at Pine Ridge is a rhetorical defense of reservation communities from potentially unfriendly outsiders.

The centrality of the reservation—a place that is both the point of departure and return in the film—aligns *Smoke Signals* with several of the most celebrated texts by Native authors: N. Scott Momaday's *House Made of Dawn* (1968) and *Ceremony* (1977) by Laguna Pueblo author Leslie Marmon Silko. These novels, to which Alexie's work has been unfavorably compared by Spokane writer Gloria Bird, helped establish the narrative structure in many works by Native authors of departure from and homecoming to a Native community. *Smoke Signals* addresses some of Bird's concerns about *Reservation Blues,* such as what she sees as excessive despair, the perpetuation of stereotypes, and the absence of lyrical evocations of the land.[30] The film depicts a strong Native community and mocks Hollywood stereotypes while the on-location filming shows the landscape of the Coeur d'Alene Reservation in a way that is not possible in a novel. The film also follows the narrative structure of *House Made of Dawn* and *Ceremony* much more closely than do the plots of Alexie's novels: *Reservation Blues*, which appears to be a consciously anti-*Ceremony* novel, ends with Thomas, Chess, and Checkers leaving the Spokane Reservation, and *Indian Killer* (1996) is about a protagonist in Seattle, John Smith, who lacks both community and reservation.

While novels by Native authors are more likely to be situated on a reservation, Hollywood films are usually set prior to or at the beginning of the reservation era. One result of Alexie's challenge to both literary and cinematic conventions is that Chris Eyre's film more closely fulfills the demands that scholars such as Bird make of Native artistic productions. In the film, the reservation almost speaks for itself, and the cinematography confirms Peone's comment that the landscape is indeed beautiful.

Culture is less important to Alexie's characters in *Smoke Signals,* therefore, than a shared community, geography, and history: the Fourth of July is a celebration of "white people's independence"; the United States is a foreign country; and the heroes are Tontos, not Lone Rangers, army officers, or explorers. Alexie even refrains from emphasizing Arnold's and Victor's mourning ritual of cutting their hair. He comments in his scene notes, "I wanted to make it more clear, but I didn't want to spoon-feed the audience. I also didn't want to make haircutting a stereotypical Indian act, done on a mountaintop or something. I mean, the symbolic act of haircutting as mourning exists in all cultures, so this wasn't an issue of generic Indian spirituality. It was an issue of personal spiritual choice" (SS, 154). Even when Alexie does include a more overt reference to traditions not practiced as frequently in non-Native cultures, such as his description in the screenplay of Thomas's "very traditionally braided hair" (SS, 7), he and Eyre do not risk making the tradition exotic narratively or visually.

Alexie is as reluctant to incorporate visible signifiers of ethnicity in the film as he is in his writing. In an interview with John Purdy in *Studies in American Indian Literatures,* Alexie says,

> There's a lot of people pretending to be "traditional," all these
> academic professors living in university towns, who rarely
> spend any time on a reservation, writing all these "traditional"
> books. Momaday—he's not a traditional man. And there's noth-
> ing wrong with that, I'm not either, but this adherence to the
> expected idea, the bear and all this imagery. I think it is danger-
> ous, and detrimental.... I want to take Indian lit *away* from that,
> and away from the people who own it now. (italics in original)

Near the end of the interview, he adds, "We shouldn't be writing about our traditions, we shouldn't be writing about our spiritual practices.... I think it's dangerous, and that's really why I write about day-to-day life."[31] In his response to Purdy's question, Alexie uses the word *dangerous* twice and thereby emphasizes what he understands is at stake in the representations of Indian culture, whether in writing or film. As Rennard Strickland (Osage and Cherokee) explains, "This question of media image is signifi-cant for Native Americans. It transcends entertainment. It influences law. It dominates resource management. The media profoundly impacts every aspect of contemporary American Indian policy and shapes both the general cultural view of the Indian as well as Indian self-image."[32] Alexie and Eyre made *Smoke Signals* with Strickland's warnings in mind.

Alexie also distinguishes the film from Hollywood productions in several other ways that—though not distinctly Native American—emphasize his desire to tell a different story and construct distinctive characters. The narrative structure of *Smoke Signals,* for example, is circular, rather than linear. Eyre follows the directions in Alexie's screenplay to use match cuts, flashbacks, wipes, and swipes to shift the story from the past to the present: the journey to Arizona. A young Victor opens a door and walks through the other side as an adult Victor, or an adult Victor looks into a mirror at a rest stop, and when the camera turns again, he is a young Victor back on the reservation. The circular narrative liberates Alexie's characters from the linear structure of so many films about the frontier that reinforce the perceived inevitability of the "progress" of civilization across the continent.

In addition, images of fire bind the characters together, much like a pattern of symbols unifies a poem or work of fiction. Victor's father, Arnold, sets fire to the Builds-the-Fire home on the Fourth of July 1976; as he narrates in voice-over, Thomas says some children are pillars of flame, and some are pillars of ash, and adds that he and Victor are children of both; Victor and Thomas argue over a barrel in which a fire burns, and Eyre positions the camera so that the fire reflects in Thomas's glasses. After Victor and Thomas have finally recovered Arnold's ashes, Eyre constructs a montage of Suzy Song setting Arnold's trailer on fire with images of the Builds-the-Fire home in flame and Victor and Thomas returning home. Alexie explains in his scene notes, "A bad fire destroyed Arnold's life. A good fire redeems him" (*SS,* 167). Finally, the film's title reclaims and revises an image in Hollywood westerns that indicates danger to the white heroes. In *Smoke Signals,* smoke and ash are the residue of a vibrant community's powerful emotions: love and anger, joy and sorrow. The smoke binds the past to the present and unites the members of the community: Thomas, Grandma Builds-the-Fire, Victor, Arnold, Arlene, and all the people who attended the Fourth of July party at the Builds-the-Fire home that ended in the death of Thomas's parents.

Thomas's storytelling, particularly about Victor's father, also binds the past to the present and the members of the community together. Thomas focuses his stories on the way that Arnold Joseph was a father figure to him, and, though the stories irritate Victor, they also give him a much more complex understanding of his father. The final scene suggests the influence that Thomas's stories have had on Victor. As Thomas recites lines from Dick Lourie's poem "Forgiving Our Fathers," Victor throws his father's ashes into the Spokane River and collapses in grief. Thomas's stories help redeem Arnold Joseph and give Victor the strength to forgive his father for leaving and to grieve.[33] Particularly when compared to other films with major distribution deals, the culmination of *Smoke Signals* is extraordinary for the way Alexie, in the screenplay, and Eyre, as the director, privilege the interior landscapes of contemporary Native men.

The participation of Indians as members of the cast and crew makes the film, for Alexie, the clearest articulation of reservation cinema. In the scene notes, Alexie mentions three times that other filmmakers should "cast Indians as Indians, because you'll get better performances" (*SS*, 158). For example, Alexie writes of the scene where Velma drives in reverse down a highway leaving the reservation, "Michelle St. John and Elaine Miles give what may be the most rezziest Indian performances in cinematic history. There is no non-Indian actor in the world who could have given these performances. These performances are not the result of years of training and study on how to 'act' like an Indian. They are the result of years of living as an Indian, of years of 'being' Indian" (*SS*, 158). Whatever Alexie's definition of being Indian is, he affirms that self-representation should take precedence over externally imposed constructions of identity. Self-representation can produce "the most rezziest of Indian performances," whereas mainstream Hollywood films depict not only misrepresentations but an absence of the tribal real.

In his voice-over at the beginning of the film, Thomas says, "I don't remember that fire. I only have the stories, and in every one of those stories, I could fly." Throughout the film, other characters make many references to telling stories, telling lies, and telling the truth. The evidence in Alexie's work suggests that he wants his audience members to see that we choose to believe particular stories about the world: we choose to believe that Billy Jack is a real mixed-blood hero, or that John Wayne and Tom Mix are real cowboys. Victor, who early in the film rigidly adheres to a particular idea of Indianness heavily influenced by Hollywood, finally chooses to act in accordance with a story that does not require him to be a stoic Plains warrior who has just returned from hunting buffalo. At the end of the film, Thomas says he will take part of Victor's father's ashes and throw them into the Spokane River, after which he will see Victor's father rise from the river as a salmon. Victor plans to participate in the same personal ritual, though he says it would be like "throwing things away when they have no use." However, when Victor releases his father's ashes, he collapses in grief. His identity is no longer beholden to the menacing, stoic warriors of Hollywood films. He is free of their influence at the end of the film and, like Thomas, can begin to construct his own identity in relation to his family and reservation community. The film ends in redemption, rather than doom. Victor is twice redeemed: from the grief of losing his father and his captivity within Hollywood definitions of who he must be as an American Indian man.

We construct our identities in reference to stories, Alexie is proposing, and, therefore, the stories we hear become defining elements in our understanding of ourselves. With their subversive humor and persistent hopefulness, Thomas's stories challenge conventional Hollywood images of Indian men and provide Victor with an alternative model of Native masculinity. At the end of the film, Victor is a Coeur d'Alene man in mourning for the Coeur d'Alene father whom he has carried home. Finally and figuratively, Victor dances with salmon.

Notes

1.   Thomas Edison made these films, which contain the first cinematic images of Indians, on September 24, 1894. He filmed a ghost dance and a buffalo dance, for example. The films can be viewed at http://memory.loc.gov/ammem/amhome.html after searching for "Edison and Indians."

2.   For a description of the way filmmakers turned Native actors into "authentic" cinematic Indians, see Archie Fire Lame Deer (Lakota) and Richard Erdoes, *Gift of Power: The Life and Teachings of a Lakota Medicine Man.* In discussing his acting career, Lame Deer describes being sprayed with body paint.

3.   See Gerald Vizenor, *Manifest Manners: Postindian Warriors of Survivance,* particularly the chapter "Postindian Warriors," for his discussion of simulated Indians and the counterimages produced by the "postindian warriors of simulations" (3). He writes, "Western movies are the muse of simulations, and the absence of humor and real tribal cultures" (6).

4.   Sherman Alexie, *Smoke Signals: A Screenplay,* xi (hereafter cited in the text as *SS*). The distinction "major distribution deal" is crucial. James Young

Dear (Winnebago), whom Beverly Singer (Santa Clara Pueblo) calls "the first Native person to become a 'movie actor'" (15) after his performance in D. W. Griffith's *The Mended Lute* (1909), continued his Hollywood career by directing *A Cheyenne Brave* (1910), *The Yaqui Girl* (1911), *Lieutenant Scott's Narrow Escape* (1911), and *Red Deer's Devotion* (1911). During the same era, Edwin Carewe (Chickasaw) directed *The Trail of the Shadow* (1917) and *Ramona* (1928). Will Rogers (Cherokee) was also a film actor, writer, director, and producer from the mid-1910s to the mid-1930s. Singer discusses specifically six of the many films and videos by Native Americans that precede *Smoke Signals*. Those films are *Hopiit* (1982), directed by Victor Masayesva Jr. (Hopi); *Lighting the Seventh Fire* (1995), directed by Sandra Osawa (Makah); *Navajo Talking Picture* (1984), directed by Arlene Bowman (Navajo); *High Horse* (1994), directed by Randy Redroad (Cherokee); *Hands of History* (1994), directed by Loretta Todd (Metis/Cree); and *A Video Book* (1994), directed by Beverly Singer.

Both Singer and Rennard Strickland catalog films from the 1960s through the 1990s in which Native Americans played an important role in writing, acting, directing, and producing. For example, both Vizenor and N. Scott Momaday (Kiowa) have screenwriting credits—Vizenor for *Harold of Orange* (1984), directed by Michael Weise, and Momaday for *House Made of Dawn* (1987), based on his novel and directed by Richardson Morse. Made-for-television films include *Medicine River* (1993), adapted by Thomas King (Cherokee) from his novel of the same name, and *Grand Avenue* (1996), which was written and coexecutive-produced for HBO by Greg Sarris (Coast Miwok) and based on his novel of the same name. After *Smoke Signals,* Eyre coproduced and directed *Skins* (2002), which was based on Adrian Louis's novel of the same name (Lovelock Paiute). Eyre directed *Skinwalkers* (2002) for PBS, and he produced *The Doe Boy* (2001), which was directed by Redroad. The Mashantucket Pequot Tribal Nation, with Red-Horse Native Productions, produced *Naturally Native* (1998), which was produced by Yvonne Russo (Sicangu Lakota) and executive-produced by Dawn Jackson (Saginaw Chippewa) and codirected by Jennifer Wynne Farmer and Valerie Red-Horse Mohl.

Indigenous-made films also gained prominence around the world in the late-twentieth and early-twenty-first centuries. Examples include the Maori films *Once Were Warriors* (1994), directed by Lee Tamahori; and *Whale Rider* (2002), directed by Niki Caro; and the Inuit film *Atanarjuat* (2001), directed by Zacharias Kunuk. Phillip Noyce's *Rabbit-Proof Fence* (2002), which is about Australia's boarding schools for Aborigines, did not have the same Indigenous control as the other three films. See Singer, *Wiping the Warpaint off the Lens: Native American Film and Video;* and Strickland, "Tonto's Revenge, or, Who Is That Seminole in the Sioux Warbonnet? The Cinematic Indian!" in *Tonto's Revenge: Reflections on American Indian Culture and Policy,* 17–45.

5. For a discussion of Indian humor, see Vine Deloria Jr. (Standing Rock Sioux), *Custer Died for Your Sins: An Indian Manifesto*. Deloria writes, "The Indian people are exactly the opposite of the popular stereotype. I sometimes wonder how anything is accomplished by Indians because of the apparent overemphasis on humor within the Indian world" (146–47; page references are to the 1988 edition).

6. Near the end of a general overview of Native American literature, Jace Weaver (Cherokee) asserts, "I would contend that the single thing that most defines Indian literatures relates to this sense of community and commitment to it." He calls this characteristic of Native American writing *communitism*. If *Smoke Signals* is representative, Weaver's statement may also apply to films made primarily by Native filmmakers. See Weaver, *That the People Might Live: Native American Literatures and Native American Community,* 43.

7. See chapter four, "Muting White Noise: The Popular Culture Invasion in Sherman Alexie's Fiction," in my book, *Muting White Noise: Native American and European American Novel Traditions.*

8. Sherman Alexie, *The Lone Ranger and Tonto Fistfight in Heaven,* 151 (hereafter cited in the text as *LRT*).

9. Sherman Alexie, *Reservation Blues,* 18 (hereafter cited in the text as *RB*).

10. As Alexie learned after several years in the movie business, Hollywood directors and studio executives are equally dangerous. See Sherman Alexie, "Introduction: Death in Hollywood," 7–11, in which he explains that he will lose his love of writing if he continues to work in Hollywood. At the time, he planned to leave after fulfilling his contractual obligation to write screenplays.

11. The three films are *Billy Jack* (1971), *The Trial of Billy Jack* (1974), and *Billy Jack Goes to Washington* (1977). Laughlin even named his company Billy Jack Enterprises.

12. Sherman Alexie, *First Indian on the Moon,* 114 (hereafter cited in the text as *FIM*).

13. Elizabeth Cook-Lynn (Crow Creek Sioux) observes that "how the Indian narrative is told, how it is nourished, who tells it, who nourishes it, and the consequences of its telling are among the most fascinating—and, at the same time, chilling—stories of our time." See "American Indian Intellectualism and the New Indian Story" in *Natives and Academics: Researching and Writing about American Indians,* 111.

14. Sherman Alexie, "I Hated Tonto (Still Do)."

15. Ibid.

16. For the Cardinal quote, see Brian D. Johnson, "Straight-Arrow Hero: Kevin Costner Touches the Native Earth," 58. Other critics such as Michael Wayne Sarf describe the way the film contains all the familiar stereotypes of cinematic Indians, and Richard Alleva and Larry Bowden denounced Costner specifically for villainizing Pawnees. See Sarf, "Oscar Eaten by Wolves,"

62–70; Alleva, "A Filmmaker's Instincts: Costner's *Dances With Wolves*," 18–19; and Bowden, *"Dances With Wolves,"* 391–96.

17. See Ward Churchill, "Lawrence of South Dakota: *Dances With Wolves* and the Maintenance of the American Empire," in *Fantasies of the Master Race: Literature, Cinema and the Colonization of American Indians,* 244.

18. Louis Owens, "Apocalypse at the Two-Socks Hop: Dancing With the Vanishing American," in *Mixedblood Messages: Literature, Family, Film, Place,* 114.

19. Ibid.

20. *Dances With Wolves,* directed by Kevin Costner (Orion Pictures, 1990).

21. See Kilpatrick, *Celluloid Indians: Native Americans and Film;* and, for a similar discussion, see Michael Hilger, *From Savage to Nobleman: Images of Native Americans in Film.* Singer also includes a chapter on Hollywood representations of Indians in *Wiping the Warpaint.*

22. Films such as *Maverick* (1994), directed by Richard Donner, and *Shanghai Noon* (2000), directed by Tom Dey, contain scenes that mock conventional Hollywood depictions of Native Americans. *Dead Man* (1996), directed by Jim Jarmusch, and *Dance Me Outside* (1995), directed by Bruce McDonald, provide more complex portraits of Native people. Though not written or directed by Native Americans, the films benefited from the participation of Native writers and/or actors. In "I Hated Tonto (Still Do)," Alexie writes about watching *Powwow Highway* (1989), directed by Jonathan Wacks: "I cried when I saw it in the theater, then cried again when I stayed and watched it again a second time. I mean, I loved that movie. I memorized whole passages of dialogue. But recently, I watched the film for the first time in many years and cringed in shame and embarrassment with every stereotypical scene."

23. See John M. Coward, *The Newspaper Indian: Native American Identity in the Press, 1820–90.*

24. Sherman Alexie, *The Toughest Indian in the World,* 23 (hereafter cited in the text as *TIW*).

25. Though Green does not mention films, her observations apply to cinematic Indian women. The quintessential princess is Pocahontas. See Rayna Green, "The Pocahontas Perplex: The Image of Indian Women in American Culture," 704, 711.

26. Contraries appear primarily in Plains cultures. The Lakota and Dakotas called their contraries *heyo'ka.* A person became a contrary after the Thunder-beings visited in a dream. For a literary example of a heyo'ka, see Dakota author Susan Power's *The Grass Dancer.* In his interviews with John Neihardt is a description of a heyo'ka ceremony in which Black Elk participated. The ceremony included the sacrifice of a dog, after which a participant offered the dog to the Thunder-beings in the west, then the north, east, and south, then the sky and the earth. In particular see the description of the heyo'kas ("sacred fool or rather sacred comedian") walking among the

audience in Raymond J. Demallie, ed., *The Sixth Grandfather: Black Elk's Teachings Given to John G. Neihardt,* 232–35.

27.   *The Business of Fancydancing* focuses on Seymour Polatkin's departure for college and return to the Spokane Reservation after a childhood friend dies. At the end of the film, one Seymour (Evan Adams) watches a second Seymour (Evan Adams) leave the reservation after the funeral. The scene suggests the hold that the reservation has on its residents. The film also contains more specific Native and Spokane cultural ceremonies and creations than *Smoke Signals,* such as powwow dancing, the Spokane traditional song "Happy Dance," and "Osinilshatin," a song written by Michelle St. John and translated by Lillian Alexie into Spokane. The lyrics reinforce the image of Seymour leaving part of himself on the Spokane Reservation: "Memories hold you tight/When there's no comfort in white arms/Loneliness will bring you back/Where you belong." See Sherman Alexie, *The Business of Fancydancing: The Screenplay,* 134.

28.   Sherman Alexie, "One Little Indian Boy," in *Edge Walking on the Western Rim: New Works by 12 Northwest Writers,* 52.

29.   Sherman Alexie, "Some of My Best Friends," 3.

30.   Gloria Bird, "The Exaggeration of Despair in Sherman Alexie's *Reservation Blues,*" 47–52.

31.   John Purdy, "Crossroads: A Conversation with Sherman Alexie," 8, 15–16.

32.   Strickland, "Tonto's Revenge," 17.

33.   See "Forgiving Our Fathers" in Dick Lourie, *Ghost Radio.* The screenplay has Alexie's original ending, and the "Scene Notes" contain a discussion of the conflict he had with Eyre about the end of the film. In the screenplay, Arnold Joseph's ashes become first a salmon and then Arnold himself rising from the river and returning to the Coeur d'Alene community.

■ *Angelica Lawson*

CHAPTER 6

Native Sensibility and the Significance of Women in *Smoke Signals*

Through Native modes of storytelling, Native authors have produced powerful texts that define a voice for Native people. Critical in this assertion is the reality of the important roles of women in Native life. These roles have been notoriously underrepresented and misrepresented in the history of American filmmaking.

As a film recognized for its decisive break from Hollywood stereotypes, *Smoke Signals* (1998) features Native women in significantly different roles from classic Hollywood portrayals. Author Sherman Alexie's screenplay successfully adapts the popular Hollywood genres of the buddy and road-trip films to tell a Native story that coincidentally reenacts an important archetype from the canons of Native oratory. As a result, the women in the film act as catalysts for both narrative and character development, furthering not only the movement of the plot but the growth of self-understanding and mutual bonds between the central male characters.

Despite Jhon Warren Gilroy's assertion that "it can, and should be argued that women play minor roles in this film," a closer look at the female characters within the context of the contemporary, historical, and mythological roles of Native women suggests they are far more complex and significant than an initial analysis indicates.[1] In fact, it can be argued that the development of the male leads would be impossible but for the influence and prominence of the female characters in this film.

Intrigued by film and its mass appeal, Alexie wrote the screenplay hoping to reach a larger audience than he had with his fiction and poetry; in particular he wanted to impact a Native audience.[2] He was careful in selecting a director and settled on Chris Eyre (Cheyenne/Arapaho), who was interested in creating a film that broke away from Hollywood stereotypes of Native people. Eyre took on the project because he recognized something of himself in the work, saying, "The material spoke to what I perceived as honesty about Indians and what I knew."[3] While studying film at New York University, Eyre claims he learned all the "rules," and *Smoke Signals* afforded him the opportunity to bend, and even break, them.

Smoke Signals initially conforms to traditional western plot development and begins by establishing the setting. A radio deejay announces, "Good Morning, Coeur d'Alene Indian Reservation. It's a rainy bicentennial Fourth of July and time for the morning traffic report." A subtitle indicates that the year is 1976. At this point, the audience is a third party simply observing the story. Both Native and non-Native audience members familiar with the American Indian Movement may recognize the deejay as John Trudell, one of its leaders. This beginning indicates that the film will be expressing a Native point of view.

This perspective becomes even more apparent as the voice-over of Thomas Builds-the-Fire usurps the western narrative form. He speaks directly to the audience in the first of many storytelling moments and encourages them to participate in and react to the story. The story takes on a mythic quality as it simultaneously presents a counternarrative to mainstream American history. Its poetic and metaphorical language evokes oral texts. The description of the way Thomas and Victor were born of flame and ash and Thomas survived fire by "flying" contributes to this impression:

> On July 4, 1976, my mother and father celebrated white people's independence by hosting the largest house party in Coeur d'Alene tribal history. I mean, every Indian in the world was

there. And then at three in the morning, after everyone had passed out on couches, chairs, the floor, a fire rose up like General George Armstrong Custer and swallowed up my mother and father.

I don't remember that fire. I only have the stories, and in every one of those stories, I could fly.

I was just a baby when Arnold Joseph saved me from that fire and delivered me into the hands of my grandmother.

And Victor Joseph was just a baby, too, when his father saved me from that fire.

You know, there are some children who aren't really children at all. They're just pillars of fire that burn everything they touch.

And there are some children who are just pillars of ash that fall apart if you touch them.

Me and Victor, we were children born of flame and ash.

The counternarrative is indicated by Thomas's saying "white people's independence." By stating this is neither his—nor his parents'—independence, he suggests an alternative interpretation of this event. In comparing the fire to George Armstrong Custer, he forces the audience to question the glorified narrative of westward expansion, alluding instead to the devastation it brought to Native people.

Framing these Native counternarratives are the familiar Hollywood genres of the buddy and road-trip film, intentionally chosen by Alexie to make the film accessible to a wider audience.[4] Eric Gary Anderson, in his discussion of *Powwow Highway* (1989), describes the road movie as a film where "two very unlike characters and their parallel, but very different, purposes begin to share the same journey," and the buddy movie as one "in which two same-sex characters gradually acquire respect and affection for each other, finally overcoming their differences to bond near the film's conclusion."[5] In *Smoke Signals*, Victor, the warrior, and Thomas, the storyteller, pair up to travel to Phoenix, Arizona, to retrieve the ashes of Victor's father, Arnold Joseph. Their relationship is uncomfortable and frequently hostile due to their opposite personalities and feelings about Arnold. Victor remembers his dad as a violent drunk who abandoned him when he was still very young and can barely tolerate Thomas's glorification of Arnold. Thomas sees Arnold as a father figure and hero who saved him from the fire that killed his parents.

Thomas is fond of telling the story about the time when he walked to "the falls" by the YMCA to have a vision: "Yeah, so I walked there, you know? I mean, I didn't have no car. I didn't have no license. I was twelve years old! It took me all day, but I walked there, and stood on this bridge over the falls, waiting for a sign." After he waited for hours, Arnold appeared and told Thomas, "All you're going to get around here is mugged!" He put his hand on Thomas's shoulder in a show of concern and then took him to Denny's for breakfast. Arnold retrieving Thomas from the city is important to the narrative. In many ways, he is a much better father to Thomas than to Victor. He rescues Thomas from the fire and the city, thus positioning himself as a positive figure.

This polarizing over Arnold is one of the central character conflicts between Victor and Thomas and marks one of the fundamental differences in their understanding and approach to life. Thomas—almost rescued from his orphanhood by Arnold—has a different perspective on the meaning of a father than does Victor, whose experience was abandonment, rather than rescue. This vastly different understanding of such an important family bond informs their overall attitude toward life and one another. The two begin to reconcile these differences as a result of their road trip to Phoenix.

The film conforms to the expectations of the buddy/road movie because Victor and Thomas eventually bond and understand themselves and one another better. However, also framing the narrative is an archetypal story in the canons of Native oratory—the hero-twin story. The character development seems to be more believable within this context because the conflict resolution is not driven by action, as in typical Hollywood buddy/road films, but rather results from the reenactment of a larger, greater story from the community. It is also within this context that the female characters become more significant.[6]

Stories centering on the actions of two brothers, often related through unconventional means, abound in Native American oral texts. The basic plot structure is frequently a journey where they find or discover their father. In some cases, the father is the sun or a star, which is often a metaphor for death. According to John Bierhorst, "one of the best known of the boy-hero myths, told throughout the Plains from Canada to Texas," is one about the violent birth of twin boys who, after many adventures, eventually return home to find their father gone. They soon learn their father has become a star, and they climb through the air to join him.[7] The Northern Arapaho have a story of two brothers born out of violence so great that the father's grief forces him to leave them. Eventually—in their late adolescence—the brothers seek him out, discovering that he has become a star. The boys then join him in the heavens. Similar stories also exist in Pueblo, Navajo, and Cherokee mythologies.

Smoke Signals echoes this basic narrative framework. Victor and Thomas, two opposites from the same community, venture together to Phoenix, Arizona, to retrieve the ashes of Victor's—and, by the extension of adoption, Thomas's—father. In the mythologies, the brothers go looking for their father to understand better who they are (often the father is unknown) as well as who their father is and why he left them. In this way, they are attempting to find their identity within their community. In the film, Thomas and Victor go to Phoenix for the same reasons.

Despite the film's emphasis on male bonding and father-son relationships, the female characters have an important presence. They serve as advisors, guides, and catalysts for action—a common role for women in hero-twin stories. In the way it depicts these women, *Smoke Signals* moves away from the typical buddy/road film: first, the female characters do not operate as a foil to the bonding of the two male characters; and second, they are not mistreated in typical Hollywood fashion.[8] Rather, the women in the film meaningfully contribute to the characters' self-knowledge and bonding.

Thomas's grandmother is his advisor. Nerdy, like Thomas, she is clearly his foundation for his place in the community. She is readily accessible to a Native audience as his guardian and mentor. It is quite common for Native children to be raised by grandparents for either social or cultural reasons. In addition, grandparents are deeply respected and considered to be the most appropriate people to turn to for advice in many Native cultures. Thomas's grandmother is not depicted as the grand old Indian wise woman of Hollywood stereotype but more realistically as the one constant in his life that he can count on.

In a wonderful scene between Thomas and his grandmother at the dinner table, both characters bow their heads as if in prayer. They are perfectly balanced in the scene, each taking up half the frame and seated directly across from each other. They both have thick braids and glasses like near mirror images. They hear a knock at the door and simultaneously look up, then at the door, then at each other, barely able to contain their joy. The staging of this scene visually establishes Thomas's relationship with his grandmother as balanced, complementary, and intimate.

By contrast, Victor is unsure of his place within both his family and community. His mother, Arlene, is also unsure about where he stands. She makes him promise to come back from Phoenix as if there is a possibility he may leave permanently as Arnold did. There seems to be little balance in this relationship, which is also visualized in a dinner scene. As Arlene makes fry bread, she stands while Victor sits.

Alexie seems to have consciously developed her character as a powerful Indian woman, who is also human and frail. Arlene—a complex Native character by Hollywood standards—does her best to raise Victor without Arnold, choosing to bring him up alone, rather than expose him to his father's alcoholism. Though this scenario comes dangerously close to repeating the Hollywood stereotype of the drunken Indian, the fact that she gives up drinking—as Arnold does eventually—challenges it. Alexie comments in his published screenplay on the scene where Arlene stands her ground on her decision not to drink or let Arnold drink, "This is a powerful scene made more powerful by Tantoo's and Gary's performances. When Arlene Joseph stands up to Arnold, she is being the kind of powerful Indian woman I've known all my life."[9]

In *The Lone Ranger and Tonto Fistfight in Heaven*—the short-story collection on which the film is based—Alexie describes Victor's mother as a powerful woman: "During all these kinds of tiny storms, Victor's mother would rise with her medicine and magic. She would pull air down from empty cupboards and make fry bread. She would shake thick blankets free from old bandanas. She would comb Victor's braids into dreams."[10]

This characterization of Arlene becomes more vivid in *Smoke Signals*. In a humorous turn that references both Native and non-Native epistemologies, Arlene steps into the role of deity in Thomas's mythical description of a feast where there were a hundred people and only fifty pieces of fry bread. In the story, Arlene "magically creates" one hundred pieces of fry bread from fifty. While the allusion to Christ's feeding thousands with only five loaves of bread is clear, a parallel one to Native female deities who appear to communities in times of great need, especially hunger, is also present. This deification of Victor's mother blurs the line between the strong Native woman in reality and her archetypal role in the broader culture, simultaneously making her larger than life and down to earth, essential to the narrative both ways.

The influence of female characters in the protagonists' own generation enters the narrative when Velma and Lucy are driving a car backward down a long and desolate reservation road where Victor and Thomas are walking to the bus stop. This comic scene is important, though brief. In exchange for a story, the women take Thomas and Victor to the bus, essentially picking up where Victor's mother and Thomas' grandmother left off as the guides who start the two men on their journey. The story Thomas tells adds to the growing collection about Arnold, essential to the identity formation of the two men.

Stories become increasingly important when Victor finally meets Suzy Song, Arnold's neighbor in Phoenix. Suzy is not an obstacle to the male bonding in the film, nor does she inhibit Victor's ability to resolve his conflict with his father. Instead, she is a catalyst for the resolution that must take place. Her presence and stories force a critical turning point in Victor's understanding of his father and himself.[11] Suzy is quite possibly the one person who really knew Arnold because she knew why he left his family.

Beginning with a series of casual stories about the way she met Arnold and what they talked about, and an anecdote Arnold related about playing basketball against Jesuits, Suzy eventually gives Victor the critical information he needs to know. She tells him that Arnold was the person who started the house fire that killed Thomas's parents. Without realizing it at the time, Victor encounters his one essential story. Throughout the various narratives, he has stumbled across huge voids that can only be filled with stories from his Native community. His father, as a member of that community, cheated Victor out of vital information in his identity-forming process. Only through understanding what he didn't know can Victor come to forgive his father and himself. In this manner, Suzy acts

as a Native sensibility. Both as a member of the Native American community, and an unknown figure who appears in a time of great need, she is a
conduit for both the mythical and communal.

As survivors of the house fire, both Victor and Thomas have to negotiate growing up without parents. Victor struggles with this most because
Thomas was too young to have known his parents before they died and
therefore doesn't realize what he has lost. In addition, he has a close relationship with his grandmother, and he willingly adopts Arnold as a father
figure. Victor, on the other hand, has to deal with the knowledge that
his father chose to abandon him. This loss drives the plot in line with a
Native sensibility, according to James Ruppert, because Native stories frequently focus on the way "an individual is encouraged to find the greater
self in the communal, and perhaps in the smallest and most essential unit
of the communal, the family" to determine his or her identity.[12] Victor is
lost and unable to deal with it because he does not know his place in his
community or family.

Nowhere in the film does this become clearer than when Victor
wakes Thomas early to leave Phoenix with Arnold's ashes. Although Victor now knows more about his father and why he left, he still has many
unresolved issues because his initial reaction to Suzy is anger and jealousy over the fact that she seems to know Arnold better than he ever
did.[13] He does not yet realize that she has given him critical pieces of
information to understand himself better. The scene that takes place as
they are driving back to the reservation in Arnold's pickup clarifies this.
Thomas begins yet another story about the time Arnold took him to Denny's when Victor yells, "I'm sick of you telling me all these stories about
my father like you know him or something." Thomas replies that he does
know Arnold and maybe Victor doesn't know himself. When accused by
Thomas of "moping around the reservation for ten years," Victor shoots
back, "What do you do all day long?" Thomas states,

> I take care of my grandma.
> Victor: And I take care of my mom.
> Thomas: You make your mom cry.
> Victor: Shut up, Thomas.

Thomas: You make your mom cry. You make her cry her eyes out, Victor. I mean, your dad left, sure. Yeah, he ran away. But you left her, too. And you're worse because you still live in the same house.

Victor does not make a positive contribution to the community because he has selfishly focused on his losses and is emotionally absent. He especially does not contribute to the most "essential unit of the communal," his family.

In the scene that follows, Victor and Thomas are in a car crash. As Victor runs for help, his mind flashes to the bits and pieces of Suzy's story, emphasizing evidence of Arnold's love for Victor because he ran into the burning house looking for his son. Overwhelmed by the stories and physical exhaustion, he collapses, only to waken to a vision of his father looming over him—huge and imposing. Victor squints at the sight of Arnold as if blinded by a bright light.

This event and vision appear to be a turning point for Victor. The trauma of the car crash causes him to relive Suzy's stories as visualized in a montage of events from the past. Finally, Victor sees Arnold standing over him, extending his hand to help him up, and he accepts. Victor's sudden acceptance of his father does not come from an elaborate psychological narrative where he spends a great deal of time looking inward for answers but, rather, suddenly as the stories from his community and family achieve a critical mass. The death of his father, the journey to Phoenix, the encounter with Suzy, and the car crash add up to the final (near) resolution for Victor, which culminates in his running through the desert to save people who are seriously hurt in the accident. In this way, he assumes his father's role in the story as rescuer.

At the hospital, Victor accepts the can of Arnold's ashes Thomas has been carrying because Victor refused to touch it. When the two return to the reservation, Victor willingly gives Thomas half the ashes. He has finally agreed to share his father with Thomas and in this way accepts Thomas as family. This gesture is Victor's first step to finding his place in the community. Thomas asks Victor yet again, "Hey, Victor? Do know why your dad really left?" Victor replies, "Yeah. He didn't mean to, Thomas." By not telling Thomas what he knows—that Arnold accidentally killed his parents by starting the house fire—Victor protects Thomas from the emotional harm of losing a father figure for a second time. In this way, he acts as an older brother and takes a responsible position in the community.

The resolution comes from forgiveness and acceptance on Victor's part but also the return of Arnold's ashes to his homeland and, more importantly, the river. References to salmon by Alexie are no coincidence; he uses this imagery frequently in his work as a metaphor for both the Spokane tribal people and the loss of a traditional way of life. These references emphasize the fact that salmon return to the place of their birth to die. Arnold's death in Phoenix disrupts the cycle because he never returns to his reservation. According to Suzy, "Arnold was always trying to get home" but failed in his struggle. The cycle is complete when the boys return Arnold to the reservation and, more importantly, the river.

The film is thick with metaphorical imagery and language borrowed from both mainstream and Native American cultures. The river and water in general are symbolic of healing and resolution, juxtaposed with the fire and conflict that begin the film.[14] Fire also correlates directly with Arnold's last residence. According to young Thomas, Arnold has "lived everywhere" since he left Victor and Arlene, but it is important that he ultimately ends up in Phoenix. After he dies, his body is cremated, and the ashes remain in Phoenix waiting for Victor and Thomas to retrieve them. The allusion to the mythological bird that rises from the ashes again and again is clear, but the ending sequence of the film also refers back to the Native twin-brother story, reinforcing both themes and making them complementary.

This sequence begins after Thomas is reunited with his grandmother. As she holds his face in her hands, she says, "Tell me what happened, Thomas. Tell me what's going to happen," and Thomas closes his eyes. The scene cuts to a bird's-eye view of a river flowing downstream as Thomas recites a poem in voice-over. As the camera follows the water, it progresses from a quiet, narrow, meandering stream to a huge rushing river that becomes more and more turbulent as it nears Victor standing on a bridge. The camera comes closer and closer to the violence of the water before swooping up to a shot of Victor from below. He is throwing the ashes into the water. As he does so with great emotional pain, the camera continues to pan up until it is at eye level with Victor for a moment before passing over his head.

What is most interesting in this sequence is that the camera catches the sun shining beside Victor as it pans up. The sun's rays grow until they flare into the camera, which then moves slightly to the right, placing the sun directly behind Victor. This natural backlighting gives Victor's silhouette enormous radiance as the film is briefly overexposed. His silhouette fades, and the frame fills with intense red and orange light all around him. Then—as the camera goes over his head—the shot quickly cuts to a view of Victor from the other side of the bridge, where the turbulent water has calmed slightly and rushes away behind him. Victor falls into a fetal position as the shot fades to black and the movie ends.

The mythic story of two brothers who search for their father—ultimately discovering that he is a star or the sun—often ends with the brothers also becoming stars. As Victor throws the ashes into the river, the camera seems to rise out of the water as it swoops up and over him, illuminating him so he radiates light like a star. According to Eyre, this was a "serendipitous moment" in filming. The camera caught the sun just right to produce this effect. Although it was a "visual accident," Eyre kept the shot because it reinforced the subtexts of the film and symbolized Victor's spiritual catharsis as he threw the ashes off the bridge.[15] Though Eyre, an Arapaho filmmaker, claims he is not familiar with the Arapaho twin-brother story and did not intentionally transform Victor into a star, that moment in the film is powerful for audience members who immediately recognize this story.

Victor throws the ashes into the river to the sound of increasingly louder Native drums and singing, and Thomas's voice-over asks, "How do we forgive our fathers? Maybe in a dream... If we forgive our fathers, what else is left?" In these final moments of the film, the visual narrative seems complete, yet the juxtaposition with the voice-over indicates otherwise. The last line creates a decidedly Native ending for the film, echoing endings in Native American oral tradition. Rather than summarize or explain the moral of the story, the film asks open-ended questions.

Alexie and Eyre's goal to move Indians in film beyond one-dimensional, polarized stereotypes is successful in Smoke Signals. The women in the narrative are instrumental in bringing Victor to a greater understanding of his relationship with his father and himself, though he must make the intuitive leap to a final catharsis through the lens of the stories. Although the women are critical to Victor's personal development, they do not co-opt his self-discovery, thus maintaining the communal function of Native American women as catalysts in opposition to the typical narrative framework of the buddy/road film, where external action causes the protagonist's catharsis. This contrast emphasizes the role of Native American women as stable arbiters of Native culture, particularly in times of crisis and personal change.

Notes

1. Jhon Warren Gilroy, "Another Fine Example of the Oral Tradition? Identification and Subversion in Sherman Alexie's *Smoke Signals*," 31.
2. See John Purdy, "Crossroads: A Conversation with Sherman Alexie," 1–18, for Alexie's comments on his desire to reach a larger Native audience. See Angelica Lawson, "A New Story: Mediation in Sherman Alexie's *Smoke Signals*" for a detailed discussion of the way the film appropriates and manipulates classic Hollywood formulas to mediate between Native and non-Native audience members.
3. Chris Eyre, interview by the author, November 24, 2000.
4. Dennis West and Joan M. West, "Sending Cinematic *Smoke Signals:* An Interview with Sherman Alexie," 29.
5. Eric Gary Anderson, "Driving the Red Road: *Powwow Highway*," in *Hollywood's Indian: The Portrayal of the Native American in Film,* 146.
6. Though Alexie acknowledges he utilized "two very classical mythic structures" in writing this screenplay, he does not specifically mention this archetype from Native oratory. West and West, "Sending Cinematic *Smoke Signals*," 29.
7. John Bierhorst, *The Mythology of North America,* 157–58.
8. Ellen Arnold, "Reframing the Hollywood Indian: A Feminist Re-reading of *Powwow Highway* and *Thunderheart*," in *American Indian Studies: An Interdisciplinary Approach to Contemporary Issues,* 347–62.
9. Sherman Alexie, *Smoke Signals: A Screenplay,* 160.
10. Sherman Alexie, *The Lone Ranger and Tonto Fistfight in Heaven,* 5.
11. Though Gilroy finds problematic Alexie's depiction of Suzy as magical, this characterization reinforces her ability to occupy both mythic and practical spaces simultaneously.
12. James Ruppert, *Mediation in Contemporary Native American Fiction,* 28.
13. Eyre interview.
14. Ibid.
15. Ibid.

■ *Susan Berry Brill de Ramírez*

CHAPTER 7

The Distinctive Sonority of Sherman Alexie's Indigenous Poetics

Although arguably the most widely known Native American poet—insofar as literary scholarship is concerned—Sherman Alexie's poetic craftsmanship has received relatively little attention. Reflecting the larger trends in literary study that emphasize the historical and sociological, much of the scholarly interest in Indigenous literature has rightfully focused more on its indigeneity, rather than its literariness. Such historically based, critical studies help to articulate the larger tribal and colonial contexts for specific texts and their authors.[1] These efforts in decolonizing literary study have taken place within the larger framework of global trends. The revolutionary turns in literary scholarship to the sociological and historical over the course of the last three decades have wrought remarkable advances in the ways we look at literary texts, but one downside of this process is that these shifts have also de-emphasized scholarly attention to poetics, prosody, and craft.[2] As Terry Eagleton laments, "What gets left out is the *literariness* of the work."[3]

As with the best of poets, Alexie has a remarkable ear for the sonority of language and the effective use of repetition, parallelism, inversions in the form of chiasmus, meter and rhythm, rhyme and para-rhyme, alliteration and assonance, punctuation, line and stanza breaks, caesura within lines, and interlinear enjambment as they affect the pacing, intricacy, and meaningfulness of his poems. Emphasizing the importance of attention to the sonority of the literary language of Native writers, Craig Womack explains, "The evolution of a word is, at least partially, in a physical act, that of speaking, which involves air and sound and movement and vibration....Even when we read a word, rather than hear one spoken, we imagine its sounds, imagine it being said out loud, hear a voice."[4] As this essay elucidates, Alexie's poetry reveals a clear appreciation for this process. Additionally his fascination with mathematics facilitates his episodically linked and numbered poetic structures that permit dialogically multiple voices and lenses to come together and cohere in larger conversively thematic poems.

The condensed nature of poetry invites close attention to the intricacies of craft in both its writing and reading. Form and content are inextricably linked in the complex expressions of skilled poets;[5] as Eagleton importantly reminds us, "The language of a poem is *constitutive* of its ideas."[6] As Alexie well knows, language is indeed constitutive of meaning, and poetry that is well crafted can elicit invaluable restorative insight and understanding. For example, when Alexie writes that "the smallest pain/ can change the world,"[7] the repeated, regular, iambic rhythm of a diiambus followed by a double iamb gives weight, and the para-rhymes and assonance of "pain/can change" draw attention away from "the smallest pain" toward the ambiguously unspecified change in the world that is potentially consequent from that pain. The poetics of these two lines from "The Unauthorized Autobiography of Lester FallsApart" underscore an insight that in many ways lies at the heart of Alexie's work: the small and enormous pains that are the reality of Indian America and, too, so much of twenty-first-century planet Earth.

To appreciate the depth and meaningfulness of Alexie's poetry, we would be well advised to delve into its language and construction, for the formal aspects of his work effectively forward its progress: expanding meaning and heightening impact regardless of whether the poems focus on the reservation community of Alexie's childhood or the diverse world of his later experience. His earlier volumes of poetry evoke reservation America and Indigenous experience in ways that assist his readers' appreciation and comprehension of stories and realities that may be unfamiliar. The poetry demonstrates the common literary device of defamiliarization in presenting the ordinary in new and different ways. Additionally, analogous to other non-dominant-culture writers, Alexie employs the reverse strategy of poetic familiarization as he "familiarizes" the unfamiliar and gives literary primacy and centrality to Indigenous America (whether reservation or urban, historical or contemporary, actual or imagined). This is profoundly evident in several of his poems that explore the meaningful intersections among the awful histories and consequents of conquest and holocaust.[8]

THE POETICS OF CONQUEST AND HOLOCAUST

In the poems "The Game Between the Jews and the Indians is Tied Going Into the Bottom of the Ninth Inning" from *First Indian on the Moon* (1993) and "Inside Dachau" from *The Summer of Black Widows* (1996), Alexie describes the all-too-analogous experiences of the genocided Other, whether indigenous or diasporic.[9] His structural choices effectively interweave the realities and stories of diverse peoples, places, and times within the coherence of each poem while integrating the telling of historical atrocity within the framework of its enduring effect upon generations of descendants. The long title of his short sonnet—"The Game Between the Jews and the Indians is Tied Going Into the Bottom of the Ninth Inning"—metaphorically depicts the histories and horrors within the framework of a baseball game. In no way does the baseball setting trivialize the seriousness of those events and their continuing consequences. Rather, the allusion to baseball mercifully lightens an otherwise painful recounting and also reminds us that baseball games eventually end or, at the very least, are called, just as history, no matter how catastrophic, will gradually fade into the legacies of storied remembrance as half and quarter lives are logarithmically reduced to iterations of lessening residues on the "children and grandchildren of survivors."[10] While the poem ostensibly refers to the competitive ending of a relationship between the Native speaker and a Jewish lover, the game and ninth-inning references are poignantly apropos because the past, present, and future of the relationship are invariably knotted up with both characters' and readers' lived and remembered histories (metaphorically the prior eight innings of the game that lead up to the final one: the end of the relationship, the final solution).[11]

It is fitting that the poetic structure that Alexie chose for this poem is the sonnet, a lyric form that has been used throughout the five centuries that span the colonization of the Americas. As Dean Rader explains in his essay on "The Epic Lyric" regarding Alexie's appropriately named "Sonnet": "Alexie irrupts our expectations, composing his sonnet with fourteen prose stanzas instead of fourteen poetic lines. Each stanza is a mini-telling, a mini-history."[12] In this way, Alexie transforms the classic lyric of Britain and Shakespeare into a vehicle that, through a love poem, speaks the history of atrocity. In the unusual, but telling, choice of the sonnet, Alexie asserts the extent to which past horrors incapacitate their descendants, but in the concluding two lines, he integrally interweaves that tale of atrocity and trauma with the interconnected story of survivance,[13] where the pain of conquest gradually lessens over generations: "we can remind each other/that we are both survivors and children/and grandchildren of survivors" (*FIM*, 80).[14]

These last two lines end the sonnet as a stand-alone couplet, concluding its three stanzas of four lines. Exemplifying Alexie's skilled use of repetition with variation, the blank-verse sonnet begins with two short parallel questions, followed by a longer, one-sentence response that runs through the final eight lines of the poem. The two questions—each three lines long—extend through the first stanza and a half, thematically and grammatically running them together; this speeds up the reading of these painful questions that point to the massacres of Sand Creek and Wounded Knee and the concentration camps of Auschwitz and Buchenwald. The response and greater part of the poem focuses on the conditions and requirements of the present generation of survivors—those who stand between the past and future—extending the poem's interlinear and interstanzaic enjambment through eight lines and three stanzas, including the concluding couplet.

The sonnet form of the poem with its separated last two lines gives greater weight to the assertion "that we are both survivors and children/ and grandchildren of survivors" (*FIM*, 80). The pairing in these lines importantly inverts the words in a chiastic crossing:

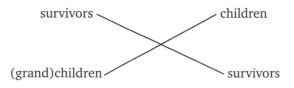

By making "survivor" the beginning and ending word in the concluding stanza, Alexie emphasizes the possibility and reality of survivance, crucially affirming that it is integrally interconnected with one's past and present familial, tribal, and historical experience. One goes forward as a survivor, but that progress stands not only upon the foundation of the prior generations' struggles, failures, and success but—perhaps even more importantly—upon each person's lived family, community, and tribal relationships.[15] The shift from the second person you and first-person I of the questions to the first person plural we in the long poetic answer suggests a relationally inclusive ambiguity that invites listener-readers to read beyond the distanced you or self-referential I into an inclusive affirmation of filial survivance.[16]

Scansion of the final stanza shows that the first line begins with a diiambus (two quick, conjoined iambs) that points forward, giving the line's emphasis to the recognition of selves as "survivors and children":

(diiambus-amphibrach-amphibrach)

that we are both survivors and children

(antispast-single beat-amphibrach)

and grandchildren of survivors. (*FIM, 80*)

The remaining metrical feet are rhythmically complete as the short-long-short pattern of the amphibrach or antispast (four beats of short-long-long-short) ascend to the middle accented beat and descend back down to their initial unaccented beat. The lone accented foot "of" becomes a conjunctive preposition connecting the speaker and his lover to their predecessors and respective survivance. As with the other poems discussed in this essay, this sonnet demonstrates the skill of form, rhythm, and sound that lyrically deepen the meaning of the poem.

The later poem, "Inside Dachau," continues Alexie's thematic focus on the parallel horrors of the conquest of America and the Holocaust of European Jewry. This connective orientation is, perhaps, closer than readers may realize. When Alexie sardonically queries—in "My Heroes Have Never Been Cowboys"—"Did you know that in 1492 every Indian instantly became an extra in the Great American Western?" (*FIM*, 102), this question applies also to the Jews of Europe, for the 1490s were the years when the Catholic Church conquered Spain and expelled the Jews and Muslims. Countries throughout the Americas are finally seeing the first generations of Indigenous heads of state—such as Evo Morales in Bolivia, Hugo Chavez in Venezuela, and formerly Toledo in Peru—but the five centuries after Columbus wrought horrific destruction upon the myriad indigenous and diasporized peoples of the world. As Elizabeth Cook-Lynn states regarding that pivotal year whose tragic consequences endure today, "The arrival of Columbus in the New World in 1492 was the beginning of a massive reign of terror and genocide that has not abated."[17]

It is especially significant that Alexie's poem "Inside Dachau" explicitly incorporates his Indigenous orientation in his poetic storying of Dachau's history. Based upon Alexie's visits to Germany and the concentration camp, the poem stories, evokes, and poignantly mythicizes the horrific experiences whose painful nearness is still too close for many Jews to attempt. As Alexie asks, "If I were Jewish, how would I remember the past? / . . . / If I were Jewish, how would I tell the stories?"[18] The passage of time is often necessary for peoples and persons to process and relate tragedy and horror; the healing panacea of distance enables the transference of past realities into the more forward-pointing, storied histories of an empowered survivance. Gloria Bird (poet and Spokane tribal member) explains the vitally restorative power of such remembrance: "Thus both witnessing and testimony become, for me, viable tools that serve the purposes of decolonization by providing detail of individual processing of the complexities of inheritance that living in the aftermath of colonization provides."[19]

The parallel, yet inextricably intertwined, genocidal histories of indigenous conquest and diasporic holocaust come together in profound ways in Alexie's poetry as the metaphors of flame and ash take form in trailer fire and Nazi ovens. His poem "Inside Dachau" is episodic and numbered—Alexie's trademark mathematical configuration that permits a longer narrative through various structures, perspectives, voices, words, and stories. The poem consists of seven separate, yet interrelated, poems each of which conveys part of Alexie's storying of the experience of being inside Dachau: as a tourist, as an American Indian, and as a Jewish prisoner. The center section, number 4, is entitled "the american indian holocaust museum" and calls for national recognition and remembrance of the genocide of Native Americans in "the construction of our museum" (*SBW,* 119–20). This section grounds the poem within Alexie's indigeneity and is the pivot round which the six other pieces circle; this express rootedness in Alexie's lived Spokane and Native identity gives the poem the depth of truths understood and lived—even in a poem about Dachau . . . especially in a poem about Dachau.

Alexie draws on the relationally conversive (conservative and transformative) power of poetry and story that makes it possible for persons to understand diverse worlds, times, and people in ways not otherwise possible.[20] Simon Ortiz makes this profoundly clear in his volume *from Sand Creek,* when he interweaves the wartime experiences of American servicemen with the larger history of the genocidal conquest of Native people, specifically relating the intertwined stories of patients in a Veteran's Administration Hospital with the nearby geography and history of Sand Creek, where Arapaho and Cheyenne people (mainly the old, the female, and the young) were massacred by the Colorado militia.[21] Analogously— as Alexie demonstrates in his poem—a deeply felt understanding of the Jewish Holocaust is possible, even by a Spokane Indian and a non-Jew.

The poem is crafted in the conversively respectful manner of a guest, inviting his listener-readers to join him in hearing the stories of Dachau. Alexie never takes the position of an authoritative voice on a place and history etched into the being of every Jew; rather, he reveals the way poetic language can become the vehicle for mutual understanding. Robin Riley Fast affirms the value of such diverse perspectives and understanding of history, geography, and the borderlands that both divide and interconnect peoples: "For different peoples and individuals, these variously realized borders may have quite different origins, appearances, and implications."[22] The complexity of the poem is such that an entire essay could be written about its seven diverse, yet interconnected, sections, including Alexie's effective use of the grounding and orienting experience of a historical trip, the integrity of personal testimony, the interrogative of rhetorically engaging questions, and the inclusiveness of the first person plural pronoun we in the first five sections, contrasted with a powerfully effective transition to the first person singular I in the final two sections: "6. after we are free" and "7. below freezing." All of these parts cohere in a tightly integrated poem that invites the reader to identify closely with the speaker (whether literally Alexie, some other literal or imagined visitor to Dachau, or the reader as an imagined and actual visitor through story).

The poem demonstrates a remarkable degree of structural sophistication. Analysis of its poetics demonstrates the extent to which language and form produce meaning. Each of the numbered sections has a unique structure, organization, and rhythm. It is significant that none of the sections of "In Dachau" are crafted in prose or block poetry; each section is in verse with line and stanza breaks that demand the respectful solemnity of silence. "7. below freezing" recreates the coldness of Dachau (physically, geographically, psychologically, climatically, spiritually) in a tightly knit repetition of phrases, sentences, rhymes, rhythm, and meter that shape a six-stanza poem of five three-line stanzas and a concluding one with four lines.

The rhythm alternates between lines of metrical feet ending on long beats that forward the movement of the poem and contrasting lines of feet ending on short beats that give it a halting motion. The first line— "Dachau was so cold I could see my breath" (*SBW,* 122)—with its syncopated rhythm moves forward with an amphimacer (-ˇ-) and iamb (ˇ-) combination that are repeated. This is a particularly strong way to begin with each foot forcefully moving the reader into the poetic visit to Dachau. This line is repeated in the concluding line of the second, fourth, and sixth stanzas, maintaining the strong forward thrust. We see this iterative pattern in the final line of the first stanza—"I have nothing new to say about death" (*SBW,* 122)—which is repeated as the ending line of the third, fifth, and sixth stanzas. Both of the repeating lines come together in the final sixth stanza as an effective and emphatic conclusion to the poem. This stanza changes the three-line form to a more forceful four-line one; the reiterative two-line ending, in turn, cycles back to the beginning that also includes both lines:

> / ˘ | / ˘ / |/ ˘ / | ˘ /
> Dachau was so cold I could see my breath.
>
> / ˘ | / ˘ / |˘ / |˘ / /
> I have nothing new to say about death. (*SBW,* 122)

It is also significant that when each of these lines ends a stanza, the first line of the next stanza picks up the metrical rhythm. In the case of the line "Dachau was so cold I could see my breath," the first line of the subsequent stanzas repeats the meter exactly:

> / ˘ / | ˘ / |/ ˘ /| ˘ /
> Everything was clean, history compressed
>
> / ˘ /|˘ / |/ ˘ /|˘ /
> I am not a Jew. I was just a guest. (*SBW,* 122)

The intricacy of this particular poem shows Alexie's craft at its best. Even with all the poem's complexity, a remarkable regularity of patterning shapes the internal meter, various forms of repetition, rhyme, alliteration, caesura, and enjambment to produce the poetic depth of understanding that relates the (hi)story that was/is Dachau. The rhyme scheme is regular: an ABA pattern that runs throughout the poem: breath, coat, death; rests, ghosts, breath; pressed, notes, death; rest, snow, breath; guest, close, death; next, smoke, breath, death. Metrically every line ends with a strong beat that moves the poem forward and also conveys the thematic strength of survival beyond the reality of Dachau. The stanzas alternate rhythmic patterns: the first, third, and fifth begin each line on a long, lone beat while the second, fourth, and sixth begin with two lines starting on a short beat, followed by a final line beginning with a long beat.

The metrical regularity is reinforced by the repetition of select words, sounds, and alliteration: was appears seven times; so, five; I, fifteen; and my, six. The repetition of first-person pronouns (twenty-one times in a relatively short poem) suggests an ambiguity that combines the speaker as author, the poem's persona, and the readers as co-creative listener-readers who become fellow speakers/thinkers as part of "a participating audience."[23] However, these first-person referents never refract the emphasis back on the speaker (or listener-reader) in solipsistic self-referentiality but, rather, focus the speaker's and listener-reader's viewpoint toward the reality that was/is Dachau.

The repetition of the hard "c" in the first line (Dachau, so cold, could see) and the fact that this is the only line that occurs four times in the poem intensify Dachau's hardness and coldness. The other repeated line includes a softer alliteration ("nothing new") that emphasizes the fact that Dachau was not a discrete event in the world. Such horrors occurred before and subsequent to Nazism—a fact well understood by Indigenous poet Alexie. Stanzas four and six repeat the alliteration of "w" in wanted, weep, wanted, weary, with, wonder, which, will, which, will. The alliteration, assonance, and para-rhyme in Jew, just, and guest in the line "I am not a Jew. I was just a guest" propel the line and heighten its intensity, deepened by the para-rhyme of guest with ghosts in the second stanza (both words end their lines).

It is important to note that particular words carry great resonance throughout Alexie's writing. When Alexie writes about expecting ghosts at Dachau, readers familiar with his work will remember lines from an earlier work that echo parallel Indigenous cultural destruction: "ghosts of drums" (*OSNS*, 41); environmental destruction: "ghosts of salmon" (*OSNS*, 73); and genocide: "the Ghost Dancers were only ghosts" (*OSNS*, 27). Words and sounds, vignettes and stories, characters and names, histories and events circle back upon each other in associative ways that create, expand, and thereby deepen meaning and insight. Alexie's lines powerfully evoke the horror that was the Holocaust, and yet, with the subtlety of the best poets and storytellers, he has crafted this poem with a prevailing humility—through the outward-looking, empathic lens and voice of the poem's persona—that poetically articulates a history that should have been unimaginable and beyond possibility. The length of the multipart poem develops the scope of a shorter lyric through the heteroglossia that the compound structure facilitates. This is evident throughout much of Alexie's work; close analysis of another poetic amalgam shows the effectiveness of this particular structure as Alexie sheds light upon Indigenous America for the diverse demographic of his broad readership.

THE COMPLEX POETICS OF INDIGENOUS AMERICA

Alexie's early collection, *First Indian on the Moon,* includes twenty-six longer poems that demonstrate his structurally disjointed, yet episodically and associatively linked, poetic technique. The stanzas and sections are separated more distinctly by his alternating pattern of prose and poetry (present in twelve pieces), his use of subtitles for different parts (used in eleven pieces), and/or his ordered numbering system (eleven times). The poem "A Reservation Table of the Elements" is one of his few works that exemplifies all three of these configurations. The poem is divided into five sections, each topically subtitled by an identifying element: aluminum, hydrogen, neon, copper, and oxygen respectively. The first, third, and fifth of these elemental sections are divided, in turn, into five numbered prose stanzas. These are punctuated by the second and fourth elemental sections, each containing a short poem of four two-line stanzas. Although Alexie's oeuvre demonstrates his consistent skill with both poetic and prose forms, he is at his best with the brevity of the lyric, communicating the raw pathos and wondrous survival of late twentieth and early twenty-first-century Indian America in strikingly moving language. As is true of a number of other Indigenous writers, Alexie's craft demonstrates his comfort with the pacing and rhythm of both poetic and block prose forms.[24]

Much of the rawness of reservation and urban Indian America requires either the speed of prose or the punctuated brevity of stanza and line breaks, giving the reader needed protective pauses from the interiority of pain, poverty, and prejudice—as well as crucial space and time for reflection—on the realities that Alexie poignantly depicts. Each of the combined poems that interweave prose and poetic structures have a distinctive pacing and rhythmic syncopation that reflect those worlds filled with the juxtaposed pace of lives lived on the edge of survival that jockey back and forth between moments of frenzied speed and slower rates of felt time. In his choice to use this mixed composition, Alexie ensures that his readers do not forget that those in the margins otherwise obscured are nonetheless evident: they are human parts of creation, interdependent persons with complex lives who desperately reach beyond the smallpox blankets of "anger and pain" to the warm giveaway blankets of "honor and grace" (*FIM*, 68). The patterning of Alexie's poems brings his readers closely, but briefly, into the worlds of the empathically heartfelt Indigenous lyric, metaphorically and metonymically presenting the reality of a blowtorch, the frozen pipes below a HUD house, and the speaker of "Copper" in "A Reservation Table of the Elements," who "crawled beneath/ . . . and discovered/ America" (*FIM*, 40).

The brevity of lyrical lines shields and distances the reader from painful emotions while the greater length of many of the prose passages protectively speeds the reader through the all-too-present tragedies that are part and parcel of contemporary America. For example, in the fifth and final block-prose part of the "Aluminum" section of the poem, Alexie pairs two specific acts of everyday violence, placing them within post-conquest America and the mythic framework of destructive vengeance wrought internally upon oneself in a tragically suffered futility: "Pick up a chair and smash it against walls, swing it so hard that your arms ache for days afterwards, and when all you have left in your hands are splinters, that's what we call history. Pick up an aluminum can and crush it in your fingers, squeeze it until blood is drawn, and when you cannot crush the can into any other shape, that's what we call myth" (*FIM*, 38).

The pace of this poem moves the reader quickly through the violent acts, much as these acts occurred rashly, without prior or concurrent reflection. The time for thinking is later—unless the pain is so great that another aluminum can of beer is more likely. Alexie's fast-moving prose includes only brief emphatic pauses through internal punctuation and the conjunction and. The poem does not offer a reflective pause until the end of the prose stanza, where the paragraph break provides the reader with the needed space to consider these events, especially noting the phrases and words given added weight through their alliteration ("arms ache," "can and crush"), para-rhyme ("splinters" and "fingers"), assonance ("smash" and "crush"), and repetition and parallelism ("Pick up . . . and smash" and "Pick up . . . and crush"; "swing it" and "crush it"; "arms ache" and "blood is drawn"; "that's what we call . . .").

The inverse pacing of the two brief, lyrical sections elicits consideration through their poetic line and stanza breaks. These second "Hydrogen" and fourth "Copper" parts provide spatial and temporal interludes from the heightened specificity and rawness in the block-prose sections.

Even so, within the prose sections, Alexie creates reflective empathic moments through minimalist storytelling, where select events and stories are recounted with such brevity that more empty space than actual text appears on the page. The long poem concludes with one such passage in the final, five-part prose section, "Oxygen." The middle piece—titled "3."—is one of Alexie's shortest, yet most powerful. It is made up of two sentences totaling twenty-eight words that, in their paucity, poignantly and tragically capture the everyday legacy of the conquest of America: "An Indian man drowned here on my reservation when he passed out and fell face down into a mud puddle. There is no other way to say this" (*FIM*, 40).

Numbering the beginning of each episodic section interrelates the parts with an associational iterative that draws attention to the rawness of repeated pain. In the poem, Alexie's direct and acerbic comment appears to be an apparently simple prose statement describing the event of one man's death, yet it, nevertheless, points to the larger reality of postconquest reservation America. What is familiar in America's margins is defamiliarized as one man's alcoholic death and given storied significance, while the all-too-common tragedy—unfamiliar in the realms of the privileged—is made evident in a literary familiarization of the death.

Alexie's turn to prose for this short passage obscures the poetic power of words that speak the awful reality underlying one man's drowning. Simple scansion of the sentence "There is no other way to say this" reveals the rhythmic importance of the ironically iterative, yet all too real, event in which one man's death must be understood as tragic, both in fact and emblematically.

$$/ \quad \smile \quad / \mid / \quad \smile \quad / \mid \smile \quad / \quad \smile$$
There is no other way to say this. (*FIM*, 40)

The sentence scans into three metrical feet whose pace is quickened by the equal length of three beats per foot. The first two feet repeat the long-short-long meter of the amphimacer, where the beginning and ending accented beats give added emphasis to the words "There," "no," and "way." Additionally the first foot ends with the vowel "o," which also begins the second foot, further fusing and accelerating the line. The repetition of "th" at the beginning, middle, and end of the line in "There," "-ther," and "this"; the internal rhyme of "way" and "say"; and the chiastic inversion of the beginning and ending consonant schemes "Th—s" and "s—th" in "There is" and "say this" demonstrate Alexie's remarkable gift for the sonority and pacing of poetic language.

The final foot inverts the pattern of amphimacers, switching to the short-long-short rhythm of the amphibrach to end the line on an unaccented downbeat that emphasizes the sadness of what is so briefly, yet powerfully, recounted. The strength of the beginning "There"—which indicates the importance of the storied event—contrasts with the weakness of the final "this"—which points to the narrator's sadness and hopelessness—moving the reader to the final point of narratorial frustration and despair at the futility and frequency of such reservation tragedies. As simple as this line seems, it is remarkably effective, directing readers with the emphatic and empathic impact of greater connection and understanding. The rhythmic impact of the line becomes clearer when contrasted with two other terse, yet poignant, lines:

> *(amphimacer-amphimacer-amphibrach)*
>
> There is no other way to say this. (*FIM,* 40)

> *(amphimacer-amphibrach-amphimacer)*
>
> There's more than one way to survive. (*FIM,* 34)

> *(amphibrach-amphibrach-amphibrach)*
>
> My heroes have never been cowboys. (*FIM,* 102)

The metrical rhythm of the first two of these lines combines with the emphasized words in each foot to clarify the contrast in what appear to be two similar lines. The first line gives rhythmical emphasis to the words "no," "way," and "say," underscoring the disempowerment of silence that yet another reservation tragedy produces. The weak beat of the final word "this" exemplifies this silencing. However, in the second line, Alexie inverts the middle and ending meter so that the line ends strongly with the long-short-long beat of the amphimacer. The rhythmically emphasized words in this line tell a very different story: "more," "one," and "sur-vive." The third line follows the same regular pattern of three feet with three beats each, but here the rhythm consists of three amphibrachs with each foot beginning and ending weakly on a short beat. There is such sad, yet insistent, poignancy in the metrical iteration of the amphibrach in "My heroes have never been cowboys" (*FIM*, 102).

The language and sonority of Alexie's poems and stories lay bare Manifest Destiny and conquest in their brutally historical, mythically storied, and personally lived realities. The fabled horses of the Plains and western tribes are invoked in the poem "I Would Steal Horses," where the retributive virility of stealing horses is conjoined with the truth of historical incapacitation, whether in the form of smallpox blankets, broken treaties, or decimated wild herds. The poem repeats the title refrain with two variations, each of which focuses on these three themes: the passing of the tribes' horse power, the loss of tribal sovereignty through the governmental violation of legal treaties, and the killing of Native people through the biological warfare of smallpox-infested blanket distributions.

Structurally the poem is tightly knit, using the fourteen-line, four-stanza sonnet form seen earlier in "The Game Between the Jews and the Indians." Although the sonnet is a well-known and commonly used poetic form—all too often tending to the forced and trite—Alexie's ear for the rhythmic and sonorous cadence of lyrical storytelling and minimal allusion creates an intriguing intricacy of form and meaning in this short poem. I would like to focus especially on the three primary, repeated refrains with their following clauses:

> / ˘ / | / ˘
> I would steal horses

> ˘ / | / ˘ ˘ | / ˘ /
> for you, if there were any left,

> . . . .
> / ˘ / ˘ | ˘ / ˘ / | //
> I would offer my sovereignty, take

> / ˘ / ˘ | / ˘ ˘ / ˘ | // | ˘ /
> every promise as your final lie, the last

. . . .

/   ˘   / | ˘ / | / ˘   /   ˘

I would wrap us both in old blankets

// | / ˘ | ˘   / | // | ˘ / | ˘   /

hold every disease tight against our skin. (*FIM,* 55)

A few singular aspects of the metrics of these paired lines merit initial explanation. The first two use interlinear enjambment to link their lines—"steal horses/for you" and "take/every promise"—and caesura for intralinear pauses—"for you, if"; "sovereignty, take"; "lie, the last"— whereas the final statement that stands alone as the sonnet's concluding two-line stanza runs steadily without the pauses in the prior assertions.

The first of the three ("I would steal horses/for you, if there were any left") has few other surprises. It consists of an independent clause and a dependent one that fill the two lines, as is also true of the ending couplet. The two lines are composed of three metrical feet of three beats and two metrical feet of two beats. While I do not believe this was mathematically intended, it nevertheless demonstrates notable parallelism and tightness of structure. Additionally the three-beat feet all feature the same metrical rhythm of the amphimacer (long-short-long). This repetition and, too, the lexical choice that produces feet that begin and end strongly come together in a poetic assertion of loss encased within the affirmative metrics of personal ability and volition. The speaker is rhythmically presented in his strength—he can and "would steal horses"; the fact that he does not do so reflects no inability on his part but, rather, historical circumstances that are out of his control.

In addition to the grammatical and semantic enjambment that closely unites the two lines, the para-rhyme ("hor-ses" and "for you"), along with the inverted meter that ends the first line with the long-short beat of a trochee and begins the second line with the inverted beats of a short-long iamb, further interweaves the two lines in a syncopation that emphasizes the strong beat of the iamb and is heightened by the pausal comma immediately following "for *you.*" The structure of these lines, where a metrical inversion combines with the repetition of the beginning metrical foot, repeats with slight variations in both sets of the other paired lines.

The second assertion—"I would offer my sovereignty, take/every promise as your final lie, the last"—consists of a metrical inversion of the first
two feet—the long-short-long-short of the ditrochaeus ("I would offer"),
then the short-long-short-long of the diiambus ("my sovereignty," where
the word is read in the more common three syllables). Both of these are
followed by a double repetition of the first foot—ditrochaeus, ditrochaeus
("every promise" and "as your final")—and end with the emphatic iamb,
"the last." Each line includes two feet with four beats followed by a long
single-beat foot that begins and ends the second clause ("take" and "lie").
Whereas the first iteration of the title assertion—"I would steal horses"—
begins the poem with a historical metaphor, the second brings the tribal
history of conquest into a poignantly lyrical relationship of broken promises and lies as the seductively powerful conquest of the heart conflates
broken treaties with false love—"I would offer my sovereignty."

The contrast that Alexie both affirms and questions in this poem is
that—unlike the power imbalance inherent in the history of Manifest
conquests and loss of tribal sovereignty—here the speaker chooses to
engage in the interpersonal relationship even if it results in loss of self
and sovereignty. The single-beat feet stress this capitulation: "take," "lie."
These words are given more importance by the repeated inverted assonance in "-sovereignty, take" ("t") and "final lie" ("l") that strengthens
their beginning consonants, giving take and lie the power of the imperative. After five hundred years of colonization, the history of deceit and
theft that underlies lives, families, and communities weight the words far
beyond the narrower scope of a single interpersonal relationship.

Building upon the single-beat emphatic foot, the syncopated combination of inverted metrical feet, and the repetition of select meter, the third
assertion brings together the mythic and historic referents of the prior
assertions in an ending couplet that again affirms and denies the personal relationship and its possibilities. Alexie concludes the poem with
the speaker asserting, "I would wrap us both in old blankets / hold every
disease tight against our skin" (*FIM,* 55). In contrast to the prior iterations, the first line scans into three feet of unequal length: an amphimacer
(long-short-long), an iamb (short-long), and a ditrochaeus (long-short-
long-short) with special emphasis on "wrap," "both," and "blankets." In
this way, the couplet begins with the predominant metrical feet of the

earlier iterations—the amphimacer and the ditrochaeus. The second line repeats the long single beat in "hold" and "tight" and the long-short pattern of the ditrochaeus in the single trochee of "every," then continues the pattern of inversion by following the trochee with three subsequent iambs that interweave the two lines with the prior iamb of "us both." The poem's final line emphasizes the words "hold," "tight," "against," and "skin," affirming the desperation of the relationship that binds the lovers tightly together with "old blankets" that ominously prefigure the smallpox reference. Smallpox mirrors the "dis-ease" of the relationship, exacerbated by the racial difference in the couple that works "against our skin." The relationship is described and deformed, and thereby defined, by its racial, gendered, cultural, and historical past and present.

The intricate structure in this poem is most evident in its powerful resonance of sound and silence, of strong and weak beats that combine in rhythmic waves in their repetitive, yet altered, iterations. The stated desire in the title—"I Would Steal Horses"—reverberates with each poetic statement of illusory and elusive desire that is passionately plaintive and assertive: "I would steal," "I would offer," "I would wrap." Tellingly no word is capitalized throughout the entire poem other than the speaker—the first-person I—who begins each sentence as the grammatical subject and whose presence and history achieve mythic status as the poem's storytelling subject. In "I Would Steal Horses"—regardless of the lack of horses, the deaths from smallpox, and the lies that wrought the loss of sovereignty and land—it is I who is the subject, the speaker, and the main topic: the Indigenous I who still speaks and asserts his subjectivity, who remembers and utters his own dreams and story that are, in fact, the much larger story of ancestry, conquest, and love. The particular patterning of this poem is not unique but rather representative of Alexie's poetical oeuvre that uses the sonnet and other tight poetic forms, reiteration of select lines, and intricate metrical structuring to interweave the Indigenous history of conquest with the everyday themes of contemporary Indian life and familiarize the unfamiliar through poetic accessibility.

As a final piece for close analysis, Alexie's poem "Blankets" continues the thematic primacy of blankets in the lives and histories of Native people. The poem exemplifies Alexie's skill in interweaving poetic and prose stanzas into a metrically integrated and coherent work. With much contemporary blank and prose verse, relatively scant attention is given to the formal metrics, whether creatively by writers or analytically by critics. This has a great cost: on the one hand, it produces poetry that could be restructured more effectively to strengthen primary themes, and on the other, it gives insufficient critical guidance to readers and writers regarding the formal strengths and weaknesses of writing.

Alexie is a writer whose poetry demonstrates his appreciation of the roles that the formal aspects of language play in sound, pacing, and emphasis. Whereas the five larger sections of "A Reservation Table of the Elements" shift back and forth between prose and poetry—both beginning, ending, and centering the poem with the block prose sections—"Blankets" inverts this order. Its five sections also alternate in form but begin, end, and center with the poetic forms that give it heightened lyricism and poignant pacing.

It is interesting that the poetic lines of "Elements" are aligned at the left, while those of "Blankets" are centered. Whether intentional or not, centering produces a poem whose appearance roughly resembles a stick-figure person, perhaps waiting to be covered by the blanket in the co-creative act of reader response. A look at the metrics of the final section/stanza of the poem exemplifies Alexie's poetic skill and some of its identifying qualities. The immediately prior fourth section of the poem in block prose ends with the beginning of the iterative refrain that repeats throughout the concluding poetic stanza: "I need you to cover me" (*FIM*, 68). This line leads into four distinct endings, each of which follows the same logical patterning "like x with y":

/ ˘ / | / ˘
like a good | blanket

˘ / | ˘ /
with warmth | and faith,

. . . .

/ ˘ | / ˘ | / ˘
like a | smallpox | blanket

˘ / ˘ | ˘ /
with anger | and pain.

....

/ ˘ | / ˘ | / ˘

like a tattered blanket

˘ / | ˘ /

with fear and shame.

....

/ ˘ | / ˘ / | / ˘

like a giveaway blanket

˘ / ˘ | ˘ /

with honor and grace. (*FIM,* 68)

Beginning the first of the four "I need you"s at the end of the prior prose stanza produces the metrical effect of breaking the first poetic line so that it scans with either a diiambus or a short-long-short amphibrach, followed by a lone, long beat of "me"—both scansions draw attention to the speaker and heighten the impact of his/her longing. Even so, the iconic blanket is given greatest weight in its thematic and trochaic repetition and placement at the end of lines: the historical and metaphoric warmth of a "good blanket"; the disease and death of conquest in the "smallpox blanket"; ancestry, poverty, and cold in a "tattered blanket"; and the tribally restorative spirit of the "giveaway blanket."

The three lines of each of the four statements are tightly knit together with similar metrical structures. One notable variation in the regular metrics of the lines occurs in the shifting descriptor of the four blankets. Each line consistently ends on the downbeat of the trochee, but the two negative descriptors—"smallpox" and "tattered"—also have a descending trochee beat, giving the line the dull monotony of three repeated trochees, while the two positive descriptors shift the metrics to the more hopeful up-down-up beat of the amphimacer that immediately precedes "blanket": "like a good/blanket" and "like a/giveaway/blanket." The final strong beat of the amphimacer strengthens the beginning beat in blanket, giving greater emphasis to the protective and restorative good, giveaway blanket.

The ending lines of each sentence alternate in rhythm, the first and third with the two iambs and the second and fourth with the amphibrach-iamb combination, whose contiguous short beats in the middle ("with anger and pain" and "with honor and grace") give added weight to the ending long beat ("pain" and "grace"). Para-rhymes interconnect lines with the same long-a vowel sound and the close final consonants "n" and "m" in "pain" and "shame", the long-a sound and the close final soft consonant sounds "th" and "s" in "faith" and "grace," and assonance in "anger" and "honor," exemplifying poetic skill that is deliberative and effective.

The poems "Blankets" (with the repeated refrain "I need you to cover me like a...blanket" and the combination of poetic and prose stanzas [*FIM* 68]), "I Would Steal Horses" (with the sonnet form and the repeated "I would..." refrain [*FIM* 55]), "The Game Between the Jews and the Indians is Tied Going Into the Bottom of the Ninth Inning" (also a sonnet with the repeated question "will you think" and "will I remember" [*FIM* 80]), and "Inside Dachau" (with the numerical stanzaic ordering [*SBW*, 117–22]), all interweave contemporary experience with the tragic, historical trajectories of conquest and genocide through close attention to poetic form and the methods by which poetic language can story worlds and times in ways that facilitate readers' entries into and understanding of those storied and lived realities. Rader describes the poetry of Alexie and other Native poets as "weapons" of empowerment: "Ultimately, these poems function as tropes of agency and contingency, for in the final scene, they empower Natives and Native culture because each writer uniquely envisions alternative modes of being."[25] Each of these poems demonstrates Alexie's craft and his sensitivity to the sonority of poetic language.

Literary criticism in the form of close reading is needed to shed light on the complex poetics that pervade the work of many Indigenous writers. Such studies will discover a remarkable array of poetic styles that reflect the diversity of Native writers' literary backgrounds, including their formal training, their tribal and regional cultural traditions, their linguistic backgrounds (e.g., monolingual, bilingual, formal, colloquial, and whether English is a first or second language), and all other relevant influences, such as national popular cultures; familiarity with, and interest in, oral storytelling traditions; and their preferred writers, literatures, genres, and styles. Scholars are just beginning to explore the depth and breadth of various Native writers' poetics and aesthetics.[26] Womack points to this trend in noting that "Native poets range widely from the more formalist writers, influenced by European forms such as meter and rhyme, to those poets trying to adapt the oral tradition"—identifying some of N. Scott Momaday's poems as examples of the former and the work of Simon Ortiz and Luci Tapahonso as representative of the latter.[27] He is correct in noting that the influence of the formalist English-language literary tradition varies from writer to writer, maintaining that "the works of Native poets lean more toward the oral-tradition influence than the formalist one."[28] I agree, as evidenced in my early exploration in my *Contemporary American Indian Literatures and the Oral Tradition* that analyzed the rhetorical range of Native literature that is more or less conversively and/or discursively informed.

However, it is important to note that the sonority of poetry requires a specificity of attention to the rich assemblage of styles and structures that generally distinguishes poetry, song, and chant from most prose.[29] Even for those poets whose work is significantly informed by their respective oral traditions, such as Simon Ortiz, Chaucer, Luci Tapahonso, Emily Dickinson, Sterling Brown, Hafiz, Homer, Edmond Jabès, and Sherman Alexie, we cannot say that their poems are without structure and style; their intricate forms will, as Womack states, demonstrate their respective poetics and prosody and the diversity of form and style evidenced synchronically and diachronically within their individual oeuvre. As one of the first scholars of Indigenous poetry even to broach the issues of craft, prosody, and style, Womack paves the way for future close studies that will further explore the rich craft that underlies and pervades Indigenous poetics.

This essay and my prior work on the poetry of Simon Ortiz begin to reveal the remarkable intricacy of that Indigenous prosody and poetics that demonstrate careful attention to an impressive array of literary techniques that combine in epistemologically deep, rhythmically complex, and emotionally rich poetry that remains, nevertheless, profoundly accessible to a broad range of readers. While studies of Alexie's short stories and novels elucidate his narrative craft, it is in the arena of poetics that we can best explicate Alexie's skill with intricate language.

Well over a decade ago, Robert Warrior critiqued "how little impact American Indian critical writers have had on each other's work."[30] While this has radically changed over the course of the last decade, analogous criticism can still be leveled regarding the literary criticism of Native poets' techniques. To date relatively little work has been done on the poetics, prosody, and craft of writers. Attention to the interwoven aspects of content and form may elucidate important "family resemblances"[31] among certain writers, revealing tribal, regional, or other affiliations and influence, what Tol Foster describes as "the *interzones* where different constituencies collide and, as a result, renegotiate their communal cultural frames."[32] This essay is offered as one contribution, beginning the elucidation of Sherman Alexie's prosody and poetic craft.

NOTES

1. Robert Warrior's exemplary volume *Tribal Secrets* demonstrates the type of work still needed to resurrect Indigenous literary histories, especially in relation to tribal, regional, and linguistic details. This neglect is largely due to the extent to which twentieth-century American literary study has failed to address the conquest of America and the concomitant struggles and enduring legacies of that history, thereby necessitating exhaustive corrective work to historicize Indigenous and other American literatures. *Tribal Secrets: Recovering American Indian Intellectual Traditions*.

2. Much of postmodern and poststructural literary studies have paid scant attention to the formal aspects of poetry as they contribute to the effectiveness of the work. While the reactive rejections of formalist literary criticism rightly critiqued the Eurocentric, ethnocentric, and androcentric biases within the New Critical, structuralist, psychoanalytic, and semiotic approaches, the blanket rejection of formalism largely turned critics away from the formal aspects of poetry. As Terry Eagleton laments in his book *How to Read a Poem,* "If most [literary scholars] have become less sensitive to literary form, some of them also look with skepticism on the critic's social and political responsibilities. In our own time, much of this political inquiry has been offloaded on to cultural studies; but cultural studies, conversely, has too often ditched the traditional project of close formal analysis." Eagleton, *How to Read a Poem,* 16.

3. Ibid., 3; italics in original. Many scholars of Indigenous literature have analyzed various aspects of the writers' poetics, such as Dean Rader's discussion of poetry that manifests "engaged resistance" ("The Epic Lyric"; "Word as Weapon," 149); Robin Riley Fast's attention to the "dialogic exchange" that she terms a "Native poetics of contested spaces" (*The Heart as a Drum,* 214, 207); Phillip Carroll Morgan's review of early Choctaw and contemporary Native literary criticism that addresses "ancient forms, structural elements, and artistic techniques" (" 'Who Shall Gainsay Our Decision?' " 130);

and Craig Womack's elucidation of the sonorous physicality of language and his call for "a compassionate criticism" that invokes a "harmony ethic" for scholarship that is "creative and life-affirming" ("Theorizing American Indian Experience," 370–71, 357). Rader, "The Epic Lyric: Genre and Contemporary American Indian Poetry," in *Speak to Me Words: Essays on Contemporary American Indian Poetry,* 122–42; and Rader, "Word as Weapon: Visual Culture and Contemporary American Indian Poetry, 147–68; Fast, *The Heart as a Drum: Continuance and Resistance in American Indian Poetry;* Morgan, " 'Who Shall Gainsay Our Decision?': Choctaw Literary Criticism in 1830," in *Reasoning Together: The Native Critics Collective,* 126–46; Womack, "Theorizing American Indian Experience," in *Reasoning Together: The Native Critics Collective,* 353–410.

4. Womack, "Theorizing American Indian Experience," 370.

5. The interrelationship of form and content is a factor in all linguistic expressions, whether literary or prosaic, textual or oral, verbal or performative. The creatively condensed nature of poetry makes it possible for the relationship of form and content to be more intricate and involved than in most other literary genres. It is important to note that the performative possibilities inherent in oral storytelling make an even more complex craft possible than what can be produced in textual form since oral stories and vignettes are created anew with each telling and audience. Phillip Carroll Morgan stresses these relationships in his essay " 'Who Shall Gainsay Our Decision?': The forms and structures of the oral stories duplicate themselves to varying degrees in the written texts" (130).

6. Eagleton, *How to Read a Poem,* 2; italics in original.

7. Sherman Alexie, *Old Shirts & New Skins,* 49 (hereafter cited in the text as *OSNS*).

8. These poems have personal resonance for me as a woman of German-Jewish ancestry through my Jewish father, who spoke only German until attending school as a young boy in New York City. While the maternal ancestry of my family reflects the genetics of conquest in our Appalachian history of mixed Indigenous, Scots-Irish, British, and Cornish blood, the Jewish lineage, although marked by its German passage, is ethnically, racially, and religiously of Middle Eastern origin.

9. The intersections and parallels between Native American and Jewish history are paramount. The history of the modern Jew of German extraction—distinctively successful prior to the Holocaust—manifests significant parallels with the renowned advances in the civilization of the Cherokees prior to the genocidal removal of the Trail of Tears. The "successful" Jewish assimilation into German society prior to the Holocaust produced a post-Holocaust psychological burden that intertwined the horrific genocide of ovens and camps with complex feelings including fear, anger, betrayal, loss, and guilt. For an extensive discussion of the Jew in Germany prior to the Nazi Holocaust, see Amos Elon's remarkable volume *The Pity of It All: A History of Jews*

in Germany, 1743–1933. Citing Fritz Stern, Elon writes "that the history of the assimilated Jews of Germany was much more than the history of a tragedy; it was also, for a long time, the story of an extraordinary success; 'We must understand the triumphs in order to understand the tragedy'" (12). Elon explains the distinctive condition and history of the more assimilated and modernized German Jews: "The history of Jewish assimilation, not only in Germany, has long been a subversive subject, which the assimilated have suppressed so as not to draw attention to themselves, and the Zionists, for equally self-interested reasons, have distorted" (12).

10. Sherman Alexie, "The Game Between the Jews and the Indians is Tied Going Into the Bottom of the Ninth Inning," in *First Indian on the Moon,* 80 (hereafter cited in the text as *FIM*).

11. The sports reference is indeed apt, for Alexie takes athletics and sports very seriously and alludes to them, especially basketball, in much of his poetry, prose, and film. The baseball imagery is also particularly relevant, for baseball is a sport that has held a central place for American Jews as one of the first competitive sports they were allowed to play and excel in (one of the most famous examples is Hank Greenberg, who sat out a World Series game because it was played on Saturday, the Jewish Sabbath).

12. Rader, "The Epic Lyric," 134.

13. Anishinaabe writer and scholar Gerald Vizenor pioneered the term *survivance,* conveying both survival and endurance. As Vizenor points out, human survivance is evidenced in verbal expression, whether active or passive: "Performance and human silence are strategies of survivance" *Manifest Manners: Postindian Warriors of Survivance,* 16.

14. Fellow Spokane poet Gloria Bird affirms the challenges in recognizing the inextricable legacy of the past as it is manifested in one's life, but she points out that this is a crucial step in the process of personal decolonization: "The hardest work is tracing back through the generations the aspects of colonization that have directly affected our lives, to identify those instances in which we have internalized what we are taught about ourselves in schools and in history books all of our invisible lives"—all as a means of "weakening...the burden of inherited shame, loss, dispossession, and disconnectedness" (30). Bird, "Breaking the Silence: Writing as 'Witness,'" in *Speaking for the Generations: Native Writers on Writing,* 26–48.

15. Native poet Duane Niatum emphasizes in his early essay about Native American poetry, "One of the oldest tribal values is the sense and need for supporting the continuity among generations" (26). Niatum, "History in the Colors of Song: A Few Words on Contemporary Native American Poetry," in *Coyote Was Here: Essays on Contemporary Native American Literary and Political Mobilization,* 25–34.

16. Simon J. Ortiz initially described the role of the reader of conversively interactive and storytelling literature: "The listener-reader has as much responsibility and commitment to poetic effect as the poet." Ortiz, *Woven Stone,* 151.

17. Elizabeth Cook-Lynn, "How Scholarship Defames the Native Voice . . . and Why," 92.

> Following upon the heels of Spain's Jewish and Muslim diaspora, three cataclysmic movements occurred that irrevocably altered the landscape of the western hemisphere: Europeans poured out of Europe seeking colonial wealth, land, and power; west Africans were horrifically diasporized into objectified forms of slavery which the world had not previously seen; and the indigenous peoples of the western hemisphere were genocided, dispossessed of their lands, relocated into slavery, and otherwise displaced, marginalized, and impoverished. . . . The perceptual shift that crystallized in 1492 magnified and globalized the objectification of lands, cultures, and persons. (162)

Susan Berry Brill de Ramírez, "Writing the Intertwined Global Histories of Indigeneity and Diasporization: An Ecocritical Articulation of Place, Relationality, and Storytelling in the Poetry of Simon J. Ortiz," in *Stories through Theory/Theory through Stories: Native American Storytelling and Critique,* 159–90.

18. Sherman Alexie, *The Summer of Black Widows,* 121 (hereafter cited in the text as *SBW*). Here I should note that as a high school student of Jewish ancestry in Switzerland, I adamantly refused to learn the German language of my father and grandparents—the linguistic connector to the homeland where we gained our family names Brill and Wolf and the country that contained the concentration camp where, as a German-speaking Jewish doctor in the United States Army, my father treated the survivors at liberation. Other than noting this fact, he never spoke further about this experience.

19. Bird, "Breaking the Silence," 29.

20. For a more detailed explanation of conversive communication in storytelling and literature, see my earlier volume, *Contemporary American Indian Literatures and the Oral Tradition;* also my introductory essay in Susan Berry Brill de Ramírez and Evelina Zuni Lucero, eds., *Simon J. Ortiz: A Poetic Legacy of Indigenous Continuance,* 25–52.

21. Simon J. Ortiz, *from Sand Creek: Rising in this Heart which is Our America.*

22. Robin Riley Fast, "Borderland Voices in Contemporary Native American Poetry," 508.

23. Ibid., 517.

24. Eric Gary Anderson makes this point: "One must take into account the fluency with which Indian poets move between poetry and still other forms of expression" (39). Anderson, "Situating American Indian Poetry: Place, Community, and the Question of Genre," in *Speak to Me Words: Essays on Contemporary Native American Poetry,* 34–55.

25. Rader, "Word as Weapon," 165.

26. At the December 2008 Modern Language Association meeting, an entire session was devoted to Native American "Indigenous Poetics" (cochaired by Sean Teuton and Susan Berry Brill de Ramírez). See note 3 for a brief list of several scholars who have explicitly addressed Native American poetics.

27. Craig S. Womack, *Red on Red: Native American Literary Separatism.*

28. Ibid.

29. Brill de Ramírez, *Contemporary American Indian Literatures.* As I have explained regarding the work of several Native women poets, "Contemporary creative work by American Indian, Alaskan Native, and Canadian First Nations peoples does not need to be in the forms of oral performance to reflect the power and presence of those oral traditions" (102). Brill de Ramírez, "The Power and Presence of Native Oral Storytelling Traditions in the Poetry of Marilou Awiatka, Kimberly Blaeser, and Marilyn Dumont," in *Speak to Me Words: Essays on Contemporary Native American Poetry,* 82–102.

30. Warrior, *Tribal Secrets,* xix.

31. The phrase "family resemblance" points to Ludwig Wittgenstein's discussion in his *Philosophical Investigations,* where he articulates that diverse realities may nevertheless bear meaningful similarities to each other and that in recognizing their family resemblances, one can gain new insights into each. Wittgenstein, *Philosophical Investigations.*

32. Tol Foster, "Of One Blood: An Argument for Relations and Regionality in Native American Literary Studies," in *Reasoning Together: The Native Critics Collective,* 272; italics in original.

CHAPTER 8

The Poetics of Tribalism in Sherman Alexie's *The Summer of Black Widows*

The transformation of tribal identity in contemporary society and culture is a concern that runs provocatively throughout the work of Spokane/ Coeur d'Alene writer Sherman Alexie. Alexie, one of the most popular Indian authors working today, has had to reckon with the ambivalence of his own rise to success. He launched his career by voicing reservation realities often filtered through speakers who are young Indian men—poised on the verge of despair but longing for something more— who reveal themselves through eloquent "rez" talk. His later stories and poems, however, have experimented with diverse materials and forms, often borrowing from Anglo-American, African American, and Western cultures to depict Indians on the move, bringing tribal identities and Native worldviews into urban and mixed-blood environments. Alexie's penchant for fusing non-Native and Native traditions in unexpected ways lies at the heart of *The Summer of Black Widows,* his acclaimed volume of poetry published in 1996.

This volume significantly thematicizes and enacts at a formal level the tensions between Alexie's tribalist, reservation roots and the writer's engagement with non-Native and multicultural materials associated with the world beyond the reservation. The poems are grouped into seven sections under headings that echo the titles of individual poems and reiterate some of the major images and themes of the volume. The collection begins with a section titled "Why We Play Basketball"; its nine poems are set on the reservation, and several mention Spokane specifically. Taken together, they summon up images of rez ball, powwows and dancing, Coyote, the Ghost Dance, and poignant details of daily life on the reservation. The collection moves through subsequent sections focusing on family affiliations, powwows, tourists, and Sasquatch, culminating in a section titled "Bob's Coney Island," which includes nine poems set in urban and global locations, including Spain, Germany, Chicago, Los Angeles, New York City, and Coney Island. Through the shifting locations of these poems, *The Summer of Black Widows* explores the way that tribalism manifests itself in diverse modes and contemporary contexts.

At a formal, technical level, the poems employ a dynamic, creative bricolage in blending Indian realities and traditional Western poetic forms. Alexie sometimes situates his work consciously within Western poetic traditions by labeling a poem a sonnet or villanelle, for instance, or referring to Anglo-American poetry icons such as Walt Whitman, Emily Dickinson, or Shakespeare. He includes Spokane and Coeur d'Alene traditions in his poems as well, using images from powwows and dancing, Sasquatch and salmon, and other markers of his specific tribal affiliations, along with allusions to tribal history and the Spokane Indian Reservation. Still other multicultural layers appear in his poems in references to African American music, mainstream pop-culture icons, and minority histories from other oppressed people. In the complex exchange of cultures, identities, and traditions that shapes *The Summer of Black Widows,* an interesting dynamic develops: as the poems move off the reservation to explore non-Native spaces, forms, and materials, they become ever so firmly rooted in tribalism. This essay explores the ways that tribalism as a worldview or critical consciousness permeates the aesthetics and ethics of the poems in *The Summer of Black Widows.*

TRIBALISM AND POETICS

In a 1997 interview with John Purdy, Alexie describes *The Summer of Black Widows* as "technically good"; "I thought it was probably my best book." He also critiques the volume—"but very few of the poems Indian people would relate to"—and comments that he wishes he could "go back to writing the kinds of poems I wrote in *Fancydancing*," his 1992 collection, which to him were more "Indian" and "accessible to Indian people."[1] In contrast to Alexie's self-criticism, some of Alexie's most insightful readers have identified *The Summer of Black Widows* as an ambitious and accomplished volume: John Newton describes it as "more affirmative" and confident about "indigenous authority"; Ron McFarland echoes Alexie's evaluation of his technique by commending the volume for its ability to "demonstrate[e] his formal range"; Susan Brill de Ramírez describes the poems as "more hopeful" and invoking the "power of the sacred to overcome the horrors of the world."[2] Alexie's comments about *The Summer of Black Widows,* however, reveal both approval and disavowal of his technical prowess and suggest that too much emphasis on poetic technique creates an uneasy detachment from Indian readers and reservation realities.

One way to navigate the relationship and tension between Native and Western poetics in Alexie's work is through the poem "Defending Walt Whitman," which stages a sometimes-comical, sometimes-inspiring encounter between young Indian men playing reservation basketball and Whitman, an iconic figure in Anglo-American poetry, who shows up at the game wanting more than anything to be a player. As Cyrus Patell observes, Alexie's poem simultaneously "pays homage to Whitman" and "shows us a Whitman who is out of place."[3] On the one hand, the poem reveals a Whitman who "cannot tell the difference between / offense and defense" and who looks ridiculous with his long beard, which "frightens / the smallest Indian boys."[4] On the other hand, Alexie's Whitman—observing the prowess of the Indian boys and young men playing basketball—is powerfully moved:

> God, there is nothing as beautiful as a jump shot
> on a reservation summer basketball court

where the ball is moist with sweat
and makes a sound when it swishes through the net
that causes Walt Whitman to weep because it is so perfect.
  (*SBW*, 14)

Whitman's appreciation—even reverence—for the game emerges from a constellation of desires: for the game itself, for young men, for brown bodies, for beauty, and for God. Erotics, aesthetics, and spirituality come together in this charged encounter.

Alexie's Indian players have their own reasons for revering basketball. It is a game that provides an escape from the wars and military stints some have served (Kuwait and "foreign wars" are both cited in the first few stanzas of the poem). More importantly, basketball becomes a way for them to express their Indianness—to be "twentieth-century warriors who will never kill"; to leap "like a salmon" heading upriver "toward home" and run like ponies with their long hair swinging freely in the wind: "bareback, skin slick and shiny" (*SBW*, 14, 15). "Defending Walt Whitman" offers an eloquent depiction of reservation basketball that recurs throughout Alexie's poetry and fiction.

But it is not clear in the poem if Whitman ever glimpses the significance of basketball for the Indian players. In fact, the poem ends with a line that suggests Whitman's implicit egocentricity: "Walt Whitman shakes. This game belongs to him" (*SBW*, 15). This arrogant claim brings us back to the title of the poem and its double (and dueling) implications—this is a poem that defends Walt Whitman (and what he symbolizes in terms of poetics and cultural encounters), but it also defends reservation life and Indian players from the prying eyes and imperialist assumptions of Whitman (himself and as a synecdoche for Anglo-Americans generally).

Rather than attempting to resolve this fundamental tension, I suggest that the power of the poem derives precisely and proportionally from the friction of this tension. Alexie's poem locates a language and rhythm that intones a commitment to the Indian players, their tribal connections, and their sense of sovereignty at the same time as it embraces Whitman's Anglo poetic and aesthetic sensibility. For it is Whitman, after all, who reveres the sensually rich details of the bright summer day, the sweat clinging to the basketball, and the swoosh of a ball that touches only net and who connects the game and the players profoundly to beauty and God. In other words, Alexie's poem—through its eloquent, poetic tribute to "rez" ball—suggests that it is possible to use Western traditions and aesthetics to strengthen tribal ties.

In his poetry, Alexie negotiates a desire for Indianness and sovereignty from within contemporary conditions in ways akin to Craig Womack's critical work on reading and interpreting Native American literature. In *Red on Red: Native American Literary Separatism* (1999), Womack demonstrates the way specific longtime tribal traditions continue to energize and preoccupy Creek writers—from oral storytellers living today to authors spanning the late-nineteenth through the twentieth centuries, including Alexander Posey, Alice Callahan, Louis Oliver, and Joy Harjo. Womack's insistent point is that, unless we read these writers in terms of tribal identity, we will make them vanish as Indians—we will fail to recognize them as Creek writers having something valuable to say about Creek traditions and sovereignty. In other words, Womack's method of reading Native writers in terms of tribal affiliations works counter to a Western model of the individual as Great Author and instead emphasizes the significant contributions Native literature can make to strengthen and sustain the political, aesthetic, intellectual, and spiritual traditions of Indian nations.

Womack is especially helpful in analyzing the ways that preconceptions about authenticity have led to misreadings of Native texts. One of the key issues he considers is literary influence: what do we do with texts by American Indian authors that reference Western canonical writers in addition to or instead of tribal and/or pantribal sources? Womack tackles this question directly in his chapter on Posey, arguing that an Indian "reading Thoreau does not—any more than an American's reading [of] Shakespeare—constitute a loss of identity. This is an argument that is only applied to Indians who, once they defy the stereotypes prevalent in popular imaginings, become suddenly less Indian."[5] Part of Womack's point is that referencing non-Native sources does not negate the Indian identity of the author or the text. But at the same time, he insists that a typical "lit-critter" interest in tracing such lines of influence can lead to overlooking important nationalist and tribalist allegiances for Creek and other Native writers.

Womack also addresses critical tendencies to privilege and romanticize oral texts, arguing that "scholars of Native literature need to break down the oppositional thinking that separates orality and literacy wherein the oral constitutes authentic culture and the written contaminated culture."[6] Such a dichotomy constructs narrow parameters to judge Natives writers and their texts, and Womack's purpose in *Red on Red* is to identify ways that all the writers he discusses have something important to contribute to Creek tribalism and sovereignty, even when they do not employ orally based poetics or see themselves specifically as Creek writers.

Womack's emphasis on tribalism suggests a useful and complex framework for reading the dynamics of Alexie's creative bricolage in *The Summer of Black Widows*. Because of the range of influences, references, and allusions in Alexie's poetry, questions of oral versus written traditions, purity versus taintedness, and real Indianness versus mixed-blood, hybrid identities naturally come up in discussions of his work. Some of the poems in *The Summer of Black Widows* follow "Defending Walt Whitman" in alluding to Anglo-American or Western cultural touchstones while also affirming tribalist affiliations. Other poems directly employ and signify on genres traditionally associated with a Western poetic tradition.

Alexie's engagement with poetic forms such as the villanelle, sestina, and sonnet and genres such as the elegy and pastoral has attracted critical attention. In her analysis of *The Summer of Black Widows*, for example, Laura Arnold Leibman argues that "for the oral tradition to combat the white world and the death Alexie's people face within it, poetry must include the strategies of the white world it fights—including its poetic forms."[7] Leibman does not go far enough in recognizing the strategic power of genre and poetics in Alexie's work: Alexie does not merely fight back against the white world but embraces and reshapes it so that Western traditions are remade as Indian ones and Western individualism yields to Indian tribalism.

As Womack emphasizes in *Red on Red*, engagement with non-Native sources or texts does not dilute the Indianness of Native writers and their texts. The potency of cross-cultural fusions in *The Summer of Black Widows* becomes dramatically clear in a seven-part sequence titled "Totem Sonnets," where Alexie carves the traditional structure of the sonnet into new forms. The sonnet, of course, is not a traditional Indigenous form, and many of the individual sonnets in Alexie's sequence incorporate non-Native peoples, films and books, and foodstuffs. But Alexie's "Totem Sonnets" hardly follows the conventions of the sonnet sequence in Western literary tradition, either. Although each sonnet has fourteen lines and can be identified as Shakespearean or Petrarchan in form, Alexie makes no attempt to follow iambic pentameter, and, more radically, he pares down the lines to names, images, or titles so that the narrative drive and assumptions of the traditional sonnet are entirely displaced.

A quick overview of topics also reveals the jarring discontinuities that structure the sequence. Sonnet one names people Alexie has elsewhere said he admires or wishes were Indian: the octet lists white people, the sestet names African Americans and Latinos. Sonnet two lists food items. Sonnet three is the most overtly Native of the sequence, citing specific notable Indian men and women. Sonnet four offers us a list of movies; sonnet five, a list of musicians; and sonnet six, a list of literary characters. Sonnet seven groups together names: biblical figures in the first quatrain, talented athletes in the second, and dead (or presumed dead) legends in the third, leading to a couplet naming the relationship "Mother/Father." This sequence—stripped down to poems of fourteen lines that offer only names, titles, or nouns without any connecting words or ideas—defies typical reading protocols for Western sonnets, let alone Native poetry. Indeed, to dwell too much on their form as sonnets may cause us to fall into what Womack terms a "lit-critter" approach that ignores tribalist allegiances or what Eric Gary Anderson identifies as "the trap of measuring American Indian poetry using non-Indian yardsticks."[8]

In "Situating American Indian Poetry: Place, Community, and the Question of Genre," Anderson argues quite compellingly that genres "are forms of identity imported from outside Native cultures and at times imposed on them; by implication, genre identities come to be associated with other suspect methods of determining Native identity, such as those that set out to calculate Indianness on the basis of blood percentiles."[9] While Anderson cautions against the abuse of this kind of outside non-Native critical perspective, Alexie's "Totem Sonnets," whose title invokes an alien, non-Native genre and which includes citations to a number of Native and non-Native persons and texts, seems to invite such analysis. Anderson also argues that American Indian poetry "works to remove or downplay any cross-cultural forces that threaten to dilute or negate its Indianness."[10] Alexie's sonnet sequence, in contrast, challenges this formulation by embracing cross-cultural fusions—perhaps to such a degree that some readers may question its authenticity as a Native poem.

I want to argue against this possible interpretation by paying close attention to the ways that the sequence invites—indeed demands—readers to locate new reading strategies through which contemporary Indian identity and tribal affiliations emerge from unexpected sources. Take sonnet two, for instance, which focuses on ordinary food that can be found in most supermarkets:

> Steamed Rice
> Whole Wheat Bagel
> Egg White
> Baked Chicken
>
> Tomato Soup
> Broccoli
> Cheddar Cheese
> Garlic Clove
>
> Grape Nuts and Non-Fat Milk
> Almonds
> Apple
> Ice Water
>
> Insulin
> Hypodermic (*SBW,* 33)

We notice, first of all, that food is an unusual subject for a sonnet, a poetic form which is typically associated with profound and lofty insights. Perhaps Alexie means to create a mock sonnet by dwelling on food (and ordinary food in this case, not even haute cuisine). Even as the list form and subject matter resist typical analytical approaches to sonnets, however, an interesting thematic emerges: the foods listed in the three quatrains may typically be identified as healthy choices—unless you are a diabetic, as the final couplet suggests, who risks dire health complications if a proper diet is not maintained consistently. This sonnet, which begins by seeming to mock the sonnet form, ultimately develops serious tribal implications: the final couplet bears witness to the epidemic of diabetes among Native people and perhaps is a personal acknowledgment of Alexie's father's diabetic illness.

The minimalist aesthetics of Alexie's sonnet sequence are also crucial to the tribalist thematic that begins to emerge from the pared-down lines, as sonnet three directly suggests:

Crazy Horse
Sitting Bull
Captain Jack
Black Kettle
Ishi
Joseph
Qualchan
Wovoka

Anna Mae Aquash
Wilma Mankiller
Tantoo Cardinal
Winona LaDuke
Buffy Sainte-Marie
Maria Tallchief (*SBW,* 34)

This sonnet functions as a chant, paying homage to leaders and artists—Indian men occupy the octave, Indian women the sestet—and Alexie enhances the totemic quality of these names by refusing to make the poem easily understood. It is also a history lesson, intoning names of leaders and elders who ought to be known if one wants to understand Alexie's poetry specifically and Indian America generally. By presenting these names in a totem sonnet without any contextual clues, Alexie exposes the politics of history and the invisibility of minority histories in mainstream America.

Most importantly, by conjoining *totem* and *sonnet,* Alexie transforms a non-Native literary form into a visually striking Native cultural and spiritual one: the totem pole. One use of traditional totem poles is to establish clan relationships.[11] Carving his figures out of words, Alexie draws into one clan—across temporal and tribal boundaries—a matrilineage and patrilineage of Indian leaders and activists.[12] The clan that Alexie unites throughout the sequence includes not only the Indian leaders of sonnet three but Native and non-Native literary characters, movies, athletes, musicians, leaders, and outlaws—from Meryl Streep and Kareem Abdul-Jabbar; to the Beatles and Robert Johnson; to Jesus Christ, Billy Mills, and D. B. Cooper. This wild and rich diversity culminates in a final couplet—"Mother/Father"—that embraces the preceding multiverse and claims its myriad voices and influences. But in the end, readers may also begin to wonder: what then makes "Totem Sonnets" an Indian or tribalist poem?

For Womack the nativeness of Native American literature becomes clear as we identify a specific tribal worldview, history, and cultural tradition in a text that reflects the writer's tribal affiliation. This reading methodology, however, is not entirely successful when applied to Alexie's "Totem Sonnets." Alexie is Spokane (through his mother) and Coeur d'Alene (through his father), and yet the poem provides few specific links to these tribal nations. Among the Native women and men in the sonnets—whether they are historical, contemporary, or fictional—none is specifically Spokane or Coeur d'Alene. (But Qualchan, the nineteenth-century Yakama warrior, and Joseph, the Nez Perce leader, come close geographically. Or perhaps we may see a subtle Coeur d'Alene connection in Cecilia Capture, the protagonist of a novel by Janet Campbell Hale, who, like Alexie, has Coeur d'Alene ancestry.)

Neither do we find any mention of salmon nor horses nor owl dancing nor the stick game, which may be expected from a Spokane/Coeur d'Alene writer; while these are powerful images in some of Alexie's other poems, not one appears in this sequence. In contrast to working with materials and images from his specific tribal affiliations, Alexie builds his poem as a totem pole—which is not a tradition practiced by either Spo-kane or Coeur d'Alene Indians, though it is historically and contempora-neously a rich heritage for coastal Salish nations in Washington, British Columbia, and Alaska.

At one level, Alexie's sonnets appear to be the kind of Native poems that are not tribally specific enough to be read through Womack's groundbreaking approach, and yet they share Womack's insistence on intellectual and spiritual sovereignty for Native writers. To read Alexie's poems as sonnets merely playing with a traditional Anglo-European form is to miss the power of this sequence, a power deeply grounded in Indi-anness. Alexie draws on his own lineage of spirit helpers in "Totem Son-nets"—some traditional (like Crazy Horse) and some quite surprising (like the Incredible Hulk). Connecting his ancestry to his contemporary location as an Indian poet, Alexie ends his poem by naming his allegiance to family: "Mother" and "Father," he writes. Rather than seeing Alexie's "Totem Sonnets" as indicative of a bicultural, bifurcated, split-at-the-root, mixed-blood, mixed-up identity, we may instead look for the presence of Indian spirits arising in both expected and unexpected places,[13] arising out of the cacophony of contemporary culture to give voice to Indian per-spectives, to clamor for recognition.

Tribalism and Ethics

Many of the poems in *The Summer of Black Widows* speak to the urgent needs of justice, spiritual renewal, and ethical obligations. What is par-ticularly striking about this volume is the degree to which Alexie fuses poetic form and technique with an Indigenous critique of white America and its assumptions. The poems gathered in *The Summer of Black Widows* employ form as a rhythmic means for creating a politically and ethically charged poetic space that articulates a tribalist worldview.

Alexie confronts one of the most contentious issues in contemporary America in his poem "Capital Punishment." The persona is a prison cook who prepares the last meal for an Indian man about to be put to death in the electric chair. Even while the speaker proclaims his detachment from the scene—"(I am not a witness)" recurs five times in the poem—he com-ments on the color of capital punishment: he casually notes that "when white people die," "dark ones" end up in the chair (*SBW*, 86). According to a summer 2006 report by the NAACP Legal Defense and Educational Fund, 55 percent of the prisoners currently on death row are people of color. An analysis by the Death Penalty Information Center also shows that the death penalty is much more likely to be recommended for minorities when the victim of the crime is white.[14] Alexie's poem does not dwell on these eye-opening statistics, however; his speaker is casual and understands that what may be news to the justice system or well-meaning white liberals is an everyday reality for minorities.

The terrors of death by electrocution are imaged in the poem when the speaker decides to turn out all the lights in the kitchen "because the whole damn prison dims / when the chair is switched on" (*SBW*, 88). Most chillingly, he recalls hearing the story of a black prisoner who was electrocuted but lived through the first execution attempt, only to be strapped into the chair again one hour later. The speaker's tone is neutral as he relates these details, and for much of the poem, readers may suspect that he is too emotionally numb to feel a sense of outrage or empathy. The two-line stanza that Alexie uses in this poem reinforces a careful, measured tone that suggests detachment or the speaker's unwillingness to see himself as a member of this desperate community.

The poem, however, reveals that the speaker's attempt to remain apart from the execution is on the verge of unraveling: he repeats the one-line refrain—"(I am not a witness)"—almost obsessively, as though to will it into being. But as the poem unfolds, that refrain gives way to a moment of recognition: "(I am a witness)," the speaker finally admits near the end. This shift in diction may seem to be a simple turn of phrase at first glance, but a closer examination links this admission to the speaker's developing collective and Indigenous consciousness. The turning point comes when the cook discusses the care with which he has prepared the prisoner's last meal:

> I want you to know I tasted a little
> of that last meal before I sent it away.
>
> It's the cook's job, to make sure
> and I was sure I ate from the same plate

and ate with the same fork and spoon
that the Indian killer used later

in his cell. Maybe a little piece of me
lodged in his mouth, wedged between

his front teeth, his incisors, his molars
when he chewed down on the bit

and his body arced like modern art
curving organically, smoke rising

from his joints, wispy flames decorating
the crown of his head, the balls of his feet. (*SBW,* 88–89)

In this remarkable exchange—via the bit of food that goes from mouth to mouth—the cook and the prisoner become intimately linked. The prisoner, to be sure, has no way of knowing what the cook has done; rather, the poem emphasizes the cook's ability to imagine this moment of reciprocity and connection, and, because of this juncture, we know that the Indian killer does not go to his death alone or unremembered. Thus, rather than serving only as a testament to the state's barbaric power to execute, the prisoner's death becomes something to be pondered and provoked by—"like modern art" (*SBW,* 89)—because of its grotesque beauty. The cook's act of imagination and affiliation allows access to a vision of the execution, which here is rendered in terms approaching martyrdom or crucifixion, obligating Alexie's readers to become witnesses to the scene as well.

The transformative possibilities of this moment become clear as the poem closes, and we find the cook has become a reluctant truth teller:

(I am a witness)

I prepared the last meal
for the Indian man who was executed

and have learned this: If any of us
stood for days on top of a barren hill

during an electrical storm
then lightning would eventually strike us

and we'd have no idea for which of our sins
we were reduced to headlines and ash. (*SBW,* 90)

By aligning lightning, an arbitrary natural phenomenon, with electrocution, Alexie's poem questions the ethics of capital punishment. By suggesting the uncertainty of knowledge—who knows why lightning strikes where it does; who knows which sins we will eventually be punished for?—Alexie's speaker reveals the fallibility of all attempts to judge innocence or culpability. This instance of recognition has important implications for critiquing capital punishment, but Alexie's method is oblique and suggestive; the political and ethical issues in the poem slowly, but firmly, take hold in the prison cook's mind and spill over to encompass Alexie's readers. In other words, the poem's ethics and aesthetics unite to enact community and collectivity for the speaker and his fellow prison workers and inmates—and readers as well. Alexie's poem insists on tribalism and collective consciousness as a way (perhaps the only way) to work toward justice.

Another significant political issue discussed in *The Summer of Black Widows* is uranium mining and poisoning, or what Ward Churchill and Winona LaDuke have called "radioactive colonialism."[15] In "Sonnet: Tattoo Tears," a fourteen-section sonnet in prose paragraphs, Alexie suggestively combines the issues of mining, fishing rights, and water ecology. Section five, for instance, includes these elegiac lines: "Disappear, brother, into the changing river, salmontravelling beneath the uranium mine, all of it measured now by half-lives and miles-between-dams" (*SBW,* 57). The flow of the Spokane River, a tributary of the Columbia, which is vital to the Northwest ecosystem, has been irrevocably altered by dams erected to produce hydroelectric power; the result is a threatened environment for salmon, endangered by the dams and environmental contamination caused by uranium mining.[16] In his poetry and prose,

Alexie frequently mourns the loss of the salmon, not only for ecological reasons but for their centrality to Spokane beliefs and traditions.

The poem "Haibun" focuses extensively on the problems of uranium mining on the Spokane Reservation. Alexie's title refers to a Japanese poetic form that combines prose paragraphs and haiku. In the genre of *haibun,* sometimes both the prose sections and the haiku are lyrical; at other times, the prose sounds prosaic, or humorous, and thus becomes a counterpoint to the haiku. In "Haibun," the prose paragraphs tell the history of mining on Spokane land while the haiku provide moments of intense clarity.

As in Leslie Marmon Silko's *Ceremony,* the story of uranium mining in Alexie's poem involves economic exploitation and greed, ecological disaster, and sovereignty. As Churchill and LaDuke point out in reference to uranium mining on Navajo lands near Shiprock from 1952 to 1980, such arrangements benefit white-owned corporations at the expense of Native people. The corporation in the Navajo case—Kerr-McGee—enjoyed "low wages, a guaranteed labor force, privileged contract status, virtually nonexistent severance taxes, and nonexistent safety regulations," and when the mine closed, the Navajo were left to deal with seventy-one acres of raw uranium tailings that were leeching into the San Juan River and a huge increase in cancer or radiation-related fatalities: by 1980, 38 of the 150 Diné who had worked in the mine had died.[17]

Alexie's poem alludes to Midnite Mine, an open-pit uranium site on the Spokane Reservation about eight miles from Wellpinit, the town Alexie grew up in. Mining operations were carried out from 1955 until 1981. Today the mine continues to be in the news. Left behind when it closed were 2.4 million tons of stockpiled ore, waste-rock piles, and two open pits partially filled with contaminated water.[18] The Environmental Protection Agency placed the site on its National Priorities list in 1999 and is presently working on a plan to clean up the area using Superfund protocols (see figures 1 and 2).

Alexie's poem critiques the repeated claim that uranium mining economically benefits Native people. The discovery of uranium in "Haibun" leads to "arguments about claim rights" and a $340,000 payment to a brother and sister, who nonetheless die young and wastefully: "Lucy died in a car wreck in 1961. In 1969, Richard choked to death on a piece

FIGURE 8.1. Pit 3 at Midnite Mine, still holding contaminated water. Spring 2002, EPA.

FIGURE 8.2. Hazard sign by core shack at Midnite Mine. Spring 2002, EPA.

of steak" (*SBW*, 29). The speaker of the poem begins to lose his innocence regarding mining when the mine closes down, reflecting,

I remember waving to the truck drivers, who were all white men. I remember they always waved back. When the mines closed down, the empty trucks rumbled away. I cannot tell you how many coffins we filled during the time of the trucks, but we learned to say "cancer" like we said "oxygen" and "love."

Grandmother died on her couch
covered with seven quilts,
one for each of her children.

The white men quickly abandoned the mine. They left behind pools of dirty water, barrels of dirty tools, and mounds of dirty landfill. They taught us that "dirty" meant "safe." After the white men left, Indians guarded the mine. My uncle worked the grave-yard shift. If he listened closely as he made his rounds, he could hear Chimakum Creek, just a few hundred feet to the south.

In this light
we can see the bones of salmon
as they swim. (*SBW*, 29–30)

The difference between the white men who drive away and the Native people left to live in a contaminated environment is stark in this passage. The uncle who guards the abandoned mine seems alienated from the landscape: does he still listen closely enough to hear Chimakum Creek while he works? And if he does, this sound is ominous since it means that the creek is close enough to be contaminated by the pilings and ore left behind.

The unflinching details of the prose in "Haibun" create an important context for parsing the haiku that follow each paragraph. In the first haiku, grandmother seems to die a peaceful death at home, comforted by tangible memories of her children, and in the second haiku, "we" may be experiencing a moment of powerful vision, seeing salmon swimming, perhaps as numerously as they did before the time of dam construction and hydroelectric power. But the prose directs readers toward an unsettling reading of the haiku. Perhaps grandmother dies alone—with none of her children in attendance—because she's been poisoned by radioactivity or they've abandoned the reservation in despair. Perhaps the vision in the second haiku is actually of environmental disaster and skeletal fish: mere shadows of a formerly vital river ecosystem. These bleak readings also lead to a pessimistic view of tribalism in the poem—as an intangible diminishing resource that results in individual isolation.

If the poem ended at this point, it might also be read as a strong ecostatement by Alexie—a stance that would be out of character for an author who commented in a 2000 interview, "I think most Native American literature is so obsessed with nature that I don't think it has any useful purpose. It has more to do with the lyric tradition of European Americans than it does with indigenous cultures."[19] But haiku and haibun—as they have been written and revised by poets working in English (rather than Japanese)—have become poetic forms for voicing serious concerns.[20] Patricia Donegan's essay "Haiku and the Ecotastrophe," for example, argues that haiku is especially vital as a genre in critiquing the destructive forces of contemporary America:

> Stopping the ecocrisis, eliminating the bomb, or spreading the world's wealth more equitably is directly connected to stopping our own greed, aggressive tendencies and overconsumptive habits. The activities and personal habits of human beings are what contribute most powerfully to ecological imbalance and destruction of nature's ecosystems. Even the writing of one haiku, and therefore some recognition of our interconnectedness, is a small positive step beyond self-interest.[21]

Donegan's emphasis on interconnectedness and interdependence—on haiku as an ethical form—is evident in the densely encoded haiku that closes Alexie's poem:

> Two suns:
> Abel fell from the sky,
> Cain rose from the lake. (*SBW,* 30)

The play on sun/son sets up the possibility of a double reading that combines the biblical allusion with a reference to uranium-fueled bombs and mining. The bombs dropped on Hiroshima and Nagasaki—and the thousands of Japanese people who lost their lives—intertwine with the uranium-contaminated runoff on Indian lands and the resulting tragic fatalities, which together are embedded in the story of Cain and Abel: two brothers whose lives were destroyed because of one's jealousy, greed, and competitiveness.[22] Alexie's "Haibun" not only shows the underside of reservation life without a strong community, but it also speaks to the urgency of renewing tribal connections and collective support systems for contemporary Indians. As demonstrated in "Haibun" and other poems from *The Summer of Black Widows,* poetic and rhythmic forms become an evocative means of articulating crucial issues of survival and sovereignty.

LOCATING TRIBALISM

The tribal consciousness that emerges through the reservation poems in *The Summer of Black Widows* becomes a mobile worldview that Alexie's Indian speakers carry with them into locations well beyond the reservation. The final group of poems appears under the heading "Bob's Coney Island" and explores the ways that tribal identity and consciousness are articulated in diverse locations; indeed, several poems depict the way urban environments especially question *and* sustain Indianness.

The long poem, "Things (for an Indian) to Do in New York (City)," treats this question at length, unfolding in thirteen sections of various perspectives and poetics. The title—with its twin sets of parentheses—suggests the complex double positioning of the poem's speaker as he considers how his Indian identity may be read in the midst of New York City. With a comic twist, he borrows the phrasing of a tourist guide to explore questions about whether it is indeed possible to be/to act like an Indian in New York and how a Native person may articulate Indianness in a non-Native, urban, capitalist environment. Alexie's speaker directly raises the politics of race, ethnicity, and class to address these issues. As a person of dark skin in New York City, the speaker easily identifies the pre(in)-scribed positions he may occupy: some white passersby will quickly note his appearance and assign him racial derogations—as a "crazy man" or a "mugger"—while men of color may see him as a "brother" (*SBW*, 124).

The poem makes clear that New York City is a potent site ethnically for the speaker as he identifies himself as "brown":

> I think how when I left the reservation
> my entire world, which had been brown, became white
> but this is New York City and everybody is brown
> but this is America, too, and everybody is still
> white.... (*SBW*, 127)

Identifying himself as brown while located in New York City allows the speaker to claim not only his personal identity as an Indian enrolled in a specific tribal nation but also the possibility of seeing himself in a tribe of other minorities. As this poem suggests, thinking in terms of tribalism for Alexie is an act of resistance to the racism and violence of white America that may be carried out locally (by claiming one's Indigenous tribal identity) and globally (by participating in broader networks of resistance).

Significantly poetry and poetics become tools that enable the speaker of Alexie's poem to articulate his voice and worldview as an Indian even in the midst of New York City. Poetry becomes a charged, dynamic space where intercultural, interracial exchanges may occur:

> Read Ted Berrigan's sonnets
> and wonder how we are all alike
> but still have absolutely nothing
>
> in common. I stop bearded men
> and beautiful women in the streets
> and they're all poets. Everybody
>
> is bearded and beautiful. Everybody
> is a poet. I roll a drunk over
> in a doorway and he quotes

> Robert Frost. My God, he's home-
> less and formalist. How much money
> should I drop into his tin cup? (*SBW*, 125)

The homeless man—both a drunk and a poet—is part of the detritus of a capitalistic economy; for Alexie's speaker, he signifies someone relegated to the margins who nonetheless has a poetic, perhaps visionary message to communicate. The speaker sees the impulse toward poetry as democratic and freely available, including him in a nation of poets. But the poem also reminds readers that the official practice and status of poetry belong to published poets such as Ted Berrigan, Robert Frost, Emily Dickinson, and Walt Whitman (referenced elsewhere in the poem), who are part of the canons of white American literature and represent non-Native, Western poetic traditions. How is it possible to be drawn into this body of work in an Indian way?

This question haunts the speaker as he walks the streets of New York:

> and I'm frightened
> because I'm an Indian
> who knows the difference
> between Monet and Manet
>
> so I just watch TV
> because I am an American
> Indian and the walk to the subway
> can break both of my hearts. (*SBW*, 128)

The world of Monet and Manet is presented in opposition to Indianness in these lines, setting up a dilemma for the speaker who may want to claim a multiverse of cultural influences. The line break between "American/Indian" deepens the bifurcation: if anything is authentically Indian in this passage, it may be the capacity to be doubly heartbroken. This mixed inheritance is both curse and blessing: it threatens to divide the speaker and unsettle his sense of his own Indianness, but it also propels him forward to find words and a poetics to articulate his condition.

In the final section of the poem, the speaker finds he is not isolated, and the potential alienation that has been hovering is pushed aside when he realizes he rides the subway with a companion—his wife—who occupies the same personal and social space:

> there is another Indian, I mean, another American
> Indian sitting on the subway seat next to me—
> really, in the seat right beside me, our legs touch
> and I am convinced that she's Indian, Native
> American, Aboriginal, beneath her clothes
> and she's Indian in her clothes, and her clothes are Indian
> because she's wearing them. (*SBW*, 129–30)

Like the speaker, the Indian woman has a potentially bifurcated identity, which splits American/Indian and Native/American across lines. But she in fact represents a way to live and act as an American Indian no matter what the outside situation or context may be. To reiterate a key image, "her clothes are Indian"—not because they are necessarily traditional or visually represent her tribal affiliation but "because *she's* wearing them" (italics added). Thus, Alexie's poem signifies on the old adage "clothes make the man" by offering a vivid image of an Indian woman who remains beautifully and integrally Indian no matter what she wears, even when she is far from her people in the heart of New York City. Her sovereign Indianness moves the speaker to consider similar possibilities for himself.

Over the course of its thirteen sections, "Things (for an Indian) to Do in New York (City)" enacts a dynamic interchange that structures *The Summer of Black Widows* as a volume: alternating between a desire for rootedness and Indianness and a movement into non-Native spaces and influences. This tension could lead to irresolution, paralysis, or tragedy. But Alexie's poems locate ways to walk in both worlds and in fact highlight the tremendous creative energy that can emerge from a collision of identities, cultures, and poetics. Catherine Rainwater, in *Dreams of Fiery Stars,* compellingly describes the ways that contemporary Native novelists negotiate cultural and power politics between Native and Anglo America. She argues that Native novelists "have written themselves into the discourse of the dominant society and encoded it with alternative notions of what it means to inhabit the earth as human beings. These writers dream of nothing less than revision of contemporary reality."[23]

Rainwater emphasizes the way narrative and fiction as genres achieve this transformation; I want to extend her analysis to another genre—Alexie's poetry. The poems in *The Summer of Black Widows* remain unequivocally tribalist in poetics and ethics, even as they broaden the term *tribe* in ways that exceed Womack's insistence on the writer's specific tribal/national identity.[24] More importantly, Alexie's evocation of and reworking of traditional poetic forms transforms our assumptions of cultural power and allows us to think of the sonnet, for example, as an Indigenous form. By working within and against poetic rules—all the while eloquently singing Native American realities—Alexie creates a borderlands poetic space where the rhythms of the sonnet, couplet, haiku, and other forms become fused/transfused/transformed with the rhythms of fancy dancing, chanting, playing basketball, powwows, salmon swimming upriver, and all the other images of his painful and loving vision of Native America.

NOTES

I am grateful to Aparajita Sagar, Marcia Stephenson, Wendy Stallard Flory, and Richard Pearce for commenting on previous drafts of this essay.

1.   John Purdy, "Crossroads: A Conversation with Sherman Alexie," 12, 7.
2.   John Newton, "Sherman Alexie's Autoethnography," 424; Ron McFarland, "Sherman Alexie," in *Twentieth-Century American Western Writers,* 9; Susan Brill de Ramírez, "Sherman Alexie," in *Native American Writers of the United States,* 10.
3.   Cyrus R. K. Patell, "Representing Emergent Literatures," 62.
4.   Sherman Alexie, *The Summer of Black Widows,* 15 (hereafter cited in the text as *SBW*).
5.   Craig S. Womack, *Red on Red: Native American Literary Separatism,* 141.
6.   Ibid., 15.
7.   Laura Arnold Leibman, "A Bridge of Difference: Sherman Alexie and the Politics of Mourning," 545.
8.   Eric Gary Anderson, "Situating American Indian Poetry: Place, Community, and the Question of Genre," in *Speak to Me Words: Essays on Contemporary American Indian Poetry,* 53.

9. Ibid., 35.

10. Ibid., 54.

11. Conversations with my colleague Wendy Stallard Flory were especially helpful in formulating this point. Carrie Etter argues that Alexie's revision of the sonnet form rejects the couplet, hence its promise of resolution, and is primarily ironic; see Etter, "Dialectic to Dialogic: Negotiating Bicultural Heritage in Sherman Alexie's Sonnets," in *Telling the Stories: Essays on American Indian Literatures and Cultures,* 143–51. My reading of his more recent sonnets suggests lyrical (rather than ironic) appropriations of the form.

12. Traditional totem poles were part of the potlatch ritual carried out by Northwest coastal Indigenous people. This reference to a tradition not associated with the Spokane or Coeur d'Alene Tribes is part of Alexie's multicultural engagement. The commonplace expression "low man on the totem pole" is a misnomer: the best carver of the group usually worked on the lower figures since those were at eye level for most observers. Also—as the acclaimed carver Norman Tait (Nisga'a) explained to Vickie Jensen—"How you go from story to design depends on how the story unfolds"; see Jensen, *Where the People Gather: Carving a Totem Pole,* 15. In other words, the story that stands behind the pole, not social or cultural hierarchy, determines the placement of figures.

13. My phrasing echoes the title and argument of Philip J. Deloria's important book *Indians in Unexpected Places.* Deloria's work compellingly points to the need to expand our ideas of Indian identity and tradition to embrace the full, complex sense of Indian lives and experiences in the twentieth century.

14. See "National Statistics on the Death Penalty and Race," Death Penalty Information Center.

15. Ward Churchill and Winona LaDuke, "Native North America: The Political Economy of Radioactive Colonialism," in *The State of Native America: Genocide, Colonization, and Resistance,* 253.

16. Blaine Harden writes about the extensive damage to the Columbia River ecosystem through damming and hydroelectric and irrigation requirements, as well as nuclear contamination; see Harden, *A River Lost: The Life and Death of the Columbia.*

17. Churchill and LaDuke, "Native North America," 247–48. Churchill and LaDuke also report the alarming situation on Laguna lands, resulting from open-pit uranium mining by the Anaconda Corporation; see 258–61.

18. These statistics come from the Environmental Protection Agency's Web site for Midnite Mine. Another mining operation on the Spokane Reservation was the Sherwood Mine and Mill, but it operated for only a short time during the 1970s and has since been cleaned up. I want to thank Ellie Hale of the EPA for her assistance with this information.

    The SHAWL (Sovereignty, Health, Air, Water, and Land) Society is a Spokane Reservation organization working to educate the public about the long-lasting dangers of uranium poisoning and speak out against some of the details of the current cleanup plan for the Midnite Mine site.

19. Joelle Fraser, "An Interview with Sherman Alexie," 63.
20. Bruce Ross has written a helpful analysis of contemporary English *haibun;* see "North American Versions of Haibun and Postmodern American Culture," in *Postmodernity and Cross-Culturalism,* 168–200.
21. Patricia Donegan, "Haiku and the Ecotastrophe," in *Dharma Gaia: A Harvest of Essays in Buddhism and Ecology,* 204.
22. There's an uncanny historical connection in these stories as well: the plutonium that fueled the bomb dropped on Nagasaki came from the Hanford nuclear site, located about 120 miles from the Spokane Indian Reservation.
23. Catherine Rainwater, *Dreams of Fiery Stars: The Transformations of Native American Fiction,* ix.
24. Alexie's views on tribalism have evolved since the publication of *The Summer of Black Widows* in 1996. He has commented to interviewers in recent years that the events of September 11, 2001, have called into question tribalism as a source of fundamentalism for him, and he currently describes himself as a member of many tribes. This emerging thread in his interviews and published works—though beyond the scope of this essay—is provocative and merits further consideration.

CHAPTER 9

Sherman Alexie's Challenge to the Academy's Teaching of Native American Literature, Non-Native Writers, and Critics

Writing in the mystery genre, Sherman Alexie (Spokane/Coeur d'Alene) offers a critique of the academy in *Indian Killer* (1996) through the character of a Spokane Indian, Marie Polatkin, who is a political activist and a University of Washington student. In chapter seven, "Introduction to Native American Literature," Marie questions the syllabus for a course taught by Dr. Clarence Mather, a white male anthropologist and wannabe Indian who "wear[s] a turquoise bolo tie, and his gray hair tied back in a ponytail."[1] As Susan B. Brill de Ramírez notes, "Dr. Mather's syllabus, lectures, and interpretations of Indian literature demonstrate his erroneous and disturbingly romanticized misconceptions about Indians and their cultures and literatures."[2]

During the first class, Marie engages Dr. Mather in a debate about the reading list he has chosen for the course, arguing for the kinds of texts and authors that should be taught in a course titled Native American Literature. As an example of a contemporary female warrior, Marie feels empowered "to harass a white professor who [thinks] he [knows] what it [means] to be Indian" (*IK*, 61). Also, through the issues that Marie raises, she offers an opportunity to explore what Alexie proposes beyond his critique of Dr. Mather's reading assignments: texts that Marie believes are neither authentic nor the most appropriate examples of Native American literature.

In *Tribal Secrets: Recovering American Indian Intellectual Traditions,* Robert Allen Warrior (Osage) writes that possibilities open up to American Indians when they remove themselves from the dichotomy of "a death dance of dependence, on the one hand, abandoning [themselves] to the intellectual strategies and categories of white, European thought and, on the other hand, declaring that [they] need nothing outside of [themselves] and [their] cultures to understand the world and [their] place in it."[3] He goes on to state, "The struggle for sovereignty is not a struggle to be free from the influence of anything outside [themselves], but a process of asserting the power they possess as communities and individuals to make decisions that affect [their] lives."[4] Marie Polatkin perfectly illustrates the possibilities that become available to a Native woman who refuses such an "either-or" detrimental model.

Marie exploits mainstream education and political activism to her own advantage and that of urban Indians. An English major in her senior year (*IK,* 34), she is also the "activities coordinator for the Native American Students Alliance at the University" (*IK,* 31). Although she grew up on the reservation, she feels somewhat isolated from her Spokane roots because she neither speaks Spokane nor dances or sings traditionally, elements often recognized as signs of authentic Indianness (*IK,* 33). Still, she remains firmly grounded in her tribal connections, as evidenced by her surprise visits home to see her parents and her welcome to Reggie Polatkin, her distant urban cousin whom she has not seen in more than a year (*IK,* 34). Marie willingly shares her dinner of Apple Jacks cereal and allows Reggie to spend the night on her couch (*IK,* 90–91, 95).

Additionally—through her involvement in protests over Indian issues and her work with the Seattle downtown homeless shelter—Marie builds community among urban Indians (*IK,* 38–39). Her intellectual sovereignty resides in her Spokane and urban tribal connections, her academic involvement, and her political and social activism—all aspects of asserting the power she possesses as a member of a community and an individual who can make decisions that affect her life.

Alexie also portrays Marie as a powerful woman. He does not place women in the traditional Euro-American patriarchal paradigm of subordination. Rather, he seems to see women through the lens of gender complementarity, as discussed by anthropologists Laura F. Klein and Lillian A. Ackerman, who see it as balanced reciprocity: "They conclude that worlds of men and women [are] different but not generally perceived as hierarchical. In other words, while there are different roles expected of men and women, neither men's roles nor women's roles are considered superior; the efforts of both women and men are acknowledged as necessary for the well-being of the society."[5]

Further evidence of Alexie's views on women's roles in labor and religion in a patriarchal culture appears in two poems from his poetry collection, *One Stick Song* (2000). In "Water" he comments on both women and men working as airport security: "I'm pleased this airport has progressed / beyond an antiquated notion of gender roles,"[6] and in the poem "Why Indian Men Fall in Love with White Women," he describes a woman working in a donut shop as "a blessed and gifted woman who wanted to be a priest, a Jesuit / an Ignatian, of all things, but was turned back by the Catholic / Church / and its antiquated notions of gender" (*OSS*, 75–76). Clearly Alexie does not limit the possibilities for women based on their gender in work or religion, and Marie is evidence of his vision.

According to Ron McFarland, Marie's "family name associates [her] with Chief Polatkin, one of whose daughters was married to Qualchan, who led the Spokane, Palouse, and Coeur d'Alene tribes in 1858 against Colonel Wright."[7] Perhaps this daughter is the model for the wife of Qualchan that Alexie depicts as a female warrior in *The Lone Ranger and Tonto Fistfight in Heaven* (1993). In Thomas Builds-the-Fire's retelling of Qualchan's hanging, Alexie includes his wife's role: a traditional female warrior: "It was then I saw the hangman's noose and made the fight to escape. My wife also fought beside me with a knife and wounded many soldiers before she was subdued. After I was beaten down, they dragged me to the noose and I was hanged with six other Indians, including Epseal, who had never raised a hand in anger to any white or Indian."[8]

Although Alexie does not name the wife and devotes only one sentence to describing her actions, she is not insignificant. Plainly she acts as an independent woman, exercising her own power to be a warrior, an example of gender complementarity. Her response does not surprise anyone, and tribal members do not condemn her behavior. This example of a strong female warrior—who fearlessly attacks soldiers, fighting alongside her husband to prevent them from hanging him and successfully wounding many before they can restrain her—paints a picture of a woman who is not limited by her gender but valued for her fierce loyalty, courage, and bravery.

Additionally Qualchan's wife prefigures the contemporary version of a female warrior in the character of Marie Polatkin. The idea of physically powerful and mentally keen women, who are grounded in gender complementarity and valued for their strength, spans 150 years in Alexie's fiction. Alexie says of Marie, "She's the strength in the book."[9] Answering an interviewer's question about the characterization of Marie, he responded, "I wanted to write...an Indian woman character...who was like *most* of the Native women I know...a very intelligent, very ambitious, very dedicated, very politically active Indian woman."[10] Alexie connects his view of strong Native women to those he knows: presumably Spokane historical figures and ones on the Spokane Reservation and in an urban environment.

in Dr. Mather's course gives Marie the opportunity to demonstrate power. She challenges "his role as the official dispenser of 'Indian education' at the University," thereby privileging her Native knowledge and authority (*IK*, 58). Mather's attitude epitomizes what educator Paulo Freire describes as the "'banking' concept of education," where

knowledge is a gift bestowed by those who consider themselves knowledgeable upon those whom they consider to know nothing. Projecting an absolute ignorance onto others, a characteristic of the ideology of oppression, negates education and knowledge as processes of inquiry. The teacher presents himself to his students as their necessary opposite; by considering their ignorance absolute, he justifies his own existence.[11]

Marie enters the classroom, however, refusing to participate in the academy's patriarchal narrative or accept the role of receptacle that

Mather assigns to her; she will not allow him as narrator to fill her with his narration, one that she knows is false.[12] As she so astutely states after seeing his reading list, "Dr. Mather [is] full of shit" (*IK*, 59). She aggressively confronts the basis of Mather's knowledge: "You think you know more about being Indian than Indians do, don't you? Just because you read all those books about Indians, most of them written by white people" (*IK*, 247). Marie decenters his teacher-centered classroom, subverts his role of authority, and resists the idea of a knowledge hierarchy, one where dominant mainstream learning is considered more valuable than others. In sum she promotes an agenda of tribal intellectual sovereignty.

Marie identifies herself as a fighter: someone who believes that "being an Indian [is] mostly about survival" (*IK*, 34, 61). Therefore, her right to confront Mather is mainly personal, stemming from the fact that she is a Spokane Indian, a cultural insider who understands the importance of working for the survival of all Indian people. Moreover, her educational background and political protest experience give her the intelligence and self-confidence to defy Mather's oppressive ideology, one that claims superior knowledge over not only students but also Indians. While she recognizes that some people, such as the white student David Rogers, see her only as the exotic Other, like Pocahontas—another brown female minority to colonize by sleeping with her—Marie does not limit her possibilities because of her ethnicity or gender (*IK*, 61, 69). In fact, her political work allows her to create lines of communication that mediate among the communities of Native students, homeless people, and urban Indians on the one hand and mainstream institutions of power represented by the university, the police, and the press on the other. Fighting with words, she is a powerful contemporary female warrior, who proclaims, "I'm talking like a twentieth-century Indian woman. Hell, a twenty-first century Indian" (*IK*, 247).

Examining Marie's objections to Mather's reading list provides insights about Alexie's attitude regarding what instructors should teach in a Native American literature course. First, Marie criticizes Mather's selection of *The Education of Little Tree* (1976) by Forrest Carter, pointing out that the author's claims of Cherokee ancestry are fraudulent (*IK*, 59). Thus, rule number one for instructors compiling Native American reading lists is to select books authored by people with legitimate claims to

Indian identity. What constitutes legitimate Indian identity, at least according to Alexie, is best left for a Native scholar to determine.[13] However, within the context of *Indian Killer,* Alexie uses Marie, a Spokane woman who was raised on the reservation, as his mouthpiece.

The second objection that Marie raises deals with autobiographies cowritten by white men, such as *Black Elk Speaks* (1932) as told to John G. Neihardt, *Lame Deer: Seeker of Visions* (1972) by John Fire/Lame Deer and Richard Erdoes, and *Lakota Woman* (1990) by Mary Crow Dog and Richard Erdoes (*IK,* 58). Perhaps the fact that publishers categorize these books as autobiographies as opposed to "told-to-" or "told-through-white-men" books is what most annoys Alexie. It appears, however, that he would continue to oppose these books on Native American reading lists even if instructors were careful to inform students about the inherent problems of filtering by white recorders. Therefore, Alexie argues that any book cowritten by a white man should not be taught in a Native American literature course.

Finally, Marie makes basically the same observation about the rest of Mather's reading list, books all associated in some way with white people: "The other seven books included three anthologies of traditional Indian stories edited by white men, two nonfiction studies of Indian spirituality written by white women, a book of traditional Indian poetry translations edited by a Polish-American Jewish man, and an Indian murder mystery written by some local white writer named Jack Wilson, who claimed he was a Shilshomish Indian" (*IK,* 58–59).

Marie protests books that are edited, translated, or written by white people and argues that they do not meet the criteria of Native American literature. She also takes exception to authors who claim to be Indian but cannot prove membership in a tribe, thereby exploiting questionable Indian identity to further their literary careers (*IK,* 67). Marie argues that for texts to be classified as Native American, the author must truly be Native American, and when called into the department chair's office, she goes further by asking, "Why isn't an Indian teaching the class?" (*IK,* 312). Thus, through the character of Marie, Alexie strongly objects to what the academy teaches in Native American literature courses and even questions who teaches them.

Craig Womack (Muskogee Creek/Cherokee) shares Alexie's concerns regarding Native American literature and makes a similar argument when he writes, "One can teach courses on Native lit, and now even on Native literary criticism, assigning as texts, books authored exclusively by Native people.... The minimal requirement for a Native studies course should be that every classroom text is written by a Native author; otherwise, how can we possibly lay claim to presenting Native perspectives?"[14] For both Alexie and Womack, then, the determining factor for a Native American reading list is that the text should represent an authentic Native American perspective, one that only genuine Indians can deliver.

Marie's critique of the academy's teaching of Native American literature, white professors, and white writers in *Indian Killer* is not an isolated topic in Alexie's fiction. His complaint about white people speaking with authority for and about Indians appears frequently in his work. In his review of Ian Frazier's *Off the Rez*, Alexie writes, "Frazier's formal use of 'the rez' marks him as an outsider eager to portray himself as an insider, as a writer with a supposedly original story to tell and as a white man who is magically unlike all other white men in his relationship to American Indians."[15] Alexie rejects white writers who believe they understand the lives of American Indians and, by writing about Indians, perpetuate the colonizing act of telling the reading public what Indians are really like.

In his short story "Dear John Wayne" from *The Toughest Indian in the World* (2000), Alexie skewers the white anthropologist, Spencer Cox, who wants to interview 118-year-old Etta Joseph, born on the Spokane Indian Reservation and now a resident of the St. Tekawitha Retirement Community in Spokane, Washington. Currently Cox is working on a "study on the effect of classical European ballroom dancing on the Indigenous powwow," but Alexie has Etta control the interview, subvert Cox's agenda, tell her story about her love affair with John Wayne, and good-naturedly poke fun at the ridiculousness of Cox's self-importance.[16] Cox considers himself more of an expert on the Salish than the Indians themselves as he cites qualifications that identify him as an authority in academic circles: "I am a cultural anthropologist and the Owens Lecturer in Applied Indigenous Studies at Harvard University. I'm also the author of seventeen books, texts, focusing on mid- to late-twentieth-century Native

American culture, most specifically the Interior Salish tribes of Washington State" (*TIW,* 190). Again Alexie makes his point that no matter how many books Cox has published, he never will be able to speak authentically about Spokane Indians' lives.

Etta tells him that his books are filled with lies and he will never know about her. To survive, she has had to live her life in a white world for "fifty-seven minutes of every hour," and when Cox asks about the other three minutes, she responds, "That, sir, is when I get to be Indian, and you have no idea, no concept, no possible way of knowing what happens in those three minutes" (*TIW,* 194). As a strong female elder, Etta is a powerful woman who does not allow Cox to colonize her life: "Those three minutes belong to us. They are very secret. You've colonized Indian land but I am not about to let you colonize my heart and mind" (*TIW,* 194).

In his short story "One Good Man," also from *The Toughest Indian in the World,* Alexie blasts another white professor from Washington State University, Dr. Lawrence Crowell, not because he is a wannabe who spent time at the 1969 Alcatraz and 1973 Wounded Knee occupations but "because he thought he was entitled to tell other Indians what it meant to be Indian" (*TIW,* 227). In these examples, Alexie seems to object most to the arrogant attitudes of whites who think that just because they study, research, write, publish, and teach about Indians or their literature, they suddenly become experts on what it means to live life as an Indian, contrary to the intellectual sovereignty demonstrated in Alexie's own writing.

Alexie voices a familiar and legitimate complaint when he says, "Indians rarely get to define our own image, and when white people do it, they often get assigned all this authority, and I guess that's what my problem is, that Indians are never even allowed the authority to self-define."[17] This same theme appears in the poem "The Unauthorized Autobiography of Me," where he notes, "Successful non-Indian writers are viewed as well-informed about Indian life" (*OSS,* 22). In the same poem, Alexie discusses the economics of publishing when he critiques the whites who write about Indians: "A book written by a non-Indian will sell more copies than a book written by either a mixed-blood or an Indian writer," and "Most non-Indians who write about Indians are fiction writers. Fiction about Indians sells" (*OSS*, 21, 22). He has suggested that white authors who write fiction about Indians at the very least should donate 10 percent of their royalties either to the American Indian College Fund or to the tribe about which they write.[18] He admits, "I'm resentful that there are many writers out there making careers off Indians and...doing absolutely nothing in return.... People ask me and I give hard-core answers. You're making money, give it back."[19] Consequently, Alexie's objections to whites writing about Indians are based not only on their arrogance and sense of authority to define Indians but also on the profits they gain from their fiction about Indians.

By introducing the general reading public to the issues surrounding the way whites teach Native American literature in the academy, Alexie raises their awareness. This is the first step in effecting change, but he does not offer anything more beyond his critique of white arrogance. No solutions can be inferred to poor choices by either unknowingly or willfully ignorant professors. He does not offer any suggestions for white scholars. His only advice recommends deferring to Native scholars and writers because they have the authority of cultural insiders. In an interview for *Indian Killer*, he expresses the following wish: "I would like to reach a larger audience and using a popular form like the mystery might enable me to do that."[20] He also has said, "First and foremost, writers like to get attention."[21] Alexie's desires to reach a larger audience, get attention, and at the same time expect that white scholars will not write about his works as they teach them in Native American literature classes call for changes that seem unlikely to happen in the near future.

According to Alexie's statements, non-Native scholars may not seem to have a role in critiquing his works because they cannot speak with the authority of cultural insiders. True, they are limited by their position, but at the same time, not all non-Native scholars attempt to speak with the authority of cultural insiders. Some white scholars consciously listen to what Native scholars and critics prescribe in approaching the literature, whether those are tribal-specific cultural and historical contexts, issues of sovereignty and connections to the land, and/or literary criticisms related to the particular tribe.[22]

In a more constructive fashion, Womack briefly addresses the roles of white critics through one of his fictional characters who asks, "How can white Lit Critters become helpers, rather than Indian experts? How can they promote the work of Native people over their own, and...keep up their own good efforts at contributing to Native literary development?"[23] Writing about American Indian history, Angela Cavender Wilson (Wahpetonwan Dakota) suggests that white scholars consult American Indian sources for cultural insiders' perspectives, and if they do not, they should acknowledge the limitations of their perspective in their work.[24] In the same way, perhaps white scholars writing about Native literature should consult Native sources or acknowledge their limited perspective.

White scholars observing all these caveats about teaching Native American texts in an academic climate that demands expertise, knowledge, and authority in their specialization may encounter problems. Negotiating the academic climate and the requests from Native writers and scholars to observe basic considerations can be difficult but not impossible. Duane Champagne (Chippewa) argues that "there is room for both Indian and non-Indian scholars within American Indian studies," but he also remarks that those involved in American Indian studies experience difficulties because their "academic colleagues operate from different values and cultural perspectives"[25] or, as Elizabeth Cook-Lynn (Crow Creek Sioux) says, "the esoteric language of French and Russian literary scholars...has overrun the lit/crit scene."[26]

Sherman Alexie maintains a sense of personal identity through connections to his Spokane tribe while engaging in a critical dialogue with the academic and larger community. In *Indian Killer*, he accomplishes this task, in part, through the character of Marie Polatkin. Alexie has argued that "there are no models of any success in any sort of field for Indians. We don't have any of that. So there is no idea of a role model existing."[27] Without a doubt, Alexie creates the role model of a successful Spokane Indian woman in Marie's character. She is a strong, autonomous, intellectually sovereign woman who, among other things, challenges the academy about who should teach Native American literature and what that person assigns to be read. As a female voice, Marie's challenge develops from gender complementarity; she knows that her community will value her role as a contemporary female warrior of words. Non-Native scholars need to heed her message.

NOTES

This essay was first presented at the American Literature Association Symposium on Native American Literature in Puerto Vallarta, November 29–December 3, 2000. I wish to thank the participants who attended the session on Sherman Alexie for their feedback and discussion following that panel.

1. Sherman Alexie, *Indian Killer,* 58 (hereafter cited in the text as *IK*).
2. Susan B. Brill de Ramírez, "Sherman Alexie," in *Native American Writers of the United States,* 10.
3. Robert Allen Warrior, *Tribal Secrets: Recovering American Indian Intellectual Traditions,* 123–24.
4. Ibid., 124.
5. Laura F. Klein and Lillian A. Ackerman, eds., *Women and Power in Native North America,* 14.
6. Sherman Alexie, *One Stick Song,* 10 (hereafter cited in the text as *OSS*).
7. Ron McFarland, "Sherman Alexie's Polemical Stories," 34.
8. Sherman Alexie, *The Lone Ranger and Tonto Fistfight in Heaven,* 98–99.
9. Bernadette Chato, "Book-of-the-Month: *Reservation Blues*," *Native America Calling.*
10. Italics added. Emerald City Productions, *Indian Killer,* audiocassette.
11. Paulo Freire, *The Pedagogy of the Oppressed,* 58–59.
12. Ibid., 58.
13. Indian authenticity is a complicated issue that I will not address here; there are various federal, state, tribal, and cultural definitions to determine who is an Indian, and they carry different degrees of validity depending on who makes the judgment. For more information, see M. Annette Jaimes, "Federal Indian Identification Policy: A Usurpation of Indigenous Sovereignty in North America," in *The State of Native America: Genocide, Colonization, and Resistance,* 123–38.
14. Craig S. Womack, *Red on Red: Native American Literary Separatism,* 10.
15. Sherman Alexie, "Some of My Best Friends," 3.
16. Sherman Alexie, *The Toughest Indian in the World,* 193 (hereafter cited in the text as *TIW*).
17. "Online Chat with Sherman Alexie," *Chats & Events,* May 1, 2000. barnesandnoble.com but no longer accessible.
18. Tomson Highway, "Spokane Words: Tomson Highway Raps with Sherman Alexie."
19. Ibid.
20. Interview by Emerald City Productions.
21. John Purdy, "Crossroads: A Conversation with Sherman Alexie," 11.
22. On October 21, 2000, my research assistant attended the book fair in Seattle, Washington, and presented Alexie with the question, "What would you recommend for white scholars who want to study Native American literature?" To date he has not responded.

23. Womack, *Red on Red,* 127.

24. Angela Cavender Wilson, "American Indian History or Non-Indian Perceptions of American Indian History?" in *Natives and Academics: Researching and Writing about American Indians,* 26.

25. Duane Champagne, "American Indian Studies Is for Everyone," in *Natives and Academics: Researching and Writing about American Indians,* 181, 188.

26. Elizabeth Cook-Lynn, "American Indian Intellectualism and the New Indian Story," in *Natives and Academics: Researching and Writing about American Indians,* 137.

27. "A Dialogue on Race with President Clinton," *The NewsHour with Jim Lehrer.*

CHAPTER 10

"Indians Do Not Live in Cities, They Only Reside There"

Captivity and the Urban Wilderness in Indian Killer

Sherman Alexie's novel *Indian Killer* (1996) has been described as a detective novel and a suspense thriller; however, these classifications are too simplistic. Alexie's novel does not set out to pose and solve a mystery, at least not in the conventional manner of detective novels. There is no sleuth, and the killer's identity is never solved. The novel reveals the injustices forced upon Native people, particularly as they journey through a modern cityscape. The Puritans who landed on the East Coast of North America saw the wilderness as symbolic of evil forces that were to test their souls, and they recorded these trying experiences with the Indigenous peoples in captivity narratives. In *Indian Killer,* Alexie plays with the concept of captivity narratives because his Native characters are trapped in an urban wilderness, dealing with the perils of modern, urban life. In one sense, *Indian Killer* is a mystery since all the characters attempt to solve their own mysteries in relation to the particular landscapes of their tribal and urban identities, and John Smith—adopted as an infant by a white family with no knowledge of his tribal heritage— seems the most lost.

John Smith is the focus of the novel, and readers follow his struggle to find his place in the Seattle wilderness. Smith was born on a reservation, and all he knows of his birth is that his mother was fourteen years old when she had him. All other information was concealed from him and his adoptive parents. As the focus of the novel, John's story deviates from the form of a more traditional detective novel. The superficial, sensational story of *Indian Killer* focuses on determining the identity of the serial killer/kidnapper and finding out whether he or she is Native. All of this seems irrelevant in relation to the story of John Smith's captivity. It's especially irrelevant because at the end of the novel, none of the characters are certain about the identity of the killer. Alexie withholds the pleasure of knowing, unequivocally, the satisfying conclusion that results from reading a standard detective novel where a suspect is singled out by a cunning detective and all questions are answered and wrapped up neatly. By the conclusion of *Indian Killer,* the killer is neither apprehended nor identified. Furthermore, John's quest similarly ends without answers.

One of the devices that Alexie employs throughout the novel follows a long tradition in Native American literature (in English), a device that I call the reverse captivity narrative. Since European settlers began coming to North America, they have written accounts of their encounters with Indigenous populations, and many of them document their captures. Among the most famous are *The Captivity of Mary Rowlandson* and the several travel journals of Captain John Smith. At the turn of the twentieth century, Native writers like Gertrude Simmons Bonnin related their captivity experiences as young children forced into boarding schools and missions. These writers used similar structures to those of the earlier colonial writers. Similarly, Alexie, at the turn of the twenty-first century, is writing about a form of captivity experienced by young Indians adopted before the Indian Child Welfare Act of 1978.

Alexie's story is not about his personal experiences as much as his generation; it is a story about Indians who are raised among whites with little or no understanding of their culture, who often do not even know the name of their tribe. Like some of the white missionaries that Bonnin had to endure, the adoptive parents of John Smith do not intend to harm their child; in fact, Alexie portrays the parents as sympathetic despite their naïveté in raising a nonwhite child and giving him a horribly ironic name. To understand *Indian Killer,* one must first examine the federal policies of Indian reform during the late twentieth century that pushed Indian people into urban environments—the wilderness that Alexie and other Native authors create—as well as the history of the reverse captivity narrative and John Smith's capture and quest for identity. Also, readers must realize why the Indian killer is never identified and defying standard detective novel format and expectations is a symbolic gesture.

The lonely urban landscapes that Alexie depicts are not uncommon to Native people. Diana Meyers Bahr reports, "Although urban Indians constitute more than 50 percent of the North American native population, Indians in the city are often considered the invisible minority."[1] The title of my essay comes from a Carroll Arnett poem, which Alexie refers to in *Reservation Blues.* In this poem, the speaker clearly expresses his feeling about urban identities: "Indians do not live in cities, they only reside there."[2] This is not to suggest that Indians only belong in pristine natural settings, but rather to clarify that the current urban environment is an unwelcoming Euro-American construction. Grappling with issues of urban identity is nothing new to Native authors. Alexie follows in a long line of Native authors critiquing the colonial imposition of termination and relocation projects in the 1950s. These projects—masked as helping Indians become part of mainstream American society—left Indian people disconnected from their tribal lands and struggling in large cities.

The termination and relocation projects began in the 1940s. In 1943 the Senate Interior Committee was ready to do away with the Bureau of Indian Affairs.[3] Committees were formed to find ways to end federal supervision of Indian tribes. By February 1954, Senator Arthur Watkins, head of the Indian Subcommittee of the Senate Interior Committee, pushed to "get rid of as many tribes as possible before the 1956 elections."[4] Termination procedures sought to abolish tribes' power and gain reservation land. Termination "was coupled with the 'Relocation Act,' a statute passed in 1956 and designed to coerce reservation residents to disperse to various urban centers around the country."[5] Along with the termination proceedings, the enactment of Public Law 280 "placed many reservations under the jurisdiction of individual States of the Union, thereby reducing the level of native sovereignty to that held by counties or municipalities."[6] Many Indians moved to large cities because of the promise of economic success, but most did not experience a better life.

Vine Deloria refers to the Relocation Act of 1956 as one of the most "disastrous" policies ever initiated. He writes, "It began as a policy of the Eisenhower administration as a means of getting Indians off the reservation and into the city slums where they could fade away."[7] Many Indians eventually returned to the reservations; however, even today, Native people are forced economically to leave reservations or other rural lands to make a living.

Many Native authors have responded to the urban experience. N. Scott Momaday's protagonist Abel in *House Made of Dawn* finds himself lost in Los Angeles, but he does not reconcile his issues of identity until he is back on his home ground. Greg Sarris's *Grand Avenue* offers a more contemporary view of Indians coping with urbanization in Los Angeles. Most of the characters go there for no other reason than work. Nila northSun writes in her poem "up & out" about her family moving off the reservation to the city to find jobs: "the city had jobs but it also / had high rent / high food high medical / high entertainment high gas / we made better money but it / got sucked up."[8] At the end of the poem, she writes, "God how I hated living on the reservation / but now / it doesn't look so bad."[9]

This awkward position of Indian people between homeland and the need for jobs to survive is best summed up in Simon Ortiz's poem "Final Solution: Jobs, Leaving," which relates the way Ortiz as a child lamented his father having to leave the Acoma Pueblo for work: "Surrounded by the United States, / We had come to need money."[10] Encroaching ranches, mining enterprises, and other economic ventures forced—and still do—Indians to take places in an ever-expanding marketplace that only seems to destroy their tribal lands and identification with these lands. When they reach the city, they are held captive by bills and other financial obligations, as well as the lifestyle. northSun writes about the way the money gets eaten up by "lunches in cute places / by drinking in quaint bars."[11]

Native authors also refer to the conspicuous invisibility of being an Indian in a city. To echo the words of the earlier Deloria quotation, relocation and termination projects caused Indians to "fade away" in an urban setting. Alexie plays with the concept of urban invisibility and alienation as well. From the beginning of the novel, he clearly establishes imagery that evokes feelings of despair about Seattle's cityscape. John is working on "the last skyscraper in Seattle," and later in the novel, he wonders "what would happen to him after the construction was complete."[12]

The city exacerbates John's agony about his identity and future. As he works on the skyscraper, he fears plummeting to his death despite using the safety precautions his coworkers take: "John was attached to the building by a safety harness, but he knew that white men made the harnesses. It would only save white men" (IK, 76). The cityscape itself is unreliable, and any connection to the structures for John—or Indians in general insofar as he represents them—means death. The city is described in terms of destruction and depression. Alexie details Seattle's early settlers' taste in developing land: "The Danes, the Swedes, and Norwegians had missed the monotonously flat landscapes of their own countries, and wanted their new country to remind them of home. Since the first days of their colonization of the Americas, European immigrants had strived to make the New World look exactly like the Old.... All John knew was that everything in this country had been changed, mutated" (IK, 73).

This city is a place of war, a national monument to colonization. To John cities represent European victory and—like the safety harnesses— are built for whites only. He looks at the city as a waste of space, and he sees the building he works on as being "pointless." Before John jumps off the skyscraper to his death, he thinks that the world around him seems to be busy and alive but the city represents death: "John knew that every building in Seattle contained the bones of fallen workers. Every building was a tomb"(IK, 405). He knows that his search for identity in the city is futile because he believes only whites can make sense of themselves in an urban setting.

Only on another plane of existence outside of the confines of the city can John achieve peace, whether in death or dreams. In the city, the only place he feels at home is the imaginary reservation of his daydreams. John's reservation of the mind is a happy place with a loving family, and "it's a good life, not like all the white people believe reservation life to be" (IK, 43). The reservation he believes he belongs to is a place of warm memories, memories that John feels have been robbed. His life in the city away from his tribe is a time of captivity.

Alexie uses this theme of captivity to make a statement about America's policies of termination and relocation, which included seizing Indian children and adopting them out to white couples so the children would have a better chance at assimilation. Captivity stories have roots deep in the American consciousness. The captivity narrative was one of the first genres of American literature. It began with *The Captivity of Mary Rowlandson* in 1682. The form became popular because of the settlers' deep religious convictions as they struggled against the evil unknown of the New World. Eric J. Sundquist asserts that "the colonial captivity narrative, such as Mary Rowlandson's, made its heroines and heroes representative of a larger community whose resolve was being tested by the satanic forces of the wilderness.... The captive's greatest risk was not death but rather the temptation to identify with the alien way of life and become a savage."[13]

The early captivity narratives of the colonists often served as justification for eradicating Indian cultures and securing the frontier by grabbing land and resources from Indian people. Alexie also uses his novel to justify the desire to eradicate white culture, especially since its conclusion references the Ghost Dance, which Wovoka hoped would rid Indian lands of Western culture.

Alexie is not the first to reverse the original form of the captivity narrative. At the turn of the twentieth century, Native authors began to employ the same techniques once popularized by their white predecessors. Gertrude Simmons Bonnin, a Yankton Sioux author also known as Zitkala-Ša, expressed to a largely white audience the alienation and suffering she had to endure as a child captive in the Carlisle Indian School. By the time she began publishing her works in 1901, the captivity narrative had merged with sentimental "women's literature" of the era and lost much of the significance it once carried. Although still widely read, the white captivity narratives had ceased to reveal an aboriginal threat to Western society since most lands had already been seized from Indian people. Bonnin cleverly brought the genre back but in different form.

Her essays—"Impressions of an Indian Childhood," "The School Days of an Indian Girl," and "An Indian Teacher among Indians"—illustrate

Bonnin's frustrations with the white world. Throughout her essays, she uses words like "confusion," "bedlam," and "frightened." One of her experiences as a child was having her hair cut by the matron: "Our mothers taught us that only unskilled warriors who were captured had their hair shingled by the enemy."[14] After trying unsuccessfully to hide from getting her hair cut, Bonnin remembers being "dragged out" and "tied fast in a chair."[15] This violence-laden language clearly describes a child held in captivity against her will.

Bonnin recounts several other grueling experiences, such as being punished for speaking her tribal language, feeling alienated from her mother on a visit home, and being ridiculed at a collegiate oratory competition. Many of her essays expressing her experiences as a captive were published in *Harper's* and *The Atlantic Monthly* and targeted specifically at white audiences. According to Dexter Fisher, "She had already become the darling of a small literary coterie in Boston whose members were enthusiastic about the autobiographical sketches, and short stories she had begun to place" in these prominent magazines.[16]

The key word that Fisher uses is "darling." Bonnin realized that she was a token in the white world. Her audiences were not responding as she wished to her essays, and although her white audience appeared to be sympathetic, its members did not understand her experience as captivity. Bonnin found herself in a difficult position; she had already become an educated outcast from her family so she could not simply return to the Yankton Reservation. She left her budding literary career to become involved in activism for Indian rights. Bonnin understood that white audiences were not ready to appreciate fully the reverse captivity narratives, and her refusal to continue writing is significant because—just as the colonists feared becoming Indian—she wanted to resist the temptation of success in mainstream America to maintain her cultural identity.

Theoretically Alexie's novel resembles Bonnin's works. The Indian characters in *Indian Killer* are constantly forced into situations that further their alienation. When they resist the white world, they are punished. Alexie is one of the first widely published authors to focus attention on the continuing captivity of Indian children. The novel's central character, John Smith, is held captive because of the rules regarding the adoption of Indian children. Before the Indian Child Welfare Act

(ICWA) in 1978, Indian children could be taken from their families and given to non-Indian families, most of them white. The government officials who assessed the living conditions of the Indian families were also mainly white. This intrusion was based on non-Indian values and assumptions.

Not many people in government agencies considered this treatment of Indian children captivity, but Indian leaders do. During the investigative hearings on the ICWA in 1980, Frank Black Elk, director of the Society of Native Peoples, eloquently made the connection:

> I have been the victim of an oppressive system called the welfare state known as social services. I was captured and held hostage until my parents would conform, but my parents refused.... I was held in captivity for 11 years and seven months.... The foster homes and institutions where I was held in bondage attempted to brainwash my mind by various means similar to control units within federal prisons which have the sole purpose of behavior modification.... The basics were cultural identity and traditional deprivation.... I was forced to believe that my culture was dead and non-existent.... A point I'd like to make is that this genocidal act of separating Native children from their natural parents must no longer prevail if we are truly concerned with the welfare and mental health of our Native children.[17]

Black Elk's testimony about his childhood uses similar language to Bonnin's and Alexie's. Fortunately for Black Elk, his tribal elders worked hard to bring him home. Later in his testimony, he tells of his happy return to tribal traditions and family ties.

Alexie sets the scene of John Smith's capture including details much like those recounted by Bonnin and Black Elk. *Indian Killer* opens with John's birth in an Indian hospital on an unidentified reservation. The opening chapter is written as though it is fantasy, but John's departure from the reservation marks the symbolic journey of a captivity narrative. The helicopter that comes to take John to his adoptive parents contains a pilot and a gunman, a situation that seems drastic considering that the adoption of a child does not usually require armed surveillance. Alexie writes, "Suddenly this is a war. The jumpsuit man holds John close to his chest as the helicopter rises. The helicopter gunman locks and loads, strafes the reservation with explosive shells...John is hungry and cries uselessly. He cannot be heard over the roar of the gun, the chopper. He cries anyway." (*IK*, 6).

This is a modern capture scene. Although Indian children were not generally taken away from their reservations with such military force, Alexie is physically representing the internal violence in taking an Indian child out of his or her community. This image of John crying against a noisy backdrop with no one to hear his suffering mirrors images in captivity narratives, especially Bonnin's, and her frustrating attempts to communicate with the missionaries. She writes of her first encounter with the government school: "Many voices murmuring an unknown tongue made a bedlam within which I was securely tied. And though my spirit tore itself in struggling for its lost freedom, all was useless."[18] This bedlam is the first thing that John encounters; Alexie also describes John's cries as "useless."

According to a report by the U.S. Bureau of Indian Affairs, "The Native American family system has been and is subjected to enormous economic, social, and cultural pressures," and the Native family structure is under attack due to ignorance about the way extended family networks function.[19] One of the conclusions of the report is that if the Native family structure had been left alone and "if this social structure were still intact, there would be no child neglect."[20] Frank Black Elk's story and Alexie's portrayal of John Smith are not aberrations but rather the norm in describing the way government involvement prior to the ICWA affected Indian families and tribal relations.

Native American author Louise Erdrich portrays the common practice for extended families to raise children in the community just as Marie Kashpaw, in *Love Medicine,* takes care of June and Lipsha. Catherine Rainwater—in explaining the real-world underpinnings of Erdrich's character Marie—contends that "the idea that biological children are somehow superior or preferred over other children who belong in a nuclear family is a Western European, not a Native American, concept."[21]

But because it was not typical of government agencies to recognize a different worldview in relation to child care, it is no surprise that stories like John Smith's exist.

The ICWA was established to battle cultural ignorance, and "it dictates exclusive tribal jurisdiction over any child custody proceeding involving a child who resides on or is domiciled within the reservation."[22] Basically no child can be placed with any foster family without permission of the tribe, and there is an established order that tribes follow when placing a child: "1. Member of the child's extended family; 2. Other members of the child's tribe; 3. Other Indian families."[23] Also, at the age of eighteen, children have the legal right to obtain any information they seek regarding their tribal affiliation and family ties. If this kind of information had been made available to people in John Smith's position, their stories could have been different.

In the early 1990s, there was a push for a grandfather clause that would let children born before 1978 have access to their personal records. In *Indian Killer,* Alexie illustrates what can happen to children who are not allowed such access. While most of the main characters suffer through one form of alienation or another, John Smith endures the greatest hardship in coming to terms with his lack of identity. In an interview with Tomson Highway, Alexie says of the adoption of Indian children: "The social problems and dysfunctions of these Indians adopted out are tremendous. Their suicide rates are off the chart, their drug and alcohol abuse rates are off the chart."[24] Accordingly Alexie's novel reasserts the importance of giving a tribe autonomy over the way its children are raised.

Adoption proceedings before 1978 were mostly clandestine. Bruce Davies states that the adoption of Indian children before 1940 was rare. He writes, "Transracial adoptions began in the 1940s and reached a high point in the 1950s and 1960s, declining in the 1970s, when Indian and Black organizations began to attack the practice."[25] In *Indian Killer,* when the Smiths are given the option of adopting an Indian baby, the agent tells them, "Now, ideally, we'd place this baby with Indian parents, right? But that just isn't going to happen. The best place for this baby is with a white family. This child will be saved a lot of pain by growing up with a white family" (*IK*, 10). These words support the arguments of Davies and others who have revealed the racist prerogative of adoption agents. By the early 1970s, minority organizations were contending that the needs of the children were not being considered; rather, the adoption agencies "were only responding to the needs of their white clientele."[26]

Since John was born in the late 1960s, he is prohibited from knowing his tribal affiliation. Alexie describes his birth mother: "John's mother is Navajo or Lakota. She is Apache or Seminole" (*IK*, 4). He is making the statement that what happened to one tribe has happened to all of them. All Indian tribes have been subjected to having their children taken away.

John's personal quest for identity throughout the novel is laden with captivity imagery. Alexie uses similar techniques to Bonnin's to describe another form of child captivity. John as a twenty-seven-year-old is depicted as having long black hair and harboring a secret desire "to carry a pair of scissors and snip off those ponytails [of young white men] at every opportunity" (*IK*, 23). His hatred of white men with ponytails echoes the significance Bonnin places on having long hair.

When John resolves to kill a white man to give what he thinks is a positive direction to his life, he thinks it should be a "white man responsible for everything that had gone wrong" (*IK*, 27). He wants to harm his tormentor, whom he perceives as the persecutor of all Indian people. In his anger, he lashes out at a system that has stolen his identity. He considers the richest white man as his victim: "John knew that Bob or Dan must have sold his soul, that slaves worked in his factories. Thousands of children. No. Indians. Thousands of Indians chained together in basements, sweating over stupid board games that were thinly disguised imitations of Scrabble and Monopoly, cheap stuffed monkeys, and primitive computer games where all the illegal space aliens were blasted into pieces" (*IK*, 28).

John projects his feelings of cultural captivity and loss upon an imaginary group of Indians being forced to work against their will for the gain of whites in an industrial setting making name-brand knock-offs. He perceives this fate as his own since he works for a construction company building the urban wilderness that is trapping him. The image of "illegal space aliens" being shot down accompanies his fear of the foreign culture where he lives. Indians made to help others create toys to teach children to kill Otherness is a striking image and again compounds John's interior-captivity visions.

John tries throughout the novel to escape his world. After work one day, he becomes overwhelmed by the voices he hears. Alexie writes, "He wanted to run. Everybody would notice. Everybody would know that he was thinking about killing white men" (*IK,* 30). His inclination to get away from downtown Seattle suggests a man in captivity looking for any possible escape.

As John searches for avenues of freedom, Alexie interjects a personal comment: "White people no longer feared Indians. Somehow, near the end of the twentieth century, Indians had become invisible, docile" (*IK,* 30). John's inability to connect to Indian identity is the result of Euro-American institutions weakening the tribes by taking away their children and trying to make them white. Perhaps one of the main reasons that the ICWA gained acceptance in Congress was because at the end of the 1970s, Indians were no longer perceived as a threat to whites. Their sovereignty issues did not interfere with most government practices. Most Indian lands were gone, and the majority of Indian children had been taught the tenets of Christianity and made to speak English. Since the end of the 1990s, there has been a push among tribal governments to convince the federal government that they deserve many more rights due sovereign nations. If they do gain more power, it will be interesting to see if they are allowed continued sovereignty over family courts. Suzanne Garner cautions, though, "without adequate funding and a responsible monitoring system it [ICWA] may never fully reach its goal."[27] Although many people support the ICWA and see it as a giant step toward tribal self-determination, there exists the reality that ultimately its success rests on the whim of federal policy.

Some may consider John Smith's visions and daydreams delusional, yet they have a ring of truth. His paranoia has five hundred-year-old roots. Contact with European and Western values has generally been detrimental for Indians. John's fear and shame of having been brought up in a white home is justified; however, Alexie does not make the Smiths terrible people. Their confusion is sympathetic, but their ignorance still produces malicious effects. Similarly the missionaries and "friends of the

Indian" of the nineteenth century who set out to help Indians often only managed to pass damaging legislation such as the Dawes Act, which was meant to give Indians a sense of individualism but caused them to lose more than half of their land.

Throughout the novel, John continually weakens his ties with his adoptive parents and tries to move closer to what he thinks he should do to assert his Indianness; however, the non-Native characters' disregard for tribal identity creates the "generic Indian" that John tries to overcome. He spends most of his life with his parents trying to understand what it means to be Indian. His mother does research on different tribes, his room is decorated with Indian art, he listens to powwow music, and his parents take him to Indian events. Alexie makes the point that simply going through the motions and associating with Indian culture is not what Indian identity is about. Being an Indian is about being a member of a tribal community. Even if someone is an outcast from his or her tribe, that person still understands who he or she is. John's only communication with his tribe is in his dreams, a fact that continues to reinforce the idea that not knowing your tribal identity means a life of loneliness and isolation.

Dying is the only way John can see to escape from captivity. He ties Jack Wilson to a beam at the top of the skyscraper that he has been helping to build. Before he captures Wilson, a detective novelist who desperately wants to be Indian, he already knows that Wilson cannot be trusted and that his misappropriation of Indian culture makes him worse than the whites who seek to enslave Indians physically. John whispers to Wilson, "Let me, let us have our own pain" (*IK*, 411). At no other time in the novel has John been able to see himself as part of an Indian community. His acknowledgment of "our pain" is the way John grasps some sense of his Indianness.

At the end of the novel, John frees himself from captivity by plunging to his death from the top of the building. But his death does not signal the end of his life or his journey to find his identity. John's ghost stands over his dead body and pulls from his pocket the photograph of his family and an article about Father Duncan and quickly puts them back into the "fallen man's" pocket. John is no longer a visible image of an Indian, no longer physically tied to what it means to look like an Indian. His ghost does not run to his next destination as the captive John has run in down-town Seattle—he walks. Even though John's death is gruesome, a calm hopefulness accompanies the event.

John's death does not answer any questions for Alexie's readers, and it shouldn't. Instead, John's story raises questions about identity and community. And just as John's death holds no definite answers, the last chapter devoted to the Indian killer does not give any more clues to his or her identity. The end of the novel may be disappointing for readers who need to know who the villain is and want to see the criminal punished. Slavoj Žižek contends that classical detective stories—like those created by Sir Arthur Conan Doyle—present an array of suspects with everyone knowing that the culprit is among the group. When the detective reveals the perpetrator, the rest of the group and the audience feel relief.[28]

Rather than delve deeply into the psychoanalytical interpretation, I prefer to focus on Žižek's idea of the way the audience is released at the end of detective novels. For Alexie the identity of the Indian killer must remain a mystery because the audience must stay implicated—captives to the severity of the message. Justice for an Indian reader might be that Wovoka's prophecy comes to pass and the continent is returned to Indigenous people. However, there is no scapegoat to relieve an audience. Alexie does not give his audience the satisfaction of feeling that Wilson and Mather will get what they deserve, that Reggie will be cleared, or that John Smith will find what he seeks.

The ending confirms the message that Indian identity is highly complex. Indian people must struggle against government policy, urban landscapes, white academia, and everyday existence to resist captivity and retain their identities as Indians. The Indian characters in *Indian Killer* are imprisoned and have their voices muffled by urban noise. Alexie offers no simple solutions, and although the novel appears to be American Indian literature or a murder mystery, the implications go far deeper than these simple categories. The quest for identity amid cultural captivity is the real focus of the novel, and readers must understand this to appreciate *Indian Killer* fully.

NOTES

1. Diana Meyers Bahr, *From Mission to Metropolis: Cupeño Indian Women in Los Angeles,* 6.
2. Carroll Arnett, *Night Perimeter: New and Selected Poems, 1958–1990,* 22.
3. Vine Deloria Jr., *Custer Died for Your Sins: An Indian Manifesto,* 55 (page references are to the 1988 edition).
4. Ibid., 62.
5. Ward Churchill, *Struggle for Land: Native North American Resistance to Genocide, Ecocide, and Colonization,* 52.
6. Ibid.
7. Deloria, *Custer Died for Your Sins,* 157.
8. Nila northSun, "up & out," in *American Indian Literature: An Anthology,* 291.
9. Ibid., 292.
10. Simon Ortiz, *Woven Stone,* 318.
11. northSun, "up & out," 291.
12. Sherman Alexie, *Indian Killer,* 24, 103 (hereafter cited in the text as *IK*).
13. Eric J. Sundquist, "The Frontier and American Indians," in *Prose Writing 1820–1865,* vol. 2 of *The Cambridge History of American Literature,* 218–19.
14. Gertrude Simmons Bonnin, *American Indian Stories,* 54.
15. Ibid., 55.
16. Dexter Fisher, "Zitkala-Ša: The Evolution of a Writer," 229.
17. Joseph Myers, *They Are Young Once but Indian Forever: A Summary and Analysis of Investigative Hearings on ICW,* April 1980, 154.
18. Bonnin, *American Indian Stories,* 52.
19. U.S. Bureau of Indian Affairs, *Young Native Americans and Their Families: Educational Needs Assessment and Recommendations,* 71.
20. Ibid., 74.
21. Catherine Rainwater, "Reading between Worlds: Narrativity in the Fiction of Louise Erdrich," 418.
22. Suzanne Garner, "The Indian Child Welfare Act: A Review," 49.
23. Ibid., 50.
24. Tomson Highway, "Spokane Words: Tomson Highway Raps with Sherman Alexie."
25. Bruce Davies, *Implementing the Indian Child Welfare Act,* 7.
26. Ibid.
27. Garner, "Indian Child Welfare Act," 50.
28. Slavoj Žižek, *Looking Awry: An Introduction to Jacques Lacan through Popular Culture,* 59.

CHAPTER 11

Indigenous Liaisons

Sex/Gender Variability, Indianness, and Intimacy in Sherman Alexie's The Toughest Indian in the World

Characters conflicted by issues concerning their Indianness (racial, spiritual, and cultural "essence") and sexual and gendered identities have featured prominently in the work of Sherman Alexie (Spokane/ Coeur d'Alene) from the beginning. With the publication in 2000 of *The Toughest Indian in the World,* however, Alexie's treatment of these issues achieved a new level of thematic intensity and breadth of expression.[1] In this collection, Alexie furthers his satiric and ironic evocation of urban "rez" experience, anchored by the rhetorical question, *"What is an Indian?"* (italics in original), that resonates throughout the book's last story, "One Good Man," and unifies the volume as a whole. Character relationships in a group of the stories reflect enmeshed indexes of sex, gender, and race as defining features of Indian identity, sometimes further complicated by their siting within interracial and/or same-sex pairings. For example, the complex question of the way sex, gender, and race contribute to defining one's sense of identity troubles a number of characters in the book, including some who are white.[2]

For one reviewer, Stephanie Holmes, "what makes these stories especially moving is that they are also love stories that explore the contradictory relationships existing both within and outside the bounds of race—between lovers, between spouses, between parents and children."[3] Indeed, most stories in *Toughest Indian* are concerned with the difficulties characters encounter in negotiating tricky border crossings of race, sex, and gender as they seek to regain through intimacy a lost or diminished sense of Indianness.

As the stories "Assimilation," "The Toughest Indian in the World," "Class," "South by Southwest," "Indian Country," and "Dear John Wayne" unfold, permutations of the question "What is an Indian?" emerge, framed within issues concerning Indianness and what I term *sex/gender variability*.[4] In their struggles with these issues, Alexie's conflicted characters mirror modern Indian attitudes and realities in a number of ways. The representations of certain couples and individuals in *Toughest Indian* reflect the disjunction between traditional Indian attitudes concerning sex and gender (sometimes extending, in fact, to the entire reservation tradition) and the relatively recent acquisition by some modern Indians of the binaristic, heteronormative sex/gender system from white dominant culture—including, more recently, homophobia and its partner, misogyny.

Whether certain characters in Alexie's stories are cognizant of their revictimization through the insidious process of inner colonization, or actively embrace the value system of the dominant culture to assimilate or advance themselves within it, anxieties of identity emerge to further complicate the nexus of race, sex, and gender. The following discussion addresses ways that certain of Alexie's characters in *Toughest Indian* subvert, adopt, or manipulate stereotypes of Indians that have been historically constructed and perpetuated by whites for various reasons; how their reinscribed identities result in behaviors that are (understandably) dysfunctional within a bicultural context; and how certain characters illustrate forms of sexuality and gender identification that once were commonplace among many Indian cultures but now are threatened with erasure.

Of course, romanticized stereotypes of American Indian sexualities, eroticized by desire and fear, long have been staples of American literature: the noble savage of Fenimore Cooper balanced against the despoiler of white women featured in countless captivity narratives; Pocahontas, depicted either as princess or squaw; the fatal attraction of miscegenation at the center of dime novels like Ann Sophia Stephens's *Malaeska: The Indian Wife of the White Hunter* (1860); and the anxieties located in the (temporary) homoerotic attraction of manly white cowboys to ambiguously attired Indian braves in numerous poems, ballads, and stories of the Old West.[5] These sexualized Indian stereotypes ultimately devolved from European accounts of the conquest of the New World, when Christian newcomers sought to reconstruct through sexual colonization (using weapons of violence, religion, and language) what they considered an appalling repertoire of "deviant" (that is, other-than-heterosexual) gendered identities among Native populations—the sex/gender variability mentioned earlier, comparable to what anthropologist Will Roscoe calls the "multiple gender paradigm" historically found in many tribes and Indian cultures.[6] For the conquerors, seeing tall, strong Indian men "effeminize" themselves by running around in "female attire" and performing "women's work"—seemingly New World versions of the androgyne, sodomite, and hermaphrodite—was disturbing, to say the least. But Indian women and men moving fluidly, even joyously, from opposite-sex to same-sex relationships (very polymorphous, very perverse, well in advance of Freud) could not be countenanced in a land imagined by the European evangelists/conquerors as the New Jerusalem.

The colonizers were right, however, in perceiving differences from the European heteronormative model in Native sexual practices and gendered identities. As historian Byrne Fone points out, the question of whether "homosexual behavior was actually practiced is not in doubt; what it meant to native peoples, however, was not what Europeans *thought they saw*. Along with the will to conquer native peoples and impose European religion and customs, Europeans imported the myth of Sodom."[7] Indeed, only the efforts of anthropologists and ethnographers over the last half century or so—notably in the work of Roscoe and Walter L. Williams—have made the dimensions of Indian sex/gender variability better understood. Lester Brown succinctly explains that "American Indian groups have at least six alternative gender styles: women and men, not-men (biological women who assume some aspects of male roles) and not-women (biological men who assume some aspects of female roles), lesbians and gays."[8]

The question of whether same-sex relationships undertaken by "not-men" and "not-women" identifies them as the "first American Indian lesbians and gays" is problematic since it conflates (and often confuses) historical concepts and terminology from radically different cultural backgrounds. Research has shown that the difficulty of the question is intensified (and possibly contaminated) by cross-cultural and cross-racial barriers. Anthropologists, sociologists, and ethnographers have discovered in interviewing members of various tribes who understand historical ways of viewing Indian gendered identities that the respondents often have difficulty understanding the common ground between the modern terms *gay* and *homosexual* (European in origin, embedded in the dominant culture's binary concept of sex and gender)[9] and traditional Native terms like *winkte* (Lakota), *hemaneh* (Cheyenne), *nádleeh* (Navajo), and *berdache*—not to mention more recent descriptions, such as "two spirit" and "third gender," for example.

Analysis of the contentious scholarly argument over terminology for American Indian persons whose sex/gender identities do not fit the dominant culture's heteronormative frame of reference is beyond the scope of this article. In fact, it is almost beside the point. The purpose of this essay is to show that modern Indians, as reflected in Alexie's portraits in *Toughest Indian,* identify themselves and pursue relationships within a broad spectrum of sex/gender possibilities; because of this, their behavior resonates with (I avoid claiming that it approximates) some tribal attitudes toward sex/gender identities of the past that may be viewed today as other-than-heterosexual. The consensus of research is clear that historic Indian attitudes frequently attributed certain spiritual and/or ceremonial powers to these gendered persons; indeed, a high percentage of tribal cultures accorded them special status and value.

One of Alexie's finest achievements in *Toughest Indian* is his nuancing of certain conflicted characters and relationships with vestigial elements of historic Indian attitudes toward multiple sexual and gendered identities, including their spirituality (more precisely for the characters, Indianness). These tribal traditions—for the most part irrecoverably buried in history and imperfectly understood today—nonetheless oscillate with and against modern concepts of sex and gender acquired from the white dominant culture.[10] That is, while some characters and relationships in

Toughest Indian reflect certain historical tribal perceptions of sex and gender, their representations in the stories are contemporary expressions of human sexual desires that are both transhistorical and transcultural. Aside from the stories' artistic value—and Alexie's work here is arguably his best since *The Lone Ranger and Tonto Fistfight in Heaven* (1993)—it is his status as both cultural hero and pop icon for his huge and loyal readership that makes *Toughest Indian* a valuable pedagogical resource; that is, it is useful not only as an argument against the recent and alarming growth of homophobia among Indians but also as a survival document that promotes ethnic renewal and heals the "cultural schizophrenia"[11] that plagues both traditional and urban Indian communities.

As I have argued elsewhere on the satirical values inherent in Alexie's work, the artistic success of much modern Indian literature depends on the use of positive and negative stereotypes that invite "a literary mode such as satire or the inflection of irony to reinvigorate them with meaning."[12] In one of his finest poems, "How to Write the Great American Indian Novel" (1996), for example, Alexie satirizes and deconstructs the entire repertoire of Indian literature's stereotypes and formulaic constructions when his speaker says, "White women dream about half-breed Indian men from horse cultures. / Indian men are horses, smelling wild and gamey. When the Indian man / unbuttons his pants, the white woman should think of topsoil."[13] Alexie's characterizations of Indian sexualities in *Toughest Indian* illustrate a dynamic based on the satirical use of stereotypes, traditional and new, and they reflect both the fluid gender indexes that exist historically in most tribal populations as well as contemporary notions of sex and gender acquired through contact with the European heteropatriarchal model.[14] In addition, the stories reveal that Alexie's urban Indians have clearly adopted the dominant culture's attitudes toward gender and sex through acculturation in proportion to the erosion of traditional tribal attitudes. Thus, a number of the stories in *Toughest Indian* reflect the desire of characters to overcome their inner colonization by renewing their sense of Indianness through the spirituality that results from sexual intimacy.

One of Alexie's favorite conceits—seen, for example, in *The Lone Ranger and Tonto Fistfight in Heaven, Indian Killer* (1996), and *Toughest Indian*—is his characters' imagining the United States as one huge reservation dotted with white population centers, where Natives who resist assimilation into the dominant culture, or who are not adept at it, lead dysfunctional lives in spaces that promote cultural and racial discontinuity. Extending their diaspora beyond the traditional reservation to the urban rez, Alexie's Indians individually and collectively reenact the dominant culture's cycle of conquest, colonization (physical and internal), demonization, exploitation, and erasure of identity.[15]

As he has done many times before, Alexie in this group of stories in *Toughest Indian* textures certain of his characters' motivations with a sense of "trophyism," enhanced by aspects of "sexual tourism." In a parallel context, sociologist Joane Nagel explains that

> racial, ethnic, and national boundaries are also sexual boundaries—erotic intersections where people make intimate connections across ethnic borders. The borderlands that lie at the intersections of ethnic boundaries are "ethnosexual frontiers." They are surveilled and supervised, patrolled and policed, regulated and restricted, but they are constantly penetrated by individuals forging sexual links with ethnic "others." Some of this sexual contact is by "ethnosexual settlers" who establish long-term liaisons, join and/or form families, and become members of ethnic communities "on the other side." Some of this sexual contact is by "ethnosexual sojourners" who stay for a brief or extended visit, enter into sexual liaisons, but eventually return to home communities. Some of this sexual contact is by "ethnosexual adventurers" who undertake expeditions across ethnic boundaries for recreational, casual, or "exotic" sexual encounters, often more than once, but who return to their sexual home bases after each excursion.[16]

Clearly, much of what Nagel discusses in this passage can support our understanding of many of the characters in Alexie's work prior to and including *Toughest Indian.*

For example, which characters in Alexie's previous work better exemplify racial/sexual colonization of Indians by "ethnosexual adventurers" than Betty and Veronica of *Reservation Blues* (1995)? Asked by radio-show host "Adam the Original" about the women's relationship with Coyote Springs band members Junior and Victor, lead singer Thomas Builds-the-Fire replies, "I'm not like a therapist or something. But I don't think it has much of a chance. I mean, I think they're all using each other as trophies. Junior and Victor get to have beautiful white women on their arms, and Betty and Veronica get to have Indian men."[17] Later—drunk in a Manhattan lounge while waiting for the band's taping with Cavalry Records—Junior ponders the racial/sexual dynamics of the relationship: "Junior knew that white women were trophies for Indian boys. He always figured getting a white woman was like counting coup or stealing horses, like the best kind of revenge against white men" (*RB*, 233). The key nuance here—as in a number of these stories from *Toughest Indian*—is that through Alexie's satire, characters manipulate white-constructed stereotypes of Indians; when these collide with other stereotypes, the satirical effect may be described as a kind of "doubling."

In the first and third stories of *Toughest Indian*—both about extramarital heterosexual tourism—Alexie constructs a new Indian stereotype: "the sophisticated, upwardly mobile urban Indian who drives a Toyota Camry, Saab, or BMW, wears Polo, Tommy Hilfiger, or designer leather, smokes chic *faux* cigarettes, and who, just as important, is espoused to a white partner."[18] Both Microsoft employee Mary Lynn of "Assimilation," herself a blooded Coeur d'Alene, and corporate lawyer Edgar Eagle Runner, the firm's trophy "scalp" in the story "Class," yearn for a racial wholeness that they imagine they can achieve through "sex with an indigenous stranger."[19] Mary Lynn views herself as suffering from "some form of sexual dyslexia" (*TIW*, 2) and, though she is happily married to a handsome, successful white man, decides to cheat on him for that very reason: "She simply wanted to find the darkest Indian in Seattle—the man with the greatest amount of melanin—and get naked with him in a cheap motel room. Therefore, she walked up to a flabby Lummi Indian man in a coffee shop and asked him to make love to her" (*TIW*, 3).

Eagle Runner, whose driver's license identifies him as Edgar Joseph, likewise attempts to break out of his inner colonization through sexual imperialism of his own; like Mary Lynn, his Indian identity has become "bleached" through assimilation and interracial marriage. Calling up an escort service and identifying himself as "Geronimo" (*TIW*, 44), he orders an "Indian" to partner him in a kind of sexual healing ceremony. Although he is hoping for Pocahontas, the princess and savior of the white man, what Eagle Runner actually discovers when he opens his hotel-room door is a version of the squaw: a white prostitute smeared with bronzer, wearing a bad Indian wig and dream-catcher earrings, and introducing herself as "Tawny Feather." As Rayna Green explains, Pocahontas demonized—the obverse of the Pocahontas-as-princess stereotype—presents a different problem for white (in Eagle Runner's case, bleached) American manhood:

> White men cannot share sex with the Princess, but once they do so with a real Indian, she cannot follow the required love-and-rescue pattern. She does what white men want for money or lust. In the traditional songs, stories, obscene jokes, contemporary literary works and popular pictorializations of the Squaw, no heroines are allowed. Squaws share in the same vices attributed to Indian men—drunkenness, stupidity, thievery, venality of every kind—and they live in shacks on the edge of town rather than in a woodland paradise.[20]

Eagle Runner, whose Indian identity has become deeply compromised by his desire to meet the racial and cultural expectations of his white law firm, is a prime example of Indian self-refashioning; the same is true of Tawny Feather, who pitifully attempts to meet Eagle Runner's expectations of "true" Indian womanhood. The reader expects no surprises, however. With perfect Alexian irony, the racial/sexual performances of these doubled caricatures dissolve to disclose a social-climbing Indian hiding his whiteness beneath a melanin wrapper and a sorry white woman masquerading behind racial cosmetics, unable to play the stereotype of Pocahontas-as-princess desired by the genetically authentic "Indian" man. As essayist Eric Liu wryly comments in another context, *"Some are born white, others achieve whiteness, still others have whiteness thrust upon them.* This, supposedly, is what it means to assimilate."[21]

Neither Mary Lynn's nor Eagle Runner's "carnal form of affirmative action" (*TIW,* 4) works out in their quests to reaffirm Indianness through intimacy, however. Jeremiah, Mary Lynn's stereotypical blond trophy husband of chilly, Nordic ancestry, crudely comments to her that "fucking an Indian doesn't make me an Indian" (*TIW*, 10); a chemical engineer (ironically), he well understands the anxiety of some of Alexie's characters about blood quantum and dilution of Indian essence. To cite another example, in *Reservation Blues,* the Warm Water sisters, Checkers and Chess, are concerned about racial dilution, the defection of Indian men's loyalty to white women, and the implications of DNA (*RB,* 82). Both Mary Lynn and Eagle Runner have "acquired a certain kind of status from pawning much of their essential Indian DNA in exchange for the spiritual emptiness of white assimilation," and both return from "their sexual excursions into 'Indian Country' to the security of their white spouses."[22] Both realize that spiritual and racial reconnection through sexual intimacy proves little more than an empty fantasy.

Throughout Alexie's works, salmon symbolizes racial essence—metaphorically, totemically, fetishistically—analogous to the way rice is viewed by some Asians.[23] Song Cho, for example, writes that "rice has many powerful resonances tied to culture and consumption. Sticky, fried or Uncle Ben's, the metaphor of rice conveys the myriad of ways we're transformed in our interaction with a white-dominant culture often to the point where we are unrecognizable to ourselves."[24] The Spokane, Alexie keeps reminding his readers, are a salmon people, very different from the Plains horse cultures supposedly most admired by whites.[25] As the nameless narrator of "The Toughest Indian in the World" puts it, "All of us, Indian and white, are haunted by salmon" (*TIW,* 21).

Similar to the motivations of Mary Lynn in "Assimilation" and Eagle Runner in "Class," the principal character's behavior in this story is motivated by the need to regain a lost sense of Indian masculinity through an act of sexual intimacy—and, for the first time in his work, Alexie depicts male/male sexual intercourse. After picking up a hitchhiking, battle-scarred Lummi boxer (significantly also nameless)—a man who "wanders" from reservation to reservation as an itinerant warrior— the narrator/journalist offers to share a room with him for the night at the Pony Soldier Motel. Remembering the episode later, the journalist remarks that "I had never been that close to another man, but the fighter's calloused fingers felt better than I would have imagined if I had ever allowed myself to imagine such things" (*TIW,* 31). During the episode itself, and prior to his allowing the boxer to penetrate him, the journalist volunteers, "'I'm not gay,'" to which the Lummi curtly replies, "'Sure'" (*TIW*, 32). Notably, the boxer seems unconcerned about sexual labels, though he clearly understands the implications of a slur from white dominant culture. Perhaps he expresses an archetypal form of Indian masculinity; unfettered by negative heterosexist terminology, the boxer seems comfortable with his sexuality. Single, or two-way denial? Perhaps both, especially on the part of the boxer, who clearly is used to male/male sex (he comes prepared with latex).

But the journalist may be operating on a different plane of Indian sex/gender identification, fulfilling a function traditionally associated with pantribal figures such as the winkte and comparable tribal gendered identities without compromising his sense of masculinity, even though he engages in what some—conditioned by heterosexist gender classification—may view as the passive sexual role. What is certain, however, is that he finds missing parts of his racial and sexual identity embodied in the "modern warrior" figure of the boxer. After the anonymous sex, the journalist remembers that he "quickly rolled off the bed and went into the bathroom. I locked the door behind me and stood there in the dark. I smelled like salmon" (*TIW*, 32).

At the story's close, the narrator watches the boxer "rise from earth to sky and become a new constellation" (*TIW*, 33), suggesting, perhaps, in its mythical aura, the spiritual powers traditionally associated with certain embodiments of Indian sex/gender variability. Alexie's narrating journalist abandons white civilization—metonymically signified by his car—and ends his story walking: "In bare feet I traveled upriver toward the place where I was born and will someday die. At that moment, if you had broken open my heart you could have looked inside and seen the thin white skeletons of one thousand salmon" (*TIW*, 34).

As opposed to Mary Lynn and Eagle Runner, the narrator of the "Toughest Indian" story does achieve a kind of spiritual salvation through intimacy; the difference, of course, resides in its gendered expression. His stiff, nervous interjection, "I'm not gay," however, reveals two things: knowledge and use of terminology acquired from the heterosexist dominant culture by some modern Indians, and concern that his intercourse with the boxer will be interpreted in ways he clearly sees as negative.

This defensive exchange between the narrator and "hypermasculine" (Indian masculinity undiluted by the enervating forces of white civilization) boxer is also indicative of enculturated homophobia, which Robert Minor defines as "fear of getting close to one's own sex."[26] Thus, while a reviewer like Stephanie Holmes may be sensitive to the interconnectedness of race, desire, and love in the stories of *Toughest Indian,* she appears to misunderstand the nuances of the encounter between the journalist and boxer in the volume's title story (as, perhaps, does the boxer himself), describing it as "homosexual," a limiting sex/gender term devised by nineteenth-century white European culture.

In fact, the story is about male intimacy as a spiritual experience through which the narrator hopes to regain his sense of Indianness—lost, it would seem (along with his name), through his immersion in white-dominant American culture. The narrator's smelling like salmon suggests that through the act of male/male sexual intimacy, he has regained a measure of Indianness. Indeed, sex can make the man, as Minor explains: "Conditioned sex...is not a process of expressing closeness by choice with one's whole being. It is tied to the desperate hope that it will finally make a man feel complete, and fully human. He will finally escape from the isolation of conditioned manhood which includes his homophobia. Here, in getting laid, he will finally feel like a man."[27] While that may be true in many cases, the journalist's sexual experience with the Lummi boxer actually helps heal his loss of Indianness to white culture.

"Salmon Boy" is the moniker bestowed on his "fat Indian" partner (*TIW,* 59) by middle-aged Seymour (aka the "Gentleman Bandit" and the "Man Who Was Looking for Love") in the story "South by Southwest" as they request one-dollar "donations" from customers in the International House of Pancakes to fund their excursion to discover love. On a mission—clearly enamored with and conditioned by the buddy-film genre and aware that its profile requires its principals to fall in love—the gentle Seymour puts it bluntly: "I aim to go on a nonviolent killing spree and I need someone who will fall in love with me along the way" (*TIW,* 58). After Salmon Boy offers to join the journey, Seymour asks, "Are you gay?...I'm not gay. Are you gay?" to which his new partner replies, "No, sir, I am not homosexual...but I do believe in love" (*TIW,* 59). The white Seymour's concern for the negative heterosexist label *gay,* as well as the

Indian's implication that love between two men needn't be considered unnatural, is a fine turn on the similar exchange between the narrator/ journalist and boxer in "Toughest Indian," where both Indian men clearly are aware of the term's implications in heterosexist white culture and contemporary Indian use.

The bonding between Seymour and Salmon Boy clearly is homosocial, and as their adventure to find love develops, it acquires a definite homo-erotic texture. As Eve Kosofsky Sedgwick explains, the term *homosocial* is "meant to be distinguished from 'homosexual.' In fact, it is applied to such activities as 'male bonding,' which may, as in our society, be char-acterized by intense homophobia, fear and hatred of homosexuality."[28] Unlike the narrator's pickup of the wandering Lummi boxer in "Toughest Indian," Seymour accepts Salmon Boy's offer of partnership condition-ally: "Only if you're one of those buffalo hunters. I can't have a nomad in my car. You just can't trust a nomad" (*TIW,* 59).

As with "Toughest Indian," this story addresses the theme of spiritual redemption of Indianness through intimacy—this time emotional, rather than sexual. Same-sex love, not physical sex, is the goal of this fourth tale from *Toughest Indian,* but neither Seymour nor Salmon Boy understands the way to achieve it, importing into their relationship conditioned notions of stereotypical heteromasculine behavior. "But how will we fall in love if we don't have sex?" wonders Salmon Boy. Unwittingly wise in his naïveté, Seymour replies with a kind of sophisticated knowledge that most men have never understood—the value of intimacy not predicated on the sexual act: "I think this is what women have wanted from men for all of our lives. I think they want to be held in our arms and fall asleep in the absence of body fluids" (*TIW,* 70).

As Robert Minor argues, the reason too many men invest the sexual act with such self-defining importance is because other avenues to inti-macy have been closed off to them:

> Women are allowed to experience and feel human closeness
> with others in numerous activities such as play, touch, caring,
> healing, attention, engagement, sharing goals, cuddling, dream-
> ing dreams together, working emotionally on their relation-
> ship together, and raising children together. Since all of these

> expressions of closeness have been taken away from men by
> the male role except for this one way, and since this one way is
> believed to be the only way, and the way by which a man can get
> all other needs met, then conditioned males feel the overwhelm-
> ing need for sex.[29]

Clearly this pair of buddies, Seymour and Salmon Boy, do not fit
Minor's definition of "conditioned males"; in fact, the only conditioning
apparent in their relationship is their homosocial/homoerotic adapta-
tion of heteronormative values associated with the buddy film. Happily
this frees them to encounter intimacy, and their relationship thus reflects
Sedgwick's notion of homosocial desire: "To draw the 'homosocial' back
into the orbit of 'desire,' of the potentially erotic...is to hypothesize the
potential unbrokenness of a continuum between homosocial and homosexual—a continuum whose visibility, for men, in our society, is radically
disrupted."[30]

One of Alexie's most poignant depictions of love and intimacy, the
story ends not defiantly—like a male version of Ridley Scott's film *Thelma
& Louise* (1991)—but with a mythical flourish, like the end of "Toughest Indian," with Seymour and Salmon Boy, pursued by police, finishing
the most important adventure of their lives by taking one another by the
hand and running "into all the south and southwest that remained in the
world" (*TIW*, 75).

Alexie's strongest depiction of a lesbian alliance to date, "Indian Country," comes midway through *Toughest Indian*. In this story, Coeur d'Alene
author Chuck "Low Man" Smith—soon after arriving in Missoula, Montana, on his latest book-promotion tour—looks up former white lover
Tracy Johnson only to learn that she is planning to marry Sara Polatkin,
a Spokane Indian. At the dinner (everyone orders salmon, of course) the
pair have arranged at the Holiday Inn to break the news to Sara's parents,
Estelle and Sid (not only Spokane, but Mormon Spokane), Low Man finds
himself rationally and physically defending Tracy and Sara's love for one
another against Sid's angry, right-wing, Christian vilification of same-sex
unions.[31] Attempting to subvert Sara's plans for same-sex marriage, her
parents have brought her "Christian forgiveness," Sid declaiming that "I
love my daughter.... And I don't want her to go to hell" (*TIW*, 145).

As the dinner-table scene escalates in intensity, Sara leaves her parents to join her partner Tracy after Sid plays the archaic, racial, blame/denial card: "My daughter wasn't, wasn't a gay until she met this, this white woman" (*TIW*, 146). Of course, blaming Western culture (and ultimately ancient Greek and Roman civilizations) for introducing the supposed "deviance" of same-sex love to otherwise "pure" (translate, heteropatriarchal) communities is one of the oldest of homophobic strategies. Once again, an other-than-heterosexual example of Indian sex/gender variability appears as not only reasonable but right because it is based on love and intimacy; the valuable insight, of course, is that Christian values have collided with, and irreparably corrupted through sexual colonization, traditional Indian values and attitudes toward gendered relationships. Because of her father's unwavering heteronormative Indianness—further conditioned by conservative Christian attitudes toward homosexuality and lesbianism—Sara's impending same-sex, interracial wedding makes her father face a bitter irony: in losing a daughter, he will not gain a son.

In some ways the most thematically satisfying and humorous story in *Toughest Indian*, "Dear John Wayne" is couched within a narrative dynamic similar to the one used by Thomas Berger in *Little Big Man* (1964).[32] Berger's novel is one of the most inclusive and authentic fictional portrayals of American Indian sex/gender variability. For example, Little Big Man describes the emergence of an Indian brother, Little Horse, as a hemaneh (*LBM*, 63; 76–77), later finding that he has become the second "wife" of Younger Bear, a "Contrary" (*LBM*, 224–26). Though Berger's narrator ribs Younger Bear for this relationship, studies by Walter Williams and David Greenberg explain this traditional behavior as customary and not to be construed as a form of homophobia.[33]

In Alexie's story, Spencer Cox—who pompously introduces himself as "a cultural anthropologist and the Owens Lecturer in Applied Indigenous Studies at Harvard University" and "author of seventeen books, texts, focusing on mid- to late-twentieth-century Native American culture, most specifically the Interior Salish tribes of Washington State"—gradually loses control of his interview with Etta Joseph, who "romantically" bills herself as being "one hundred and eighteen years old and...the Last of the Spokane Indians" (*TIW*, 190). The year is 2052, and the setting is the

St. Tekawitha Retirement Community on the one-hundredth birthday of Etta's identical twin "boys," Marion and John, who are also residents of the home.

Etta and her author have a great deal of fun deflating the pretensions of Cox, the stereotypical "bad" white anthropologist—one who is motivated to "preserve" Indian cultures (while advancing his academic career), asks the wrong questions, misinterprets responses, and hears what he wants to hear.[34] After playing into Etta's traps a number of times—she tells him that there can be "good" lies, admits that "I'm having fun with you" (*TIW,* 192), and states that "having fun is very serious" (*TIW,* 193)—Cox surrenders control and lets Etta tell him the story about herself that she wants him to hear: how, as a naïve eighteen-year-old Indian extra on the set of John Ford's film *The Searchers* (1956), she surrendered her virginity to the ultimate macho movie-cowboy icon, John Wayne. (Etta insists that the date of the film was 1952, which supports her implication that her twin boys were fathered by the Duke.)

Like the previous stories discussed, "Dear John Wayne" is about acting, playing parts, subverting stereotypes—and intimacy. Etta learns from their lovemaking that John Wayne—the definitive film stereotype of white American manhood—actually is just a vulnerable man, Marion Morrison, looking for intimacy and love. One might expect that his macho movie-star identity would make John Wayne what Minor calls a "conditioned male" in privileging the importance of the sexual act; in fact, however, the man hidden by the stereotype is drawn out by Etta through intimacy: "'John Wayne is the star. I'm Marion, I'm just Marion Morrison.' She held him for a good long time" (*TIW,* 200). And the doubled John Wayne/Marion Morrison learns much from Etta as well.

After he enters the makeup trailer and catches his (white) sons "happily covering their faces with lipstick and mascara" (*TIW,* 202), Marion Morrison (rather than "John Wayne") delivers a speech that reveals his transformed nature. In consoling the crying boys—terrified that their father will gender them as girls—Marion replies, "Oh, sons, you're just engaging in some harmless gender play. Some sexual experimentation. Every boy does this kind of thing. Every man likes to pretend he's a woman now and again. It's very healthy" (*TIW,* 203). Admitting to them that "I try to embrace the feminine in myself" (*TIW,* 203), Marion (sounding a little like Seymour in "South by Southwest") reveals a truth about sex, gender, and intimacy that he could only have learned from Etta Joseph, the love of his life: "If you want to make a woman happy, really happy, there's only one thing you got to do," and that is to "listen to her stories" (*TIW*, 203–4).

Perhaps the story's cultural anthropologist also learns something important about Indians from Etta Joseph: Indians are real people with real stories, not simply bundles of data available for exploitation before they die off in the captivity of the last rez: the retirement home. At the end of "Dear John Wayne," Cox realizes that "he could destroy the tape or keep it; he could erase Etta's voice or transcribe it. It didn't matter what he chose to do with her story because the story would continue to exist with or without him" (*TIW*, 207–8). In some cases, intimacy and love conspire to fashion a higher form of historical truth.

As it informs his poetry, short fiction, novels, and films, the transmission of cultural values clearly is vital to Alexie's artistic mission, much in the same spirit as Gerald Vizenor's concept of *survivance,* which Will Roscoe explains as "the capacity of native North Americans, against overwhelming odds, to pass on ideas, symbols, identities, and cultural forms from one generation to the next."[35] In its satiric inversions and implosions of racial, cultural, and sexual stereotypes, *Toughest Indian* adds to a body of work that, considered in terms of the accretionary power that typifies the oral tradition, comprises Alexie's "artistic vision of a survival document—a defiantly realistic coping mechanism for modern reservation 'warriors.'"[36]

In terms of their pedagogical value, the representations of sex/gender variability in *Toughest Indian* may be useful in addressing a relatively new and insidious incursion from white dominant culture, one that Alexie himself earlier recognized as developing on both traditional and urban reservations: homophobia. For example, in the story "Somebody Kept Saying Powwow" from *The Lone Ranger and Tonto Fistfight in Heaven,* Alexie's narrator, Junior, comments on Norma's seemingly ambiguous sex/gender identity (what some today call bisexuality): "Some people said that Norma took a woman home with her once in a while, too. Years ago, homosexuals were given special status within the tribe. They had powerful medicine. I think it's even more true today, even though our tribe has assimilated into homophobia. I mean, a person has to have magic to assert their identity without regard to all the bullshit, right?" He adds that "Norma held on to her status within the tribe despite all the rumors, the stories, the lies and jealous gossip."[37]

Alexie's concern regarding Indian homophobia also finds expression in *Reservation Blues,* when the Spokane rock band Coyote Springs comes upon a same-sex couple while killing time before their big gig:

> Everybody climbed back into the van. With Thomas as driver
> and Chess and navigator, Coyote Springs soon found a market.
> Along the way, they noticed there were brown people in Seattle.
> Not everybody was white. They watched, dumbfounded, as two
> men held hands and walked down the street.
>   "Jeez," Junior said, "look at that."
>   "Those men are two-spirited," Thomas said.
>   "They're too something or other," Victor said. (*RB,* 149–50)

This passage illustrates three things of vital importance in anticipation of Alexie's depiction in the stories of *Toughest Indian* of the inseparable nexus of Indian sex/gender variability, modern notions of Indianness, and intimacy: Thomas's (and Alexie's) awareness of a tribal history of broadly defined notions of sex and gender roles; their joint awareness that, historically, individuals who did not fit into the heterosexist pattern for sex and gender imposed on tribes by white Europeans once were accorded special powers, status, and respect; and the knowledge shared among Alexie, his narrator, and his readers that the rise of homophobia among Indians in recent years is ultimately a lamentable manifestation of the effects of European colonization.

Therefore, the enforced regulation by European colonists of early Indian sex/gender roles and practices must be viewed through a more complex historical prism: not only as the righteous bringing of the earliest inhabitants of the Americas to Christian salvation and civilization but also as the loss through that acculturation of an essential feature of Native tribal identity. That loss has been exacerbated in recent years by the gradual adoption of another of the dominant culture's power constructs for regulating simplistic, "Christianized" concepts of gender, sex, and desire—homophobia.

On this trend, Alexie has been quite candid and outspoken. For example, in an interview with Georgia Pabst, he commented that homophobia is "the only universally accepted hatred across all religions and cultures and it makes no sense." Questioned by Robert Capriccioso on Indian reaction to his film *The Business of Fancydancing* (2002), Alexie stated that "the Indian world is incredibly homophobic. It's so funny, all these white liberals think that Indians are so loving and peaceful and sacred, but you know, Indians are a bunch of rednecks," adding that "long before this movie, I was talking to an Indian elder…and he was talking about gay people and how evil they are. I said to him, you know, all these things you're saying have been used against Indians, you know, quoting the Bible." And in a brief article on the film that he wrote for *Out* magazine, Alexie remarked that "Indian country is homophobic, so many Indians hope I'm not gay. Why don't they want me to be gay? Well, I'd obviously be much less cool, right? And heck, they might have to kick me out of the club."[38]

Sadly, the extreme results of contemporary Indian homophobia are apparent in the growing number of acts of violence directed toward other-then-heterosexual Indians.[39] An example from real life illustrates a number of the points made in this discussion. In the winter of 1999–2000, a battle between competing Native sex/gender ideologies—that is, between a historically traditional attitude, more tolerant and inclusive of what today are called lesbian/gay identities and "lifestyles," versus a "modern," restrictive, antihomosexual stance that, implicitly at least, enforces heterosexism (itself a form of homophobia)—erupted at Haskell Indian Nations University, established in Lawrence, Kansas, in 1884 to eradicate Indianness and promote assimilation of Natives into white-dominant American culture.[40] The purpose was to discredit, silence, and render invisible Prentice Crawford (Cherokee/Dakota), then president of Haskell's student senate.

In December of 1999, Crawford had outed himself in an interview with Deb Taylor, a reporter for Kansas's lesbian/gay publication, *The Liberty Press*. Crawford argued that historic Indian concepts of male homosexuality gave those men extraordinary spiritual powers, adding that "some even viewed winktes as a manifestation of the Creator." Homosexuality as a form of Indian sex/gender variability, Crawford continued, "began to take on the more white attitude of negativity and deviance" after contact between American Indian tribes and white European colonizers. Furthermore, Crawford claimed that as much as 5 to 10 percent—perhaps more—of Haskell's students were lesbian or gay, most of them closeted for self-protection. Taylor reported that "Crawford believes that for some, 'all they need to know is that it's okay to be true to themselves.'"[41]

Days after Crawford's resignation under pressure in January 2000, Don Bread, then dean of Haskell's School of Business, wrote in a letter to *The Liberty Press*, "Let me say without hesitation that our Native American people DO NOT consider the practice of homosexuality as a natural and desirable practice. Homosexuality is not considered to be a lifestyle that is revered or in any way considered anything but what it is—an unnatural practice that goes against the nature of our existence."[42]

He then resorted to the racial blame/denial strategy that continues to be leveled at oppressed groups: "Concerning contemporary lifestyles among Native Americans, homosexuality is a reality. As Native Americans were assimilated into white society, the Native American became exposed to all aspects of the value systems and lifestyles of the 'white man,' including homosexuality." Then Bread added that "I find no reference of such practices in the oral histories of our Indian people. Neither do I find scholarly references of such practices."[43]

The denial and lack of knowledge demonstrated in this response is troubling. How can an educator at an institution such as Haskell be unaware of the rich variety of sex/gender manifestations that are the historical legacy of most American Indian tribes? Of the meticulous research conducted on Native sex/gender variability by white and Indian anthropologists and ethnographers, like Roscoe's germinal studies *The Zuni Man-Woman* (1991) and *Changing Ones* (2000), Williams's *The Spirit and the Flesh* (1986), and the studies of Indian lesbians by Beatrice Medicine, Terry Tafoya, and others? Of the already-rich and growing literature about and authored by gay and lesbian authors such as Maurice Kenney, Paula Gunn Allen, and others; or the groundbreaking anthology of lesbian/gay Indian letters edited by Roscoe, *Living the Spirit* (1988)? Of the historical pantribal tradition of *berdachism* that survives today, even on some urban reservations.[44]

Perhaps most troubling about the attitudes expressed by Bread is that he seems to be playing a taxonomic shell game: Indian homosexuals do exist today, but that is due to the insidious influence of deviant white culture; gay Indians today aren't like the traditional same-sex Indian figures, and they lack the spiritual qualities once attributed to those people. In other words, Bread depicts contemporary lesbian and gay Indians negatively in the light of modern Euro-American perceptions. Like some others—such as Alexie's character of Sid Polatkin—he cites the "point of contact" theory as responsible for these negative behaviors, thereby allowing him to blame European white culture for them while at the same time disavowing, silencing, and rendering invisible modern, self-identified lesbian and gay Indians.

In a larger sense, the posture is potentially destructive and harmful in allowing homophobic attitudes to grow among modern Indian communities, whether within traditional or urban reservations or on college campuses. With not a little irony, it allows inner-colonized, assimilated Indians living anywhere to justify homophobic behavior directed toward members of their communities (redemonizing them, as it were) for the same practices deemed deviant by original Euro-American colonizers.

Clearly a literary cult hero for many young Indians today, Alexie's Native and "reservation tourist" readers alike find practical value in the "imaginative literary realism"[45] that he achieves in works like *Toughest Indian,* where his authorial persona functions in ways similar to the ancient trickster/Coyote figure. Coyote, as Barbara Babcock and Jay Cox explain, "is the crazy, creative Indian negotiating urban America. Polysemic as well as multifunctional, coyote and his stories just keep 'going along,' somewhere beyond interpretation, epitomizing resistance and survival."[46] This is the reason why I have asserted from the beginning of this essay that a work like Alexie's *Toughest Indian* has exciting pedagogical potential for countering emerging Native homophobia and demonstrating, through its characters' searches for intimacy, a need for tolerance for persons who represent a broad spectrum of sex/gender variability. In his interview with Taylor, Crawford rightly noted the treble discrimination experienced by lesbian and gay Indians, which in fact exists for those members of any minority racial or ethnic group due to layers of race or ethnicity, gender identification, and sex—even within lesbian and gay communities themselves.[47]

Representations of Indian sexual and gendered identities in works such as Alexie's *Toughest Indian* may help readers to have the confidence to answer questions like one posed by a member of another triply oppressed group, gay Asian Americans: "When we look in the mirror and see a stereotype, who do we believe, the mirror or ourselves?"[48] On another important level, Alexie's widespread and fiercely loyal readership makes *Toughest Indian* an especially valuable resource for affirming modern Native identity and an inspirational bulwark for withstanding the continuous erosion of values traditionally inherent in Indianness by white dominant culture. Indeed, as the variety of sexual and gendered identities in the relationships in *Toughest Indian* suggests, one can respond simply enough to the question "What is an Indian?" by acknowledging that Indians, like people of all races and cultures throughout history, are sexual beings who need and deserve cultural space to fulfill their desires—however identified and enacted—through intimacy. Again, in Prentice Crawford's words, "All they need to know is that it's okay to be true to themselves."[49]

NOTES

1.   While this essay limits its discussion primarily to the stories of *Toughest Indian,* much that is argued here can be extended to Alexie's characters and themes in earlier novels, the subsequent volume of short stories *Ten Little Indians* (2003), and his film *The Business of Fancydancing:* (2002). For an in-depth discussion of the latter, see Quentin Youngberg, "Interpenetrations: Re-encoding the Queer Indian in Sherman Alexie's *The Business of Fancydancing,"* 55–75. Youngberg's article appeared after this essay was accepted for publication in this volume.

2.   African American perspectives on the question are offered by Horace Griffin, "Their Own Received Them Not: African American Lesbians and Gays in Black Churches," in *The Greatest Taboo: Homosexuality in Black Communities,* 110–21; John L. Peterson, "Black Men and Their Same-Sex Desires and Behaviors," in *Gay Culture in America: Essays from the Field,* esp. 150–55; and Robert F. Reid-Pharr, *Black Gay Man: Essays.* Editor Song Cho's introduction to the anthology *Rice: Explorations into Gay Asian Culture + Politics*

considers the issues from an Asian American point of view, as does Joseph Carrier's essay, "Miguel: Sexual Life History of a Gay Mexican American" (in *Gay Culture in America,* 202–24), from a Mexican American perspective. For a collection of same-sex interracial perspectives, see Kai Wright et al., "Sexing the Archetype: Interracial Dating and Mating," 60–65, 76. See also Eve Kosofsky Sedgwick's theoretical discussion of the issues in *Epistemology of the Closet,* 30–34, 58–62.

3.   Stephanie Holmes, review of *The Toughest Indian in the World* by Sherman Alexie.

4.   Sue-Ellen Jacobs, Wesley Thomas, and Sabine Lang explain that "the word *variance* implies subjective departure from a norm; 'variability,' however, implies agency operating in context of a range of possibilities" (15n1). Jacobs, Thomas, and Lang, eds., introduction to *Two-Spirit People: Native American Gender Identity, Sexuality, and Spirituality,* 1–18. The term that I use in this essay, *sex/gender variability,* is intended to be more suggestive of the fluidity of traditional Indian concepts of sex and gender; that is, it is less restrictive than variance. In fact, the fluidity of traditional Indian gender attitudes in some ways resembles those in the European early modern period that define sex as biological and gender as socially and culturally determined. For the origins of gender concepts as they emerged from the discoveries of sexual biology, see Thomas Laqueur, *Making Sex: Body and Gender from the Greeks to Freud.* Terry Tafoya's article on modern Indian lesbians specifically addresses the concept of sex/gender fluidity. Tafoya, "Sex and Spirit: Native American Lesbian Identity."

5.   The double stereotype of the noble savage/hypermasculine Indian provided the thrilling subtext of many captivity narratives, as June Namias's analysis of the genre shows: "Nineteenth century captivity materials offered mixed messages for women [readers]: excitement, possible romantic bliss, but the chance of sexual harassment. The big, dark Indian was pictured simultaneously as a thrill and a sexual threat to white women and consequently a competitive sexual threat to white men." Namias, *White Captives: Gender and Ethnicity on the American Frontier,* 109.

6.   Will Roscoe, *Changing Ones: Third and Fourth Genders in Native North America,* 126.

7.   Byrne R. S. Fone, *Homophobia: A History,* 319; italics added. Fone's discussion of New World Indigenous sexual practices includes a useful analysis of European reactions and attitudes (319–26, 451–54). Jonathan Katz reprints valuable extracts and source materials on impressions of Indian sexualities that span more than four centuries (281–334). Katz, "Native Americans/Gay Americans 1528–1976," in *Gay American History: Lesbians and Gay Men in the U.S.A.—A Documentary by Jonathan Katz.*

8.   Lester B. Brown, "Women and Men, Not-Men and Not-Women, Lesbians and Gays: American Indian Gender Style Alternatives," 6.

9.   In *Epistemology of the Closet,* Eve Kosofsky Sedgwick explains that

> the word "homosexual" entered Euro-American discourse during the last third of the nineteenth century—its popularization preceding, as it happens, even that of the word "heterosexual."...What *was* new from the turn of the century was the world-mapping by which every given person, just as he or she was necessarily assignable to a male or female gender, was now considered necessarily assignable as well to a homo- or hetero-sexuality, a binarized identity that was full of implications, however confusing, for even the ostensibly least sexual aspects of personal existence. It was this new development that left no space in the culture exempt from the potent incoherences of homo/heterosexual definition. (2)

10. In *Changing Ones,* Roscoe includes detailed pantribal tables for these sex/gender identities: "Glossary of Native Terms for Alternative Gender Roles and Sexuality by Language Family" (213–22) and "Tribal Index of Alternative Gender Roles and Sexuality" (223–47). Please note the different spellings within tribal cultures for expressions of sex/gender variability. For discussions of terminology, consult Jacobs, Thomas, and Lang, eds. (1–18, as well as other essays in their *Two-Spirit People*); chapters 1, 5, and 6 of Roscoe's *Changing Ones;* and Lester Brown, "Women and Men." The best sources of information on the *berdache* remain Charles Callender and Lee M. Kochems, "The North American Berdache," 443–70); Will Roscoe, *The Zuni Man-Woman;* and Walter L. Williams, *The Spirit and the Flesh: Sexual Diversity in American Indian Culture.* For the sacred status historically accorded the berdache by some tribes, see Williams, 31–43.

11. The term *cultural schizophrenia* is adopted from Richard Fung, a contributor to the anthology *Rice,* edited by Song Cho, who writes that "creating an Asian gay culture may be the only way to overcome what Richard Fung describes as the 'cultural schizophrenia' of Asian gay existence in which 'I related on the one hand to a heterosexual family that affirmed my ethnic culture and, on the other hand, to a gay community that was predominantly white'" (4).

12. Stephen F. Evans, "'Open Containers': Sherman Alexie's Drunken Indians," 50.

13. Sherman Alexie, "How to Write the Great American Indian Novel," in *The Summer of Black Widows,* 95.

14. See Roscoe, "Tribal Index of Alternative Gender Roles and Sexuality," in *Changing Ones,* 223–47.

15. Evans, "'Open Containers,'" 64–65.

16. Joane Nagel, "The Color of Sex: Race, Ethnicity, and Sexuality in America."

17. Sherman Alexie, *Reservation Blues,* 158 (hereafter cited in the text as *RB*).

18. Evans, "'Open Containers,'" 66.

19. Sherman Alexie, *The Toughest Indian in the World,* 1 (hereafter cited in the text as *TIW*).

20. Rayna Green, "The Pocahontas Perplex: The Image of Indian Women in American Culture," 711.

21. Eric Liu, "Notes of a Native Speaker," in *The Accidental Asian,* 34–35; italics in original.

22. Evans, "'Open Containers,'" 66.

23. See Lisa Tatonetti, "Sex and Salmon: Queer Identities in Sherman Alexie's *The Toughest Indian in the World,*" 201–20, which was published after this essay was accepted for publication.

24. Cho, introduction to *Rice,* 1.

25. Compare the speaker's humorous iterative references to features of horse cultures supposedly admired by whites in Alexie's "How to Write the Great American Indian Novel."

26. Robert N. Minor, *Scared Straight: Why It's So Hard to Accept Gay People and Why It's So Hard to Be Human,* 51. For Minor homophobia extends well beyond a negative heterosexual attitude toward gay and lesbian relationships. It is a broader anxiety that encompasses fear of intimacy between same-sex "straights" as well—a form of enculturated, internalized homophobia (51–52).

27. Ibid., 116.

28. Eve Kosofsky Sedgwick, *Between Men: English Literature and Male Homosocial Desire,* 1–2.

29. Minor, *Why It's So Hard,* 115–16.

30. Sedgwick, *Between Men,* 1–2.

31. For Mormon policy statements on homosexuality, see Ron Schow, Wayne Schow, and Marybeth Raynes, eds., *Peculiar People: Mormons and Same-Sex Orientation,* 314–15.

32. Analogous to the relationship of Etta Joseph and Spencer Cox in this story, Thomas Berger's 111-year-old Jack Crabb/Little Big Man recounts his picaresque adventures "in the glorious history of the Olden Time Frontter" for historian Ralph Fielding Snell. Berger, *Little Big Man,* xxiv (hereafter cited in the text as *LBM*). The narrative (un)reliability of Crabb and Etta Joseph is elusive and illusory for their recorders and reading audiences alike and is one source of the artistic tension in both works.

33. See Williams, *The Spirit and the Flesh,* 39–41; and David Greenberg, "Why Was the Berdache Ridiculed?" 179–90. For Crabb's explanation of the tribal figure of the contrary, see *LBM,* 170.

34. Here and elsewhere Alexie enjoys lampooning the pretensions and duplicity of white academics. See, for example, his portraits of Dr. Clarence Mather, teacher of Native American literature, and mystery novelist Jack Wilson, who poses as a Shilshomish Indian, in the novel *Indian Killer* (1996). The name Cox may remind some readers of anthropologist Matilda Coxe Stevenson, who conducted work on the Zuni berdache during the late-nineteenth and early-twentieth centuries (see Williams, *Spirit and the Flesh,* 57–58 and elsewhere). In 1831 an explorer named Ross Cox published an account of

his travels and experiences among various Indian tribes, including the Spokane, among whom he identified an alternative male gender role. Beyond these parallels, it is also possible that James Cox, Alexie's maternal grandfather, is the source for this recurring surname.

35. Roscoe, *Changing Ones,* 167. For Gerald Vizenor's concept of *survivance,* see his chapter on "Postindian Warriors" (1–44) and "Epilogue" (163–78) in *Manifest Manners: Postindian Warriors of Survivance.*

36. Evans, "'Open Containers,'" 48.

37. Sherman Alexie, *The Lone Ranger and Tonto Fistfight in Heaven,* 203. In "Assimilation" Mary Lynn also experiences desire for another woman:

> A few summers ago, during Crow Fair, Mary Lynn had been standing in a Montana supermarket, in the produce aisle, when a homely white woman, her spiky blond hair still wet from a trailer-house shower, walked by in a white T-shirt and blue jeans, and though Mary Lynn was straight—having politely declined all three lesbian overtures thrown at her in her life—she'd felt a warm breeze pass through her DNA in that ugly woman's wake, and had briefly wanted to knock her to the linoleum and do beautiful things to her. (*TIW,* 2)

Compare also the same-sex experiences acknowledged by Grace Atwater and Roman Gabriel Fury in the *Toughest Indian* story "Saint Junior."

38. Georgia Pabst, "Alexie Sends Strong Signals: Writer Spares No One from Barbs"; Robert Capriccioso, "Sherman Alexie: American Indian Filmmaker/ Writer Talks with Robert Capriccioso"; and Sherman Alexie, "Dancing Fancy: Celebrated Writer-Director-Poet Sherman Alexie Comes Out?" 32–33.

39. See, for example, reports of the brutal murder of Justin Fidelis Enos written by Dennis Wagner, "Ex-con Pleads Guilty in 2000 Hate Killing"; and Ann Rostow, "Gay Murders Continue." On the bludgeoning death of Fred Martinez, "an openly gay or transgendered Navajo teen," see Aspen C. Emmett, "Murphy Pleads Guilty to Murder."

40. For a brief history of Haskell's evolution from an industrial training school to a modern university, see http://www.haskell.edu

41. Deb Taylor, "Saving the *Indian*: A Story of Two-Spirit, Sacred People. Native Queers," 34–35.

42. Don Bread, "Not My Idea of Native Acceptance," 7.

43. Ibid.

44. Will Roscoe, *The Zuni Man-Woman;* and Roscoe, ed., *Living the Spirit: A Gay American Indian Anthology.* For a brief overview of lesbian/gay Indian literature, see Roscoe, "Native North American Literature," in *The Gay and Lesbian Literary Heritage: A Reader's Companion to the Writers and Their Works, from Antiquity to the Present,* 513–17. See also Tafoya's "Sex and Spirit"; Lisa Tatonetti and Daniel Heath Justice, "Indigenous Literature with a Queer/ LGBT Two-Spirit Sensibility"; and Tatonetti, "The Emergence and Importance of Queer American Indian Literatures; or 'Help and Stories' in Thirty

Years of SAIL," 143–70. As previous notes suggest, literature on the berdache is quite extensive. For instances of the so-called modern berdache,
see, for example, Berdache Paul, "My Life as an Intersex," 10–11, 34; and
contributors to Roscoe, ed., *Living the Spirit,* 9–93, 217–22. Tatonetti's article
appeared after this essay was accepted for publication.

45. Evans, "'Open Containers,'" 64.

46. Barbara Babcock and Jay Cox, "The Native American Trickster," in *Handbook of Native American Literature,* 100.

47. Taylor, "Saving the *Indian*," 35. Social worker Karina L. Walters would
agree: "Indian gays and lesbians have a double or triple (e.g., American
Indian, lesbian, woman) minority status and experience discrimination
within their own culture (as a gay person); within the gay and lesbian community (as an ethnic minority); and within the dominant group (as both
an ethnic person and as a gay or lesbian person)." Walters, "Urban Lesbian
and Gay American Indian Identity: Implications for Mental Health Services
Delivery," 54. Brian Joseph Gilley's powerful monograph, *Becoming Two-
Spirit* (published since this article was accepted for publication), vividly
depicts the efforts to achieve acceptance within homophobic Native communities by various groups of men. In his preface, Gilley writes that

> what concerned the men the most was the fact that they felt socially
> and personally separated from their families and communities because
> of their sexuality. They knew full well, through direct experience or lis-
> tening to fellow Natives talk, that their sexuality was a source of shame
> and disdain. They also feared homophobia so much that it often kept
> them from participating in the social and spiritual practices that their
> families taught them were so important to their Native identity.

Gilley, *Becoming Two-Spirit: Gay Identity and Social Acceptance in Indian
Country,* ix.

48. Cho, introduction to *Rice,* 2.

49. Taylor, "Saving the *Indian*," 35.

■ *Margaret O'Shaughnessey*

CHAPTER 12

Sherman Alexie's Transformation of "Ten Little Indians"

When Sherman Alexie titled his 2003 collection of stories *Ten Little Indians,* he was actually using a phrase he had employed several times in his earlier writings, notably in *The Lone Ranger and Tonto Fistfight in Heaven* (1993). In one story in this collection, "The Only Traffic Signal on the Reservation Doesn't Flash Red Anymore," Victor describes a group of Indian boys walking by: "I'd like to think there were ten of them. But there were actually only four or five."[1] For Victor—as for Alexie—ten Indians seems to be a particularly meaningful entity, suggesting more than, say, a large number. The significance becomes clear in another story, "The Approximate Size of My Favorite Tumor," when, in the middle of James Many Horses's wedding, the drunken Raymond stands and tells his memories of James:

> "I remember once when he and I were drinking at the Powwow Tavern when all of a sudden Lester FallsApart comes running in and says that ten Indians just got killed in a car wreck on Ford Canyon Road. *Ten Skins?* I asked Lester, and he said, *Yeah, ten.* And then Jimmy starts up singing, *One little, two little, three little*

Indians, four little, five little, six little Indians, seven little, eight little, nine little Indians, ten little Indian boys."

Everyone in the wedding laughed some more, but also looked a little tense after that story. (*LRT,* 161; italics in original)[2]

What James sings is, of course, the refrain from the well-known—though politically incorrect—nursery rhyme, "Ten Little Indians." Written in 1868 by Septimus Winner for American minstrel shows, the piece had many imitators from the outset, including a version a year later by the English ballad writer Frank Green, who altered the racial identity of the title figures to what seemed more fitting for British minstrel shows. In changing "Injuns" into "Nigger Boys," Green simply translated the inherent prejudice from one despised group of people to another. The fact that this minstrel song became a standard counting rhyme for children does not lessen its offensiveness.

The rhyme itself, in all of its versions, describes the demise of each "Injun" or "nigger" one after the other, as in the first stanza: "Ten little Injun boys went out to dine,/One choked his little self, and then there were nine." Not only do the boys choke to death, they also chop themselves in half, fall overboard, break their neck, shoot each other, and get stung by bees, swallowed by a fish, and "hugged" by a bear, as well as suffer less violent, but equally deadly, mishaps as becoming "frizzled up" and "fuddled."[3] As Lucy Rollin perceptively remarks, "Such a description of the gradual disappearance of a dark-skinned people through their own carelessness or ignorance, coupled with the pleasant rhythm and the gleeful ending, 'And then there were none,' can hardly be less than wish fulfillment."[4] Although some versions of the rhyme have substituted a happy ending where the last little "Injun" marries and raises a family, oral tradition has discarded this variation as "unnecessarily sentimental."[5]

Familiarity with the rhyme increased after Agatha Christie used it in her murder mystery, *Ten Little Indians,* originally published in 1939 in England as *Ten Little Niggers* and in the United States as *And Then There Were None* (the last line of one version of the rhyme). Christie also adapted the narrative into a stage play in 1940, and over the course of the next fifty years, it was made into five films. In Christie's mystery, ten strangers are lured to a party on a secluded island, where, one by one, they are killed by their host for crimes they supposedly committed. Although the final lines of the stage play suggest that the two survivors will marry, the original novel—where the rhyme appears as a poem on parchment hanging over the fireplace—ends with everyone dead: "One little Indian boy left all alone; / He went and hanged himself and then there were none."[6]

What makes everyone "a little tense" after Raymond sings the rhyme in Sherman Alexie's "The Approximate Size of My Favorite Tumor" is, of course, the implication that the Indian boys are dying off one after the other, that on the reservation this is the normal condition. In this sense, the rhyme is a reflection of what Louis Owens calls "doomed Indianness," where the Indian "is supposed to vanish, to die, culturally and literally."[7] It is also the sentiment expressed in Teddy Roosevelt's words about Indians cited in Alexie's novel *Flight* (2007): "I don't go so far as to think that the only good Indians are dead Indians, but I believe nine out of ten are, and I shouldn't inquire too closely into the case of the tenth."[8]

And Sherman Alexie has certainly depicted today's Indian—on the reservation and off—as inherently self-destructive: "Indian boys always find some way to die," although in most instances, such deaths can be traced to larger societal forces, ones that may incite nihilistic behavior.[9] Death and general loss are so widespread among Indians that even "one Indian killing another did not create a special kind of storm. This little kind of hurricane was generic. It didn't even deserve a name" (*LRT,* 3). A sense of loss is pervasive among Indians—"*They're all gone, my tribe is gone*" (*LRT,* 17; italics in original)—and awareness of this loss becomes a lament: "*One more gone, one more gone, and our world fills with all of our dead.*"[10] Though aware of what is happening to them, Alexie's Indians seem to be unable to do anything about it: "Sometimes it seems like all Indians can do is talk about the disappeared" (*LRT,* 222). They hardly ever expect a good outcome from a situation: "Believe me, everything looks like a noose if you stare at it long enough" (*LRT,* 178). Experience has reinforced their sense of hopelessness: "I was looking for a happy ending / but instead found a refrigerator / abandoned on East Fifth Street."[11]

It is clearly his depiction of "doomed Indianness," his "unflinchingly bold depiction of the dysfunctional nature of contemporary reservation life," that has made Alexie's work controversial—if not distasteful—to some fellow Indian writers.[12] But what these critics have failed to recognize is that Alexie describes this condition precisely to show the need to do something about it. From early on, survival is a main concern in his writing. Not only does he insist that "we all want to survive"[13], he points out somewhat paradoxically that "Indians have a way of surviving" (*LRT*, 49). Again, "*How do you explain the survival of all of us who were never meant to survive?*" (*OSNS*, 90; italics in original). That several of these citations come from *Old Shirts & New Skins* (1993) is particularly significant, for "the idea of survival in its various permutations" may well be "the overarching theme" of this work.[14] It is therefore not surprising that an especially pertinent expression of Alexie's feelings about survival should appear in one of its prose pieces, "Red Blues":

> Late at night, I take inventory of what I have lost, make plans for the future, but there's only so much I know about survival. The television is white noise and the midnight movie is just another western where the Indians lose. Nothing changes. So, I keep counting, *one little, two little, three little Indians*, all the way up to ten little Indian boys, stop, then start again, until I count the entire world. These small measurements are all I have as defense against inertia. (*OSNS*, 87; italics in original)

Notwithstanding all the gloom, in focusing on the refrain, Alexie is actually doing the reverse of what the rhyme spells out in its various stanzas. Instead of depleting the Indians—reducing them from ten to nine and down to one or none—he is in effect multiplying them. Over and over he counts "all the way up to ten little Indians boys," then starts again until he counts "the entire world," until he gives all Indians identity and life. What Alexie does is give meaning to a favorite phrase of his: "Survival = Anger × Imagination. Imagination is the only weapon on the reservation" (*LRT*, 150). Elsewhere, for the word "Survival" in this equation, he substitutes "Poetry," suggesting what—for him at least—survival is all about.[15]

"Ten Little Indians" is not the only nursery rhyme in Alexie's writings. In "The Fun House"—after experiencing a mouse running up her pant leg—Aunt Nezzy repeats over and over what happened: "'One dumb mouse tore apart the whole damn house. One dumb mouse tore apart the whole damn house,' she chanted at them, sang it like a nursery rhyme, like a reservation Mother Goose" (*LRT,* 81). Moreover, despite Harrison Snake Church's telling his son's third-grade teacher that "Indians didn't believe in using numbers, that the science of mathematics was a colonial evil,"[16] "Ten Little Indians" is not the only counting song in Alexie's writing. In "Saint Junior," from *The Toughest Indian,* Alexie explains the origin of the "indigenous songs called '49s'":

> Some say those songs were invented after fifty Indian warriors went out to battle and only one came back alive. Distraught, the lone survivor mourned his friends by singing forty-nine songs, one for each of the dead. Others believe the 49s were invented when fifty warriors went out to battle and forty-nine came back alive. Distraught, they remembered the lost one by singing forty-nine songs, one by each of the living. Still others believe the 49s were invented by a woman who fell in love with forty-nine men and had her heart broken by each and every one of them. And still more believe the 49s were invented by forty-nine men who mourned the loss of one good woman. However they were invented, those songs have always been heavy with sadness and magic.[17]

Everybody on the reservation sang them "because they understood what it meant to be Indian and dead and alive and still bright with faith and hope."[18] Though based on loss, the songs transform this negative feeling, converting it into something positive and even celebratory.

This is precisely what Alexie is doing with the "Ten Little Indians" rhyme. It is what Victor meant when he watched a group of Indian boys walk by and said he would "like to think there were ten of them" (*LRT,* 44). And on one level, it is what the drunken James was doing when he started singing the rhyme after hearing that ten Indians had been killed in a car wreck. Although the wedding guests respond by laughing and looking "a little tense," this counting song—like the 49 in "Saint Junior"—becomes a vehicle for memorializing, commemorating, and getting beyond the obvious waste.

Far from callously depicting his fellow Indians' failures and demise, Alexie actually wants to celebrate their survival, in fact to insist on it over and over: "Indians fight their way to the end, holding onto the last good thing, because our whole lives have to do with survival" (*LRT,* 32). Although like the Jews, they are "the eternal survivors" (*LRT,* 11)—as the title of one of his poems, "The Game Between the Jews and the Indians is Tied Going Into the Bottom of the Ninth Inning," expresses it—the Indians can pride themselves on having survived: "We can remind each other/that we are both survivors and children/and grandchildren of survivors" (*FIM,* 80).

Even more significantly, Alexie insists that "there is nothing we cannot survive" (*OSNS,* 47); or, as he spells it out, "I know some of you will die in car wrecks. I know some of you will die of cirrhosis. I know some of you will die of a broken heart. But more than that, I know some of you will live, will learn how to breathe this twentieth century oxygen/and learn how/to dance a new dance" (*FIM,* 108). His affirmation continues, "Believe me, the Indian men are rising from the alleys and doorways, rising from self-hatred and self-pity, rising up on horses of their own making" (*FIM,* 108).

The image of horses is probably Alexie's most vivid embodiment of this sentiment. As he expresses it elsewhere in *First Indian on the Moon* (1993), "I would close my eyes and dream of something strong, dream of horses exploding, rising into the air, their hearts beating survive, survive, survive" (*FIM,* 51). In *Reservation Blues* (1995), this image dominates the song that Thomas, Chess, and Checkers sing at the end as they leave the reservation: "Big Mom taught them a new song, the shadow horses' song, the slaughtered horses' song, the screaming horses' song, a song of mourning that would become a song of celebration: we have survived, we have survived" (*RB,* 306). These Indians are finally victorious. Whether or not Victor, who appears throughout Alexie's early fiction, is a literal victor, his name is not accidental. In one of "The Alcoholic Love Poems" in *First Indian on the Moon,* Alexie both differentiates between the terms "victor" and "victim" and links them (*FIM,* 36), a distinction not always easy to make, though one that is finally necessary for him.

Throughout his writings, Alexie seems to go out of his way to mention ten Indians, appealing to what seems an inherent mythic dimension in the number. "The Unauthorized Autobiography of Me" begins with the assertion that on a late summer night on the reservation, "ten Indians are playing basketball on a court barely illuminated by the streetlight above them" (*OSS,* 13). Regardless of the fact that ten is the customary number of players—at least in regulation—here the phrase is the important thing, reinforcing what Alexie spells out: the Indians will keep on playing until conditions make it impossible.

Similarly, when the fourth-grade music teacher tells his students to line up behind the instrument they want to learn to play and "all ten Indian boys line up behind the drum" (*OSS,* 15), the number acquires a life of its own or, again, a mythic significance. Meaning more than "many" or "a lot," it creates a sense of totality, suggesting that all the Indian boys in the world would choose the drum. In like manner, in the story "South by Southwest" in *The Toughest Indian in the World* (2000), Salmon Boy says that when he was a boy and lost his moccasins in the river while at a powwow in Flagstaff, "my auntie spanked me until I cried like ten Indians" (*TIW,* 59). There cannot be, he suggests, a sound louder than that. In "Jesus Christ's Half-Brother Is Alive and Well on the Spokane Indian Reservation," when tired and impatient Indians are trying to dig a grave for Jesse WildShoe, Alexie describes the way they pour kerosene on the frozen ground and light it: "There we were ten little Indians making a hell on earth for a fancydancer who already had enough of that shit" (*LRT,* 122). Though these "ten little Indians" may well be the losers suggested by the rhyme, their number provides a mythic context for the death and thereby redefines the nature of the survivors.

A similar ambiguity exists in Alexie's use of the rhyme in the movie he wrote and directed, *The Business of Fancydancing* (2002). Its title notwithstanding, the film is an original reworking of several previous writings, not just the collection of poems and stories he published ten years earlier. The "Ten Little Indians" tune—initially played on the violin by the self-destructive Mouse—recurs as an important element in the incidental music of the film, especially during the final credits. Although obviously ironic, the tune—besides giving a mythic dimension to the death and destructiveness—allows Alexie a way to commemorate, even celebrate, his people.

Because the phrase persists in Alexie's writings, it is not surprising that he finally used it as a book title—*Ten Little Indians* (2003)—or that references to the nursery rhyme appear in this collection of stories. In "Flight Patterns," William tells the Ethiopian taxi driver that he is Indian: "not jewel-on-the-forehead Indian," rather "bows-and-arrows Indian":

> "Oh, you mean ten little, nine little, eight little Indians?"
> "Yeah, sort of," said William. "I'm that kind of Indian, but much smarter." (*TLI,* 115)

William, successful as "a fully recognized member of the notebook-computer tribe" (*TLI,* 109) and an urban Indian who does not smoke, drink, or eat processed sugar, is smarter because he is not self-destructive like the Indians in the rhyme and the ones who people Alexie's early writing, especially the stories in *The Lone Ranger and Tonto Fistfight in Heaven* and the novel *Reservation Blues.*

On the other hand, since Alexie's literary concerns have increasingly moved off the reservation and his characters are more and more an integrated part of the modern American world, it is surprising that after ten years of incorporating the rhyme in his writings, he should highlight it as a title. *Ten Little Indians* as the title of, say, his first collection of stories—*The Lone Ranger and Tonto Fistfight in Heaven* might have been more expected—and perhaps more appropriate, despite there being twenty-two stories in the collection (expanded to twenty-four in the 2005 reprint)—though his Indian audience might well have found it distasteful. That other contemporary Indian writers have not used the rhyme is hardly surprising. Those who are primarily concerned with the image of the modern Indian would certainly shun it, while others would regard it as a demeaning racial slur.[19]

Whereas he once courted approval, Alexie—now accustomed to disapproval from many of his fellow Indians—may simply not care if his title offends. Besides—given that Ten Little Indians collectible dolls are now available from Friends of the Feather and the nursery rhyme has been recast as a popular song by the Beach Boys and used by Harry Nilsson as a musical setting for the Ten Commandments—the public climate may simply not be an issue. Nevertheless, *Ten Little Indians* seems an inappropriate title for Alexie's collection because it leads the reader to expect to find ten stories—one per Indian—recording death, destruction, and loss. The fact that the collection actually comprises only nine stories may at first be disconcerting, but it should make the thoughtful reader pause. By including only nine stories is Alexie suggesting that the loss stops there; that—like the alternative happy ending of the rhyme—the Indians do not extinguish themselves after all? Or is he metaphorically singing, as does the 49—at least the version that originates with the surviving fiftieth warrior—to commemorate the dead forty-nine? Is Alexie in effect this survivor: the tenth (or fiftieth) Indian, celebrating those who have been lost? In this sense, he would be like the poet Seymour who—visually doubled at the end of *The Business of Fancydancing*—both remains on the reservation with the family and friends he has reconnected with at Mouse's funeral and returns to the successful life he has established as a poet and proud gay man in the larger world. The violin rendition of the nursery rhyme in the final credits thus suggests—like the 49—not merely loss but triumphant survival.[20]

At the same time, these interpretations—and others like them—may all be far-fetched given that nine is also the number of stories in Alexie's previous short fiction collection, *The Toughest Indian in the World.* Initial announcements of *Ten Little Indians* had the volume containing eleven stories. When asked at a book signing about this change, Alexie explained simply that "nine is a much funnier number than eleven."[21] It may also be worth noting that in all of Alexie's previous collections— whether poems or stories—the title of the volume comes from one of the selections. Not so with *Ten Little Indians,* where the title seems to be designed as a container for everything within, a way of defining the nine stories, functioning in the same way as the titles of his two novels, *Reservation Blues* and *Indian Killer.* In this light, it is interesting that some of the early advertising for *Ten Little Indians* that printed part of the opening story, "The Search Engine," called it Chapter One.[22]

If one can draw any conclusion about the relationship of title to stories, it may be that Alexie has in effect used it to deconstruct the rhyme: his characters have rendered it, at least in its traditional sense, meaningless. In essence, this is what he did with the phrase "Indian killer" in his

1996 novel when he played with its meanings of both an Indian who kills and a killer of Indians.[23] Moreover, in that work, he reverses the meaning of "Ten Little Indians," for white men—not Indians—are being systematically murdered. Who then are the ten little Indians Alexie is writing about? To whom does the title refer? If it is simply the main character in each story, then of course there are not ten. If it is the main Indian characters in each story, there are more than ten. At the same time, the Indianness of several of these people is questionable—not because they live in Seattle or the white world or are—like Richard in "Lawyer's League"—biracial. Harlan Atwater in "The Search Engine," who pretended to be an Indian poet—"Indian is easy to fake" (TLI, 40)—was raised by whites, has not been to the reservation in thirty years, rejected his birth mother, and now wants only to care for his aged white parents whom he considers "the two best, the two most honorable and loyal people in my life": "So," he asks, "what kind of Indian does that make me?" (TLI, 52).

That question may be asked of other characters in Ten Little Indians. The race of the unnamed victim of the bombing in "Can I Get a Witness?" is incidental, especially since she sees in the disaster an opportunity to disappear, to walk away from her Indian husband and two sons and "start a new life, a better life" (TLI, 94). Also incidental is the ethnic identity of David and Sharon in "Do You Know Where I Am?" Although when young they viewed themselves as "native American royalty, the aboriginal prince and princess of western Washington" (TLI, 151), being Indians is finally of no significance to them. When sent each summer to the reservation by his white mother so that he could keep in touch with his "tribal heritage," David merely read spy novels to his grandfather and went to garage sales with his grandmother. In his mind, the reservation was "a sedate version of Disneyland" (TLI, 150–51). Even the narrator and his mother in "The Life and Times of Estelle Walks Above" are ill-informed about their heritage. Whereas the mother changed her name from Estelle Miller to Estelle Walks Above to impress her white friends, the son does not know "what an Indian is supposed to be": "To this day, I rarely look in the mirror and think, I'm an Indian" (TLI, 134). Being an Indian is, he decides, "number three" on the list of things he is (TLI, 135).

A super-Indian like Corliss Joseph in "The Search Engine" may know her tribe, her clan, and both her public and secret Indian names but still realize that "everything else she knew about Indians was ambiguous and transitory" (*TLI*, 52). And even though Jackson Jackson in "What You Pawn I Will Redeem" gets back his grandmother's powwow regalia and, dancing in it, becomes his grandmother, what is of greatest importance in this story is his recognition of goodness in the world: "Do you know how many good men live in this world? Too many to count!" (*TLI*, 194).[24]

More to the point, the stories in *Ten Little Indians* are less about what makes one distinctively Indian than being human and alive. This is what William in "Flight Patterns" demonstrates when—after learning from his Ethiopian taxi driver to find pleasure in the simple here and now—he desperately calls his wife to tell her "I'm here" (*TLI*, 123). This and other stories in the collection are "redemption stories," where the characters are "forever saving someone, or at least making the attempt"; but even when unsuccessful, they do not come across as victims.[25] They, in other words, redeem the nursery rhyme. Like the husband and wife in "Do Not Go Gentle," who use the giant vibrator as a magical drumstick to bring their baby out of a coma, Alexie's stories transform the rhyme so that it is no longer simply about death and loss or even Indians. We are all ten little Indians, and Alexie is counting us as he did in "Red Blues," counting until he finally realizes that he is able to "count the entire world" (*OSNS*, 87) or—as Jackson Jackson puts it in "What You Pawn I Will Redeem"— we are "too many to count" (*TLI*, 194).

NOTES

1. Sherman Alexie, *The Lone Ranger and Tonto Fistfight in Heaven*, 44 (hereafter cited in the text as *LRT*).
2. Alexie also uses this story—though with some changes—in *The Business of Fancydancing: The Screenplay*, 32. Unfortunately, the scene was omitted in the final version of the film.
3. Iona and Peter Opie, eds., *The Oxford Dictionary of Nursery Rhymes*, 327–28.
4. Lucy Rollin, *Cradle and All: A Cultural and Psychoanalytic Reading of Nursery Rhymes*, 125.
5. Opie, *Oxford Dictionary of Nursery Rhymes*, 328. Also see the positive finger-play rhyme in Gloria T. Delamar, *Children's Counting-Out Rhymes, Finger-plays, Jump-Rope and Bounce-Ball Chants and Other Rhythms*, 19.
6. Agatha Christie, *Ten Little Indians*, 30.
7. Louis Owens, *Mixedblood Messages: Literature, Film, Family, Place*, 70.
8. Sherman Alexie, *Flight*, 25.

9. Sherman Alexie, *First Indian on the Moon*, 50 (hereafter cited in the text as *FIM*). See Jan Johnson's essay in this volume for more on the relationship between trauma and nihilism.

10. Sherman Alexie, *Reservation Blues*, 246 (hereafter cited in the text as *RB;* italics in original).

11. Sherman Alexie, *The Summer of Black Widows*, 127.

12. Stephen F. Evans, "'Open Containers': Sherman Alexie's Drunken Indians," 46. Along with offering a particularly detailed defense of Alexie, Evans gives a good account of the controversy among Indians about his writing.

13. Sherman Alexie, *Old Shirts & New Skins*, 68 (hereafter cited in the text as *OSNS*).

14. Evans, "'Open Containers,'" 55.

15. Sherman Alexie, *One Stick Song*, 20 (hereafter cited in the text as *OSS*). "Poetry" also appears in *Old Shirts & New Skins*, xi.

16. Sherman Alexie, *Ten Little Indians*, 217 (hereafter cited in the text as *TLI*).

17. Sherman Alexie, *The Toughest Indian in the World*, 152–53.

18. Ibid., 153.

19. An interesting appearance of the rhyme occurs in the film version of Adrian C. Louis's novel *Skins* (2002). The novel (1995) does not contain the scene. Rudy comes upon his drunken brother, Mogie, shooting at beer bottles and singing the words, "One little, two little, three little VCs" as he aims and fires. For the obnoxious term "Injun" (or "nigger") in the original, Mogie substitutes the Viet Cong enemy he knew in Vietnam, thus not only extending and perpetuating the prejudice that was the basis of the original rhyme in the nineteenth century but also, through the mindless, systematic shooting of what is essentially his mirror image, revealing the self-destructiveness of the Indian.

20. The ending of the screenplay is notably different. Though its publication postdates the film, the screenplay should properly be viewed as a draft of the final film.

21. Jayme Meyers, "Review, *Ten Little Indians*," *Contemporary Literature.* Online at http://contemporarylit.about.com/ but no longer accessible.

22. See, for example, *Denver Post,* June 29, 2003. Available online at http://www.denverpost.com/Stories/0,1413,36%7E27%7E1481604,99.html; and *Washington Post Online,* June 20, 2003. Available online at http://www.washingtonpost.com/wp-srv/style/longterm/books/chap1/tenlittleindians.html

23. See also what Alexie does with the phrase in "Capital Punishment," a poem that appeared the same year in *The Summer of Black Widows* (86–90).

24. Alexie plays with this equation in "One Good Man" in *The Toughest Indian in the World,* where "What is an Indian?" is repeated over and over, intersecting with the title.

25. David Kipen, "Way off the Reservation: The Indians in Alexie's Fiction Are Out for Redemption."

CHAPTER 13

Healing the Soul Wound in *Flight* and *The Absolutely True Diary of a Part-Time Indian*

Flight (2007), Sherman Alexie's first novel since *Indian Killer* in 1996, addresses themes he has explored throughout his career: absent or imperfect fathers, fathers and sons, alcohol and alcoholism, colonialism, history, notions of masculinity, love and family, and the search for identity. Like the protagonist of *Indian Killer,* the main character in *Flight* is a young, emotionally wounded male Indian orphan adopted into a white family.[1] But the two novels create very different visions of redemption for their protagonists, a contrast that attests to the distance Alexie has traveled over the past decade in contemplating the ravages of colonialism, racism, and violence, as well as the possibilities of reconciliation and healing.

Alexie has said that he sees *Flight* as his answer to *Indian Killer's* nihilist vision.[2] While his works have frequently attempted to narrate historical trauma, *Flight,* and Alexie's subsequent novel for young adults, *The Absolutely True Diary of a Part-Time Indian* (2007), implicitly explore the possibilities for healing the tragic legacy of genocide and colonialism in ways that no earlier works have. In these two novels, empathy, compassion and forgiveness mark a possible way out of suffering and grief. *Flight* and *Diary* convey hopefulness not apparent earlier in Alexie's career.

Flight's protagonist is a shame- and rage-filled adolescent who commits mass murder in the lobby of a Seattle bank. As Alexie embarked on the book tour for *Flight* in April of 2007, the massacre at Virginia Tech had just occurred; Alexie seemed attuned to the many alienated, angry, and hurting young people in the United States. Due to the novel's teenage protagonist, some reviewers read *Flight* as a young adult novel: "Was it perhaps meant as a young-adult book—a morality tale of a teenager battling issues of identity and history, alcoholism and acne, who, through some strange 'back-to-the-future' fantasy trip, arrives at an understanding of himself and his country?"[3] Alexie's next novel, *The Absolutely True Diary of a Part-Time Indian,* published approximately six months after *Flight,* was indeed written for and marketed to a young adult audience to significant acclaim.[4]

While adolescent readers can undoubtedly enjoy both *Flight* and *Diary,* the gravity of the issues they imaginatively address make for a powerful adult reading experience with themes as vital as those addressed by the essays of James Baldwin in *The Fire Next Time* and Cornel West in *Race Matters:* the despair of young people living in communities ravaged by racism, poverty, and hopelessness.[5] This is not to say that Native American and African American historical experience that results in widespread despair is the same but that Baldwin and West's proposals for curing the illness of despair seem to be reflected in Alexie's new works, more so than interventions recommended by theorists of Native American trauma or Native healers.[6] Native American historical trauma theories, however, are highly appropriate as a context for reading Alexie's work.

The "soul wound" caused by the colonization of American Indians is a theoretical concept specific to Native Americans that illuminates Alexie's treatment of cultural trauma. I want to discuss *Flight* and *Diary* in terms of Alexie's "thematization of suffering"[7] and the soul wound,[8] the deep, long-lasting anguish that began with the arrival of Columbus on Turtle Island and the subsequent death, dispossession, and denigration of millions of Native people in the Americas. This wounding of the soul results from the trauma of colonialism and genocide and the dominant culture's lack of acknowledgement of the American Indian holocaust: "Historical trauma response has been identified and is delineated as a constellation of features in reaction to the multi-generational, collective, historical and cumulative psychic wounding over time, both over the life span and across generations."[9] Theorists of Native American historical trauma have formulated several phases that include contact with Europeans, economic competition, an invasion/war period, a subjugation and reservation period, a boarding-school period, a forced-relocation and termination period, and ongoing forms of colonialism.[10]

In "The American Indian Holocaust: Healing Historical Unresolved Grief," Maria Yellow Horse Brave Heart and Lemyra DeBruyn identify high rates of suicide, homicide, accidental deaths, domestic violence, child abuse, and alcoholism as "the product of a legacy of chronic trauma and unresolved grief across generations[;] racism and oppression, including *internalized oppression* are continuous forces which exacerbate these destructive behaviors."[11] The soul wound, historical trauma, or historical unresolved grief originate from "the loss of lives, land, and vital aspects of Native culture promulgated by the European conquest of the Americas."[12]

Flight and *Diary* are narratives of trauma that bear witness to American Indian history and experience and seek witnesses to their characters' ongoing suffering. Recognizing the traumatized victim can alleviate "disenfranchised grief... grief that persons experience when a loss cannot be openly acknowledged or publicly mourned,"[13] or the sense among many Indian people that negative constructions of them as subhuman and lacking a full range of human qualities and emotions make them seem incapable of having feelings, the capacity to mourn, and therefore no need or right to grieve.[14]

Furthermore, many of Alexie's characters—*Flight's* protagonist Zits in particular—can be recognized in Lisa Poupart's claim that "the intense historical unresolved grief and pain that exists is [sic] accompanied by an extreme rage at the dominant culture for abuses past and present. And, like Indian grief and pain, this rage is also invalidated by the dominant culture and denied avenues of expression."[15] This rage is generally turned inward and expressed through depression, anxiety, substance abuse, and suicide, and manifested externally within families and communities through domestic and other forms of violence.[16] When Alexie was asked by Åse Nygren if there is a central narrative of violence in Indian literature, he responded, "Well, yes, I think so. After all, we come out of genocide, and our entire history is filled with murder and war. Perhaps violence is not the right word, though. But there is definitely a lot of humiliation in Native literature. We write about being humiliated a lot. And that takes physical forms, emotional forms and mental forms. I think Native literature is the literature of humiliation and shame."[17]

Hence, Alexie feels that—as a result of this grim history—suffering and even trauma are fundamental to the experience of being Native American. Ceaseless suffering attains an epistemological status, as Alexie told Nygren:

> The fact is you cannot separate our identity from our pain. At some point it becomes primarily our identity. The whole idea of authenticity—"How Indian are you?"—is the most direct result of the fact that we don't know what an American Indian identity is. There is no measure anymore. There is no way of knowing, except perhaps through our pain. . . . As for the characters—I make them suffer! I specifically designed them to be suffering. John Smith [from *Indian Killer*], for instance, there's no redemption there; there's no healing, there's no talking cure. For a lot of the characters there's no cure. All there is, is suffering. The whole point of their identity is suffering. What keeps coming back to me is that when I think about Indians all I think about is suffering. My first measure of any Indian is pain.[18]

I argue that Alexie's stories are narratives of trauma seeking witnesses to his characters'—and, by extension, Native peoples'—grief and pain. Alexie wants to dramatize Native history, experience, and suffering to disrupt widespread historical amnesia. Nancy J. Peterson argues that ethnic American writers tell history through "literature as a genre because 'what really happened' is often so excruciatingly painful that to articulate these events as American history would be to invite utter disbelief."[19] Alexie incisively characterizes those who don't recognize or validate the vast pain of Native people: "The romantic idea is that if people are feeling a lot of pain you'd wish that people would empathize more. I wish that was true.... Honestly, I think that people who can't empathize with the [Indian] mascot [issue] or with feminism, for instance, are not so far removed from a criminal. The inability to understand why something might be offensive is a form of sociopathy."[20]

For Native Americans, historical trauma is not merely a matter of painful legacies; suffering is ongoing and maintained by present-day forms of colonialism, including—to cite one well-known example—the reduction of Indian religious traditions to sports mascots. Because of this continuing abuse, Nancy Van Styvendale argues that trauma theory is "crucial to the field of Native literatures[:]...One of my functions as literary critic is to recognize the fact of trauma in Native literatures (with all the attendant benefits and dangers of such a move) by using the lexicon of trauma to make sense of the constructions of history, woundedness, recovery, and temporality that I see expressed within this literature."[21] Van Styvendale challenges the assumption "of trauma as rooted in event, where 'event' is defined, as it most commonly is, as a singular, recognizable, and chronologically bounded incident" and insists it be understood as "cumulative, collective, intergenerational, and intersubjective[;]...the trauma of Native peoples, when understood as trans/historical, exceeds any attempt to fix its location or define its event, even as it demands our attention to historically specific atrocities."[22] For example, Van Styvendale thinks the removal of *Indian Killer*'s protagonist from his Indian mother to a white family and his subsequent loss of identity and resulting psychosis reflects a widespread practice of adopting out Indian children that the Bureau of Indian Affairs began in the late 1950s and was stopped only by the Indian Child Welfare Act of 1978.[23] This specific, historical removal is linked to the many removals, dispossessions, and relocations of Native people through time.

Van Styvendale insists on the efficacy of trauma theory to elucidate Native people and their literature for several reasons: "The deployment of this language provides Native communities with a means through which they can give expression to their collective and individual pain [through] linguistic and diagnostic categories that, because they are sanctioned within the dominant culture, hold out the hope of having this pain recognized, legitimated, and compensated for."[24] She argues further that the lack of research on Native trauma "reveals an institutional complicity in larger, nationwide attempts to forget the trauma of Native peoples. This repression ameliorates 'white guilt' for the theft of the North American land base and obfuscates the need for Euroamericans to take responsibility for privileges that continue to accrue from this theft— and its denial."[25] Just as importantly, Van Styvendale contends that seeing trauma as an "event outside the norm…allows the 'norm' itself to go unrecognized as the site of multiple traumas, an oversight that in relation to the systemic oppression of Native North Americans, justifies the status quo of domestic colonialism."[26] One of the many accomplishments of *Flight* and *Diary* is the exploration of the multiple traumas of ongoing colonialism (as well as the violence of American culture) as the unrecognized norm.

Flight's protagonist, Zits, is a fifteen-year-old, acne-scarred, half-Indian, half-Irish orphan who lives in Seattle. Because his Indian father abandoned him and his mother when he was born, and his Irish mother died of breast cancer when Zits was six, he has bounced from foster family to jail to foster family for the past nine years. He has lived in and escaped from twenty of these foster homes by the time the novel opens and has attended twenty-two schools. He has just enough clothes to fit in a small backpack and, currently, forty-seven pimples on his face. Zits's counting—the need to take stock—may be part of his response to trauma, an attempt to quantify his otherwise-incomprehensible experience.[27] He has suffered extensive mental, sexual, and physical abuse and has little sense of self-worth. He is angry, bitter, filled with shame, and resentful of those who don't share his rotten life.

Zits takes what solace he finds in his beloved books and getting drunk with homeless Indians "who wander around downtown Seattle.… Those street Indians enjoy my company.… Of course, those wandering Indians are not the only Indians in the world, but they're the only ones who pay attention to me."[28] Zits's observation reveals his need for attention to himself and his despair. Furthermore, his camaraderie with other Indians reflects his awareness that his situation is not just personal and individual; he is part of a much larger group of suffering Indians. Yet these homeless and wounded Indians are probably not the people who can give him the help he needs.

During one of his many brief stays in jail, Zits comes under the influence of a young white man who calls himself Justice. Justice gives Zits the attention he craves and convinces him that an extraordinary act of violence—a violent form of the Ghost Dance—will bring back his parents and give him the revenge, relief, and justice he desperately seeks. This act—a massacre in a downtown bank—sends Zits hurtling through space and time. He finds himself consecutively in the bodies of a white male FBI agent in 1975 who participates in the killing of an American Indian activist; a mute Sioux child at the Custer battlefield in 1876; an old Indian tracker for the Seventh Cavalry, who tries to save a Sioux child; a middle-aged white flight instructor, who cheats on his wife and unknowingly teaches a 9/11-type terrorist to fly;[29] his drunken father, "shambling" and vomiting through a Tacoma alley; and, finally, his own fifteen-year-old body as a transformed young man. This time-travel paradigm creates a "bodily epistemology" that makes traumas of the past present for Zits and readers.

I want to read Zits's embodiment as his father through the lens of Native trauma theory because American Indian historical grief is widely understood to be transmitted intergenerationally and this situation has a thematic relationship to Alexie's recurring exploration of fathers and sons, abandonment, and the complexities of forgiveness. These are issues he addressed in his first collection of short stories, *The Lone Ranger and Tonto Fistfight in Heaven* (1993), and the screenplay *Smoke Signals* (1998). In *Flight* Alexie explores this most painful of issues by locating his narrator, the abandoned son, within the body of his missing father.[30]

Initially Zits does not know he is inside his father; he simply wakes up on the ground staring at a rat and vomiting blood (*Flight*, 132). He realizes he is "a street drunk, a loser whose belly is torn apart by booze" (*Flight*, 132). When a "pretty white" couple approach him and he asks them if he is white (he'd most recently inhabited the body of the white flight instructor), they tell him he is Indian: "I look down at my dirty T-shirt, emblazoned with a black-and-white photograph of the Apache warrior Geronimo and the ironed-on caption FIGHTING TERRORISM SINCE 1492" (*Flight,* 132).

Appearing soon after the 9/11 attacks, this popular T-shirt expresses many American Indians' perspective of having been invaded, terrorized, and colonized and the patriotism of American Indians in their struggle to retain their land, lives, and culture. But the grief and rage that result from Indians' awareness of the ongoing reality of colonization and the dominant culture's denial of it are registered in this man's drunken state. Alcohol numbs the pain of trauma and disenfranchised grief: the sense that the dominant culture neither recognizes this tragic history nor cares about the pain caused by its injustice.

Many symptoms and expressions of the soul wound become apparent in the ensuing scene: when the man again vomits blood, the passersby tell him he is dying and call 911 (*Flight,* 135). But Zits/the man is disgusted by the good Samaritans' compassion and tells them "it's all your fault" and "white people did this to Indians" (*Flight,* 136). Zits tells us, "I don't even know if I believe that. But this fifty-year-old guy wants to blame someone for his pain and his hunger.... This homeless guy's anger is even stronger than my anger. And anger is never added to anger. It multiplies" (*Flight,* 136). He insults the caring woman but realizes, "Maybe I can't defeat her with my rage and self-hatred" (*Flight,* 137). After being punched in the face by the woman's partner, the man/Zits awakes, aware that he is in an alley in downtown Tacoma, only thirty miles from home in Seattle. As he "shambles" out of the alley, his bloody face horrifies the people on the street: "'I want some respect,' I say. Nobody hears me. Worse, nobody understands me" (*Flight,* 141).

I read this desire for respect and understanding as a direct expression of disenfranchised grief—the sense that no one recognizes or cares about the suffering of Native people. Though this man may be one of many homeless in the city looking for respect, in the context of American Indian colonization and trauma, he articulates one of the most painful issues of being Indian in America: the history and legacy of genocide are ignored and occluded.

Zits/the man finally feels he has gotten respect when he convinces a man to tell him a story. Afterward the stranger pulls out his wallet to show Zits/the man a photo of his family and then asks if he has kids. Zits is startled—"I don't know this homeless Indian's name, let alone if he has any kids"—and pulls out a wad of photos and receipts held together by a rubber band (*Flight*, 149). He spots a "familiar photo" and realizes, "It is me, the five-year-old me. The five-year-old Zits. The real me" (*Flight*, 150). Confused, he looks into the side-view mirror of a nearby truck: "I stare at my bloody reflection. I am older than I used to be. I am battered, bruised and broken. But I know who I am. I am my father" (*Flight*, 150). Zits realizes he's staring into the face of his betrayer—the man he should kill—but "what satisfaction is there in killing a man who wants to die?" (*Flight*, 151).

Zits asks the questions he has always wanted to ask his father: "Why did you leave me, why did you want to carry a photograph of me but not me?" (*Flight*, 152). These are questions his father/the man doesn't want to answer: "I can feel him fighting me. He doesn't want to remember the day he left me" (*Flight*, 152). But Zits forces his father to remember and learns that his father was not only sexually molested but cruelly—actually horrifically—ridiculed by his own father to believe he was utterly worthless: "My father wants to weep. He wants to cry out for his father. He wants to be forgiven, to be loved. But if he speaks he will only be ridiculed again. He will only be diminished" (*Flight*, 155). Now inside his father's memories at the hospital where Zits's mother is giving birth to him, he realizes, "My father cannot be a participant. He cannot be a witness. He cannot be a father" (*Flight*, 156). Zits understands that his father has been so damaged by abuse that he does not have the strength or confidence to raise his own son and perhaps fears that he will inflict the same abuse on him that he received from his father.

The word "witness" is important because of its multivalence to trauma. Victims of historical trauma desperately need someone to validate their pain by acknowledging their grief. Without some sort of efficacious intervention, the traumatized person cannot understand or witness the sources of their suffering and thereby gain relief from its continual haunting.[31] Because Zits is now a witness to his father's abuse and understands why he was abandoned, there is hope that he can forgive his father, perhaps find relief from his own suffering, and stop the intergenerational transmission of historical trauma. When Zits suddenly finds himself back in his body in the lobby of the bank where his time traveling began, he remembers "the dirtiest secret" he owns: his own sexual molestation by his aunt's boyfriend soon after his mother's death (*Flight*, 159). Now aware of the source of his shame, he may be able to stop blaming himself for his victimization. In *Flight's* final chapters, Zits discovers his father's soul wound and, through it, his own.

Alexie provides hope for Zits's healing through a remarkably happy ending, one that seems too perfect given the degree of trauma the narrative describes. His new foster family is comprised of his friend, Police Officer Dave; Dave's brother, a fireman; and his brother's wife, a nurse, all of whom are white, although Zits notices the woman's cheekbones are like "Indian cheekbones" and "wonder[s] if she's a little bit Indian" (*Flight*, 175).

How are we to read these "Dick and Jane Patriot" types? Ironically? Can those without many material benefits or power do much to ameliorate the widespread and devastating suffering of young people like Zits? Or is Alexie suggesting that white or non-Native people can do some of the very important—perhaps necessary—work of acting as allies to Native people?[32] That the soul wound can be healed at least partly through cross-racial alliances?[33] Still, I find myself asking, why not create an Indian father and family for Zits, considering the identity and legal issues presented by extratribal adoption?[34] What is Alexie suggesting through offering these caring, almost too-good-to-be-true white folks as Zits's new family?[35]

I think that this hopeful, interracial conclusion to *Flight* reflects a shift in Alexie's vision that has been so marked by anger throughout his career.[36] Perhaps after expressing his anger and frustration at the effects of colonialism in many of his works, he is now offering possibilities for healing this painful legacy. Alexie stated that he was changed by the 9/11 terrorist attacks[37]; he told Åse Nygren that he realized that "everybody's pain is important."[38] Speaking of his early career, he continued, "I was fundamental. I was so focused on Indian identity I didn't look at details. So having children, having friends, my life diversifying—all that has changed me.... Worrying about racism is easy! Easy! Dealing with racism is easy, compared with dealing with love."[39]

Although the legacy of genocide and colonialism that creates nihilism in Alexie's characters such as John Smith in *Indian Killer* and Zits in *Flight* persists, his vision of the way to address the widespread despair among Indian people has changed. His new perspective brings his recent work into implicit conversation with African American chroniclers of cultural trauma, especially James Baldwin and Cornel West. This move is a departure from models offered by Native American trauma theory, which emphasize healing through decolonization and interventions based on tribal cultural traditions and traditional ceremonies.[40]

Baldwin in *The Fire Next Time* and West in *Race Matters* address the nihilism and despair that results from severe, extended oppression. In the introduction to *Race Matters,* West writes, "We have created rootless, dangling people with little link to the supportive networks—family, friends, school—that sustain some sense of purpose in life." He continues, "Let us hope and pray that the vast intelligence, imagination, humor, and courage of Americans will not fail us. Either we learn a new language of empathy and compassion, or the fire this time will consume us all."[41] In the essay "Black Nihilism," West avers:

> *Nihilism is to be understood here not as a philosophic doctrine that there are no rational grounds for legitimate standards or authority; it is, far more, the lived experience of coping with a life of horrifying meaninglessness, hopelessness, and (most important) lovelessness.* The frightening result is a numbing detachment from others and a self-destructive disposition toward the world. Life without meaning, hope, and love breeds a coldhearted, mean-spirited outlook that destroys both the individual and others.[42]

West stresses the need for compassion and empathy to interrupt the scourge of nihilism, and this is what Alexie's new work suggests as well. The condition of much of the black community that West describes is in some ways analogous to the situation of American Indian people suffering from the soul wound of historical trauma that is vividly portrayed in Alexie's work. West offers a prescription to relieve nihilism that may resonate with those who suffer from American Indian historical trauma, suggesting that through an ethic of community—what we may call cross-racial kinship—we can all have a role to play in this badly needed healing:

> Like alcoholism and drug addiction, nihilism is a disease of the soul. It can never be completely cured, and there is always the possibility of relapse. But there is always a chance for conversion—a chance for people to believe that there is hope for the future and meaning to struggle.... Nihilism is not overcome by arguments or analyses; it is tamed by love and care. Any disease of the soul must be conquered by a turning of one's soul. This turning is done through one's own affirmation of one's worth— *an affirmation fueled by the concern of others.* A love ethic must be at the center of a politics of conversion.[43]

I think that something akin to the "love ethic" and "new language of empathy and compassion" that Alexie hints at in *Flight* is clearly evident in his latest novel, *The Absolutely True Diary of a Part-Time Indian.* In the highly autobiographical *Diary,* the fourteen-year-old Spokane Indian protagonist, Arnold Spirit, chooses to go to high school in the nearby white town of Reardan, despite this making him a "traitor" to his tribe. Arnold identifies alcohol and hopelessness as the plagues affecting his tribe and reservation and believes that an education and interaction with people who are not burdened by these afflictions will allow him to create a better life for himself. One of the strongest messages in *Diary* in relation to healing the soul wound comes from Arnold's dying grandmother, who utters the words "forgive him" after being hit and fatally injured by a drunk driver.[44] I think for Arnold this means forgiving his alcoholic, but loving, father, his tribe for considering him a traitor for leaving the reservation, and himself for leaving the reservation. In *Diary* Arnold mourns the loss of his grandmother and his father's best friend, Eugene, and finally that of his sister, all of whom die alcohol-related deaths. He cries because he knows "five or ten or fifteen more Spokanes would die during the next year, and that most of them would die because of booze.... I cried because so many of my fellow tribal members were slowly killing themselves and I wanted them to live. I wanted them to get strong and get sober and get the hell off the rez," which he likens to a prison constructed to make Indians die and disappear (*ATD*, 216).

Perhaps this sentiment suggests why the family that adopts Zits in *Flight* is white: they are archetypes for caregivers and have the clout that comes from being linked into social power structures. They are not burdened by historical trauma and can offer the love that Zits so desperately needs. Maybe these people will actually nurture and sustain Zits's Indian identity. In *Diary* rejecting alcohol and even the reservation becomes for Arnold an act of resistance to ongoing colonialism and cultural genocide.[45]

The language of *Diary*—particularly its concluding chapters—reflects compassion and empathy. It upholds a love ethic that suggests a way out of nihilism and perpetual grief. Arnold's father is an alcoholic, but he deeply loves his son. Arnold expresses love for his father, his family, his tribe, and his reservation but believes he must leave to escape the hopelessness and despair that can overwhelm even wonderful, loving people. Alexie told an interviewer that *Diary*'s "theme is about escape" and he hopes "it encourages all sorts of trapped people to feel like they can escape."[46] In leaving his reservation, Arnold compares himself to an American immigrant—"millions of other Americans who had left their birthplaces in search of a dream" (*ATD*, 257). He realizes that he is in fact a member of many "tribes" (*ATD*, 257).

In relation to healing the soul wound, both *Flight* and *Diary* have an important message, one that may not be heard by all who suffer from historical trauma but one that holds out hope for Zits, Arnold Spirit, and perhaps Alexie as well: the efficacy and necessity of forgiveness. In the final scene of Alexie's film *Smoke Signals*—as Victor Joseph pours his father's ashes into the Spokane River and screams with grief—we hear Thomas Builds-the-Fire recite Dick Lourie's poem, "Forgiving Our Fathers": "Do we forgive our fathers in our age or in theirs? Or in their deaths? Saying it to them or not saying it? If we forgive our fathers, what else is left?"[47] The film, *Flight,* and *Diary* are, to use the words of James H. Cox earlier in this collection, "extraordinary in the ways that they privilege the interior landscapes of contemporary Native men."[48] Through his narrative strategy, Alexie forces us to ask difficult questions: to grieve and heal, must wounded sons forgive their fathers? Must victims forgive their oppressors, even when they do not receive an apology from them? Can victims of colonialism and historical trauma heal without an apology? Is an apology meaningful if the oppressed do not receive some kind of reparation for their spiritual and material losses?[49]

Smoke Signals, Flight, and *Diary* suggest—to quote Desmond Tutu—that there is "no future without forgiveness"[50] and cross-racial alliances and communities of concern can play a powerful role in healing those afflicted by the soul wound of colonialism. *Flight* and *Diary* provide validation and inspiration for Indians seeking to heal the soul wound of historical trauma. Yet I argue that one of the most important effects of Alexie's latest works—particularly since he admits the majority of his readers are white—is making Native American historical trauma and the occluded truth of American Indian history visible. As one thoughtful student exclaimed during a recent classroom discussion of *Flight,* "He wants us to see Native trauma and grief so that we'll do something about it!" This comment suggests that Alexie's work—and perhaps all Native American trauma narratives—ask readers "to bear some sort of ethical responsibility for the stor[ies] they read"; when readers turn from private encounters with novels to the public history these texts reflect, a wider discussion on the efficacy and limits of apology, forgiveness, reconciliation, and reparation can begin.[51]

Notes

1. For a discussion of the protagonist of *Indian Killer* as traumatized as a result of his adoption into a white family, see Margaret Homans, "Adoption Narratives, Trauma, and Origins," 4–26.
2. Elijah Elk Center, Saginaw Chippewa Tribe, presentation at the Native American Literature Symposium, Mt. Pleasant, MI, March 9, 2007.
3. Anderson Tepper, "A Boy's Life, Zits and All."
4. *The Absolutely True Diary of a Part-Time Indian* won the 2007 National Book Award for young adult literature.
5. James Baldwin, *The Fire Next Time;* Cornel West, *Race Matters.*
6. See Eduardo Duran and Bonnie Duran, Maria Yellow Horse Brave Heart, and Susan Yellow Horse-Davis, "Healing the American Indian Soul Wound," in *International Handbook of Multigenerational Legacies of Trauma,* 341–54. See also Eduardo Duran, *Healing the Soul Wound: Counseling with American*

Indians and Other Native Peoples; and Eduardo Duran and Bonnie Duran, *Native American Postcolonial Psychology.*

7.   Åse Nygren, "A World of Story-Smoke: A Conversation with Sherman Alexie," 149.

8.   Duran and Duran, Brave Heart, and Yellow Horse-Davis, "Healing the American Indian," 341.

9.   Ibid., 342.

10. Ibid., 343–44.

11. Maria Yellow Horse Brave Heart and Lemyra M. DeBruyn, "The American Indian Holocaust: Healing Historical Unresolved Grief," 60; italics in original. The term *internalized oppression* comes from Paulo Freire's seminal study *The Pedagogy of the Oppressed.*

12. Ibid.

13. Ibid., 66.

14. Lisa Poupart, "The Familiar Face of Genocide: Internalized Oppression among American Indians," 90.

15. Ibid., 89.

16. Ibid.

17. Nygren, "World of Story-Smoke," 155.

18. Ibid., 157, 165.

19. See Nancy J. Peterson, *Against Amnesia: Contemporary Women Writers and the Crises of Historical Memory,* 7. Peterson continues, "To even begin to tell these kinds of stories, then, requires the capacity to exceed normative narrative expectations. And so, of necessity, wounded histories are written as literature, or fiction, and not as history, for only literature in our culture is allowed the narrative flexibility and the willing suspension of disbelief that are crucial to the telling of these histories" (Ibid).

20. Nygren, "World of Story Smoke," 159.

21. Nancy Van Styvendale, "The Trans/historicity of Trauma in Jeanette Armstrong's *Slash* and Sherman Alexie's *Indian Killer,*" 204.

22. Ibid., 203.

23. Ibid., 221. See also note 7.

24. Ibid., 205.

25. Ibid., 205–6.

26. Ibid., 206.

27. I am grateful to my colleague David Sigler for this insight.

28. Sherman Alexie, *Flight,* 7 (hereafter cited in the text).

29. Alexie initially thought about organizing the entire novel around the flight instructor, whose appearance in a documentary fascinated him. "He started crying—I forget which of the terrorists he taught—but he said, 'He and I were friends; he would come to my apartment and drink. Some nights he'd get too drunk to go home, so he'd sleep on my couch.' In the midst of this epic tragic event, there was this smaller, more human betrayal, and it seemed to me that nobody has really talked about the way those terrorists

betrayed friends." See Rod Smith, "The Metamorphoses: Sherman Alexie Delivers a New Novel and a Shape-Shifting American Indian."

30. When an interviewer recently asked Alexie if it was hard writing about his father now that he had passed on, Alexie replied, "It's always tough, you know. But as somebody pointed out, my whole career has been writing about my father. I've been causing myself pain for fifteen years. I think that's the big thing that drives my career and drives my success. I mean, certainly, it's the Indian thing, but it's the failing father thing bigger than anything else." See Stephanie Dunnewind, "Sherman Alexie Captures the Voice, Chaos and Humor of a Teenager," 4. See also Alexie's discussion of his alcoholic father in relation to Theodore Roethke's poem "My Papa's Waltz" in "A Conversation with Sherman Alexie" by Diane Thiel.

31. See Bessel Van Der Kolk, Alexander McFarlane, and Lars Weisaeth, eds., *Traumatic Stress: The Effects of Overwhelming Experience on Mind, Body, and Society.*

32. I define *allies* as people who work to be agents of social change, rather than instruments of oppression. See Maurianne Adams, Lee Anne Bell, and Pat Griffin, *Teaching for Diversity and Social Justice,* 106.

33. Alexie explicitly discusses the necessity of cross-racial alliances in Silja Talvi, "Sherman Alexie Isn't Who You Think He Is," *Colors NW Magazine,* December 6, 2003. Originally online but no longer accessible.

34. See Homans, "Adoption Narratives."

35. Jeff Berglund has generously given me a partial description of fathers in Alexie's more recent short fiction: "a dedicated white father in 'Assimilation' who is married to a white woman (*Toughest Indian in the World*); a great, loving Indian father in 'One Good Man' who through divorce now must share his son with his ex-wife's white husband (*Toughest Indian in the World*); a passionate and grieving Indian father in 'Do Not Go Gentle' in *Ten Little Indians*—with his wife he tries to fight for his infant son's life; a good Indian father in 'Flight Patterns' in *Ten Little Indians,* but one who is absent on business trips/speaking engagements; a grieving Indian father in 'Class,' who has lost his child (and who is married to a white woman) in *Toughest Indian;* finally, in 'Whatever Happened to Frank Snake Church' (*Ten Little Indians*), Frank has amazing, loving parents; Frank is an adult, but he keeps them in his memory when he tries to achieve in different undertakings." Jeff Berglund, e-mail message to author.

36. Alexie told Åse Nygren that

> it is only in the last few years that my politics has found a way into my work that feels natural [he explains he wrote "politically" to defend himself from people who claimed he was employing stereotypes when he was writing about his own life]. Part of the reason is because you grow older. The way I think about it is that I used to spend more time looking inside myself, looking internally. Now I look at more of the world and wider range of people. "World of Story-Smoke," 153.

37. Elijah Elk Center, March 9, 2007.
38. Nygren, "World of Story-Smoke," 156.
39. Ibid., 168.
40. See Duran and Duran, Brave Heart, and Yellow Horse-Davis, "Healing the American Indian."
41. West, *Race Matters,* 9, 13.
42. Ibid., 22–23; italics in original.
43. Ibid., 29; italics added.
44. Sherman Alexie, *The Absolutely True Diary of a Part-Time Indian,* 157 (hereafter cited in the text as *ATD*).
45. I do not believe, however, that Alexie is suggesting that healing can only come through Indians leaving the reservation and assimilating into white families and culture.
46. Dunnewind, "Sherman Alexie Captures the Voice," 4.
47. Sherman Alexie, *Smoke Signals: A Screenplay* (New York: Hyperion, 1998), 148–49.
48. James H. Cox, "This is What It Means to Say Reservation Cinema: Making Cinematic Indians in *Smoke Signals*," in *Sherman Alexie: A Collection of Critical Essays*, 74. In his interview with Diane Thiel, Alexie suggests this trend will continue:

    > I am currently working on my first non-fiction, a big book about four generations of Indian men in my family, and our relationship with war, and I've broken it down into [a] fiction, non-fiction project, and poetry, so I'm really looking for a hybrid work here.... In some sense, I feel this new book is a summation of all my themes until now. After this book, I think I'll be looking in some radical new directions.

    Alexie's *Face* (2009) devotes some space to the relationship between fathers and sons, as well as military service.
49. In "Teaching Smoke Signals: Fatherhood, Forgiveness, and 'Freedom,' 123–46, Ralph Armbruster-Sandoval urges the creation of a U.S. Truth Commission that will document the atrocities committed against Indian people, put pressure on the United States government to apologize formally and express remorse to Indian people for their suffering, and provide reparations.
50. Desmond Tutu, *No Future without Forgiveness.*
51. See Dean Franco, "What We Talk about When We Talk about *Beloved,*" 415–39.

CHAPTER 14

The Business of Writing:

Sherman Alexie's Meditations on Authorship

I'm not going to try to speak for everybody. I'm one individual
heavily influenced by my tribe. And good art doesn't come
out of assimilation—it comes out of tribalism.

—SHERMAN ALEXIE, "ALEXIE'S TRIBAL PERSPECTIVE"[1]

I don't think they stay up late worrying about my career. I'm an
artist; I'm not supposed to be accepted where I am from. My only
purpose is to teach children to rebel against authority figures. You
think tribal councils want that? Our politicians are just as corrupt as
theirs. You know, we've been electing George W. for 120 years.

—SHERMAN ALEXIE, "AMERICAN INDIAN FILMMAKER/WRITER"[2]

I try to write about every day Indians,
not just that whole "corn pollen, four directions,
Mother Earth, Father Sky" Indian thing where everybody
starts speaking slowly, and their vocabulary shrinks down

> *until they sound like Dick and Jane. And it's all*
> *about spirituality, and it's all about politics.*

—Sherman Alexie, Sixty Minutes II[3]

> *The following are all good things: the ecstatic and disdainful reviews;*
> *the enraptured and bored audiences; the fans and the enemies; the*
> *skeptics and the faithful . . . when Indians love you and hate you for*
> *making a movie about Indians; and so on and so on. Trust me. The*
> *whole damn universe of response to your art, to your tiny little cre-*
> *ation, is a beautiful, amazing thing.*

—Sherman Alexie, preface to The Business of Fancydancing[4]

> *I'm a narcissist, as all artists and writers are,*
> *but how can I be of service?*

—Sherman Alexie, "Voice of the New Tribes"[5]

Sherman Alexie has explored his evolving role as author as completely, if not more obsessively, than James Joyce in *The Portrait of an Artist as a Young Man*. In structuring a very early poem titled "Portrait of the Indian as a Young Man"—an obvious allusion to Joyce—Alexie uses two phrases: "Some stories remain," and "some stories change."[6] As with the fictional Stephen Daedelus, the burden of history for Alexie is manifold: simultaneously personal, cultural, historical, religious, political, and artistic. As he notes in an early story from *The Lone Ranger and Tonto Fistfight in Heaven* (1993)—"A Drug Called Tradition": "Your past is a skeleton walking one step behind you, and your future is a skeleton walking one step in front of you."[7]

Caught between the genocidal history of the past and the presumptive, if not imminent, tragedy of the future—possibly succumbing to high mortality rates and levels of suicide, higher-than-average incidence of diabetes, substandard health care, poverty, and crime—Alexie's characters allow him to explore the possible role of tradition as a means of escaping the death march. He seems to characterize tradition, though, as a drug because some characters view it as a cure, some see it as release, some relish it as retreat, some interpret it as the source of meaning, and some seek it as a means of mediating between experiences in this world and the mysteries of the spirit world. For many, tradition is impossible to recover, access, or understand. As Alexie once noted in an interview, "In my dictionary, 'Indian' and 'nostalgic' are synonyms. As colonized people, I think we're always looking to the past for some real and imaginary sense of purity and authenticity."[8]

It's clear that Alexie, since the beginning of his publishing career, has had to contend with others' expectations of him as a writer who is American Indian. Is he an American Indian writer? Is he a writer who is American Indian? Is he an American writer who happens to be Indian? As an American Indian writer, what are his obligations to his tribal community? To other Indigenous people? What are his obligations to art? To earning a living? To his family? To his readers?

As theoretically provocative as the well-known and diverse scholarship in American Indian studies—Louis Owens's *Other Destinies* (1992) and *Mixedblood Messages* (1998), Gerald Vizenor's *Manifest Manners* (1994); Robert Warrior's *Tribal Secrets* (1995); Elizabeth Cook-Lynn's *Why I Can't Read Wallace Stegner* (1996) and *Anti-Indianism in Modern America* (2001); and Craig Womack's *Red on Red* (1999)—Alexie's fiction and poetry offer his readers an exploration of the ontology of writing and authorship for an individual self-identifying as Indian and publicly publicized as Native American.[9] Of course, Alexie's writing, however confessional, will never directly reveal the true person of its author. But that's beside the point. Although Alexie's views on any subject—including writing and authorship—have shifted over his career, he has stated on more than one occasion that he's moved to explore certain subjects not just because they shed light on the experiences of American Indian people but because they lead to a deeper understanding of aspects of himself or his thoughts at a particular moment. For example, in an interview in 1999, Alexie noted,

> There's always a huge difference between public persona and private person. In my art I try to keep that as narrow as possible. I try to write about that kind of Indian I am, the kind of person I

> am and not the kind of person or Indian I wish I was.... It's the
> difference between writing with imagination about an imaginary
> world and writing with imagination about a real world. I try to
> write with imagination about a real world.[10]

An inextricable actor in this circuit of meaning, of course, is the reader
or, more appropriately, readers because there are many types with mul-
tiple—and often competing—needs, interests, and ideological stakes.
From early defensive poems such as "In Response to Elizabeth Cook-
Lynn's Pronouncement..." (1993)[11] to "How to Write the Great Indian
Novel" from *The Summer of Black Widows* (1996) to "The Unauthorized
Autobiography of Me" and "Open Books" from *One Stick Song* (2000)
to "Indian Country" from *The Toughest Indian in the World* (2000) to his
directorial debut, *The Business of Fancydancing* (2002), to "The Search
Engine" from *Ten Little Indians* (2003) to "Oral Tradition" and a later
defensive poem, "Eagle Feather Tuxedo," both from *Face* (2009), and
"Fearful Symmetry" from *War Dances* (2009), Alexie has returned to the
subject of authors and their readers, examining the way readers fulfill
and frustrate authorial desires and authors satisfy and disappoint readers. Directly in interviews and autobiographical poetry—and indirectly in
his fiction—he has commented on the history of American Indian literature, readers' expectations shaped by it, and his own resistance to others'
expectations and models of creativity (for example, an attention to tra-
ditionalism within a tribal context or a focus on tribal nationalism and
Indigenous sovereignty).

All writers—it goes without saying—struggle with the burden of history, but American writers of color whose histories and cultures have
been previously ignored or misrepresented by mainstream culture have
an even greater burden of expectation placed upon them—by members
of their own communities as well as progressives from outside. Layered
on top of that—for the Indigenous writer—are the beautiful complex
of traditions, versions of history, spirituality, cosmology, and philosophies that any tribally affiliated writer must choose whether to explore
in his publications. Tribal members, through the generations, evolve
new traditions and ways of being in the world. Tradition is not static or
opposed to innovation, and it reacts to political and social exigencies; in

contrast, romanticized notions of tribal people assume that tradition is unchanging.

To avoid assumptions about the way older expressive traditions influence his writing, Alexie consciously and repeatedly eschews terms like *storyteller* and *storytelling,* as well as the framework of the oral tradition, as narrow interpretations of his own inspirations, motives, and interests. As he shared in "The Unauthorized Biography of Me": "'How does the oral tradition apply to your work?' 'Well,' I say, as I hold my latest book close to me, 'It doesn't apply at all because I typed this. And when I'm typing, I'm really, really quiet.'"[12]

In interview after interview, Alexie has fashioned and refashioned his authorial persona. By becoming a public intellectual—one of the most well-known living American Indian authors—he has bridged the pop, academic, and literary divide. He has discoursed on the state of Native literary studies and his sometimes-uncomfortable fit within this sphere. For example, in an often-cited interview with John Purdy, Alexie noted he wanted to reach twelve-year-old readers living on the reservation; he yearned to "take literature from what it is now"; and he critiqued writers for selling out their culture, saying they are doing what no other Indian people would: "No Indian will stand on the roadside singing traditional songs for money—this is what writers do when they put it in a book and sell it."[13] With the publication of *The Absolutely True Diary of a Part-Time Indian* (2007), winner of a National Book Award, Alexie has realized some of these hopes, although in the meantime, he has revised his profile of his ideal readership, particularly based on the fan base for his film *The Business of Fancydancing:* "You know who I depend on? There are about 75,000 college-educated white women in the country who buy all of my books and go to all of my movies. I mean, if I had to depend on Indians for a career? No way! No chance."[14]

Alexie's meditations on authorship and readership continue to circulate and reframe scholarly and nonscholarly conversations about the role of writers—particularly American Indian writers and intellectuals—as well as readers, whether they be pleasure readers or research scholars engaged in literary analysis and the advancement of new perspectives on the way literature and culture should be interpreted—by whom, for whom, and using what methodologies. This essay frames such wide-ranging meditations within an analysis of two primary works: Alexie's film, *The Business of Fancydancing,* and "The Search Engine" from his short-story collection *Ten Little Indians*, both released a decade after his early publications. In both narratives, a recognized tribal member has chosen—for different reasons—to live in urban Seattle, away from his home reservation; each is a writer identified as contributing to Native American literature, though one leaves it all behind early in his career while the other pursues commercial and critical success, consciously capitalizing on aspects of his own identity.

Balancing the demands of art and reality is dangerous business. Alexie explores this explicitly in his film *The Business of Fancydancing,* which focuses on Seymour Polatkin, a Spokane poet, who leaves his reservation to attend college. In college Polatkin realizes he is gay, undertakes his poetic avocation, and begins to grapple with his alcoholism. That's all backdrop to the film's primary narrative: Polatkin's difficult return to the reservation—after gaining literary acclaim—to attend funeral services for his childhood friend, Mouse, a talented violinist who succumbed to the demons of his addictions. In an interview, Alexie noted that Seymour Polatkin is "a slightly more exaggerated autobiographical version of me—with more regrets.... Plenty of people saw my leaving as a betrayal. I felt guilty, but I've forgiven myself, and most of my reservation has."[15] Throughout the film, Polatkin appears at readings and book signings, surrounded by his non-Indian, primarily white fans. He has commodified his identity and knowingly tapped into his readers' interest in all things Indian. His life with his primarily white male partners has increased his separation from his childhood community, though, notably, it is not his sexuality that has caused this sense of estrangement.

If anything, Polatkin's sexuality may be a screen on which the author's outsider status is projected. Polatkin is "queer," not because he is gay, but because he is an artist-outsider who steals from his culture.[16] Aristotle, a childhood friend, clearly feels Polatkin's successful career as a poet has led him to turn his back on his friends and community to profit from their stories. *The Business of Fancydancing* meditates on the politics of creativity: a writer's complex personal dance between personal and communal memory, between tribal tradition and history, and between private profit, artistic acclaim, and responsibilities to home. What happens to the friend or family member when sold into literary servitude, transformed into the subject of consumable fiction, poems, stand-up routines?

The film's title, taken from a poem by Alexie, makes this connection between art and commerce, between the individual artist and the communal audience. In competitive powwows, the fancy dancers demonstrate profound athletic ability and originality. They wear double bustles with brightly colored feathers, breechcloths, yokes, anklets, bells, beaded moccasins, armbands, and porcupine headdresses. This style of dance requires great endurance. Among the dances for men at competitive powwows, fancy dancing is a fan favorite. Its origins are interesting. While it had its roots in Plains cultures, it became formalized during Wild West shows before it was incorporated into the powwow circuit. It is recognized as a dance that became popular partially because it fulfilled audience expectations for who and what an Indian man should be, in fact, as Tara Browner puts it, "Fancy dancing [is] iconic of pow-wow dancing (and Indians in general) to the outside world."[17] Fancy shawl dancing—also practiced by Seymour in the film, who crosses traditional gender lines to participate in a dance reserved for women—has a similar origin in Wild West shows before it became a feature on the competitive powwow circuit.[18] Alexie's poem makes these connections explicit and offers a gloss on creative artists generally:

> We watch him dance
> and he never talks. It's all a business we
> understand. Every drum beat is a promise
> note written in the dust, measured exactly. Money
> is a tool, putty to fill all the empty
> spaces, a ladder so we can reach
>
> for more. A promise is just like money.
> Something we can hold, in twenties, a dream we can reach.
> It's business, a fancydance to fill where it's empty.[19]

Fancy dancing figures into this film beyond the title. Interspersed between action in the past and present are what the screenplay calls "IN-BETWEEN" where the characters inhabit a dark stage. In these interludes, at times characters soliloquize, at times a journalist interrogates Seymour, at times Seymour and his former girlfriend, Agnes, shawl-dance together. When Seymour appears fancy dancing, though, it is always just before or after he makes a public appearance as a poet, reading or speaking about being an Indian to primarily white audiences.

A scene early in the film establishes that Seymour is a commodity for sale. Viewers see a storefront setting during National Indian Month. Seymour's reading of Alexie's poem, "How to Write the Great American Indian Novel," reminds us that consumers are interested in buying certain kinds of Indians. Even the title of Seymour's book, *All My Relations,* recalls a commonly used phrase that evokes a mythic pan-Indian community. The book buyer observes Seymour from a distance, the way a zoo-goer might examine an exotic specimen. Overlaying his reading are two quite different critical commentaries: *The New York Quarterly* praises his poems for evoking tragedy, while the grassroots Web site, indianz.com, notes that Polatkin is "full of shit."

Three other scenes in the film show Seymour performing his Indian-ness before primarily white or non-Indian audiences. Alexie has alluded to scenes such as this one, where a Native writer is reading to almost exclusively white audiences. "The Unauthorized Autobiography of Me" in *One Stick Song,* for example, asks this rhetorical question: "Have you ever stood in a crowded room where nobody looks like you? . . . Since I left the reservation, almost every room I enter is filled with people who do not look like me. . . . Often I am most alone in bookstores where I am read-ing from my own work. I look up from the page at white faces" (*OSS,* 22). In these scenes in the film, men and women alike flock to get Seymour's autograph. As we later see, this reception is incredibly different from the one he receives when he returns home.

This pandering to romanticized or stereotypical notions of Indianness sharply contrasts with Alexie's commentary on this phenomenon within the literary field: "I want us to write about the way we live. . . . When I see words like the Creator, Father Sky, Mother Earth, Four Legends, I feel like we're colonizing ourselves. These words, this is how we're supposed to talk—what it means to be Indian in white America. But it's not who we really are; it's not what it means to be Navajo or Spokane or Coeur d'Alene."[20] This tension exists for Alexie and other Native artists who want the rest of the world to pay attention. Thomas Builds-the-Fire, Alexie's storyteller alter ego in *Reservation Blues* (as well as other works), tries to explain why he started up the band that achieves acclaim—at the risk of sustaining clichéd and stereotypical ideas of Indianness: "'I heard voices,' Thomas said. 'I guess I heard voices. I mean, I'm sort of a liar, enit? I like the attention. I want strangers to love me. I don't even know why. But I want all kinds of strangers to love me.'"[21] In a more confessional vein, in "The Unauthorized Autobiography of Me," Alexie alludes to the fulfillment of similar desires when he formed a band in his youth: "We are heroes. We are loved. I sing with everything I have inside of me: pain, happiness, anger, depression, heart, soul, small intestine. I sing and I am rewarded with people who listen.... This is why I am a poet" (*OSS,* 20).

In *The Business of Fancydancing,* the tension within Seymour that grows more obvious as his negative criticism increases finds expression in an in-between scene when a journalist questions, "Where do your poems come from?" Seymour answers, "I knew that writing poems was what I wanted to do my whole life," to which the interviewer replies, "Standard literary answer number two." Seymour continues, "Sometimes I think that nothing is real until I write it first." The interviewer follows up, "That doesn't leave a lot of room for the rest of us, does it?" to which Seymour responds, "I go to this place and it's dark there—like inside a machine, or inside the belly of a whale, and all of my dreams are there—my memories and lies, they get mixed up and spin, spin, spin—that's when a poem happens."

The exaggeration and blurring of truth in art is a common theme in Alexie's writing, clearly expressed in a poem from his book *One Stick Song* titled "Open Books": "Let us now celebrate / poets and liars, liars and poets / for we are both of those things.... Let us now celebrate the lies / that should be true because they tell us so much" (*OSS,* 30). For the poet, finding truth in lies and appropriating and modifying others' truths and experiences are not problematic in themselves. When Seymour continues his discussion, he tells his interlocutor (most likely an imaginary projection of his unconscious attempt to wrestle with his own demons): "Ari and I are so close, our memories have blended together; we're a little more than kin and less than kind." A jump cut replaces Seymour with

Aristotle, who narrates a childhood experience about stolen apples. This voice-over narration alternates between Aristotle and Seymour. Seymour's version is the calculated, well-crafted voice of the poet who has recollected this "personal" story countless times. Significantly, Aristotle notes that Seymour was the best apple thief on the reservation and he pinned the blame on the others. Viewers learn that in Seymour's version of these events, he is the only one who is caught after the others turn him in.

Seymour's poem's distortion of Aristotle's and his friends' version of the true experience is Exhibit A in the case indicting Seymour's character. At another point in the film—in a flashback to a time long before Mouse died, before his addictions spiraled out of control—Aristotle and Mouse are criticizing Seymour's new publication, *All My Relations,* and discussing the way he has cannibalized their personal experiences. Mouse feels stripped of his own memory, as if he is already dead.

Later in the film—when Seymour has returned to the reservation for Mouse's memorial—he and Aristotle exchange insults. When Aristotle questions why Seymour has turned his back on his friends, he points out that Seymour has been living an illusory existence and reminds him that on the reservation, "it's real." Seymour objects and criticizes Aristotle's lack of self-perception: "I bet you don't even recognize yourself in my stories. I have more insight into you than you ever will; that's why I write about you." Aristotle implies that Seymour wasn't around to do the real work of trying to save Mouse. Of course, Aristotle couldn't save Mouse, either, in spite of his proximity. Seymour retorts, "I'm supposed to come back and save your ass? I'm supposed to save every sad Indian ass that ever lived? What is this? Open season on Seymour Polatkin? Do you know how often this happens to me? Every goddamn place I go. Some stupid Indian with an attitude problem—think I haven't heard it all before? I deserve a better life than what I was born into. I made it better. I got no help from these goddamn Indians." Aristotle, however, has the last word: "You write about these goddamn Indians. They help you every day, every one of them. We've been helping you since you were born."

Seymour has likely always wrestled with his role as a writer—an insider and outsider simultaneously. While we may not see Seymour undergoing an immediate transformation, the end of the film implies that he is questioning his motives. In the penultimate interlude, we see him fall to the ground while fancy dancing, just before he is supposed to deliver his eulogy. The audience hears him scream, but we realize this, too, is a projection of his internal state. In the aftermath of his once-close-friend's death, the wordsmith, the professional poet, has no words to share. As he backs out of the driveway to begin his journey back to Seattle, we see a mirror image of Seymour being left behind, suggesting that this insider/outsider split will never be reconciled. This sequence is followed by shots of Aristotle in the rearview mirror mockingly performing a fancy dance. Next—in the film's final interlude scene—we see Seymour stripping off his regalia. He sheds his iconic trappings of Native identity. Naked, he rejoins his lover in bed as the memorial music swells.

If *Business* shows us tribally related readers disappointed in the commodified version of their own experiences—an allegorical exploration of critiques leveled at Alexie by tribal members or other Native writers and scholars—"The Search Engine" explores the flip side: a reader who desperately yearns for writing that mirrors her specific experiences, someone with whom she can identify. But these are expectations that cannot be met by any one individual. In this story, Corliss Joseph, a nineteen-year-old Spokane student at Washington State University, learns of Harlan Atwater's book of poetry published almost thirty years earlier. She is intrigued by his claimed tribal affiliation—Spokane, like her own—and is hopeful that she has finally found a fellow writer and lover of literature who shares a similar background.

Corliss's English-major tastes are cosmopolitan to be certain, and she holds her own in the best academic discussions and debates; for example, she is deeply moved by W. H. Auden, John Donne, Elizabeth Bishop, Emily Dickinson, Gerard Manley Hopkins, and Langston Hughes.[22] Prior to college, she learned to be an intellectual Robin Hood, stealing knowledge from an elite prep school. Corliss reads and finds an emotional and philosophical home in words, living with books as if they are her siblings; she is obviously starved for reflections of her own experiences in what she reads.[23] A chance finding of *In the Reservation of My Mind* by a Spokane writer, Harlan Atwater—never before checked out from the university library, though it was acquired in 1972—sets her on a journey of self-discovery, primarily focused on the assumptions she makes about authors she reads and the difficulties Native writers face in juggling multiple responsibilities and expectations, not to mention complicated and private personal lives.[24]

In her obsession to track down Atwater in person to authenticate his identity, Corliss resorts to Internet search engines like any contemporary student. In obvious ways, Alexie's story title puns on the age-old racial epithet, "injun," reminding readers that Corliss's pursuit of authenticity will meet with the typical pitfalls created by stereotypical thinking. The story is thus a meditation on reader desires, needs, hope, and expectations as well as writers' inextricable entanglement in the web of cultural pressures that may include commercial success or some form of cultural capital.

At first Corliss uses the lenses of academia to understand Atwater's work: she notes, for example, that he has used the sonnet form. Although she finds some of his poems "amateurish and trite," she is moved by his description of shared experiences and familiar places: "Corliss had swum the Little Spokane River. She'd floated down the river in a makeshift raft. She'd drifted beneath bridges and the limbs of trees. She'd been in the physical and emotional places described in the poem. She'd been in the same places where Harlan Atwater had been, and that made her sad and happy" (*TLI,* 17). This passage reminds us what processes of identification readers bring to bear on any text. For example, when Corliss first reads Atwater's poems, she thinks, "How could [I] ever be alone if Harlan Atwater was somewhere out there in the world" (*TLI,* 16).

Corliss's insider cultural knowledge creates a different set of interpretative criteria and raises the bar for realism and/or authenticity, the responsibility not only of artist truth tellers, generally, but any artist connected to a community whose world is depicted for those outside the group. In the case of Native writers, questions are thus raised about the way the tribe and tribal members are depicted, places are described, sacred and/or privileged knowledge is shared or restricted, and public accounts of tribal and personal experience hurt or benefit the group as a whole.

With these concerns in mind, Corliss then follows a path familiar to contemporary scholars in American Indian literary studies—she looks for tribal verification of Atwater's identity and the authenticity of his artistic vision. First, Corliss tries to find out if Harlan is known in his tribal community, or if he capitalized on a fake affiliation; secondly, she attempts to find out whether Harlan is known within the community of successful Native American writers. Her mother and father have never heard of him, nor have luminaries such as Joy Harjo, Simon Ortiz, Adrian Louis, and Leslie Marmon Silko. Corliss looks in public records and considers all sorts of reasons for possible name changes and an absence from tribal or federal records since typically, "every moment of an Indian's life is put down in triplicate on government forms, collated, and filed" (*TLI*, 20).

Alexie has explored this subject before in his novel *Indian Killer,* where his author character, Jack Wilson, possesses a questionable tribal identity; even more directly, Alexie has commented on having themes from his writing stolen by Nasdijj, who led publishers and writers to believe he was writing memoirs of his experiences as a Navajo/Diné person.[25] Alexie's "The Unauthorized Autobiography of Me" and "How to Write the Great American Indian Novel" similarly allude to non-Native readers' fascination with all things Indian, particularly if produced by non-Indians or questionable Indian people. In *War Dances* (2009), one white male academic is described as being "addicted to the indigenous."[26] Corliss also knows this about white people: "No matter how smart, [they] were too romantic about Indians. White people looked at the Grand Canyon, Niagara Falls, the full moon, newborn babies, and Indians with the same goofy sentimentalism. Being a smart Indian, Corliss had always taken advantage of this romanticism" (*TLI*, 11).[27]

Ironically, Corliss also is the victim of romanticism in this story. Her search eventually turns up an interview from the early 1970s published in *Radical Seattle Weekly.* Through this interview, readers can see that Atwater is playing into expectations for Native writers—more pronounced because Alexie has so often commented on related issues in interviews. Atwater notes, for example, that Native writing is connected to the oral tradition (*TLI*, 21), that everything he writes is "all about the elders.... If I think the tribal elders would love the idea, then to me, it's an idea worth turning into a poem" (*TLI*, 22), that "it's all about ceremony. As an Indian, you learn about these sacred spaces. Sometimes, when you're lucky and prepared, you find yourself in a sacred space, and the poems come to you.... Sometimes the whole tribe is writing the poem with me"

(*TLI,* 22-23), and that he is more influenced by "the natural rhythms of the world" than other writers (*TLI,* 23). Such responses fly in the face of Alexie's personal sentiments expressed in numerous interviews and commentaries, including a quote used earlier in this essay.

Interspersed throughout "The Search Engine's" mock interview, however, are nuggets of truth that resemble comments made by Alexie. For example, Atwater says, "There's been so much junk written about Indians.... So much romanticism and stereotyping. I'm just trying to be authentic" (*TLI,* 22). Like his author/creator, Atwater calls humor a survival tool and sees that extreme tribalism leads people to fight against one another. Atwater takes this gesture to authenticity to the next level, however: "I think you're going to find I'm writing the most authentic Indian poems that have ever been written. I'm trying to help people understand Indians. I'm trying to make the world a better place, full of more love and understanding.... I believe that poetry can save the world. And shoot, that one has always been a radical thought, I guess. So maybe I am a radical, you know?" (*TLI,* 22).

When Corliss finally tracks down the first published Spokane author, she is disappointed to find not only a man who was coerced to play Indian in the late 1960s but also one who has no interest or connection to his tribal people. In fact, it has been a long time since he's talked to an Indian: "I'm of the urban variety, bottled in 1947, but I haven't been to the rez in thirty years, and you're the first Spokane I've talked to in maybe twenty years. So if I'm still Spokane, I'm not a very good one" (*TLI,* 26). When she talks about the merits of his writing, Atwater responds, "Don't try to flatter me.... Those poems are mostly crap" (*TLI,* 26). He regales her with stories of his love for his white adoptive family; his deep disdain for his birth mother, an addicted woman who often lives on the streets; and his momentary popularity back when women were turned on by his Indian act. Rather than being flattered by Corliss's interest in his work, Atwater seems troubled to be taken back to this period. Like Seymour Polatkin and perhaps Alexie himself, he is asked to explain how and why he has become distanced from his reservation and tribal identity.

Alexie creates an interesting character for his readers to consider: Atwater is far from an ethnic imposter—he is actually Spokane by birth—but he is willfully culturally bereft. He has rejected tribalism and the duplicity of playing into stereotypical notions of an Indian writer. His bloodline is not in question, but his unwillingness to fulfill the social expectations that others have—including Corliss, who is Native herself—encourages readers to examine expectations of all authors, particularly Native ones, as well as their relationship and connection to tribe and community.

In many respects, this story explores in reverse an early experience Alexie had with a negative review of *Reservation Blues* from fellow Spokane writer Gloria Bird. Her review of the novel, entitled "The Exaggeration of Despair," critiques numerous elements, suggesting that it is colonialist and "preys upon a variety of native cultures," that it is a funhouse filled with self-referential "traps of popular culture," that it "omits the core of native community... Spokane culture or traditions," and that it exaggerates "despair without context." In addition to these points, Bird also indicts Alexie's description of the natural landscape by comparing his work to other Native writers, N. Scott Momaday and Leslie Marmon Silko:

> The community of Wellpinit and its surroundings are intimate props, familiar scenery that is vacant of any emotional investment. There is none of the sweeping, lyrical prose of Momaday's *The House Made of Dawn* whose lines like, 'The canyon is a ladder to the plain,' stay in the mind for years. Neither is there the detail of Silko's *Ceremony* wherein description of the New Mexican landscape is dense with meaning.[28]

Bird's review captivated Alexie enough that he responded—in addition to e-mails and LISTSERV postings—with a poem mimicking her title, "The Exaggeration of Despair," where he catalogues a litany of despairs facing Native people, including members of his own family, something he takes up again in "One Stick Song," a poem that tries to sing back/bring back all of those whom the speaker has lost from this world.[29]

But in "The Search Engine," Atwater's rebuff of Corliss confuses her and stalls what she has fashioned—more than a search for his identity— as an identity quest about herself. She is disappointed because her expectations of him—her desires about him—don't match up to who Atwater actually is. As Alexie emphasizes in "Open Books," the declaration "poets are liars" is less a value judgment than a definition. Put another way, "poetry is lying." Through Corliss's experience, Alexie reminds readers that no one can make assumptions about the truth of claims made through fiction or poetry, that art may exaggerate, and that it relies in so many ways on the tension between truth and artifice. Literature is no singular vehicle for exploring a person or culture, and readers who expect literary works and their creators to function this way are bound to be disappointed.

While Alexie draws attention to the obvious fact that artists reshape the world in their fiction, this is not enough to appease some critics who demand more from an American Indian writer with such a significant readership. Many feel that Native people have been misrepresented for too many centuries. Rather than attempting to reconcile the age-old tensions between politics and art, I want to emphasize what we all gain from reading Alexie's statements on authorship: we come to a deeper understanding of the complexities of the tangled mix of ideological and communal desires that condition expectation and determine critical authority. As Henry Giroux explains, "The construction of meaning, authority, and subjectivity is governed by ideologies inscribed in language and which offer different possibilities for people to construct their relationships to themselves, others, and the larger reality."[30] The rise of literary theories about tribal nationalism has exerted an authority that creates expectation to be sure. Shifts in critical sensibility have occurred in literary studies in each decade of the twentieth century; since 1977, the field of American Indian literary studies has been refining and testing paradigms that resist both ethnographic and extracultural approaches.[31] The lively discussion and critique of Elvira Pulitano's controversial *Toward a Native American Critical Theory* (2003)—which garnered multiple reviews in *American Indian Quarterly* and in-depth point-by-point analysis by Craig Womack in *American Indian Literary Nationalism* (2006) and again in *Reasoning Together: The Native Critics Collective* (2008)—are but one example of reactions to claims of authority established by tribal/nationalist theories.[32]

What does this have to do with Alexie? It certainly impacts his writing and the expectations placed on him as a Native American author. Different paradigms of interpretation condition the way readers receive his work. Unfortunately, misunderstandings about tribally specific approaches or aesthetic theories linked to nationalism have too often dismissed a popular, defiant, wiseass writer such as Alexie. Rather than analyze Alexie's work in opposition to such thinking, it's worth considering the specific ways his writing demonstrates key elements of a culturally centered approach, which, at its core, is interested in the tension among past, present, and future traditions within a particular framework. Alexie's writing focuses attention on the heterogeneous nature of tribal life and the reinterpretations of traditions that are accompanied by vital intracultural debates (i.e., sovereignty, tradition, nationalism, and so forth). Just in the space of "The Search Engine" and *The Business of Fancydancing*, a Spokane/Coeur d'Alene writer introduces us to two fictional writers who are Spokane but very different from one another and bear some traces of their creator/author; we also see many different Spokane readers, each with different expectations of the writers. We discover that reader expectation and writerly intent are not—or shouldn't be?—reconciled, something also clearly illustrated by Alexie's exchanges with Gloria Bird about *Reservation Blues*.

If one reviews many of the seminal works on tribal/nationalist approaches, this heterogeneous nature becomes evident: Craig Womack's *Red on Red* assembled diverse Muscogee writers and even created a colloquial persona to respond to the work of a "lit critter."[33] Robert Warrior's interest in *Tribal Secrets* was to gather intellectual traditions as an evolving canon, not create a unified narrative of tribal philosophy and cosmology. Daniel Heath Justice's *Our Fires Survive the Storm* applies the theoretical framework of *Red on Red* to Cherokee writing; in writing about the experience of researching this book, Justice acknowledges that his

> initial supposition that there was a single, unitary idea of 'Cherokeeness' was both naive, and, ultimately, impossible, especially given the long and tangled realities of Cherokee social history. Yet I also came to realize that though there are many different ways of understanding what it is to be Cherokee— some more suited for the preservation of Cherokee nationhood,

communitism, and decolonization than others—each way is still an attempt to give shape to an idea of what it is to be, think, and live Cherokee. Thus, easy assertions of a unitary definition break down, and the complicated living realities of the Cherokee people are revealed.[34]

This sounds remarkably like the experiences that Alexie has fictionally represented in his construction of Spokane characters. While there are shared histories and even mutually recognized obligations and centering principles, there is no unified portrait of a people. And, if there are requests to establish an authoritative perspective, his work tells us that such appeals should be met with skepticism. In sum Alexie's writing on authorship encourages us to reexamine our simplistic interpretation and/or application of theories.

It's also worth noting that Alexie shares another interest with tribal/nationalist theorists: claiming sovereignty over one's intellect and imagination and their contributions to the communal cultural imagination.[35] His fictional characterizations of English professors (*Indian Killer*, "One Good Man" from *The Toughest Indian*), anthropologists ("Dear John Wayne" from *The Toughest Indian*), and film producers (his new story "Fearful Symmetry" from *War Dances* (2009)), to name but a few stock characters, examine the history and continuing resistance to non-Native influence on the interpretation of Native people and culture. In public forums, interviews, and op-ed pieces, Alexie has commented about ethnic fraud (Nasdijj), outsiders' interpretations of Native people (Ian Frazier's *On the Rez*), and non-Natives cashing in on Indian themes (Tony Hillerman and Barbara Kingsolver). Taken together, these fictional and factual expressions seem to demonstrate that Alexie and the tribal/nationalist theorists share some of the same ideas; indeed, as indicated by one of the epigraphs that opened this essay, Alexie noted in 2000 that "good art" comes out of tribalism, not assimilation, though he has also linked extreme fundamentalism to tribalism (but not necessarily exclusively in art).

Alexie's work on authorship exposes us to the tensions that emerge when American Indian writers allied with tribal groups are thought to represent or misrepresent the community. This dynamic, though, takes us back to the point I've been making: tribal communities are composed of diverse perspectives, so the challenge of the individual to represent the whole, the collective, is unachievable. Despite different perspectives, Alexie has suggested that he recognizes an obligation as a member of a tribe, rather than an individual artist who elevates art as the highest value, which is the "Western civilization idea of the artist: that the artist as the individual is responsible to his or her personal vision. Certainly, yeah. But you have to be a member of a tribe. You have to be a member of a family. You have to be responsible and held accountable."[36]

The questions about reception and community response prompted by Alexie's writing force readers to consider the value of art and literature in the lives of individuals, whether it be inspirational rescue ("Survival = Anger × Imagination"), intellectual nourishment, political action, public service, aesthetic pleasure, entertainment, escapism, fancy and wonder, avocation, vocation, or any combination. As a form of art, literature serves different purposes; its definition and value have been contested over time. Those who want to define its role in our lives—or are threatened by its repurposing—often have a stake in the current definition and somehow benefit from sustaining its current purpose and value.

Through the years, *literature* became inextricably linked with *author*. Today we define authorship as a profession, which presumes a unified subject, an individual with a muse, someone with a purpose and vision, an auteur, a genius, a fancy dancer, if you will, but these notions emerged over the last three or four hundred years, coinciding with the rise of capitalism and its link with publication and sale of the written word. And thus, the act of writing, rather than the actions of relaying cultural narratives, singing songs, doing prayer work, participating in communal entertainment, was transformed. Just as in later centuries, the traditional Plains dances were transformed into the commercially viable fancy dances in North America.

The category of author has tremendous influence today, despite Roland Barthes's proclamation in "The Death of the Author."[37] As Michel Foucault later explained, the "author function" is special in discourse, still carries weight, and is markedly different from everyday speech.[38] Employing the Foucauldian definition, it is worthwhile to examine how Alexie's name, as a metonym for his body of work, impacts this particular mode of communication. Alexie is among only a handful of living writers whose reputation precedes his work. Just as distorted or exaggerated notions about writers such as Ernest Hemingway, Virginia Woolf, Emily Dickinson, and William Shakespeare precede and exceed their respective works, so does Alexie's public persona. Developed across his writing in multiple genres and public forums, it influences and hovers over all past, present, and future work. For example, his public-opinion pieces, especially in 2002–3 during the lead-up to U.S. engagement in the Iraq War, all staged intellectual interventions, meant to spark debate.[39] All of his works—some transformed by his public-speaking engagements, others recycled and incorporated into his fiction, poetry, and screenplays—illustrate a writer at work, in process, influenced by audience reaction, reshaping and transcending the limits of any particular generic tradition. Witnessing this dynamic requires readers and listeners to be actively engaged, more so than when reading any single novel, any single story, any single poem.

Alexie may share his individual goals for writing with readers, but there is no assurance that his words will be understood or break free of presumptions readers make based on their own needs and desires.[40] This is the case with the fictional Mouse, Aristotle, and Corliss. Nor will his words be easily untangled from readers' preconceptions about who Alexie is, what American Indian writers should engage in, and what U.S. writers in the early twenty-first century should take responsibility for. We may be like Mouse and Aristotle, carping about Alexie's representation of X or Y; we may be like Corliss, yearning for a model writer; we may be like Harlan Atwater, disinterested, purposefully removed; we may be like Seymour, both confused and committed, open to the process of exploration. Alexie's manifestations of authorship demonstrate to readers that the writer is but one source of meaning, and the reader's desires are only another in an ongoing chain of signification. Alexie's works hold a mirror up to us, asking us why we need what we think we need and why we expect an author, this author, to deliver it.

Notes

1. Ron Franscell, "Alexie's Tribal Perspective Universal in Its Appeal," 11.

2. Robert Capriccioso, "Sherman Alexie: American Indian Filmmaker/Writer Talks with Robert Capriccioso."

3. "The Toughest Indian in the World," *Sixty Minutes II.*

4. "What I've Learned as a Filmmaker," preface to *The Business of Fancydancing: The Screenplay,* 8.

5. Duncan Campbell, "Voice of the New Tribes."

6. Sherman Alexie, "Portrait of the Indian as a Young Man," 1.

7. Sherman Alexie, *The Lone Ranger and Tonto Fistfight in Heaven,* 21.

8. Diane Thiel, "A Conversation with Sherman Alexie."

9. See Louis Owens, *Other Destinies: Understanding the American Indian Novel,* and *Mixedblood Messages: Literature, Film, Family, Place;* Gerald Vizenor, *Manifest Manners: Narratives on Postindian Survivance;* Robert Warrior, *Tribal Secrets: Recovering American Indian Intellectual Traditions;* Elizabeth Cook-Lynn, *Why I Can't Read Wallace Stegner and Other Essays: A Tribal Voice,* and *Anti-Indianism in Modern America: A Voice from Tatekeya's Earth;* and Craig Womack, *Red on Red: Native American Literary Separatism,* and Craig Womack, Daniel Heath Justice, and Sean Teuton, eds., *Reasoning Together: The Native Critics Collective.*

10. Juliette Torrez, "Juliette Torrez Goes Long Distance with Sherman Alexie."

11. Sherman Alexie, "In Response to Elizabeth Cook-Lynn's Pronouncement That I [Am] One of the New, Angry (Warriors) Kind of Like Norman Schwarzkopf and Rush Limbaugh," 9.

12. Sherman Alexie, "The Unauthorized Autobiography of Me," in *One Stick Song,* 16 (hereafter cited in the text as *OSS*). In "Dear John Wayne," Etta Joseph tells Spencer Cox, the anthropologist, "Don't give me that oral tradition garbage. It's so primitive. It makes it sound like Indians sit around naked and grunt stories at each other." Sherman Alexie, *The Toughest Indian in the World,* 193.

13. John Purdy, "Crossroads: A Conversation with Sherman Alexie," 16.

14. Capriccioso, "Sherman Alexie."

15. Maya Jaggi, "All Rage and Heart."

16. The best analysis of this film to date is Quentin Youngberg's "Interpenetrations: Re-encoding the Queer Indian in Sherman Alexie's *The Business of Fancydancing,*" 55–75. Youngberg argues that,

> through the use of cultural codes endemic to the film's "text," Alexie situates the issue of Indian homosexuality within a nexus of other themes in a way that renders an understanding of sexual conflict as indispensable to understanding the racial tensions in the film. In the end *The Business of Fancydancing* enacts a process of interpenetration between Indian and queer coding practices that mutually reinforce one another and serve to complicate the viewer's understanding of cultural conflict by dramatizing an intersection between ostensibly separate cultural phenomenon, namely ethnic and sexual identities." (58)

17. Tara Browner, *Heartbeat of the People: Music and Dance of the Northern Pow-Wow,* 59. Browner continues, "The men's [fancy] dancing style developed as a result of intersections between traditional warrior society dances and Wild West shows, where dancing was performed as an exhibition event for audiences unfamiliar with the meanings behind more (comparatively) sedate styles of war dances" (58). See also Clyde Ellis, *A Dancing People: Powwow Culture on the Southern Plains.*

18. Quentin Youngberg discusses Seymour's Shawl Dance in depth and suggests that while the dance relates to the Butterfly Dance—reserved primarily for women whose husbands have been lost in battle—it is linked to Seymour's coming out. Importantly, Youngberg acknowledges that the Shawl Dance was a modern addition to powwows—"a flashy addition to competitive dance"—and thus "comes as a bearer of the sell-out theme in two senses: that of the native American poet selling out to the white world outside the reservation, and that of the homosexual male selling out his gender." This last point requires some explanation: Youngberg means that he's a sellout because of heteronormative standards, not that a homosexual character is a sellout. "Interpenetrations," 64.

19. Sherman Alexie, "The Business of Fancydancing," in *The Business of Fancy-dancing,* 69.

20. Susan Berry Brill de Ramírez, "Fancy Dancer: A Profile of Sherman Alexie," 57. David Treur's discussion of Alexie's reaction to the Nasdijj fraud case is interesting:

> Nasdijj and Alexie and Carter all use the mark of authenticity to provide much of their magic.... The hoax and subsequent discussions...once again focused on identity not writing, and those who were hoaxed will now require even more proof of cultural citizenship...what the Nasdijj drama should show us if we tried to think about it productively is that by foregrounding authenticity we treat Native American fictions as artifacts, not art: fictions animated by what we imagine to be the origins of the author, not the originality of the writing. *Native American Fiction: A User's Manual,* 190.

21. Sherman Alexie, *Reservation Blues,* 213. In "Oral Tradition" from *Face* (2009), Alexie writes, "I turn each reading into a test / Of my humor and masculinity. / It's cheap, but I want strangers to want me / Naked on their shelves if not their beds. / Who doesn't know that reading is like sex?" *Face,* 89.

22. In "Eagle Feather Tuxedo" from *Face,* Alexie shares the way he was influenced—and rescued—by great writers, most of whom were quite different from him: "And if you study what separates me, / The survivor, from the dead and the car-wrecked, / Then you'll learn that my literacy / Saved my

ass. It was all those goddamn texts / By all those damn dead white writers and female writers / That first taught me how to be a fighter" and

"I wasn't saved by the separation of cultures; I was *reborn* inside the collision of cultures" (*Face,* 80; italics in original).

23. Sherman Alexie, *Ten Little Indians,* 5 (hereafter cited in the text as *TLI*).

24. This title comes from a repeated line in Adrian C. Louis's poem "Elegy for the Forgotten Oldsmobile" in *Fire Water World.* Alexie has noted that this poem profoundly inspired him as a young writer. From interview with Tomson Highway, "Spokane Words: Tomson Highway Raps with Sherman Alexie."

25. Sherman Alexie, "When the Story Stolen Is Your Own."

26. Sherman Alexie, "Go, Ghost, Go," in *War Dances,* 22.

27. Part of this line is reworked in Alexie's screenplay for *49?,* a short film about the genre of songs called "49s" but also about American Indian creative expression generally.

28. See Gloria Bird, "The Exaggeration of Despair in Sherman Alexie's *Reservation Blues,"* 47–52. The quotation comes from the republished version available online at http://www.hanksville.org/storytellers/gbird/poems/RezBlues.html

29. Alexie also has a long-running quarrel with Elizabeth Cook-Lynn, as mentioned earlier in this essay. In a footnote in *New Indians, Old Wars,* she says that "Alexie is to Indian Country what Larry McMurtry is to Texas, perhaps, a figure in a broad landscape, a rare and exceedingly accessible writer who becomes a 'tourist' attraction" (220n2). See also her often-cited "American Indian Intellectualism and the New Indian Story," 57–76.

30. Henry Giroux, "Reading Texts, Literacy, and Textual Authority," 85.

31. I regard the Flagstaff meeting of the MLA division on American Indian literature as the watershed moment.

32. Jace Weaver, Craig Womack, and Robert Warrior, *American Indian Literary Nationalism;* and Elvira Pulitano, *Toward a Native American Critical Theory.* See also *American Indian Quarterly* 29, nos. 1 and 2 (winter and spring 2005).

33. In "Theorizing American Indian Experience" from *Reasoning Together,* Craig Womack writes,

> I have taken great pains to imagine a Muscogee Creek response to my own theorizing and even written literary criticism that includes comic dialect letters where Creek people talk back to my text (that is, to say, Creek people who I have invented in my imagination, not actual letters from Creek readers, though I get those too). This is an imperfect measure of the community, to be sure: nonetheless, this is my attempt to try to think about how those I am writing about might respond to what I am saying about them, or at least to consider that. I use the one tool

most immediately available to me to unite my experience with theirs—my imagination. (369)

34. Daniel Heath Justice, "'Go Away, Water!': Kinship Criticism and the Decolonization Imperative," in *Reasoning Together*, 153.

35. In "Eagle Feather Tuxedo" from *Face,* Alexie notes,

> But my sobriety does give me sovereignty. Most Indians use "sovereignty" to refer to the collective and tribal desire for political, cultural, and economic independence. But I am using it here to mean "the individual Indian artist's basic right to be an eccentric bastard." I am using it here to attack Elizabeth Cook-Lynn, the Sioux Indian writer and scholar who . . . believes that "tribal sovereignty"/Should be our ethos. (*Face,* 79–80)

36. Torrez, "Juliette Torrez Goes Long Distance."

37. Roland Barthes, "The Death of the Author," in *Falling into Theory: Conflicting Views on Reading Literature,* 222–26.

38. Michel Foucault, "What Is an Author?" in *The Foucault Reader,* 107.

39. See the bibliography at the end of this collection for an extensive list of these essays or opinion pieces.

40. Interestingly, within the field of American Indian literary studies, *The Business of Fancydancing* has met with criticism, in particular, what is deemed a failure on Alexie's part to create a gay Native man who is an integral part of his community, not living in exile from it with a white man (and having dated almost exclusively non-Native men). Alexie's graphic portrayal of Mouse's huffing has also prompted criticism. (Native American Literature Symposium, March 2003, Mystic Lake, Minnesota).

As I was doing final editing work on this chapter, Lisa Tatonetti published a provocative article on this very subject, "Visible Sexualities or Invisible Nations: Forced to Choose in *Big Eden, Johnny Greyeyes,* and *The Business of Fancydancing,* 157–81. I mention these points at the end of my article as a reminder of readerly responses and the selectivity of interpretative approaches; my reading—in its emphasis on Alexie's philosophy on authorship—has led me to see Seymour's sexuality as an element of his character and a feature of his public persona as a gay Native author: his sexuality has become one additional performative element in his repertoire. The flaws in Seymour's character are purposeful, I believe, created by Alexie to support his larger argument about the professional fancy dancer. If Alexie had focused on Seymour's sexuality as a motor for the narrative, then I would agree that its representation is flawed.

Contributors

ELIZABETH ARCHULETA teaches in Arizona State University's Women and Gender Studies program. She has published articles in *Wicazo Sa Review, Studies in American Indian Literatures, American Indian Quarterly, New Mexico Historical Review,* and *Indigenous Peoples' Journal of Law, Culture & Resistance.* Her essays also appear in *The National Museum of the American Indian: Critical Conversations* and *Simon J. Ortiz: A Poetic Legacy of Indigenous Continuance.* She is a 2008–9 Ford Diversity postdoctoral fellowship recipient and was also awarded the Gilberto Espinosa Prize for the best article of 2007 from *New Mexico Historical Review.*

JEFF BERGLUND is an associate professor of English and a President's Distinguished Teaching Fellow at Northern Arizona University, where he teaches contemporary Native literature and Indigenous film. He is the author of *Cannibal Fictions: American Explorations of Colonialism, Race, Gender, and Sexuality* (University of Wisconsin Press, 2006) and his essays have appeared in *Simon J. Ortiz: A Poetic Legacy of Indigenous Continuance, Studies in American Indian Literatures, American Indian Quarterly, Camera Obscura,* and *Studies in American Fiction.* He was the recipient of an NEH grant for his project Remembering the Long Walk to Hwééldi: Diné (Navajo) Memorial Histories.

SUSAN BERRY BRILL DE RAMÍREZ, professor of English at Bradley University, is the author of *Wittgenstein and Critical Theory* (1995), *Contemporary American Indian Literatures and the Oral Tradition* (1999), and *Native American Life-History Narratives: Colonial and Postcolonial Navajo Ethnography* (2007). She is completing work on Native American women's ethnography, coediting a volume on orality in Native and medieval literatures, and exploring the concept of "geographies of belonging" for their critical relevance in indigenous and diasporic literatures.

JAMES H. COX is an associate professor of Native American and American literatures at the University of Texas at Austin. He has published essays in *Studies in American Indian Literatures* (on Alexie) and *American Indian Quarterly* (on Thomas King), and his book, *Muting White Noise: Native American and European American Novel Traditions,* was published by the University of Oklahoma Press. He also has an essay on Choctaw author Todd Downing in *MELUS.*

STEPHEN F. EVANS teaches a broad range of courses—including American Indian literature, technical writing, Shakespeare, and gender studies—at the University of Kansas. His examination of Alexie's satiric techniques, "'Open Containers': Sherman Alexie's Drunken Indians," appeared in *American Indian Quarterly* in 2001.

P. JANE HAFEN is a professor of English at the University of Nevada, Las Vegas. She is editor of *Dreams and Thunder: Stories, Poems and The Sun Dance Opera* by Zitkala-Ša and coeditor, with Diane Quantic, of *A Great Plains Reader.* She is also the author of the monograph *Reading Louise Erdrich's* Love Medicine, part of the Western Writers series.

PHILIP HELDRICH is an associate professor in the Interdisciplinary Arts and Sciences program at the University of Washington, Tacoma. He is the author of two books, most recently *Out Here in the Out There: Essays in a Region of Superlatives* (2005), winner of the Mid-List Press First Series

Award in creative nonfiction. He directs the Southwest Texas Popular and American Culture Associations.

PATRICE HOLLRAH is the director of the Writing Center at the University of Nevada, Las Vegas, and teaches in the Department of English. She is the author of various publications in the field of American Indian literature, including *"The Old Lady Trill, the Victory Yell": The Power of Women in Native American Literature* (Routledge, 2003). She also served as the president of the Association of Studies in American Indian Literatures (ASAIL) from 2008 to 2009.

MEREDITH JAMES is an associate professor of English at Eastern Connecticut State University, where she teaches American and Native American literatures. She received her PhD from the University of Oklahoma and is the author of *Literary and Cinematic Reservation in Selected Works of Native American Author Sherman Alexie.*

JAN JOHNSON, an assistant professor of English at the University of Idaho, teaches ethnic American literature, Native American literature and film, and the literature of environmental justice. She has published essays on salmon, environmental sovereignty and Columbia Plateau tribal literature, Nez Perce recolonization resistance during the Lewis and Clark bicentennial, and Nez Perce jazz bands of the twentieth century. Her essay in this volume intersects with broader research projects involving historical trauma and healing in Native literature and communities.

ANGELICA LAWSON is a graduate of the University of Arizona's PhD program in American Indian studies. She was the recipient of the prestigious Charles A. Eastman Dissertation Fellowship at Dartmouth College. She is an assistant professor of Native American studies at the University of Montana, where she teaches Native American film.

MARGARET O'SHAUGHNESSEY teaches Native American literature as well as environmental literature at the University of North Carolina at Chapel Hill. She has also published several articles on the role of medievalism, especially Arthurian legend, in modern literature and the use of art in American literature.

Nancy J. Peterson is professor of English and an affiliated faculty member of the American Studies and Women's Studies programs at Purdue University. She focuses on contemporary American literature and culture in her research and teaching, with a particular interest in ethnic American literatures. She is the author of *Beloved: Character Studies* (Continuum, 2008) and *Against Amnesia: Contemporary Women Writers and the Crises of Historical Memory* (University of Pennsylvania Press, 2001) and the editor of *Toni Morrison: Critical and Theoretical Approaches* (Johns Hopkins University Press, 1997) and *Conversations with Sherman Alexie* (University Press of Mississippi, 2009).

Jan Roush is an associate professor of English at Utah State University, where she has previously served as director of the American Studies program and the director of the Writing Center. From 1986 to 2005, she wrote the annual research column for the Western Literature Association. She is co-editor of *Pulling Leather: Being the Early Recollections of a Cowboy on the Wyoming Range* a reissued edition of the book by Ruben Millins. Her various articles on Sherman Alexie, Tony Hillerman, and cowboy poets have appeared in *Western American Literature, A Literary History of the American West,* and *US Icons and Iconicity.* She teaches courses in Native American literature, Western American literature, and folklore.

Lisa Tatonetti is an associate professor at Kansas State University, where she teaches American Indian and multiethnic American literatures. She has published articles on both queer Native literature and images of the 1890 Ghost Dance and Wounded Knee massacre in American Indian literature. Her essays have appeared in *Studies in American Indian Literatures, MELUS, GLQ: A Journal of Lesbian and Gay Studies,* and *Studies in American Fiction,* which featured her article on Sherman Alexie's depiction of queer identities in *The Toughest Indian in the World.*

Bibliography

To make it easier for the reader to navigate through the many references both written by and about Sherman Alexie, the editors have divided the bibliography for this collection of critical essays into two major divisions. The first section lists works written by Alexie or directly related to him, such as interviews, reviews, or analyses of his writing. Furthermore, since Alexie has written so prolifically across genres, the section detailing his works is subdivided according to type: poetry and multigenre works; fiction; films, videos, and screenplays; and articles and essays. Interviews with Alexie and multigenre related materials comprise another subsection, and books and articles analyzing his writing make up the last subsection.

The second division is devoted to secondary works that contributors to this collection have used in their analyses of facets of Alexie's writing.

Works by and about Sherman Alexie

Works Written by Sherman Alexie

Poetry and Multigenre

The Business of Fancydancing. Brooklyn: Hanging Loose Press, 1992.
Dangerous Anatomy. Boise, ID: Limberlost Press, 2005.
Face. Brooklyn: Hanging Loose Press, 2009.

First Indian on the Moon. Brooklyn: Hanging Loose Press, 1993.

"In Response to Elizabeth Cook-Lynn's Pronouncement That I [Am] One of the New, Angry (Warriors) Kind of Like Norman Schwarzkopf and Rush Limbaugh." *Wicazo Sa Review* 9, no. 2 (autumn 1993): 9.

I Would Steal Horses. Niagara Falls, NY: Slipstream Press, 1992.

Old Shirts & New Skins. Los Angeles: American Indian Studies Center, UCLA, 1993.

One Stick Song. Brooklyn: Hanging Loose Press, 2000.

"Portrait of the Indian as a Young Man." *Studies in American Indian Literatures* 4, no. 4 (winter 1992): 1.

Seven Mourning Songs for the Cedar Flute I Have Yet to Learn to Play. Walla Walla, WA: Whitman College Book Arts Lab, 1994.

The Summer of Black Widows. Brooklyn: Hanging Loose Press, 1996.

Water Flowing Home. Boise, ID: Limberlost Press, 1996.

The Man Who Loves Salmon. Boise, ID: Limberlost Press, 1998.

Fiction

The Absolutely True Diary of a Part-Time Indian. Art by Ellen Forney. New York: Little, Brown, 2007.

Flight. New York: Grove Press, 2007.

"Ghost Dance," *McSweeney's* 10 (2003): 350–64.

The Lone Ranger and Tonto Fistfight in Heaven. New York: Atlantic Monthly Press, 1993.

Indian Killer. New York: Atlantic Monthly Press, 1996.

Reservation Blues. New York: Atlantic Monthly Press, 1995.

Ten Little Indians. New York: Atlantic Monthly Press, 2003.

The Toughest Indian in the World. New York: Atlantic Monthly Press, 2000.

War Dances. New York: Grove Press, 2009.

Films, Videos, Screenplays

The Business of Fancydancing. Written and directed by Sherman Alexie. Starring Evan Adams, Michelle St. John, Gene Tagaban, Swil Kanim. A FallsApart Production with Outrider Pictures, 2002.

The Business of Fancydancing: The Screenplay. Brooklyn: Hanging Loose Press, 2003.

'49? Directed by Eric Frith. Performed by Gene Tagaban. Seattle: Flyfilmmaking/Byrd Productions, 2003.

Smoke Signals. Directed by Chris Eyre. Screenplay by Sherman Alexie. Starring Evan Adams, Adam Beach, and Irene Bedard. Miramax Films, 1998.

Smoke Signals: A Screenplay. New York: Hyperion, 1998.

Articles and Essays

"Chapter & Verse: Reclaiming God from Pro-War Hypocrites—and Unmasking Bush as Lousy Christian." theStranger.com, March 27, 2003. Available online at http://www.thestranger.com/2003-03-27/feature3.html

"Dancing Fancy: Celebrated Writer-Director-Poet Sherman Alexie Comes Out?" *Out* (November 2002): 32–33.

"Every Teen's Struggle: Speaking to a Universal Need." *Publishers Weekly,* February 18, 2008. Available online at http://www.publishersweekly.com/pw/by-topic/columns-and-blogs/soapbox/article/14017-every-teen-s-struggle-.html

"George and Dick." theStranger.com, May 15, 2003. Available online at http://www.thestranger.com/2003-05-15/reservations.html

"Green World." *Harper's,* June 2009, 42–44. Available online at http://www.harpers.org/archive/2009/06/0082529

"I Hated Tonto (Still Do)." *Los Angeles Times,* June 28, 1998. Available online at http://articles.latimes.com/1998/jun/28/entertainment/ca-64216

"An Imaginary Interview." theStranger.com, May 1, 2003. Available online at http://www.thestranger.com/2003-05-01/reservations.html

"Introduction: Death in Hollywood." *Ploughshares* 26 (winter 2000): 7–11.

"Killing Indians: Myths, Lies, Exaggerations." Lecture, Hall Center Humanities Series, University of Kansas, Lawrence, October 29, 2003.

"Lefties Need to Love, Love, Love the White Working Class." theStranger.com, April 17, 2003. Available online at http://www.thestranger.com/seattle/reservations/Content?oid=13968

"Love, Hunger, Money." *High Country News* 26, no. 17 (September 19, 1994). Available online at http://www.hcn.org/servlets/hcn.URLRemapper/1994/sep19/dir/essay.html

"Net Profit." theStranger.com, November 7, 2006. Available online at http://www.thestranger.com/seattle/net-profit/Content?oid=101518

"One Little Indian Boy." In *Edge Walking on the Western Rim: New Works by 12 Northwest Writers,* edited by Bob Peterson and Mayumi Tsutakawa, 52–65. Seattle: One Reel/Sasquatch Books, 1994.

"Relevant Contradictions: In Defense of Humor, Irony, Satire, and a Native American Perspective on the Coming War in Iraq." theStranger.com, February 27, 2003. Available online at http://www.thestranger.com/2003-02-27/feature2.html

"Sixteen Words vs. Ten Words." theStranger.com, August 14, 2003. Available online at http://www.thestranger.com/2003-08-14/reservations.html

"Sixty-One Things I Learned during the Sonics Trial: A Sonics Love Story." theStranger.com, July 29, 2008. Available online at http://www.thestranger.com/seattle/Content?oid=631015

"Some of My Best Friends." Review of *On the Rez* by Ian Frazier. *Los Angeles Times,* January 23, 2000, 3.

"Sonics Death Watch." 26 installments (January 17–July 10, 2008). theStranger.com, available online at http://www.thestranger.com/ seattle/Author?oid=14116

"Superman and Me." *Los Angeles Times,* April 19, 1998. Available online at http://fallsapart.com/superman.html

"Three Reasons Independent Film Will Survive." *MovieMaker* 49, February 3, 2003. Available online at http://www.moviemaker.com/issues/49/indiealive2.html

"Vouch for Me." theStranger.com, May 29, 2003. Available online at http://www.thestranger.com/2003-05-29/reservations.html

"The Warriors." In *Home Field: Nine Writers at Bat,* edited by John Douglas Marshall. Seattle: One Reel/Sasquatch Books, 1997.

"What Sacagawea Means to Me." *Time,* July 1, 2002. Available online at http://www.time.com/time/2002/lewis_clark/lprocon.html

"When the Story Stolen Is Your Own." *Time,* January 29, 2006. Available online at http://www.time.com/time/printout/0,8816,1154221,00.html

"White Men Can't Drum." *New York Times Magazine,* October 4, 1992, 30.

Interviews with Sherman Alexie

Collected Interviews

Peterson, Nancy J, ed. *Conversations with Sherman Alexie.* Jackson: University of Mississippi Press, 2009.

Selected Individual Interviews (including video and audio)

"Author Sherman Alexie Talks *Flight.*" *Talk of the Nation,* April 11, 2007, transcript. Available online at http://www.npr.org/templates/story/story.php?storyId=9517855 [site includes audio].

Baker, Jeff. "Native American Writer Sherman Alexie Enjoys Being an Offensive Threat." *Oregonian,* October 3, 2009. Available online at http://www.oregonlive.com/O/index.ssf/2009/10/post.html

Blewster, Kelley. "Tribal Visions." *Biblio* 4, no. 3 (March 1999): 22–29.

Brill de Ramírez, Susan Berry. "Fancy Dancer: A Profile of Sherman Alexie." *Poets & Writers* 27, no. 1 (January–February 1999): 54–59.

Butler, Kiera. "Don't Call Me Warrior." *Mother Jones,* November–December 2009. Available online at http://www.motherjones.com/interview/2009/11/sherman-alexie-dont-call-me-warrior-extended

Campbell, Duncan. "Voice of the New Tribes." *The Guardian,* January 4, 2003. Available online at http://www.guardian.co.uk/books/2003/jan/04/arts-features.fiction

Capriccioso, Robert. "Sherman Alexie: American Indian Filmmaker/Writer Talks
    with Robert Capriccioso." *Identity Theory,* March 23, 2003. Available online
    at http://www.identitytheory.com/interviews/alexie_interview.html

Chapel, Jessica. "Atlantic Unbound Interview." June 1, 2000. Available online at
    http://www.theatlantic.com/unbound/interviews/ba2000-06-01.htm

Chato, Bernadette. "Book-of-the-Month: *Reservation Blues." Native America Call-
    ing,* KUNM 89.9 FM, Albuquerque, NM, June 26, 1995. American Indian
    Radio on Satellite (AIROS), transcript. Available online at http://www.
    airos.org//

"Conversations with KCTS 9: Sherman Alexie." July 11, 2008, video. Available
    online at http://www.kcts9.org/video/sherman-alexie-leaving-rez [site
    includes multiple interview segments].

Crispin, Jen. "A Conversation with Sherman Alexie." *Bookslut.* Available online
    at http://www.bookslut.com/features/0203/alexie.htm

Curan, Katie. "Straight Talk with Filmmaker Sherman Alexie." *The Flagstaff Tea
    Party:* 3, no. 3 (March 2002). Available online at http://www.flagsteaparty.
    org/Publications/Headlines/Pages/2002/March_April2002/Straight

Daley, Lauren. "Novelist Draws on Wellspring of Experience." *SouthCoast
    Today,* August 29, 2009. Available online at http://www.southcoastto-
    day.com/apps/pbcs.dll/article?AID=/20090829/NEWS/908290310/-1/
    LIFE18#STS=fzmaip07.17f5

Dellinger, Matt. "Q&A: Redeemers." *The New Yorker,* April 21, 2003.
    Available online at http://www.newyorker.com/
    printable/?online/030421on_onlineonly01

Emerald City Productions. *Indian Killer.* San Bruno, CA: Audio Literature, 1996.
    Audiocassette.

Fielding, Julien R. "Native American Religion and Film: Interviews with Chris
    Eyre and Sherman Alexie." *Journal of Religion and Film* 7, no. 1 (April 2003):
    19.

Fraser, Joelle. "An Interview with Sherman Alexie." *Iowa Review* 30, no. 3 (win-
    ter 2000–2001): 59–70.

Harris, Emily. "Northwest Passages: Sherman Alexie." *Think Out Loud,* October
    8, 2009, transcript. Available online at http://www.opb.org/thinkoutloud/
    shows/northwest-passages-sherman-alexie/ [site includes audio].

Highway, Tomson. "Spokane Words: Tomson Highway Raps with Sherman
    Alexie." *Aboriginal Voices* (January–March 1997). Available online at
    http://www.fallsapart.com/art-av.htm

Jaggi, Maya. "All Rage and Heart." *The Guardian,* May 3, 2008. Available online
    at http://www.guardian.co.uk/books/2008/may/03/featuresreviews.
    guardianreview13

Margolis, Rick. "Song of Myself: Interview with Sherman Alexie." *School Library
    Journal,* August 1, 2007, 29. Available online at http://www.schoollibrary-
    journal.com/article/CA6463515.html

McDonald, Christine. "An Interview with Sherman Alexie." *Multicultural Review*
    11, no. 4 (2002): 48–51.

Neff, Renfreu. "An Interview with: Sherman Alexie." *Creative Screenwriting* 5, no. 4 (July–Aug 1998): 18–19, 59.

Nygren, Åse. "A World of Story-Smoke: A Conversation with Sherman Alexie." MELUS 30, no. 4 (winter 2005): 149–69.

"Online Chat with Sherman Alexie." *Chats & Events,* May 1, 2000. Barnesandnoble.com. Online at http://www.barnesandnoble.com/co.../transcript.asp?userid=24L2DFWCYO&eventId=218 but no longer available.

Pabst, Georgia. "Alexie Sends Strong Signals: Writer Spares No One from Barbs." *Milwaukee Journal Sentinel,* March 10, 2002. Available online at http://www.jsonline.com/enter/books/mar02/25632.asp

Purdy, John. "Crossroads: A Conversation with Sherman Alexie." *Studies in American Indian Literatures* 9, no. 4 (winter 1997): 1–18.

Rose, Charlie. "A Conversation with Native-American Author Sherman Alexie." *Charlie Rose,* June 26, 1998, video. Available online at http://www.charlierose.com/view/interview/4848

"Sherman Alexie." *The Colbert Report,* October 28, 2008, video. Available online at http://www.colbertnation.com/the-colbert-report-videos/189691/october-28-2008/sherman-alexie

"Sherman Alexie, Sitcom American." National Public Radio, August 18, 2003, transcript. Available online at http://www.npr.org/templates/story/story.php?storyId=1397737 [site includes audio].

"Six Questions: Border Talk." *POV Borders* (*A New Web Series*), 2002, transcript. Available online at http://www.pbs.org/pov/pov2002/borders/talk/dialogue010_sa_6q.html

Smiley, Tavis. "Sherman Alexie." *Tavis Smiley,* April 27, 2007, transcript. Available online at http://www.pbs.org/kcet/tavissmiley/archive/200704/20070427_alexie.html [site contains audio].

Spencer, Russ. "What It Means to Be Sherman Alexie." *Book Magazine* (July–August 2000): 32–36. Available online at http://www.bookmagazine.com/archive/issue11/alexie.shtml

Thiel, Diane. "A Conversation with Sherman Alexie." *Crossroads* 61 (spring 2004). Available online at http://www.poetrysociety.org/journal/articles/salexie.html

Torrez, Juliette. "Juliette Torrez Goes Long Distance with Sherman Alexie." (*Sic*) *Vice & Verse,* August 31, 1999. Available online at http://poetry.about.com/library/weekly/aa083199.htm?once=true&terms=alexie

"The Toughest Indian in the World." *Sixty Minutes II,* March 20, 2001, transcript. Available online at http://www.cbsnews.com/stories/2001/01/19/60II/main265512.shtml [site includes video].

"UCSD Guestbook: Sherman Alexie." University of California Television, 27-minute video. Available online at http://www.uctv.tv/search-details.aspx?showID=6190

West, Dennis, and Joan M. West. "Sending Cinematic Smoke Signals: An Interview with Sherman Alexie." *Cineaste* 23, no. 4 (fall 1998): 28–32.

Williams, Mary Elizabeth. "Without Reservations." Salon.com, July 2, 1998. Available online at http://www.salon.com/entertainment/movies/int/1998/07/02int.html

Related Multimedia Materials

Boyd, Jim. *Reservation Blues*. Inhelium. WA: Thunderwolf Productions, 1995. CD.
"A Dialogue on Race with President Clinton." *The NewsHour with Jim Lehrer,* July 9, 1998, transcript. Available online at http://www.pbs.org/newshour/bb/race_relations/OneAmerica/transcript.html
"National Book Award Acceptance Speech." November 14, 2007, video. Available online at http://www.youtube.com/watch?v= 6AbxJxDoI8
Sherman Alexie's official Web site. http://www.fallsapart.com
Smoke Signals: Music from the Miramax Motion Picture. N.p.: TVT Productions, 1998. CD.
"Up All Night." *Now with Bill Moyers,* October 4, 2002, transcript. Available online at http://www.pbs.org/now/printable/transcript_alexie_print.html

Books and Articles about Sherman Alexie

Allen, Chadwick. "Postcolonial Theory and the Discourse of Treaties." *American Quarterly* 52, no. 1 (March 2000): 59–89.
Andrews, Scott. "A New Road and a Dead End in Sherman Alexie's *Reservation Blues." Arizona Quarterly* 63, no. 2 (summer 2007): 137–52.
Archuleta, Elizabeth. "Refiguring Indian Blood through Poetry, Photography, and Performance Art." *Studies in American Indian Literatures* 17, no. 4 (winter 2005): 1–26.
Armbruster-Sandoval, Ralph. "Teaching *Smoke Signals:* Fatherhood, Forgiveness, and 'Freedom.'" *Wicazo Sa Review* 23, no. 1 (spring 2008): 123–46.
Banka, Ewelina. "'Homing' in the City: Sherman Alexie's Perspectives on Urban Indian Country." *European Review of Native American Studies,* 20, no. 1 (2006): 35–38.
Banks, Wishelle. "Alexie Finds Inspiration in His Home, Humor in His Family and Their Life." *The Native Voice* (1995). Available online at http://fallsapart.com/art-nv.html
Belcher, Wendy. "Conjuring the Colonizer: Alternative Readings of Magic Realism in Sherman Alexie's *Reservation Blues." American Indian Research and Culture Journal* 31, no. 2 (June 2007): 87–101.
Berglund, Jeff. "Facing the Fire: American Indian Literature and the Pedagogy of Anger." *American Indian Quarterly* 27, nos. 1–2 (winter–spring 2003): 80–90.
———. "Turning Back the Cannibal: Indigenous Revision in the Late Twentieth Century." In *Cannibal Fictions: American Explorations of Colonialism,*

Race, Class, Gender, and Sexuality, 130–70. Madison: University of Wisconsin Press, 2006.

Bird, Gloria. "The Exaggeration of Despair in Sherman Alexie's *Reservation Blues." Wicazo Sa Review* 11, no. 2 (fall 1995): 47–52.

Blumberg, Janet. "Sherman Alexie: Walking with Skeletons." In *Literature and the Renewal of the Public Sphere,* edited by Susan VanZanten Gallagher and M. D. Walhout, 122–38. Basingstoke, UK: Palgrave Macmillan, 2000.

Bolt, Julie. "Teaching Notes." *Radical Teacher* 72 (spring 2005): 43–44.

Bowers, Maggie Ann. "'Ethnic Glue': Humour in Native American Literatures." In *Cheeky Fictions: Laughter and the Postcolonial,* edited by Susanne Reichl and Mark Stein, 247–55. Amsterdam: Rodopi, 2005.

Brill de Ramírez, Susan Berry. *Contemporary American Indian Literatures and the Oral Tradition.* Tucson: University of Arizona Press, 1999.

———. "Sherman Alexie." In *Native American Writers of the United States,* edited by Kenneth M. Roemer, 3–10. Dictionary of Literary Biography 175. Detroit: Gale Research, 1997.

Brodbeck, Jane. "Hybridism as a Means of (De)Constructing the Old Paradigm: The Good Guys (White) versus the Bad Ones (Red)." In *Disability & Indigenous Studies,* edited by James Gifford and Gabrielle Zezulka-Mailloux, 124–32. Edmonton: CRC Humanities Studies, 2003.

Bruce, Heather E., Anna E. Baldwin, and Christabel Umphrey. *Sherman Alexie in the Classroom: "This Is Not a Silent Movie. Our Voices Will Save Our Lives."* Urbana, IL: National Council of Teachers of English, 2008.

Cain, M. Celia. "Red, Black and Blues: Race, Nation and Recognition for the Bluez." *Canadian Journal for Traditional Music* 33 (2006): 1–14.

Carroll, Kathleen L. "Ceremonial Tradition as Form and Theme in Sherman Alexie's *The Lone Ranger and Tonto Fistfight in Heaven:* A Performance-Based Approach to Native American Literature." *Journal of the Midwest Modern Language Association* 38, no. 1 (spring 2005): 74–84.

Chen, Tina. "Toward an Ethics of Knowledge." *MELUS* 30, no. 2 (summer 2005): 157–73.

Christie, Stuart. *Plural Sovereignties and Contemporary Indigenous Literature.* New York: Palgrave Macmillan, 2009.

———. "Renaissance Man: The Tribal 'Schizophrenic' in Sherman Alexie's *Indian Killer." American Indian Culture and Research Journal* 25, no. 4 (2001): 1–19.

Claviez, Thomas. "Cosmopolitanism and Its Discontents: The Politics of Sherman Alexie's *Reservation Blues* and Leslie Marmon Silko's *Almanac of the Dead." Litteraria Pragensia* 15, no. 30 (2005): 17–27.

Cline, Lynne. "About Sherman Alexie." *Ploughshares* 26, no. 4 (winter 2000–2001): 197–202. Available online at http://www.pshares.org/issues/article.cfm?prmArticleID=502.

Cobb, Amanda J. "This Is What It Means to Say *Smoke Signals:* Native American Cultural Sovereignty." In *Hollywood's Indian: The Portrayal of the Native*

American in Film, edited by John E. O'Connor and Peter C. Rollins, 206–28. Lexington: University Press of Kentucky, 1998.

Cook-Lynn, Elizabeth. "American Indian Intellectualism and the New Indian Story." In *Natives and Academics: Researching and Writing about American Indians,* edited by Devon A. Mihesuah, 111–38. Lincoln: University of Nebraska Press, 1998.

Coulombe, Joseph L. "The Approximate Size of His Favorite Humor: Sherman Alexie's Comic Connections and Disconnections in *The Lone Ranger and Tonto Fistfight in Heaven.*" *American Indian Quarterly* 26, no. 1 (winter 2002): 94–115.

Cox, James H. *Muting White Noise: Native American and European Novel Traditions.* Norman: University of Oklahoma Press, 2006.

———. "Muting White Noise: The Subversion of Popular Culture Narratives of Conquest in Sherman Alexie's Fiction." *Studies in American Indian Literatures* 9, no. 4 (winter 1997): 52–70.

Crank, James. "The Saddest Joke: Sherman Alexie's Blues." In *Dark Humor,* edited by Harold Bloom and Black Hobby, 219–28. Bloom's Literary Themes. New York: Chelsea House Publishers, 2010.

Cummings, Denise K. "'Accessible Poetry'? Cultural Intersection and Exchange in Contemporary American Indian and American Independent Film." *Studies in American Indian Literatures* 13, no. 1 (spring 2001): 57–80. Available online at http://oncampus.richmond.edu/faculty/ASAIL/SAIL2/131.html

Cutter, Martha J. *Lost and Found in Translation: Contemporary Ethnic American Writing and the Politics of Language Diversity.* Chapel Hill: University of North Carolina Press, 2005.

Dean, Janet. "The Violence of Collection: *Indian Killer's* Archives." *Studies in American Indian Literatures* 20, no. 3 (fall 2008): 29–50.

Delicka, Magdalena. "The Dynamics of Contemporary Cultural Politics in Sherman Alexie's Reservation Blues." *American Studies* 18 (1999): 73–80.

DeNuccio, Jerome. "Slow Dancing with Skeletons: Sherman Alexie's *The Lone Ranger and Tonto Fistfight in Heaven.*" *Critique: Studies in Contemporary Fiction* 44, 1 (fall 2002): 86–96.

Dix, Andrew. "Escape Stories: Narratives and Native Americans in Sherman Alexie's *The Lone Ranger and Tonto Fistfight in Heaven.*" *Yearbook of English Studies* 31 (2001): 155–67.

———. "Red, White and Black: Racial Exchanges in Fiction by Sherman Alexie." In *American Fiction of the 1990s: Reflections of History and Culture,* edited by Jay Prosser, 63–75. London: Routledge, 2008.

Doenges, Judy. Review of *The Toughest Indian in the World,* by Sherman Alexie. *Seattle Times,* May 14, 2000.

Donahue, Cecilia. "Travels in Salinas and Spokane: John Steinbeck and Sherman Alexie as Cultural Explorers" *Steinbeck Review* 5, no. 1 (spring 2008): 27–34.

Donahue, Peter. "New Warriors, New Legends: Basketball in Three Native American Works of Fiction." *American Indian Culture and Research Journal* 21, no. 2 (1997): 43–60.

Dunnewind, Stephanie. "Sherman Alexie Captures the Voice, Chaos and Humor of a Teenager." *Seattle Times,* September 8, 2007.

Elliot, Michael A. "Indian Patriots on Last Stand Hill." *American Quarterly* 58, no. 4 (December 2006): 987–1015.

Etter, Carrie. "Dialectic to Dialogic: Negotiating Bicultural Heritage in Sherman Alexie's Sonnets." In *Telling the Stories: Essays on American Indian Literatures and Cultures,* edited by Elizabeth H. Nelson and Malcolm A. Nelson, 143–51. New York: Peter Lang, 2001.

Evans, Stephen F. "'Open Containers': Sherman Alexie's Drunken Indians." *American Indian Quarterly* 25, no. 1 (winter 2001): 46–72.

Falquina, Silvia Martínez. "From the Monologic Eye to Healing Polyphonies: Dialogic Re/Vision in Native American Narratives." *Revista Alicantina de Estudios Ingleses* 16 (November 2003): 239–53.

Fast, Robin Riley. *The Heart as a Drum: Continuance and Resistance in American Indian Poetry.* Ann Arbor: University of Michigan Press, 2000.

Fitz, Karsten. "Native and Christian: Religion and Spirituality as Transcultural Negotiation in American Indian Novels of the 1990s." *American Indian Culture and Research Journal* 26, no. 2 (2002): 1–15.

Ford, Douglas. "Sherman Alexie's Indigenous Blues." *MELUS* 27, no. 3 (fall 2002): 197–216.

Franscell, Ron. "Alexie's Tribal Perspective Universal in Its Appeal." *Denver Post,* May 21, 2000, II.

Fritsch, Esther, and Marion Gymnich. "'Crime Spirit': The Significance of Dreams and Ghosts in Three Contemporary Native American Crime Novels." In *Sleuthing Ethnicity: The Detective in Multiethnic Crime Fiction,* edited by Dorothea Fischer-Hornung and Monika Mueller, 204–23. Madison, NJ: Fairleigh Dickinson University Press, 2003.

Gillan, Jennifer. "Reservation Home Movies: Sherman Alexie's Poetry." *American Literature* 68, no. 1 (March 1996): 91–110.

Gilroy, Jhon Warren. "Another Fine Example of the Oral Tradition? Identification and Subversion in Sherman Alexie's *Smoke Signals.*" *Studies in American Indian Literatures* 13, no. 1 (spring 2001): 23–42.

Gordon, Stephanie. "'The 7-11 of My Dreams': Pop Culture in Sherman Alexie's Short Fiction." *Studies in American Culture* 24, no. 2 (October 2001): 29–36.

Grassian, Daniel. *Understanding Sherman Alexie.* Columbia: University of South Carolina Press, 2005.

Hafen, P. Jane. "Rock and Roll, Redskins, and Blues in Sherman Alexie's Work." *Studies in American Indian Literatures* 9, no. 4 (winter 1997): 71–78.

Hearne, Joanna. "John Wayne's Teeth: Speech, Sound, and Representation in *Smoke Signals* and *Imagining Indians.*" *Western Folklore* 64, nos. 3–4 (2005): 189–208.

Heldrich, Philip. "Black Humor and the New Ethnic Writing of Tony Diaz and Sherman Alexie." *Pennsylvania English* 23, nos. 1–2 (spring 2001): 47–58.

Herman, Matt. "Authenticity Reconsidered: Toward an Understanding of a Culturalist Reading Paradigm." *Northwest Review* 35, no. 3 (1997): 125–33.

Hollrah, Patrice. *"The Old Lady Trill, the Victory Yell": The Power of Women in Native American Literature.* New York: Routledge, 2003.

———. "Sherman Alexie's Challenge to the Academy's Teaching of Native American Literature, Non-Native Writers, and Critics." *Studies in American Indian Literatures* 13, nos, 2–3 (summer–fall 2001): 23–35.

Holmes, Stephanie. Review of *The Toughest Indian in the World* by Sherman Alexie. *Pacific Rim Voices*, December 16, 2001. Available online at http://www.pacificrimvoices.org/rvarchive/alexie.html

Homans, Margaret. *"Adoption Narratives, Trauma, and Origins." Narrative* 14, no. 1 (January 2006): 4–26.

Italie, Hillel. "The Many Lives of Sherman Alexie." *News from Indian Country,* July 2000, 14B–15B.

James, Meredith K. *Literary and Cinematic Reservation in Selected Works of Native American Author Sherman Alexie.* Native American Studies 18. Lewiston, NY: Edwin Mellen Press, 2005.

Jorgensen, Karen. "White Shadows: The Use of Dopplegangers in Sherman Alexie's *Reservation Blues." Studies in American Indian Literatures* 9, no. 4 (winter 1997): 19–25.

Kane, Katie. "Nits Make Lice: Drogheda, Sand Creek, and the Poetics of Colonial Extermination." *Cultural Critique* 42 (spring 1999): 81–103.

Keegan, James. "'Y'all Need to Play Songs for Your People': Reservation versus Assimilation and the Politics of White-Indian Encounter in Sherman Alexie's Fiction." *Revista Canaria de Estudios Inglesses* 39 (November 1999): 115–34.

Kilpatrick, Jacqueline. *Celluloid Indians: Native Americans and Film.* Lincoln: University of Nebraska Press, 1999.

Kipen, David. "Way off the Reservation. The Indians in Alexie's Fiction Are Out for Redemption," *San Francisco Chronicle*, June 29, 2003. Available online at http://www.sfgate.com/cgi-bin/article.cqi?f=/chronicle/archive/2003/06/29/RV110120.DTL.

Klopotek, Brian. "'I Guess Your Warrior Look Doesn't Work Every Time': Challenging Indian Masculinity in the Cinema." In *Across the Great Divide: Cultures of Manhood in the American West,* edited by Matthew Basso, Laura McCall, and Dee Garceau-Hagan, 251–74. New York: Taylor & Francis, 2001.

Krumrey, Diane. "Subverting the Tonto Stereotype in Popular Fiction: Or, Why Indians Say 'Ugh.'" In *Simulacrum America: The USA and the Popular Media,* edited by Elisabeth Kraus and Carolin Auer, 161–68. Rochester, NY: Camden House, 2000.

Krupat, Arnold. "The 'Rage Stage': Contextualizing Sherman Alexie's *Indian Killer."* In *Red Matters: Native American Studies,* 98–121. Philadelphia: University of Pennsylvania Press, 2002.

Lawson, Angelica. "A New Story: Mediation in Sherman Alexie's *Smoke Signals."* Master's thesis, University of Wyoming, 2000.

Leibman, Laura Arnold. "A Bridge of Difference: Sherman Alexie and the Politics of Mourning." *American Literature* 77, no. 3 (September 2005): 541–61.

Lincoln, Kenneth. "Futuristic Hip Indian: Alexie." In *Sing with the Heart of the Bear: Fusions of Native American Poetry, 1890–1999,* 267–76. Berkeley: University of California Press, 2000. Also included in *The Trickster,* edited by Harold Bloom and Blake Hobby, 9–18. Bloom's Literary Themes. New York: Chelsea House Publishers, 2010.

Mariani, Giorgio. "From Atopia to Utopia: Sherman Alexie's Interstitial Indians." In *America Today: Highways and Labyrinths,* edited by Nocera Gigliola, 582–91. Siracusa, Italy: Grafia, 2003.

Marx, Doug. "Sherman Alexie: A Reservation of Mind." *Publishers Weekly,* 243, no. 38 (September 1996): 39–40.

Matchie, Thomas. *"Miracles at Little No Horse:* Louise Erdrich's Answer to Sherman Alexie's *Reservation Blues." North Dakota Quarterly* 70, no. 2 (2003): 151–62.

———. "Writing about Native Americans: The Native and Non-Native Critic/Author." *Midwest Quarterly* 42, no. 3 (spring 2001): 320–33.

McCracken, Kathleen. "Appropriation with a Purpose: Cinematic Contexts and Narrative Strategies in the Fiction of Sherman Alexie." *Irish Journal of American Studies* 7 (December 1998): 21–40.

McFarland, Ron. "Sherman Alexie." In *Twentieth-Century American Western Writers,* edited by Richard H. Cracroft, 3–10. *Dictionary of Literary Biography* 206. Detroit: Gale Research, 1999.

———. "Sherman Alexie's Polemical Stories." *Studies in American Indian Literatures* 9, no. 4 (winter 1997): 27–38.

———. "Teaching Sherman Alexie's *Reservation Blues." Wicazo Sa Review* 16, no. 2 (fall 2001): 139–47.

McGrath, Jacqueline L. "The Same Damn Stories': Exploring a Variation on Tradition in Sherman Alexie's *The Lone Ranger and Tonto Fistfight in Heaven." Southern Folklore* 57, no. 2 (winter 2001): 94–105.

McNally, Joel. "Sherman Alexie." *The Writer* 114, no. 6 (June 2001): 28–31.

Meyers, Jayme. "Review, *Ten Little Indians." Contemporary Literature.* Online at http://contemporarylit.about.com/cs/currentreviews/fr/tenlittleindian.html but no longer available.

Mihelich, John. "Smoke or Signals? American Popular Culture and the Challenge to Hegemonic Images of American Indians in Native American Film." *Wicazo Sa Review* 16, no. 2 (fall 2001): 129–37.

Miles, Jonathan. "Sherman Alexie's Cultural Imperialism." Salon.com, February 14, 2000. Available online at http://www.salon.com/books/log/2000/02/14/alexie/index.html

Moore, David L. "Sherman Alexie: Irony, Intimacy, and Agency." In *The Cambridge Companion to Native American Literature,* edited by Joy Porter and Kenneth Roemer, 297–310. Cambridge: Cambridge University Press, 2005.

Newton, John. "Sherman Alexie's Autoethnography." *Contemporary Literature* 42, no. 2 (summer 2001): 413–28.

Owens, Louis. *Mixedblood Messages: Literature, Family, Film, Place.* Norman: University of Oklahoma Press, 1998.

Pasquaretta, Paul. "African-Native American Subjectivity and the Blues Voice in the Writings of Toni Morrison and Sherman Alexie." In *When Brer Rabbit Meets Coyote: African-Native American Literature,* edited by Jonathan Brennan, 278–92. Urbana: University of Illinois Press, 2003.

Patell, Cyrus R. K. "Representing Emergent Literatures." *American Literary History* 15, no. 1 (spring 2003): 61–69.

———. "The Violence of Hybridity in Silko and Alexie." *Journal of American Studies of Turkey* 6 (fall 1997): 3–9.

Peeterse, Natalie. "Can the Subaltern Speak... Especially without a Tape Recorder?: A Postcolonial Reading of Ian Frazier's *On the Rez." American Indian Quarterly* 26, no. 2 (spring 2002): 271–85.

Porzio, Allison. "Absolute Critical Literacy for Part-Time Critical Readers: Sherman Alexie's *The Absolutely True Diary of a Part-Time Indian* and Cultural Studies." *English Record* 58, no. 1 (2008): 31–38.

Quirk, Sarah A. "Sherman Alexie." In *American Novelists Since World War II.* Fifth series, edited by James R. Giles and Wanda H. Giles, 3–10. Detroit: Thomson Gale, 1996.

Rader, Dean. "I Don't Speak Navajo: Esther G. Belin's In the Belly of My Beauty." *Studies in American Indian Literatures* 12, no. 3 (fall 2000): 14–34.

———. "Word as Weapon: Visual Culture and Contemporary American Indian Poetry." *MELUS* 27, no. 3 (fall 2002): 147–68.

Richardson, Janine. "Magic and Memory in Sherman Alexie's *Reservation Blues." Studies in American Indian Literatures* 9, no. 4 (winter 1997): 39–51.

Robins, Barbara K. "Teaching Sherman Alexie's 'Every Little Hurricane.'" *Eureka Studies in Teaching Short Fiction* 3, no. 2 (spring 2003): 25–35.

Roppolo, Kimberly, and Chelleye L. Crow. "Native American Education vs. Indian Learning: Still Battling Pratt after All These Years." *Studies in American Indian Literatures* 19, no. 1 (spring 2007): 3–31.

Roush, Jan. "Trickster Tracks in the Works of Sherman Alexie." In *US Icons and Iconicity*, edited by Walter W. Höbling, Klaus Rieser, and Suanne Rieser, 205-217. Vienna: Lit Verlag GmbH, 2006.

Sabatier, Diane. "L'Ecriture rouge de Sherman Alexie: L'Example de 'The Sin Eaters.'" *Journal of the Short Story in English* 45 (autumn 2005): 123–34.

Schroeter, Beate. "History in Oblivion: The Critique of America in Native American Literature." In *The Image of America in Literature, Media, and Society,* edited by Will Wright and Steven Kaplan, 117–23. Pueblo, CO: Society for the Interdisciplinary Study of Social Imagery, 1999.

Simon, Michael. "Getting Special Delivery: An Essay about Teaching Sherman Alexie's Short Story 'Special Delivery.'" *Eureka Studies in Teaching Short Fiction* 3, no. 2 (spring 2003): 73–77.

Singer, Beverly. *Wiping the Warpaint off the Lens: Native American Film and Video.* Minneapolis: University of Minnesota Press, 2001.

Slethaug, Gordon E. "Hurricanes and Fires: Chaotics in Sherman Alexie's *Smoke Signals* and *The Lone Ranger and Tonto Fistfight in Heaven." Literature/Film Quarterly* 31, no. 2 (2003): 130–40.

Smith, Rod. "The Metamorphoses: Sherman Alexie Delivers a New Novel about a Shape-Shifting American Indian." *TimeOut New York* 600, March 29–April 4, 2007. Available online at http://newyork.timeout.com/articles/books/1773/the-metamorphoses

Stokes, Karah. "'Was Jesus an Indian?' Fighting Stories with Stories in Sherman Alexie's *Indian Killer*." *Kentucky Philological Review* 16 (2002): 44–47.

Tatonetti, Lisa. "Sex and Salmon: Queer Identities in Sherman Alexie's *The Toughest Indian in the World*." *Studies in American Fiction* 35, no. 2 (autumn 2007): 201–20.

———. "Visible Sexualities or Invisible Nations: Forced to Choose in *Big Eden, Johnny Greyeyes,* and *The Business of Fancydancing. GLQ: A Journal of Lesbian and Gay Studies* 16, no. 1–2 (2010): 157–81.

Tellefsen, Blythe. "America Is a Diet Pepsi: Sherman Alexie's Reservation Blues." *Western American Literature* 40, no. 2 (summer 2005): 125–47.

Tepper, Anderson. "A Boy's Life, Zits and All." Review of *Flight* by Sherman Alexie. *Village Voice*, March 13, 2007.

Tillett, Rebecca. "'Resting in Peace, Not in Pieces': The Concerns of the Living Dead in Anna Lee Walters's *Ghost Singer*." *Studies in American Indian Literatures* 17, no. 3 (fall 2005): 85–114.

Treur, David. *Native American Fiction: A User's Manual.* St. Paul: Graywolf Press, 2006.

Troyer, Robert A. "Dialogue and Discourse Structure: A Speech Move Analysis of Sherman Alexie's Story 'What You Pawn I Will Redeem.'" In *The State of Stylistics,* edited by Greg Watson, 303–331. Amsterdam: Rodopi, 2008.

Van Styvendale, Nancy. "The Trans/historicity of Trauma in Jeannette Armstrong's *Slash* and Sherman Alexie's *Indian Killer*." *Studies in the Novel* 40, nos. 1–2 (spring–summer 2008): 203–23.

Whittemore, Katharine. "'The Toughest Indian in the World' by Sherman Alexie." Review of *The Toughest Indian in the World*. Salon.com, June 5, 2000. Available online at http://www.salon.com/books/review/2000/06/05/alexie

Williams, Sarah T. "Man of Many Tribes." *Star Tribune,* December 31, 2007. Available online at http://www.startribune.com/entertainment/books/11435616.html?elr=KArksUUUoDEy3LGDiO7aiU

Winkler, Scott A. "Dreams Like Baseball Cards: Baseball, Bricoleur, and the Gap in Sherman Alexie's *The Lone Ranger and Tonto Fistfight in Heaven*." *Aethlon* 21, no. 2 (spring 2004): 87–98.

Youngberg, Quentin. "Interpenetrations: Re-encoding the Queer Indian in Sherman Alexie's *The Business of Fancydancing*." *Studies in American Indian Literatures* 20, no. 1 (spring 2008): 55–75.

OTHER BOOKS AND ARTICLES CITED IN THIS COLLECTION

Adams, Maurianne, Lee Anne Bell, and Pat Griffin. *Teaching for Diversity and Social Justice: A Sourcebook.* New York: Routledge, 1997.

Aldridge, John W. *Time to Murder and Create: The Contemporary Novel in Crisis.* New York: McCay, 1966.

Allen, Chadwick. "Blood (and) Memory." *American Literature* 71, no. 1 (March 1999): 93–116.

Alleva, Richard. "A Filmmaker's Instincts: Costner's *Dances With Wolves.*" *Commonwealth,* January 11, 1991, 18–19.

Anderson, Eric Gary. "Driving the Red Road: *Powwow Highway.*" In *Hollywood's Indian: The Portrayal of the Native American in Film,* edited by Peter C. Rollins and John E. O'Connor, 137–52. Lexington: University Press of Kentucky, 1998.

———. "Situating American Indian Poetry: Place, Community, and the Question of Genre." In *Speak to Me Words: Essays on Contemporary American Indian Poetry,* edited by Janice Gould and Dean Rader, 34–55. Tucson: University of Arizona Press, 2003.

Arnett, Carroll. *Night Perimeter: New and Selected Poems, 1958–1990.* Greenfield Center, NY: Greenfield Review Press, 1992.

Arnold, Ellen. "Reframing the Hollywood Indian: A Feminist Re-reading of *Powwow Highway* and *Thunderheart.*" In *American Indian Studies: An Interdisciplinary Approach to Contemporary Issues,* edited by Dane Morrison, 347–62. New York: Peter Lang, 1997.

Babcock, Barbara, and Jay Cox. "The Native American Trickster." In *Handbook of Native American Literature,* edited by Andrew Wiget, 99–106. New York: Garland Publishing, 1996.

Bahr, Diana Meyers. *From Mission to Metropolis: Cupeño Indian Women in Los Angeles.* Norman: University of Oklahoma Press, 1993.

Baker, Houston. *Blues, Ideology and Afro-American Literature: A Vernacular Theory.* Chicago: University of Chicago Press, 1984.

Bakhtin, Mikhail. *The Dialogic Imagination.* Translated by C. Emerson and M. Holquist. Austin: University of Texas Press, 1981.

———. *Rabelais and His World.* Translated by Helene Isnolsky. Cambridge, MA: MIT Press, 1968.

Baldwin, James. *The Fire Next Time.* 1961. Reprint, New York: Vintage Books, 1993.

Baraka, Amiri. "Black Art." In *Transbluesency: The Selected Poems of Amiri Baraka/LeRoi Jones* (1961–1995), edited by Paul Vangelisti, 142. New York: Marsilio, 1995.

Barthes, Roland. "The Death of the Author." In *Falling into Theory: Conflicting Views on Reading Literature,* edited by David H. Richter, 222–26. Boston: Bedford/St. Martin's, 1999.

Basso, Keith. "'To Give Up on Words': Silence in Western Apache Culture." In *Western Apache Language and Culture: Essays in Linguistic Anthropology,* chapter 5. Tucson: University of Arizona Press, 1990.

Berger, Thomas. *Little Big Man.* New York: Delta/Seymour Lawrence, 1989.

Bhabha, Homi. *The Location of Culture.* New York: Routledge, 1994.

Bierhorst, John. *The Mythology of North America.* New York: Quill William Morrow, 1985.

Bird, Gloria. "Breaking the Silence: Writing as 'Witness.'" In *Speaking for the Generations: Native Writers on Writing,* edited by Simon J. Ortiz, 26–48. Tucson: University of Arizona Press, 1998.

Bonnin, Gertrude Simmons. *American Indian Stories.* Lincoln: University of Nebraska Press, 1985.

Bowden, Larry. *"Dances With Wolves." Cross Currents* 41 (1991): 391–96.

Brave Heart, Maria Yellow Horse, and Lemyra M. DeBruyn. "The American Indian Holocaust: Healing Historical Unresolved Grief." *American Indian and Alaska Native Mental Health Research* 8, no. 2 (1998): 60–82.

Bread, Don. "Not My Idea of Native Acceptance." Letter to the editor, *The Liberty Press* (Kansas City edition) 6, no. 6 (2000): 7.

Brill de Ramírez, Susan Berry. "The Power and Presence of Native Oral Storytelling Traditions in the Poetry of Marilou Awiatka, Kimberly Blaeser, and Marilyn Dumont." In *Speak to Me Words: Essays on Contemporary American Indian Poetry,* 82–102.

———. "Writing the Intertwined Global Histories of Indigeneity and Diasporization: An Ecocritical Articulation of Place, Relationality, and Storytelling in the Poetry of Simon J. Ortiz." In *Stories through Theory/Theory through Stories: Native American Storytelling and Critique,* edited by Gordon Henry, Silvia Martinez-Falquina, and Nieves Pascual Soler, 159–90. Lansing: Michigan State University Press, 2009.

Brill de Ramírez, Susan Berry, and Evelina Zuni Lucero, eds. *Simon J. Ortiz: A Poetic Legacy of Indigenous Continuance.* Albuquerque: University of New Mexico Press, 2009.

Brown, Lester B. "Women and Men, Not-Men and Not-Women, Lesbians and Gays: American Indian Gender Style Alternatives." In *Two Spirit People: American Indian Lesbian Women and Gay Men,* special issue of *Journal of Gay and Lesbian Social Services* 6, no. 2 (1997): 5–20.

Browner, Tara. *Heartbeat of the People: Music and Dance of the Northern Pow-Wow.* Urbana: University of Illinois Press, 2004.

Callender, Charles, and Lee M. Kochems. "The North American Berdache." *Current Anthropology* 24, no. 4 (August–October 1983): 443–70.

Carrier, Joseph. "Miguel: Sexual Life History of a Gay Mexican American." In *Gay Culture in America: Essays from the Field,* edited by Gilbert Herdt, 202–24. Boston: Beacon Press, 1992.

Champagne, Duane. "American Indian Studies Is for Everyone." In *Natives and Academics: Researching and Writing about American Indians,* edited by Devon A. Mihesuah, 181–89. Lincoln: University of Nebraska Press, 1998.

Cho, Song, ed. Introduction to *Rice: Explorations into Gay Asian Culture + Politics,* 1–5. Toronto: Queer Press, 1998.

Christie, Agatha. *Ten Little Indians.* Greenway ed. New York: Dodd, Mead, 1978.

Churchill, Ward. "Lawrence of South Dakota: *Dances With Wolves* and the Maintenance of the American Empire." In *Fantasies of the Master Race: Literature,*

Cinema and the Colonization of American Indians, edited by M. Annette Jaimes, 239–42. Monroe, ME: Common Courage, 1992.

———. *Struggle for Land: Native North American Resistance to Genocide, Ecocide, and Colonization.* San Francisco: City Lights Books, 1994.

Churchill, Ward, and Winona LaDuke. "Native North America: The Political Economy of Radioactive Colonialism." In *The State of Native America: Genocide, Colonization, and Resistance,* edited by M. Annette Jaimes, 241–66. Race and Resistance Series. Boston: South End Press, 1992.

Coleman, William E. *The Voices of Wounded Knee.* Lincoln: University of Nebraska Press, 2000.

Conley, John, and William O'Barr. *Just Words: Law, Language and Power.* Chicago: University of Chicago Press, 1998.

———. *Rules Versus Relationships: The Ethnography of Legal Discourse.* Chicago: University of Chicago Press, 1990.

Cook, Nancy L. "Speaking in and about Stories." *University of Cincinnati Law Review* 63 (1994): 95.

Cook-Lynn, Elizabeth. "American Indian Intellectualism and the New Indian Story." In *Natives and Academics: Researching and Writing about American Indians,* 111–38.

———. *Anti-Indianism in Modern America: A Voice from Tatekeya's Earth.* Urbana: University of Illinois Press, 2001.

———. "How Scholarship Defames the Native Voice . . . and Why." *Wicazo Sa Review* 15, no. 2 (autumn, 2000): 79–92.

———. *New Indians, Old Wars.* Urbana: University of Illinois Press, 2007.

———. *Why I Can't Read Wallace Stegner and Other Essays: A Tribal Voice.* Madison: University of Wisconsin Press, 1996.

Cover, Robert M. "Violence and the Word." *Yale Law Journal* 95 (1986): 1601, 1604.

Coward, John M. *The Newspaper Indian: Native American Identity in the Press, 1820–90.* Urbana: University of Illinois Press, 1999.

Davies, Bruce. *Implementing the Indian Child Welfare Act.* Washington, DC: Legal Services Corporation Research Institute, 1981.

Davis, Angela. *Blues Legacies and Black Feminism: Gertrude "Ma" Rainey, Bessie Smith and Billie Holiday.* New York: Vintage Books, 1999.

Davis, Arthur P., J. Saunders Redding, and Joyce Ann Joyce, eds. *The New Cavalcade: African American Writing from 1760 to the Present.* Washington, DC: Howard University Press, 1992.

Death Penalty Information Center. "National Statistics on the Death Penalty and Race." Available online at http://www.deathpenaltyinfo.org/article.php?scid=5&did=184

Delamar, Gloria T. *Children's Counting-Out Rhymes, Fingerplays, Jump-Rope and Bounce-Ball Chants and Other Rhythms. A Comprehensive English-Language Reference.* Jefferson, NC: McFarland, 1983.

Deloria, Philip J. "American Indians, American Studies, and the ASA." *American Quarterly* 55, no. 4 (December 2003): 669–80.

———. *Indians in Unexpected Places.* Lawrence: University Press of Kansas, 2004.

Deloria Jr., Vine. *Custer Died for Your Sins: An Indian Manifesto.* New York: Macmillan, 1969. Reprint, Norman: University of Oklahoma Press, 1988.

Demallie, Raymond J., ed. *The Sixth Grandfather: Black Elk's Teachings Given to John G. Neihardt.* Lincoln: University of Nebraska Press, 1984.

Donegan, Patricia. "Haiku and the Ecotastrophe." In *Dharma Gaia: A Harvest of Essays in Buddhism and Ecology,* edited by Allan Hunt Badiner, 197–208. Berkeley: Parallax Press, 1990.

Duncan, Patti. *Tell This Silence: Asian American Women Writers and the Politics of Speech.* Iowa City: University of Iowa Press, 2004.

Duran, Eduardo. *Healing the Soul Wound: Counseling with American Indians and Other Native Peoples.* New York: Teachers College Press, 2006.

Duran, Eduardo, and Bonnie Duran. *Native American Postcolonial Psychology.* New York: State University of New York Press, 1995.

Duran, Eduardo, and Bonnie Duran, Maria Yellow Horse Brave Heart, and Susan Yellow Horse-Davis. "Healing the American Indian Soul Wound." In *International Handbook of Multigenerational Legacies of Trauma,* edited by Yael Danieli, 341–54. New York: Plenum Press, 1998.

Eagleton, Terry. *How to Read a Poem.* Oxford: Blackwell, 2007.

Ellis, Clyde. *A Dancing People: Powwow Culture on the Southern Plains.* Lawrence: University Press of Kansas, 2003.

Elon, Amos, *The Pity of It All: A History of Jews in Germany,* 1743–1933. New York: Metropolitan Books, 2002.

Emmett, Aspen C. "Murphy Pleads Guilty to Murder." *Cortez Journal,* February 8, 2002.

Environmental Protection Agency. Midnite Mine statistics. Available online at http://www.epa.gov/superfund/sites/npl/nar1546.htm and http://yosemite.epa.gov/R10/CLEANUP.NSF/sites/midnite

Fast, Robin Riley. "Borderland Voices in Contemporary Native American Poetry." *Contemporary Literature* 36, no. 3 (fall 1995): 503–36.

Finley, Lucinda. "Breaking Women's Silence in Law: The Dilemma of the Gendered Nature of Legal Reasoning." *Notre Dame Law Review* 64 (1989): 886–909.

Fisher, Dexter. "Zitkala-Ša: The Evolution of a Writer." *American Indian Quarterly* 5, no. 3 (August 1979): 229–38.

Fone, Byrne R. S. *Homophobia: A History.* New York: Metropolitan Books, 2000.

Foster, Tol. "Of One Blood: An Argument for Relations and Regionality in Native American Literary Studies." In *Reasoning Together: The Native Critics Collective,* edited by Craig Womack, Daniel Heath Justice, and Sean Teuton, 265–302. Norman: University of Oklahoma Press, 2008.

Foucault, Michel. *The History of Sexuality.* Vol. 1, *An Introduction.* Translated by Robert Hurley. New York: Random House, 1980.

———. "What Is an Author?" In *The Foucault Reader,* edited by Paul Rabinow, 101–20. New York: Pantheon, 1984.

Franco, Dean. "What We Talk about When We Talk about *Beloved.*" *Mfs* (*Modern Fiction Studies*) 52, no. 2 (summer 2006): 415–39.

Freire, Paulo. *The Pedagogy of the Oppressed.* Translated by Myra Bergman Ramos. New York: Herder and Herder, 1970.

Friedman, Bruce Jay. Foreword to *Black Humor.* Edited by Bruce Friedman. New York: Bantam, 1965.

Garner, Suzanne. "The Indian Child Welfare Act: A Review," *Wicazo Sa Review* 9, no. 1 (spring 1993): 47–51.

Gilley, Brian Joseph. *Becoming Two-Spirit: Gay Identity and Social Acceptance in Indian Country.* Lincoln: University of Nebraska Press, 2006.

Giroux, Henry. "Reading Texts, Literacy, and Textual Authority." *Journal of Education* 172, no. 1 (1990): 84–103.

Glenn, Cheryl. *Unspoken: A Rhetoric of Silence.* Carbondale: Southern Illinois University Press, 2004.

Green, Rayna. "The Pocahontas Perplex: The Image of Indian Women in American Culture." *Massachusetts Review* 16 (winter 1975): 698–714.

Greenberg, David. "Why Was the Berdache Ridiculed?" *Journal of Homosexuality* 11, nos. 3–4 (1985): 179–90.

Griffin, Horace. "Their Own Received Them Not: African American Lesbians and Gays in Black Churches." In *The Greatest Taboo: Homosexuality in Black Communities,* edited by Delroy Constantine-Simms, 110–21. Los Angeles: Alyson Books, 2000.

Harden, Blaine, *A River Lost: The Life and Death of the Columbia.* New York: Norton, 1996.

Harjo, Joy. *The Woman Who Fell from the Sky.* New York: Norton, 1994.

Harris, Angela P. "Race and Essentialism in Feminist Legal Theory." In *Critical Race Theory: The Cutting Edge,* edited by Richard Delgado and Jean Stefanic, chapter 25. Philadelphia: Temple University Press, 2000.

Herman, Matt. "Authenticity Reconsidered: Toward an Understanding of a Culturalist Reading Paradigm." *Northwest Review* 35, no. 3 (1997): 125–33.

Hilger, Michael. *From Savage to Nobleman: Images of Native Americans in Film.* Lanham, MD: Scarecrow, 1995.

Hittman, Michael. *Wovoka and the Ghost Dance.* Researched, compiled, and written by Michael Hittman and edited by Don Lynch. Lincoln: University of Nebraska Press, 1990.

Horton, Andrew. "The Bitter Humor of *Winter in the Blood.*" *American Indian Quarterly* 4, no. 2 (May 1978): 131–39.

Jacobs, Sue-Ellen, Wesley Thomas, and Sabine Lang. Introduction to *Two-Spirit People: Native American Gender Identity, Sexuality, and Spirituality,* edited by Jacobs, Thomas, and Lang, 1–18. Urbana: University of Illinois Press, 1997.

Jaimes, M. Annette. "Federal Indian Identification Policy: A Usurpation of Indigenous Sovereignty in North America." In *The State of Native America: Genocide, Colonization, and Resistance,* 123–38.

Jenson, Richard, R. Eli Paul, and John E. Carter. *Eyewitness at Wounded Knee.* Lincoln: University of Nebraska Press, 1991.

Jensen, Vickie. *Where the People Gather: Carving a Totem Pole.* Seattle: University of Washington Press, 1992.

Johnson, Brian D. "Straight-Arrow Hero: Kevin Costner Touches the Native Earth." *Maclean's,* November 19, 1990, 58.

Justice, Daniel Heath. "'Go Away, Water!': Kinship Criticism and the Decolonization Imperative." In *Reasoning Together: The Native Critics Collective,* 147–68.

Katz, Jonathan. "Native Americans/Gay Americans 1528–1976." In *Gay American History: Lesbians and Gay Men in the U.S.A.—A Documentary by Jonathan Katz,* 281–334. Rev. ed. New York: Thomas Y. Crowell Company, 1992.

Kehoe, Alice Beck. *The Ghost Dance: Ethnohistory and Revitalization.* Ft. Worth, TX: Holt, Rinehart and Winston, 1989.

Klein, Laura F., and Lillian A. Ackerman, eds. *Women and Power in Native North America.* Norman: University of Oklahoma Press, 1995.

Lame Deer, Archie Fire, and Richard Erdoes. *Gift of Power: The Life and Teachings of a Lakota Medicine Man.* Santa Fe: Bear and Company, 1992.

Laqueur, Thomas. *Making Sex: Body and Gender from the Greeks to Freud.* 1990. Reprint, Cambridge, MA: Harvard University Press, 1992.

Lincoln, Kenneth. *Indi'n Humor: Bicultural Play in Native America.* New York: Oxford University Press, 1993.

Liu, Eric. "Notes of a Native Speaker." In *The Accidental Asian,* 33–56. New York: Vintage/Random House, 1999.

Louis, Adrian C. *Fire Water World.* Albuquerque: West End Press, 1989.

Lourie, Dick. *Ghost Radio.* Brooklyn: Hanging Loose Press, 1998.

McGregor, James H. *The Wounded Knee Massacre from the Viewpoint of the Sioux.* 1940. Reprint, N.p.: Fenwyn Press Books, 1969.

Minh-ha, Trinh T. *Woman, Native, Other: Writing Postcoloniality and Feminism.* Bloomington: Indiana University Press, 1989.

Minor, Robert N. *Scared Straight: Why It's So Hard to Accept Gay People and Why It's So Hard to Be Human.* St. Louis: HumanityWorks!, 2001.

Mooney, James. *The Ghost Dance Religion and the Sioux Outbreak of 1890.* 1896. Reprint, Lincoln: University of Nebraska Press, 1991.

Moraga, Cherríe. *Loving in the War Years: Lo Que Nunca Pasó por Sus Labios.* Boston: South End Press, 1983.

Morgan, Phillip Carroll. "'Who Shall Gainsay Our Decision?': Choctaw Literary Criticism in 1830." In *Reasoning Together: The Native Critics Collective,* 126–46.

Myers, Joseph. *They Are Young Once but Indian Forever: A Summary and Analysis of Investigative Hearings on ICW, April 1980.* Oakland, CA: American Indian Lawyer Training Program, 1981.

Nagel, Joane. "The Color of Sex: Race, Ethnicity, and Sexuality in America." Lecture, Hall Center Humanities Series, University of Kansas, Lawrence, November 15, 2001.

Namias, June. *White Captives: Gender and Ethnicity on the American Frontier.* Chapel Hill: University of North Carolina Press, 1993.

Niatum, Duane. "History in the Colors of Song: A Few Words on Contemporary Native American Poetry." In *Coyote Was Here: Essays on Contemporary Native American Literary and Political Mobilization,* edited by Bo Schöler, 25–34. Aarhus, Denmark: Seklos, 1984.

northSun, Nila. "up & out." In *American Indian Literature: An Anthology,* edited by Alan Velie, 291. Norman: University of Oklahoma Press, 1979.

Opie, Iona and Peter, eds. *The Oxford Dictionary of Nursery Rhymes.* Oxford: Clarendon Press, 1951.

Ortiz, Simon J. *from Sand Creek: Rising in this Heart which is Our America.* Tucson: University of Arizona Press, 1981.

———. *Woven Stone.* Tucson: University of Arizona Press, 1992.

Owens, Louis. *Other Destinies: Understanding the American Indian Novel.* Norman: University of Oklahoma Press, 1992.

Paul, Berdache. "My Life as an Intersex." *White Crane Journal* 50 (fall 2001): 10–11, 34.

Peterson, John L. "Black Men and Their Same-Sex Desires and Behaviors." In *Gay Culture in America: Essays from the Field,* 147–64.

Peterson, Nancy J. *Against Amnesia: Contemporary Women Writers and the Crises of Historical Memory.* Philadelphia: University of Pennsylvania Press, 2001.

Poupart, Lisa. "The Familiar Face of Genocide: Internalized Oppression among American Indians." *Hypatia* 18, no. 2 (spring 2003): 86–100.

Power, Susan. *The Grass Dancer.* New York: G. P. Putnam's Sons, 1994.

Pratt, Alan R. *Black Humor: Critical Essays,* edited by Alan R. Pratt. New York: Garland, 1993.

Price, Darby Li Po. "Laughing without Reservation: Indian Standup Comedians." *American Indian Culture and Research Journal* 22, no. 4 (1998): 255–71.

Pulitano, Elvira. *Toward a Native American Critical Theory.* Lincoln: University of Nebraska Press, 2003.

Rader, Dean. "The Epic Lyric: Genre and Contemporary American Indian Poetry." In *Speak to Me Words: Essays on Contemporary American Indian Poetry,* 123–42.

Rainwater, Catherine. *Dreams of Fiery Stars: The Transformations of Native American Fiction.* Philadelphia: University of Pennsylvania Press, 1999.

———. "Reading between Worlds: Narrativity in the Fiction of Louise Erdrich," *American Literature* 62, no. 3 (September 1990): 405–22.

Reid-Pharr, Robert F. *Black Gay Man: Essays.* New York: New York University Press, 2001.

Rollin, Lucy. *Cradle and All: A Cultural and Psychoanalytic Reading of Nursery Rhymes.* Jackson: University of Mississippi Press, 1992.

Roscoe, Will. *Changing Ones: Third and Fourth Genders in Native North America.* New York: St. Martin's Griffin, 2000.

———, ed. *Living the Spirit: A Gay American Indian Anthology,* compiled by gay American Indians. New York: St. Martin's Press, 1988.

———. "Native North American Literature." In *The Gay and Lesbian Literary Heritage: A Reader's Companion to the Writers and Their Works, from Antiquity to* the Present, edited by Claude J. Summers, 513–17. 1995 Reprint, New York: Holt/Owl, 1997.

———. The Zuni Man-Woman. Albuquerque: University of New Mexico Press, 1991.

Ross, Bruce. "North American Versions of Haibun and Postmodern American Culture." In Postmodernity and Cross-Culturalism, edited by Yoshinobu Hakutani, 168–200. Madison, NJ: Fairleigh Dickinson University Press, 2002.

Rostow, Ann. "Gay Murders Continue." Texas Triangle Online, January 24–30, 2003.

Ruby, Robert H., and John A. Brown. The Spokane Indians: Children of the Sun. Norman: University of Oklahoma Press, 1970.

Ruppert, James. Mediation in Contemporary Native American Fiction. Norman: University of Oklahoma Press, 1995.

Sarf, Michael Wayne. "Oscar Eaten by Wolves," Film Comment 27 (1991): 62–70.

Schlicke, Carl P. General George Wright: Guardian of the Pacific Coast. Norman: University of Oklahoma Press, 1988.

Schow, Ron, Wayne Schow, and Marybeth Raynes, eds. Peculiar People: Mormons and Same-Sex Orientation. Salt Lake City: Signature Books, 1991.

Sedgwick, Eve Kosofsky. Between Men: English Literature and Male Homosocial Desire. New York: Columbia University Press, 1985.

———. Epistemology of the Closet. Berkeley: University of California Press, 1990.

SHAWL (Sovereignty, Health, Air, Water, and Land) Society. Information on cleaning up the Midnite Mine site. Available online at http://www.thefigtree.org/jan06/shawl.html

Stimson, William. A View of the Falls: An Illustrated History of Spokane. Northridge, CA: Windson Publications, 1985.

Strickland, Rennard. "Tonto's Revenge, or, Who Is That Seminole in the Sioux Warbonnet? The Cinematic Indian!" In Tonto's Revenge: Reflections on American Indian Culture and Policy, 17–45. Albuquerque: University of New Mexico Press, 1997.

Sundquist, Eric J. "The Frontier and American Indians." In Prose Writing 1820–1865. Vol. 2 of The Cambridge History of American Literature, edited by Savan Bercovitch, 175–238. Cambridge: Cambridge University Press, 1995.

Tafoya, Terry. "Sex and Spirit: Native American Lesbian Identity." Augsburg Now, August 26, 2001.

TallBear, Kimberly. "DNA, Blood and Racializing the Tribe." Wicazo Sa Review 18, no. 1 (2003): 81–107.

Tatonetti, Lisa. "The Emergence and Importance of Queer American Indian Literatures; or 'Help and Stories' in Thirty Years of SAIL." Studies in American Indian Literatures 19, no. 4 (winter 2007): 143–70.

Tatonetti, Lisa, and Daniel Heath Justice. "Indigenous Literature with a Queer/LGBT Two-Spirit Sensibility." Available online at http://oncampus.richmond.edu/faculty/ASAIL/Two-Spirit.htm

Taylor, Deb. "Saving the *Indian*: A Story of Two-Spirit, Sacred People. Native Queers." *The Liberty Press* (Kansas City edition) 6, no. 4 (December 1999): 34–35.

Tutu, Desmond. *No Future without Forgiveness*. New York: Image, 2000.

U.S. Bureau of Indian Affairs. *Young Native Americans and Their Families: Educational Needs Assessment and Recommendations*. Lawrence, KS: Haskell Press, 1976.

USGenNet. "History of the Pacific Northwest, Oregon and Washington, 1889." Available online at http://www.usgennet.org/usa/or/county/union1/1889v ol1/1889volumeIpage621-639.htm

Utley, Robert M. *Frontiersmen in Blue, the United States Army and the Indian, 1848–1865*. Lincoln: University of Nebraska Press, 1967.

———. *The Indian Frontier of the American West, 1846–1890*. Albuquerque: University of New Mexico Press, 1984.

Van Der Kolk, Bessel, Alexander McFarlane, and Lars Weisaeth, eds. *Traumatic Stress: The Effects of Overwhelming Experience on Mind, Body, and Society*. New York: Guilford Press, 1996.

Vangen, Kate. "Masking Faces: Defiance and Humour in Campbell's *Halfbreed* and Welch's *Winter in the Blood*." In *The Native in Literature,* edited by Thomas King, Cheryl Calver, and Helen Hoy, 188–205. Toronto: ECW Press, 1987.

Velie, Alan. *"Winter in the Blood* as Comic Novel." In *Critical Perspectives on Native American Fiction,* edited by Richard F. Fleck, 189–94. Washington, DC: Three Continents, 1993.

Vizenor, Gerald. *Manifest Manners: Narratives on Postindian Survivance*. Lincoln: University of Nebraska Press, 1999.

———. *Manifest Manners: Postindian Warriors of Survivance*. Middletown, CT: Wesleyan University Press, 1994.

Wagner, Dennis. "Ex-con Pleads Guilty in 2000 Hate Killing." *Arizona Republic,* August 14, 2002.

Walters, Karina L. "Urban Lesbian and Gay American Indian Identity: Implications for Mental Health Service Delivery." *Journal of Gay and Lesbian Social Services* 6, no. 2 (1997): 43–65.

Warrior, Robert A. *Tribal Secrets: Recovering American Indian Intellectual Traditions*. Minneapolis: University of Minnesota Press, 1995.

"Washington Territorial Timeline." Available online at http://www.secstate. wa.gov/history/Timeline/default.aspx

Weaver, Jace. *That the People Might Live: Native American Literatures and Native American Community*. New York: Oxford University Press, 1997.

Weaver, Jace, Craig Womack, and Robert Warrior. *American Indian Literary Nationalism*. Albuquerque: University of New Mexico Press, 2006.

West, Cornel. *Race Matters*. New York: Vintage Books, 1993.

Williams, Walter L. *The Spirit and the Flesh: Sexual Diversity in American Indian Culture*. 1986. Reprint, Boston: Beacon Press, 1992.

Wilson, Angela Cavender. "American Indian History or Non-Indian Perceptions of American Indian History?" In *Natives and Academics: Researching and Writing about American Indians,* 23–26.

Wittgenstein, Ludwig. *Philosophical Investigations.* Translated by G. E. M. Anscombe. Oxford: Basil Blackwell, 1984.

Womack, Craig S. *Red on Red: Native American Literary Separatism.* Minneapolis: University of Minnesota Press, 1999.

———. "Theorizing American Indian Experience." In *Reasoning Together: The Native Critics Collective,* 353–410.

Wright, Kai, Lisa Kennedy, Eric Gutierrez, Alexander Chee, and Peter McQuaid. "Sexing the Archetype: Interracial Dating and Mating." *Out,* August 2002, 60–65, 76.

Yazzie, Robert. "'Life Comes from It': Navajo Justice Concepts." *New Mexico Law Review* 24 (1994): 175–90.

Žižek, Slavoj. *Looking Awry: An Introduction to Jacques Lacan through Popular Culture,* Cambridge, MA: MIT Press, 1991.

Index

PS 3551 .L35774 Z87 2010

Sherman Alexie